Dear Susan,
Merry Christmas.
Hope this helps you on your
journey to learn Russian.
Love,
Sophie

**Vladislav Zubok** is Professor of International History at the London School of Economics and Political Science (LSE). He has previously taught at Temple University and has served as a fellow at the National Security Archive, a non-governmental organization at the University of George Washington. His publications include *A Failed Empire: The Soviet Union in the Cold War from Stalin to Gorbachev* and *Zhivago's Children: The Last Russian Intelligentsia*.

'Dmitri Likhachev, who narrowly escaped death in the Gulag, was as much revered by Russians as Alexander Solzhenitsyn. But unlike that Old Testament thunderer, he spoke with the voice of scholarly reason. He passionately believed that Russia's history and culture were an essential part of a wider European tradition. In his fluent and meticulous account, Vladislav Zubok reminds us both of a significant historical figure, and of an enduring truth about a great country which is contested both by today's noisy Russian nationalists and by those who denounce them in the West.'

— Sir Rodric Braithwaite

'In this marvellous biography, Vladislav Zubok brings to life Dmitry Likhachev, a social thinker and scholar who evoked the glory of Russian culture over a long life. Zubok reveals this important story at a time when the Russian identity is under grim duress. Likhachev opposed Russia's repressive authoritarian traditions as did Tolstoy, Akhmatova, Pasternak, Grossman, and many others. Bravo for Zubok!'

— Jeffrey Brooks, Professor of History, Johns Hopkins University

'Dmitry Likhachev's biography is a journey through the twentieth century, taking us from pre-revolutionary Petersburg to the Gulag and the blockade, the rediscovery of old Russian culture, the reframing of national identity, and the commanding heights of cultural politics. Vladislav Zubok does full justice to the life of this remarkable representative of the Russian intelligentsia.'

— Michael David-Fox, Georgetown University

'Dmitry Likhachev was an astonishing figure: unique in his long, goal-directed life, his rather abstruse scholarly endeavour that somehow developed into a public role, yet at the same time an exemplary personality, telling us much about Russia itself. Vladislav Zubok's balanced, well-rounded and non-sentimentalized book should do him full justice.'

— Robin Milner-Gulland, Emeritus Professor of Russian and East European Studies at the University of Sussex

'Amidst the whirlwinds of war, revolution, and state terror, few Russians did more to maintain the finest traditions of "Old Russia" and to assert the inviolability of the individual than Dmitry Likhachev, brilliant scholar, cultural preservationist, and public intellectual. Vladislav Zubok's masterful biography of the man dubbed "Russia's conscience" not only recounts one of the most remarkable Russian lives of the twentieth century, it offers a timely reminder that even during its darkest hours Russia has been home to indomitable defenders of humanism and democratic values.'

— Douglas Smith, author of *Rasputin: Faith, Power, and the Twilight of the Romanovs*

# THE IDEA OF RUSSIA

## THE LIFE AND WORK OF DMITRY LIKHACHEV

VLADISLAV ZUBOK

I.B.TAURIS
LONDON · NEW YORK

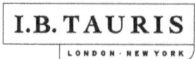

Published in 2017 by
I.B.Tauris & Co. Ltd
London · New York
www.ibtauris.com

Copyright © 2017 Vladislav Zubok

The right of Vladislav Zubok to be identified as the author of this work has been asserted
by the author in accordance with the Copyright, Designs and Patents Act 1988.

All rights reserved. Except for brief quotations in a review, this book, or any part thereof,
may not be reproduced, stored in or introduced into a retrieval system, or transmitted,
in any form or by any means, electronic, mechanical, photocopying, recording or otherwise,
without the prior written permission of the publisher.

Every attempt has been made to gain permission for the use of the images in this book.
Any omissions will be rectified in future editions.

References to websites were correct at the time of writing.

Library of Modern Russian History 8

ISBN: 978 1 78453 727 2
eISBN: 978 1 78672 053 5
ePDF: 978 1 78673 053 4

A full CIP record for this book is available from the British Library
A full CIP record is available from the Library of Congress

Library of Congress Catalog Card Number: available

Typeset in Garamond Three by OKS Prepress Services, Chennai, India
Printed and bound by CPI Group (UK) Ltd, Croydon, CR0 4YY

# CONTENTS

*List of Plates* vi
*Preface   A Russian Fox* ix
*Acknowledgements* xii
*A Note on Russian Names* xiv

1. Vanishing Russia, 1906–1921                         1
2. Patriotism of Pity, 1921–1928                      14
3. Through the Gulag and Great Terror, 1928–1941      32
4. The Great Fatherland War, 1941–1945                54
5. Patriotism Defiled, 1945–1955                      72
6. Advocate of Cultural Legacy, 1955–1965             88
7. The Making of a Wise Man, 1966–1976               105
8. Recognition, 1976–1988                            121
9. Preparing for Collapse, 1988–1991                 138
10. The Smoke of the Homeland, 1991–1999             157

Conclusion   Death and Beyond                        177

*Notes*                                              181
*Select Bibliography and Further Reading*            218
*Index*                                              221

# LIST OF PLATES

Plate 1. Likhachev's parents, Sergei Likhachev and Vera Konyaeva, around 1900 (Likhachev Foundation, St Petersburg).

Plate 2. *Dachniki* (summer-folk) from St Petersburg on a Finnish gulf beach before the revolution (original source unknown).

Plate 3. Sergei Alexeyev (Askoldov) influenced Likhachev's philosophy and educational choices (Institute of Russian Literature, St Petersburg).

Plate 4. Likhachev in 1927, on the eve of his arrest (Likhachev Foundation, St Petersburg).

Plate 5. Map of Solovki concentration camp (Likhachev Foundation, St Petersburg).

Plate 6. A sketch of the Solovki kremlin. The dots mark the path that Likhachev took every day to and from his work in Krimkab for three years between 1929 and 1931 (Institute of Russian Literature, St Petersburg).

Plate 7. Likhachev's pass that allowed him to move around Solovki (Institute of Russian Literature, St Petersburg).

Plate 8. Reverend Nikolai Piskanovsky, who saved Dmitry's life (public domain).

Plate 9. Likhachev with his father and mother, on their visit to Solovki, after the night of executions, November 1929 (Likhachev Foundation, St Petersburg).

Plate 10. Likhachev and his friend, Ukrainian poet Vladimir Korolenko, incised their names on a boulder in Solovki. Korolenko was executed in 1937 (photo by Oleg Leikind, Likhachev Foundation, St Petersburg).

# List of Plates

Plate 11. Likhachev during his illness with ulcers works at home proofreading, after 1933 (Likhachev Foundation, St Petersburg).

Plate 12. Likhachev and Zina Makarova, married with twins in Leningrad, 1938 (Likhachev Foundation, St Petersburg).

Plate 13. Carrying corpses in Leningrad during the Siege, 1942 (Institute of Russian Literature, St Petersburg).

Plate 14. Likhachev and his students at Leningrad University, 1953. Two of the students in the picture would later join his department (Likhachev Foundation, St Petersburg).

Plate 15. Three generations of the Pushkin House. Likhachev is in the middle in the second row, 1955 (Department of Old Russian Literature, Institute of Russian Literature, St Petersburg).

Plate 16. Likhachev and Nikolai Voronin, who launched the movement to preserve old Russian legacy, late 1950s (Likhachev Foundation, St Petersburg).

Plate 17. Likhachev with his wife and department colleagues on a field trip to an old Russian city, around 1967 (Department of Old Russian Literature, Institute of Russian Literature, St Petersburg).

Plate 18. Likhachev in the department; Lurie and others mentioned in the text are in the picture, 1967. During this time Likhachev helped A.I. Solzhenitsyn to write *The Gulag Archipelago* (Institute of Russian Literature, St Petersburg).

Plate 19. Likhachev, honorary doctor of Oxford University, 1967 (Institute of Russian Literature, St Petersburg).

Plate 20. Likhachev with his family, including his brothers, daughters, cousins, and wife (Likhachev Foundation, St Petersburg).

Plate 21. Likhachev on a trip, possibly in Solovki in 1966. He explored the archipelago by boat, travelling to the Big Zaitsky Islands, Muksalma, and Anzer (Department of Old Russian Literature, Institute of Russian Literature, St Petersburg).

Plate 22. Likhachev, full member of the Academy of Sciences, with friend Dmitry Kalistov, and granddaughter Vera, in Komarovo around 1971 (Likhachev Foundation, St Petersburg).

Plate 23. Likhachev and Raisa Gorbacheva at the Cultural Foundation, Moscow, *c.* 1986 (The State Museum of History of St Petersburg).

Plate 24. Likhachev and Yeltsin at the funeral of Andrei Sakharov, 1989 (photo by Lev Sherstennikov).

Plate 25. Likhachev and Nicky Oppenheimer, 1992. Oppenheimer sponsored a cultural programme to collect and preserve Russian manuscripts (Likhachev Foundation, St Petersburg).

Plate 26. Likhachev and Prince Charles, 1994 (photo by A. Riv, from the State Museum of History, St Petersburg).

Plate 27. Likhachev and George Soros (on right), c. 1995 (Likhachev Foundation, St Petersburg).

Plate 28. Likhachev dictates his memoirs (Institute of Russian Literature, St Petersburg).

# PREFACE

# A RUSSIAN FOX

In his classic book on Russian thinkers, Isaiah Berlin quoted from the Greek poet Archilochus, who wrote: 'The fox knows many things, but the hedgehog knows one big thing.' Dostoyevsky in Berlin's classification was a classic 'fox' and Tolstoy was a 'hedgehog'. The same can be said about Russian thinkers who lived and acted during communism. An American historian of Russia selected two names of the 'main national ideologues of contemporary Russia': Aleksandr Solzhenitsyn and D.S. Likhachev.[1]

Solzhenitsyn was a hedgehog in Berlin's definition: he knew and proselytized one thing: a long-suffering Russia. His *Gulag Archipelago* revealed the horrors of communist terror and thereby helped destroy the fateful grip of communist ideology on intellectuals. In his epic *Red Wheel*, Solzhenitsyn wrote how the revolution, a product of Western communism and liberalism, destroyed the Old Russia he venerated. He also advocated, without success, the restoration of 'a Russian nation state' combining the Russian Federation, Ukraine and Belorussia. And he ended up backing Vladimir Putin.

The *Encyclopedia Britannica* describes Dmitry Sergeevich Likhachev (1906–1999) as a 'Russian intellectual, literary historian, and author of more than 1,000 scholarly works who devoted his life to defending his country's Christian and cultural heritage'.[2] He was much more than this curt description. Among Russian thinkers of the last century he was a 'fox' who knew and understood many things: medieval Russian culture, avant-garde literature and art of St Petersburg, but also the South Slavic cultures, and English and Scottish literature. He provided leadership for a number of national editorial and publishing projects; he was elected to the top Soviet legislative assembly and convinced its delegates to elect Mikhail Gorbachev as the first Soviet president. He created and chaired the first national foundation for culture in the Soviet Union. Gorbachev and Boris Yeltsin considered him a leader of the 'national intelligentsia' and heeded his advice on the issues of nationalities and cultural policies. Jews in Russia turned to him to protect them from anti-Semitism; Russian émigrés around the world responded to his call to 'return' to Russian museums many pieces of cultural legacy in their private possession.

He also, like Solzhenitsyn, loved his country. During the second decade of his life, Dmitry (Mitya) Likhachev looked upon Russia as a 'dying mother', a victim of the revolution and Bolshevik dictatorship. In his recollections he 'wanted to collect the Motherland's images ... tell the tale of her sufferings'.[3] His idea of Russia, however, was much more dynamic, open, and liberal than Solzhenitsyn's. He did not idealize the heritage of old Russia; rather he expected to preserve it for cultural evolution and study, as a foundation for a tolerant and democratic Russian culture. And this is what he spent his life accomplishing until he died in 1999, at the age of 92. He searched for an answer to a major contradiction of Russian history: how to form a national identity that would be dignified and not hostile to others. School children read the oldest Russian literary texts in his translation; and astronomers gave his name to a newly discovered small planet. And yet outside Russia, D.S. Likhachev remained not as widely acknowledged and recognized as he should have been.

Perhaps he was an exotic thinker who had nothing to say to the world? This book argues to the contrary. It reveals to readers a Russia they have hardly known. After decades of Cold War propaganda, two images of Russia became imprinted on Western public opinion: a land that rejected its dark and backward past and sought to build a communist future; and a hostile militarist empire that opposed freedom and democracy. Likhachev's story differed from the stories of communism and the Cold War: it is an extraordinary saga of a person seeking to preserve his personal dignity in revolution, terror and war. It is also a story of moral fortitude and the perseverance of a man struggling to preserve the 1,000-year-old legacy of Russian culture. Those who come to Russia to admire St Petersburg and its palaces, to see the medieval churches and monasteries of ancient Russian cities, to look at icons and frescoes, should thank D.S. Likhachev.

His focus on 'national cultures' acquires a new meaning today, when liberal globalization suddenly produced new issues and challenges. The global culture of consumption and entertainment complicated old 'national' identities, and at the same time leaves many people with a yearning for 'a little motherland' for their cultural belonging and identity. This quest may inspire xenophobic tribalism or, even worse, aggressive nationalism and fundamentalism. Likhachev's approach to Russian culture pointed in the opposite direction: he framed a search for cultural identity not in the language of tribalism and nationalism, but in the common framework of humanism and personal dignity. This framework, he believes, was not an abstract ideology: it is the product of European culture, as it emerged after centuries of evolution and interaction with other cultures. 'A concert of national cultures', Likhachev explained, was not a return to the era of romantic nationalisms. Instead, in the age of globalization, this approach can reconcile the search for one's own identity with empathy to other cultures and religions.

The shifts in Russian identity during the last 25 years underline the wisdom of Likhachev's approach. In 1991, when the Soviet Union collapsed, many Russians had a crisis of identity. An idea of new liberal Russia lacked both economic and cultural foundation. While many Eastern Europeans, Balts and Ukrainians could celebrate their 'national independence', the case for Russian celebration was unclear. This vacuum of identity was filled by cultural nihilism, cynicism, and anti-American resentment. Liberal Russian politicians and figures of culture concentrated their efforts on integration with the West, but most ordinary Russians were left behind, to struggle with their complex frustrations. As a result, the liberal globalization waltzed over Russia, but instead of a national consensus, produced a backlash; the latter trend became dominant during the presidency of Vladimir Putin.

Likhachev's voice was absent recently, when Vladimir Putin took over Crimea and Russian troops engaged in a war in East Ukraine. This was a nightmare the scholar of Russian culture had anticipated and feared for years would happen. If Russian–Ukrainian common cultural space breaks down, he warned in Kiev in 1982, this would be a victory for nationalism and cultural provincialism on both sides. Another nightmare for him would have been to learn that Russia decided to turn away from Europe, as a result of a dispute between the European Union and the Russian Federation over Ukraine. In contrast to Solzhenitsyn and numerous Russian nationalists, 'the Russian fox' from St Petersburg strongly believed that Russia's place was squarely in Europe and its culture should remain anchored in a European cultural heritage.

# ACKNOWLEDGEMENTS

In 1996 Likhachev was ready to transfer his personal archives to the Institute of Russian Literature (IRLI), the place where he worked for almost 60 years. 'A small part of [my archives] is sorted and filed', he explained in a letter to his associate in Moscow. 'The bulk, however, will be sorted some day, not soon. I really count on it. When they go through my letters, all the people who are mentioned in them will not be alive anymore ... There is also plenty of rubbish. After the war I did not destroy any materials.'[4] Likhachev did not oblige his future researchers and biographers; on the contrary, he sealed away most of his private papers for many years to come. Indeed, unto this day 'the collection of D.S. Likhachev' remains closed for researchers.

I am deeply thankful to Vera Zilitinkevich-Tolz, granddaughter of D.S. Likhachev and a professor of history at the University of Manchester, who helped me to gain access to some papers from this vast collection. My special thanks also to T.S. Tsarkova, of the Manuscript Department of IRLI, and to I.V. Fedorova from the Department of Old Russian Literature at IRLI, for facilitating this task. I am also grateful to the Department of Old Russian Literature at IRLI; N.V. Ponyrko, G.M. Prokhorov, and I.A. Lobakova shared with me their memories of Dmitry Sergeevich and helped with the archival access. Vera Zilitinkevich-Tolz also provided me with assistance in other ways: showed me personal notebooks of her grandfather; answered numerous questions, ranging from family history to the academic life in Leningrad; supplied pictures from family albums, and all this without ever imposing her own views and opinions.

A number of foundations and research centres helped me with their resources. The Russkyi Mir Foundation in Moscow gave me the Seed Grant to start research on a completely new topic and complete the first English language book on D.S. Likhachev. The Kennan Institute at the Wilson Center for International Scholars in Washington DC granted me a scholarship and access to its unique intellectual environment. The US Library of Congress, the institution that D.S. Likhachev admired and worked collaboratively with, was a great resource for my research. From beginning to end, I have benefited from the friendship and assistance of the Likhachev Foundation in St Petersburg, a non-government academic group with a mission to preserve and propagate the legacy of D.S. Likhachev. In the Foundation, A.V. Kobak, O.L. Leikind, N.K. Korsakova, D.Ia. Severiukhin and others shared with me archival findings, publications, photographs and films. They also helped me to learn about the academic, intellectual, and cultural life in Leningrad and St Petersburg – everything that I wanted to know in order to write this book.

Other archival documentation for the book came from the State Archive of the Russian Federation (GARF), with the assistance of its director S.M. Mironenko, from the Russian Academy of Sciences (ARAN) with the assistance of I.G. Tarakanova, and from the Russian State Archive of Literature and Art (IRLI), with the assistance of T.L. Latypova and E.V. Bronnikova, who produced a collection of hundreds of letters between D.S. Likhachev and numerous correspondents. The Director of the Institute of History in St Petersburg, V.N. Pleshkov, gave me access to the unpublished letters of Ya. S. Lurie and A.A. Zimin, friends and historians, both of them scholarly opponents of D.S. Likhachev. In Boston, in the archive of the Massachusetts Institute of Technology (MIT) I read the letters of D.S. Likhachev to American–Russian scholar Roman Yakobson; in the Bodleian Library of Oxford, British archivists showed me the documentation about the honorary doctorate D.S. Likhachev received in 1967. My research also greatly relied on the meticulous archival research and publications of L.I. Sokolova about the discussion on the origins of *The Lay of Igor's Campaign* in 1963–1965.

Many people found time to share with me information about a Likhachev they knew. Among them V.S. Zilitinkevich-Tolz, D.A. Granin, A.B. Roginsky, I.E. Ganelina, B.A. Uspensky, Ya.A. Gordin, A.V. Kobak, M.I. Milchik, V.M. Paneyakh, L.V. Nazarova, I.Yu. Yurieva, K.A. Barsht, E.V. Lukin, Vladimir Tolz, James Billington, Frederik E. Starr, Robin Milner-Gulland, Will Ryan, Vittorio Strada and Clara Strada; also the late S.O. Shmidt, R.Sh. Ganelin and Edward Keenan.

A number of people read the manuscript or selected chapters, and helped me to correct errors of facts and to come up with better arguments. Among them Boris Ostanin, Galina Boguslavskaia, Robin Milner-Gulland, Yuri Slezkine, Michael David-Fox, and anonymous reviewers from I.B.Tauris. Last, but the most important reader and judge of the book is my wife Lena

Vitenberg, who met with D.S. Likhachev (I never did), inspired me to write about him, and helped me to preserve my balance and stamina during the long research and writing process. My particular gratitude goes to I.B. Tauris, its founder Iradj Bagherzade, and my editor Joanna Godfrey. They did not know about D.S. Likhachev before, yet had the vision and courage to introduce this remarkable personality to readers around the world.

# A NOTE ON RUSSIAN NAMES

I am delighted that this book introduces British and international readers to many new figures from the recent Russian and Soviet cultural history. Those who have already delved into this subject should be familiar with the sound and sight of Russian names and patronymics (second name after one's father that Russians must use to address each other respectfully). For others it may be a bit confusing. The main protagonist of the book has different names throughout the text: 'Mitya' and 'Dima' when he was a child and a young man; 'Dmitry' and 'Dmitry Sergeevich' for adulthood, and 'D.S.' as his colleagues around the world called him. Likhachev was a complicated person, and it is befitting for a Russian fox to have several names. Calling him just 'Dmitry' would sound dry and formal, and would take away personal nuances that makes Russian culture so special.

# CHAPTER 1

# VANISHING RUSSIA, 1906–1921

> We can't forget those awful years,
> From days of war and freedom lingers
> The glow of blood on every face.
> *Aleksandr Blok to Zinaida Gippius, 1914*

One morning in early 1992, 85-year-old Dmitry Likhachev sat at his desk in his office in St Petersburg, Russia, and wrote about his childhood. Winter mornings are dark in the northern city, and a table-lamp shed light across the piles of manuscripts. Ceiling-high bookshelves were crammed with books and memorabilia. In the corner of his office was a padded coat that had saved him many decades ago, when he was in Stalin's camp and later, during the war in the Siege of Leningrad. On the wall to the left of the desk was a reproduction of Andrei Rublev's icon 'Trinity', and there were family photos, as well as the photos of many people now dead: friends, writers, poets and priests. One picture was the last Russian emperor Nicholas II, with his melancholic wife Aleksandra, and their only and very sick son Alexei. The Tsarevich was only two years older than the man who now was writing his memoirs.

Mitya (Dmitry) Likhachev was born on 28 November (15 November of the old Julian calendar) 1906, the second son of electrical engineer Sergei Likhachev and his wife Vera Konyaev. His family did not belong to the imperial elites of power, culture and wealth. They came from merchant families (*iz detei kupecheskikh*) – people who made their living in trade and commerce. The founder of the clan came to St Petersburg from the north-east, where Russians had never lived in bondage and conducted an entrepreneurial life of husbandry and trade. Emperor Nicholas I bestowed on Pavel Likhachev the title of a hereditary honorary citizen of the city; this was testimony to his wealth.

Mitya's grandfather Mikhail was a person of strong religious beliefs, involved in various charities. An elder of St Vladimir Cathedral, he arranged the funeral of Feodor Dostoyevsky in 1881. At home, he was a family despot, ruling many children from his first and then second marriage in a way reminiscent of wilful Russian characters created by playwright Aleksandr Ostrovsky.[1]

Mitya's father Sergei, along with his uncles, aunts and in-laws, already belonged to a socially dynamic and rapidly modernizing part of Russian society. Sergei Likhachev moved out of his father's house to study, became an engineer, and ended up as a successful employee in the Ministry of Posts and Telegraphs. Handsome and energetic, Sergei also excelled on the dance floor. During a ball at a fashionable club in Shuvalov, a suburban place near St Petersburg, he met Vera Konyaev. Vera and her two younger sisters, Liubov and Alexandra, came from a well-to-do family of Old Believers who joined the official Orthodoxy: Semen Konyaev was a wealthy merchant, but also, like his brother, a socialite, a good singer and conversationalist, a billiard player and a gambler. Anathematized in 1666 by the Orthodox Church, Old Believers cultivated a stubborn conservatism and preserved a tradition of literacy and a work ethic. Their Russian identity was rooted in religion, simple and strong as a rock.[2] Vera Konyaev was accustomed to a life of comfort and brought to Sergei a sizeable dowry. In marriage Sergei and Vera had three sons: Mikhail (Misha), Dmitry (Mitya) and finally Georgy (Yura).

From his grandfather Mikhail and numerous aunts and uncles little Mitya learned about 'Holy Russia' – a sacred space of memories and worship for millions of Russians. People prayed to this notion in the grand cathedral that housed the Holy Mother of Kazan; they went to the cloisters of St Sergius, St Daniil and St Savva to touch the relics of Russian saints. 'People', wrote Likhachev, thought of Holy Russia 'when they received bad news about war or famine'. The Lord, they prayed, could punish Russians for their sins, but would not let Holy Russia perish. Monasteries, churches, icons, cults of saints created for millions of Russians another reality – which rose above the despotism of the Russian state, the slavishness of people, and the cruelty of Russian history.[3]

Vera Konyaev taught her children to say a prayer and make the sign of the cross over their pillows before going to bed. Every evening Mitya kneeled, together with his mother, and prayed to the icons in rich silver encasings. On Good Friday and for matins on Easter Day, the family went to a chapel of the ministry where Sergei worked. 'We left our coats in the cloakroom and went upstairs. The parquet floors in the church were highly polished' and reflected the electric light well. It was one of the first cathedrals in Russia with electricity, the special pride of Likhachev's father who wired the church.

An attendant brought elegant Viennese chairs for the family, as a sign of respect, so that they could take some rest during the long services.[4]

Engineer Likhachev reached a rank that granted him personal nobility. He could not, however, pass this privileged status to his children. At the same time in the emerging new urban culture sons and daughters of the merchants 'moved comfortably into intelligentsia roles and identified strongly with intelligentsia values'. Sergei and Vera did not aspire to a life of culture and refinement, and rather thought of themselves as part of the professional strata, that included engineers, physicians and teachers.[5] Still, they read a lot and were interested in all cultural news. Among their favourites were Russian poets who gave a lyrical description of the Russian peasantry, full of love and sympathy for the hard life and kindness of Russia's people, especially the peasants.[6] They also loved the novels of Nikolai Leskov, a literary chronicler of Holy Russia and its characters, who was more popular in their milieu than Tolstoy, Turgenev and Dostoyevsky.[7] Mitya would be the first in the family who would 'move comfortably into the intelligentsia's roles' – making the issues of culture and art his profession and passion.

## Small Homelands

In the late nineteenth century three Russians, Orientalist Viktor Rozen, historian of Byzantine art Nikodim Kondakov and the literary historian Aleksandr Veselovsky asked themselves a question: What does it take to become a Russian citizen? For half a century this question was debated between Westernizers and Slavophiles. From the 1870s, Russian nationalists began to demand 'Russification' of non-Russian borderlands of the empire; and the Tsarist administration translated some of these ideas into policies. Transforming multi-ethnic imperial populations into 'Russians' generated more problems than expected: the resistance of non-Russians, particularly in the borderlands, destabilized the empire and filled the ranks of anti-systemic radicals. Rozen, Kondakov and Veselovsky had a different approach. Their idea was to construct a conscious sense of belonging to Russia, a foundation of citizenship, by cultivating an individual attachment to a 'small homeland' (*malaia rodina*) – just as German writers and intellectuals did before and after German unification. This meant taking children to local museums, the publication of historical-artistic guides to cities and localities, trips by students to historical and natural sites, a movement to preserve old monuments, and exhibitions and museums devoted to local pride and local memories. If applied energetically, this cultural work would in time turn Russia into a 'modern' country with patriotic citizens like Germany or France.[8]

St Petersburg was an ideal place to implement this concept.[9] The dreamchild of Peter the Great, it was visible proof of how culture could be 'constructed'. Its magnificent centre became a small homeland for little Mitya. The Likhachevs rented apartments in the district between St Isaac's Cathedral and the Mariinsky Theatre, where streets were lined with the adorned facades of palaces and other monumental edifices. In 1977, a man of 70, Likhachev wrote about his former professor as if he wrote about himself: 'His daily road became ... a kind of excursion that helped him to master Russian history and literature. [He] walked past many historical buildings of Petersburg, where the spectres of great Russian writers of the 19th century still seemed to be present ... It was the same city where [famous Russian poets] Blok and Akhmatova lived.'[10]

At the time of Mitya's birth, the city's aesthetic value was already inspiring a whole generation of artists and poets. The World of Art, an aesthetical movement created by Aleksandr Benois and Serge Diaghilev, poet Aleksandr Blok and writer Andrei Belyi, viewed the city as a setting for their cultural imagination.[11] Mitya's parents became great fans of the imperial ballet. Sergei and Vera paid annual fees for a third-tier box of the Mariinsky Theatre and attended performances religiously. Mitya's first ballet experience was at the age of five; in 1911 the imperial ballet was at its glorious peak: Tatiana Karsavina and Olga Spessivtseva were the stars of all performances. The miracle of the brightly lit scenery contrasted with the glitter in the darkened hall – there the light only dimmed during the performance, and the jewellery of the ladies in the audience gave the effect of moonlight on a shimmering lake.[12]

Aristocratic Petersburg remained a fascinating attraction for the boy. Children flocked to the palace square to watch the parade of the Guards regiments, Semenovsky and Preobrazhensky, admire their scarlet-red and navy-blue uniforms, and listen to the military bands of these regiments. Officers wore spurs on their boots and clicked melodiously as they marched on the cobbled pavement.[13] With his nanny Katerinushka, Mitya went daily to aristocratic-looking parks, with Chinese pagodas and little Japanese gardens. He fell in love with parks for the rest of his life. He later called them 'books about the past', that retained the spirit of 'olden times' better than dynamic urban landscapes.[14] A very sensitive boy, he noticed the haughty caste-like spirit of the Petersburg aristocrats. Arrogant manners, the caste spirit offended Mitya.[15] And there was also 'another Petersburg' of the slums, 'rootless and poor' that 'accumulated venom towards aristocratic dwellers of the city'. 'Another Petersburg' spawned 'the most extreme and inhuman forms of vengeance – revolutionary terror, ideologists of self-destruction'.[16] Mitya could see 'proletarians' everywhere in Petersburg: cobblers in the streets cut stone with a deafening noise, construction workers carried stacks of bricks on their backs up the perilous catwalks, contracted peasants heaved a huge cargo from the barges to the embankments. Mitya 'almost chafed with pity' at the plight of those workers, and recited with his father, who stood at his side, the poetry of Nikolai Nekrasov about poor Russian *muzhiks*.[17] Had he been a bit older, he might have become a socialist. Yet Mitya grew up after the first Russian revolution of 1905–1907. He never learned to hate the tall and arrogant *Gorodovye* (policemen) or the Cossacks on horses who slaughtered revolutionary-minded students and Jews. He considered Petersburg the best place in the world and was patriotic. And he was not an exception. Under the Duma Monarchy of 1905–1913, millions of Russians for the first time began to identify not only with monarchy or religion, but with an idea of a great country.[18]

Mitya's idea of Russia was developed by the family trips. In 1911–1912 Sergei Likhachev stayed in Odessa on a business commission. During the summer he, Vera and the children rented a summer place in nearby Crimea. This beautiful peninsula had long become the favourite resort of the Romanovs, the Petersburg aristocracy and the Russian professional classes. Poets, artists, architects, biologists and sculptors from Petersburg built, decorated, gardened and extolled the 'Russian Riviera'. Vladimir Nabokov, who lived in Gaspra in 1919 after fleeing from revolutionary Petrograd, wrote about Crimea: 'The whole place seemed completely foreign: the smells were not Russian, the sounds were not Russian …'[19] Little Mitya, however, discovered Russian history in Crimea. The family went to the battle sites of the Crimean war of 1853–1856, including the monuments to Sevastopol's defences and the Genovese fortress of Balaklava where the British–French expeditionary force had their base. The stories about the defeat of Russian troops during the Crimean war caused 'personal grief' to six-year-old Mitya. The Likhachevs even managed to purchase a bureau that had once belonged to Rear Admiral Vladimir Istomin, killed in Sevastopol during the siege of 1855.[20]

Another experience of Russia for Mitya was a family trip down the Volga river in May 1914 on a luxury steamboat used by the 'Caucasus and Mercury Co.'. Mitya saw the Volga as a mythical 'great Russian river' which connected lands populated by the Mordva, the Tatars, the Chuvash and others. Russia's economic power was on the rise: fleets of snow-white and flamingo-coloured cruiseships added to the busy traffic, passing numerous barges and commercial vessels, and endless rows of logs on top of which the loggers lived in colourful tents and even cooked on their fires. Many river ports teemed with commerce, with cargo-haulers and stores of piled-up cargo, and a local market with local delights. Peasants, cargo-haulers and marines were Russians, but the bazaars were full of Persians, Tartars and Kalmuks, who dressed differently and spoke their own languages. In Saratov Mitya saw Volga Germans, who had resettled there at the invitation of Catherine the Great. And all those people lived, worked and traded together in one mighty country! Even the names of other steamships reminded one of Russian history: *Prince Pozharskii* and *Kuzma Minin* celebrated the principal organizers of the liberation of Moscow from the Polish occupation in 1613. Another new ship was proudly named *1812* in memory of the recent celebration of the first centennial of Russia's Great Fatherland War against Napoleon. From the deck Mitya saw Russian medieval cities, snow-white monasteries and churches capped by gilded onion-domes. Many years later Likhachev recalled this trip with special feeling: 'I saw the Volga!'[21]

Most summers before the revolution the Likhachevs rented a dacha in Kuokkala on the northern side of the Gulf of Finland, the territory of the Duchy of Finland, then a part of the Russian empire. *Dachniki* (summer-folk) commuted from Petersburg, but mostly stayed in their rented Finnish plywood houses, among lovely pine trees, far from urban noise and tension. Stephen Lovell writes that it was in dacha settlements that a modern middle-class Russian culture was created, 'between aristocratic sociability and popular culture'.[22] Sergei and Vera befriended people outside their social and professional circle: among them the daughter of ballet choreographer Marius Petipa, who played in the Mariinsky orchestra; Maria Puni, from a family of artists involved in ballet scenery, and the the Annenkovs, a family of old nobility that gave Russia many artistic talents. Mitya played with their children.[23]

The Kuokkala dacha community attracted artistic bohemia. Writers Leonid Andreev and Maxim Gorky lived there. Theatre innovator Vsevolod Meyerhold staged performances in the local theatrical studio, attracting his fans and critics. Likhachev would later believe that the Russian cultural avant-garde of the 1900s 'was born from the jokes, pranks, and joy' on the beaches of Kuokkala.[24] This democratic, avant-garde spirit contrasted with the pompous city, but also with the milieu along the opposite, southern coast of the Finnish gulf. There, the Tsarist palaces of Peterhof, the Constantine Palace and Oranienbaum lined up: the world of court and aristocracy. More academic and conservative figures of Petersburg's cultural scene rented dachas there or had their summer properties there. Among them were Aleksandr Benois and other artists who founded the movement The World of Art. The tension between the two coasts made possible remarkable cultural fusion such as the 'Russian Ballets' of Sergei Diaghilev.

The Petersburg culture of the 1910s is often called the Silver Age, and it meant many things: tension and anxiety, cultural decadence and whacky intellectual extremism. Historian of art John Bowlt called the Silver Age an original Russian cultural movement and suggested its role in the formation of Russian identity, linked to the idea of 'greater destiny'.[25] Indeed, not only many artists, but also scholars and scientists in the Academy of Sciences considered themselves as cultural missionaries of Europe on the expanses in the East. From that new sense of destiny came, according to historian Vera Tolz, 'a rare example of healthy Russian patriotism – an uncommon feature in Russian society, in which patriotism has often taken the form of xenophobia and anti-Semitism, with the majority of Westernized liberals being cautious of expressing patriotic feelings'.[26]

This kind of patriotism was an idea that Peter Struve (1870–1944) had in mind. From a family of Russified Germans, Struve passionately believed that the empire was not an obstacle, but rather an opportunity to build a modern Russian nation. Following in the steps of Veselovsky, Rozen and Kondakov, Struve was convinced that only Russian culture and language could be the foundation for a future liberal nation state. Instead of suppressing the non-Russians, Struve suggested, they should be given greater cultural autonomy. He conceded that Poles and Finns were beyond assimilation and were 'ready' for their own nation state. Yet he vehemently resisted any idea of separating Ukrainians and Belorussians from the Russians. He was also remarkably optimistic about the eventual assimilation of Jews – one of the most 'alien' groups of tsarist Russia. 'The Russian intelligentsia,' he wrote, 'has always considered Jews to belong to us, the Russians.' As for the Russians themselves, Struve admitted that aggressive and reactionary forms of Russian nationalism were growing, too. However, he optimistically believed that cultural and educational work would take care of this problem.[27] This was a liberal idea of Russia based not on hatred and exclusion, but on common culture and common destiny.

## The End of Petersburg

On 1 August (19 July in the Julian Russian calendar) 1914, Germany declared war on the Russian empire. This war brought a mobilization of Russian nationalism to an unprecedented level. Thousands of people prayed for victory over the 'Teutons' in the Cathedral of Our Mother of Kazan. Russian newspapers of every kind wrote about 'the second Patriotic war – in defence of the very foundations of our Motherland'.[28] Numerous liberal-minded intellectuals became Russian chauvinists; many *dachniki* returned to the city to join spontaneous demonstrations under Russian flags and flocked to the palace square, where the Russian Tsar Nicholas II came out to greet the enormous crowd. Many fell to their knees. The police were visibly absent. Twenty thousand Petersburg Jews, fearing pogroms, came to the palace square on another day and prayed for the soul of the Tsar. Pogroms did indeed happen, but against Russified Germans, an integral part of the elites and middle classes of St Petersburg and Moscow. The nationalist mob looted German-owned cafes and set fire to the German embassy near St Isaac's Cathedral. On 18 August, Nicholas II renamed Petersburg, which was suddenly too German for patriotic ears, as Petrograd.[29]

The chauvinistic enthusiasm did not last. The Great War revealed Russia's fateful capacity to turn even its temporary successes into failures.[30] When facing the better-organized German army, the Russians suffered horrendous losses. In the disastrous retreat of 1915 Russia lost 1.5 million officers and men and abandoned Western Ukraine and Poland. Millions of refugees from the lost borderlands streamed eastward. Almost overnight, patriotic fervour gave way to defeatism, while adoration of the Tsar disappeared like a summer night's dream.[31] People rumoured: 'The Tsar with his entire family is under the sway of Grishka Rasputin, a lecherous drunkard. The Tsaritsa stoops to treason. Ministers openly sell the motherland ...'[32] The murder of Rasputin on 17 December 1916 by a group of aristocrats and monarchists could not stop a further meltdown of the Tsar's authority. A pebble – a few days of difficulties with bread in Petrograd – produced a revolutionary avalanche. The garrison troops, 200,000 in all, and even the Cossacks, joined the riot. On 2 March 1917 Nicholas abdicated unconditionally on the part of himself and his son Alexei.

When the revolution began, Mitya Likhachev was already an elementary school student, in a privileged minority receiving excellent education.[33] The Karl Mai School for Boys, where his older brother had already studied, practised the newest kind of European liberal pedagogy, with an outstanding and devoted faculty. The school rejected many 'isms' – elitism, hierarchism, chauvinism and clericalism. The main mission was to raise citizens of a future democratic Russia. There were also students from British and French families, Jews, Germans, Swedes, Finns and Estonians. The school janitor addressed students in Russian, German and Italian.[34] The Mai students participated in patriotic activities, such as collecting clothing for the soldiers and materials for the treatment of the wounded soldiers. They also knitted woollen wristbands and balaklavas, which the Russian soldiers could wear in winter under their helmets. Mitya had a map of Europe at home, where he pinned little French and British flags for the much smaller Western front, and small Russian flags across the giant Eastern frontline. When Russia began to lose the war, the line of Russian flags had to be relocated further and further eastward on the map. Mitya was 'beyond himself with grief'. Before bed, every night, he prayed for the salvation of Holy Russia. A chance opened his eyes to the negative side of war nationalism. His parents hired a Polish refugee student to help Mitya with his school lessons. At some point, the girl began to tell Likhachev about Polish history. In the Russian empire, any narratives of Polish national history remained banned. Mitya indignantly exclaimed: 'Polish history does not exist!' He was stunned to see the girl crying. He learned an important lesson: his patriotism could be insulting to others. At family meals, Mitya overheard the rumours about Rasputin and 'German dominance' around the Tsar, but also about the 'inherent flaws of the Russian nation': carelessness and lack of foresight, a deficit of self-organization.[35]

The Tsar's abdication took the Likhachevs, like everyone else, by surprise. And like everyone, they joined the 'celebration of freedom' that swept through the city. Many felt pride that Russia had finally become a full member of 'the great family of democracies' against 'the Teutonic tyranny' of Germany.[36] In the meantime without the traditional authority of the Romanovs, Russian statehood precipitously went to ruin. The Provisional Government in Petrograd, consisting of well-meaning liberals and socialists, was powerless, lacked enforcement tools and feared its own troops. Aleksandr Kerensky, a self-proclaimed 'dictator of the Republic', believed in the rule of law, refused to introduce martial law and believed that the Tsarist generals posed more danger to 'the Republic' than Lenin, Trotsky and other Bolsheviks. Before long, Lenin and Trotsky ousted Kerensky and ended the brief spell of liberal intellectualism in power.

Petrograd ceased to be a modern metropolis. In the absence of police, crime was rampant everywhere. The armed soldiers and sailors, called 'the pride of the revolution', dominated the central streets, and shopped in expensive stores, accompanied by prostitutes. The drunken mob broke into liquor stores, gutted splendid squares and parks, and systematically looted aristocratic districts. They filled the pavements of the glorious Nevsky Prospect with chaff, scraps and cigarette butts. Filth and the stench of urine replaced the wonderful smells of wealth, trade and tidiness that Mitya Likhachev admired. Aristocratic chic and officers' braids and spurs vanished. The Bolshevik victory sealed the fate of aristocrats, but also of many other Russians. According to the revolutionary taxonomy, all educated and propertied groups of the former empire, all members of the privileged estates of nobility and clergy became *byvshiie* or 'former people' – disenfranchised, their property prone to confiscation. Those people, many of them with a strong Russian identity and the ethos of citizens, were a future basis for a modern Russian nation that Struve dreamed about. Now they became the victims of revolutionary fury.[37]

All members of the Likhachev and the Konyaev clans became 'former people' as well. Sergei and Vera felt very lucky in not owning any property, aside from furniture and family valuables. Sergei Likhachev, always a dandy at heart, stopped sporting his fancy costumes, and began to dress in a modest and shabby way, trying to blend into the new 'proletarian' style. In September 1917, some workers criticized Sergei's 'bourgeois ways' and he had to leave his work at the power plant of the Chief Directorate of Posts and Telegraphs. Fortunately, he was immediately 'elected' to a similar position by a workers' committee of the First State Printing House. He was glad and proud to win 'proletarians' trust'. New times required survivalist skills. Sergei began to acquire useful 'friends' and patrons among Bolsheviks. And then the Red Terror began. At night, Mitya could hear the crackling sound of shots: the revolutionary jailers 'liquidated', without trial or decree, hundreds of prisoners – Grand Dukes, aristocrats, priests, lawyers, liberal politicians, landowners and army officers.[38]

Sergei's job in effect protected the family from revolutionary excesses. He won the trust of the Bolshevik Ilya Ionov (Bernshtein), a hysterical workaholic and the head of the Petrograd State Publishers (Petrogosizdat). Ionov's influence came also from the fact that his sister Zlata Lilina was a wife of Grigory Zinoviev, Lenin's associate, who would become for several years a dictatorial ruler of Petrograd. The family also lived in a large flat, owned by the Printing House. This was a luxury at the time, when people could not stay safe in their own flats, and when the Bolsheviks abolished the ownership of real estate and forced former house-owners to accept 'proletarian tenants'. Bourgeois flats turned into communal apartments with communal kitchens and toilets.[39] The Likhachevs preserved enough room for a big library and for all the family possessions, including Vera Konyaev's dowry: old furniture, icons in silver casings and jewellery. Mitya liked to look at the albums of photographs Sergei had taken with his Kodak camera in the Crimea, on the Volga and in other places before 'the times of trouble'. The family even continued with their habit of renting a summer dacha. Kuokkala was now in independent Finland, and the family went by train from the Petrograd to the nearby villages of Olgino and Toksovo.

Still, the Likhachevs faced the same problems as the millions: the Bolshevik policy of 'war communism' created economic ruin. Central heating stopped, and the crude metal stove that replaced it warmed only a small space around. In revolutionary times, peasants and traders no longer stored and dried thousands of cubes of wood for winter heating. At night in winter in 1919–1922 the house temperature fell below zero degrees celsius, and the Likhachevs, like thousands of other families in the city, slept in impromptu 'tents' made out of rolled carpets, warming themselves with their body heat and breathing. The school was unheated as well: few students continued to attend it. Mitya was among those who still did, and he had to wear thick gloves and a fur-coat in class. Likhachev recalled that his hands 'grew swollen' from cold and malnutrition.[40] The giant city was hungry: under the Bolsheviks money became worthless, due to hyperinflation, and private trade was banned. Ever resourceful, Sergei still could not obtain bread, but the family had *duranda* – a sort of millcake. Bread, when obtained, consisted of coarsely ground oat mixed with wild herbs. The family silver could be exchanged for a bag of frozen potatoes from the peasants, who braved the Red Guard block-posts at the risk of death. Mitya's older brother Mikhail undertook dangerous trips to the countryside by dark, on cold trains. He returned with cereal, flour, milk and even cottage cheese – bartered for clothes and Vera's jewels. The family lived in anticipation: 'Such a life simply cannot last forever.'[41]

Dmitry also suffered in a spiritual sense. His beloved city was degraded, and in March 1918 the Bolsheviks stripped it of its status as the capital, moving their government to Moscow, further away from the advancing German armies. It was 'an evil act, cowardly, destructive, and blind. It killed the magnificent city and threw the country far back.'[42] One visitor observed: 'Petersburg remained like a giant, stylish country mansion whose old owners had abandoned it. And the new nomads who have conquered it still have to find their bearings in its giant premises.' He also found the city hauntingly beautiful in a 'heart-rending' way.[43] As Bolshevik rule unfolded, patriotic Russians, who despised Lenin and Trotsky, had a severe case of identity crisis. When Ukraine declared its 'independence' under a German armed protectorate, Russia became a phantom, 'disintegrated like a house of cards'.[44]

As Trotsky and then his successor Abram Yoffe negotiated with the Germans over the terms of peace, Russian liberals faced an impossible choice: Bolshevik dictatorship vs German occupation. On the one hand, all patriotic Russians felt outrage at Germany's intent to dismember Russia, but on the other hand, they fervently hoped that Germans would come to finish off Bolshevism and restore Russia's statehood. The Bolsheviks turned out to be smart beyond anticipation. They signed the Treaty of Brest-Litovsk and surrendered to the German Reich 78,000 square kilometres of territory populated by 56 million people – one third of the pre-war population of the Russian empire. Also, Lenin's government pledged to pay Germany billions of reparations in gold, food and other resources. The German leaders decided to pocket the huge gains and keep the Bolsheviks for a while as their satellites. The news of the Treaty of Brest-Litovsk shook many Russians. Historian Evgeny Tarle, a Russified Jew and a fervent enemy of Germany, wrote that it 'means death to Russia as a sovereign political body'.[45] Even those who considered anti-Semitism despicable earlier, now vented their venom against 'the Jews' who were so visible in the Bolshevik leadership.[46] Likhachev recalled: 'When the scandalous peace of Brest-Litovsk was concluded, it was impossible not to believe that it was plain and simple treason, the work of the enemies of our Motherland.'[47] Some of the Russian youth with military training fled to the south of Russia to form the White movement.

In July 1918 came more devastating news, this time about the execution of the last Russian Tsar in Yekaterinburg by a Bolshevik firing squad. The majority in Petersburg spoke about the death of Nicholas Romanov with indifference; some people were full of venom and contempt. Mitya, however, felt great pity of the last Tsar. Later he learned from Igor Anichkov, his English language tutor, who in 1918 fought briefly in the White army of Admiral Kolchak, that the whole family of the Tsar was killed, including the girls and little Tsarevich.[48] Mitya, however, was too little and timid to do anything aside from going to school. Sergei Likhachev did everything to keep his sons from trouble. The terrible slaughter of the civil war bypassed the family entirely – they were extraordinarily fortunate. The only real loss in the family was the departure of Vera's little sister, Alexandra (Shura) Konyaev: she married Valentin Andrealetti, an engineer from a family with Italian roots, and in the early 1920s the young couple left Russia. They would never return.

In 1920, when Mitya was 13, his parents found another school for him just a few blocks from home. 'Lentovka' was a private school established in 1907 by philanthropist Lidia Lentovskaia. Its faculty consisted of teachers with 'progressive views' who had lost their jobs in the state educational system during the first Russian revolution. The school director kept Marxist revolutionary brochures in his office and encouraged select senior students to read them. Democratic-minded, socialist-leaning intellectuals preferred Lentovka to the schools controlled by the imperial Ministry of Education. Lentovka's teachers welcomed the revolution. After the Bolshevik coup they continued to espouse Social Democratic views. Their real creed, however, was Russian literature and art; they worshipped classical and European culture, and viewed it as a foundation for Russia's development.[49]

At that school Mitya met the teachers who influenced him for life. The most important among them was Leonid Georg, with German roots and a remarkable dedication to art and theatre. Vladimir Veidle, Georg's younger cousin, recalled that 'Lelya' unveiled to him the beauty of Petrograd, the works of Shakespeare, Pushkin and Aleksandr Blok.[50] With his students, Georg staged *Twelfth Night*, Gogol's *Inspector-General* and Pushkin's *Little Tragedies*. His idols were Anton Chekhov and Konstantin Stanislavsky; imbued with 'a delicate sense' of beauty, Georg wanted to convey this sense to his students, to protect them from disillusionment and cynicism. From him Mitya learned the principles of 'kindness to people, intellectual tolerance, and discussions about life and its meaning'.[51] During the 'war communism' the Lentovka teachers, along with their colleagues in Petrograd, decided to practise *rodinovedeniie* – to give students the sense of Russia that the revolution seemed to have destroyed. They began to take their classes to the places of cultural memory, and also outside the city on excursions and field trips.[52] Boris Lossky, son of Mitya's favourite philosopher, recalled how important school excursions became for shaping his Russian identity. Teachers took him and other students to the Russian Museum, later the Hermitage, and the palaces of the Russian aristocracy, which the Bolsheviks had confiscated and opened to the public. In summer they toured the palaces and parks of Peterhof, Tsarskoye Selo and Pavlovsk, and even travelled to ancient Pskov.[53]

In the summer of 1921, the school organized a multi-week field trip to the Russian North. Remarkably, Sergei and Vera allowed Mitya, on whom they doted, to join his class. The students took a long train ride from Petrograd to Murmansk on the White Sea. Then they continued on a steamboat across the White Sea to Archangel, then again by steamer up the river Dvina, and then by rail back to Petersburg. The timing of this excursion was ideal: the British occupation of this area had ended shortly before, and the Russian North was still free from the gulag labour camps that would cover its territories a few years later.[54] This trip became for Dmitry an even greater revelation than the Volga voyage. The Russian North at the time preserved many monuments of ancient Russian culture, and the dignified lifestyle of free Russian peasants who had never known serfdom. Its cultural history resonated strongly with the ancestral roots of the Likhachevs and Konyaevs. This was the land of the Old Believers, of their ancient religious books and icons, oral folklore, music and songs. Mitya could see peasants from the Russian North in pre-war Petersburg: they brought their goods for trade using waterways; their barges in Moika and Fontanka smelled of fresh forest and tar. Now he saw for the first time their beautiful wooden churches, where peasants still sang their prayers, using an ancient version of musical notation. He and his classmates even fished together with local peasants in the Barents Sea. 'When I saw *Pomory* in their peasant huts, heard their songs and fairy-tales, saw how simply and without affectation those beautiful people behaved, I was absolutely stunned,' Likhachev recalled in his old age. 'Their way of life impressed me as ideal: they worked at a measured pace, with great satisfaction.' Mitya finally saw what Holy Russia could be like.[55]

# CHAPTER 2

# PATRIOTISM OF PITY, 1921–1928

> Any national feelings are allowed in this country, except for Great Russian feelings.[1]
> *Lidia Ginzburg, Russian-Jewish philologist, notes of 1925–1926*

After winning the Civil War in 1921, the Bolsheviks declared other 'frontlines', education being one of them. The new regime turned its gaze from the defeated Whites and political rivals to Russian schools, universities and academic scholarship. Some Bolsheviks, like Anatoly Lunacharsky, opted for a 'softer' policy: to organize the 'enlightenment' of the masses with the help of the old cultural elites. Lenin, Trotsky, Zinoviev and the Bolshevik secret police, the Cheka, pursued a 'hard line': to eliminate the Russian intelligentsia and replace them with 'proletarian' cadres.[2] Mitya Likhachev was educated in the midst of Bolshevik policies. Instinctively, and because of his early upbringing and social habits, Mitya ended up in the milieu of 'former people', intellectuals who struggled for autonomy of thinking and conscience in the face of the advancing Bolshevik police-state. When he reminisced about his life in the early 1990s, Likhachev argued that he was part of the first cohort of 'dissidents' in Soviet history – four decades ahead of Andrei Sakharov and Aleksandr Solzhenitsyn. Mitya attended several informal associations of the embattled intelligentsia, so-called *kruzhki*; this allowed him to develop the quality he would cherish later as one the greatest gifts of his life. It was the inner habit of freethinking, free speech, and conscience.

## Democracy of *Kruzhki*

In 1921 a new teacher Ivan M. Andreyevsky (1894–1976) began to teach psychology in Mitya's class at Lentovka. Charismatic and energetic, he had a rich biography: a radical socialist in his youth, he knew some prominent

Bolsheviks, and was arrested during the first revolution. Later he studied psychology at the Sorbonne, and listened to the lectures of Henri Bergson. By 1917 Andreyevsky was already a conservative Orthodox thinker, a devotee of St Serafim of Sarov and Bishop Ioann of Kronstadt. He was professor of philosophy at Petersburg University and came to Lentovka to teach part-time. Andreyevsky invited some of his students, including Mitya, to come to his apartment, where he organized a *kruzhok*. It was named flamboyantly 'The Academy of Art, Literature, Philosophy, and Science' (Helfernak). Among the members were medievalist Vsevolod Bakhtin and philosopher and linguist Mikhail Bakhtin, pianist Maria Yudina, scholar of Dostoyevsky Vassily Komarovich, writer Evgeny Ivanov, a close friend of Aleksandr Blok. From Lentovskaia school came Leonid Georg and Igor Anichkov – Mitya's older friend from the Kuokkala dacha community. All who attended the *kruzhok* signed their names in the Helfernak journal; every presentation was announced and recorded.[3]

Petrograd in the early 1920s was a hive of intelligentsia associations and ventures. Among the most important was the Institute of Art History ('the Zubov House'). The wealthy art lover Count Valentin Zubov invented his 'Institute' in his former palace near St Isaac's Square and made it a second home for hundreds of individuals and artists. In 1921–1923 the Institute housed research centres on the history of art, the history of music and linguistics. The brilliant group of Formalists worked there, among them Victor Zhirmunsky, Boris Eichenbaum, Boris Tomashevsky and Victor Shklovsky.[4] Another formal association was the Free Philosophical Association ('Volfila'), set up in November 1919 in the House of Arts, another confiscated palace, by a group of leftist intellectuals. It had sections on the 'philosophy of man', Russian literature, philosophic and literary creativity, ethics, the philosophy of religion, anarchism and communism. Public lectures drew an audience of hundreds; among the speakers were Blok, Bely and Meyerhold.[5]

After the Civil War ended, the Bolsheviks began to view these associations as a threat to their ideological and cultural monopoly. Russian culture to them was synonymous with White counter-revolution.[6] In June–July 1921 the Cheka announced the so-called 'Tagantsev conspiracy' that allegedly involved hundreds of Petrograd professors, scientists, engineers, literary and artistic figures. They were found guilty of organizing a 'combat organization' and preparing an insurrection. In reality, geographer Vladimir Tagantsev, a graduate of the Karl Mai School, organized a loose network of citizens to rescue Petrograd's cultural heritage from looting – in case the Bolshevik regime would implode. The Cheka executed Tagantsev, his wife, poet Nikolai Gumilev, pro-rector of Petrograd University and almost 60 other intellectuals and prominent cultural figures. Many others were sent to a concentration camp. Yakov Agranov, Lenin's secretary and plenipotentiary in Petrograd, cynically commented: 'In 1921 seventy per cent of the Petrograd intelligentsia had one foot in the enemy camp. We had to cauterize that foot'.[7]

Western public protests made Lenin, Trotsky, Zinoviev and the Cheka officials conceive another plan: to 'purge Russia' of the intelligentsia by deporting the top intellectuals to Western Europe. In Petrograd, the head of the OGPU-NKVD (the new name for the Cheka) Iosif Unshlicht gathered a group of 'experts' to make lists for deportation; one of these experts was Ilya Ionov, influential sponsor of Sergei Likhachev. The Bolsheviks approached the German government, and it agreed to accept the deportees. On 28 September 1922 the German ship *Oberbürgermeister Hacken* started from Petersburg harbour, carrying a large group of Moscow intellectuals, above all philosophers, sociologists and public intellectuals. In November a smaller German ship, the *Preussen*, took the Petrograd intellectuals with their families to Germany.[8] In 1924 OGPU-NKVD shut down the Volfila. In response, the remaining members of the Russian intelligentsia formed *kruzhki* which continued in the private apartments of intellectuals. One of them was Andreyevsky's Helfernak. They became the next line of defence for the intellectuals, their cultural autonomy and freedom of speech and thought.

In Andreyevsky's flat, Mitya Likhachev found the milieu he badly lacked at home, among his narrowly pragmatic parents and brothers. He met people who shared his passion for philosophy, literature and ethics, something he learned from his teachers at Lentovka. Likhachev's favourite was Henri Bergson, a philosopher who rejected positivist fact-accumulation and emphasized the primary role of the energy of the human mind, intuition and *elan vital*. He also read Nikolai Lossky, a philosopher of Russian intuitivism, who left Russia on board the *Preussen* in November 1922. One of Helfernak's members was Lossky's family friend Sergei Alexeyev (Askoldov), a mathematician who became a religious philosopher and a thinker of great originality. In August 1918, he published an essay about the Russian Revolution, explaining it as a result of a split within the Russian people. Russian liberals, he claimed, failed to understand the Russian national character which was composed of great polarities and conflicting features. Like his colleague Andreyevsky, Alexeyev encouraged Mitya to borrow books from his library. He taught him that knowledge had an indivisible nature, that borders between natural science and humanities were artificial, and that intuition was no less important for making discoveries than deduction from facts.[9]

At one meeting of Helfernak, Alexeyev asked Dmitry to take notes of his presentation about the nature of time. There were many levels and dimensions of time, Alexeyev reported. In our physical time everything perishes and vanishes without a trace. Yet there are higher time-systems, he continued. Within them, the past stays, and therefore in the Christian meaning of resurrection, 'death loses its sting'.[10] Mitya was greatly impressed: this blended religious beliefs with a deeply personalist philosophy of ethical responsibility. When 1923 began, Mitya came to Alexeyev for advice on his future studies. His time at Lentovka was almost over, and Likhachev wanted to study humanities at the university. Unfortunately for him, the Bolsheviks abolished all university courses on history. Bolshevik Mikhail Pokrovsky argued that the past, including history and archaeology, was just 'reactionary and useless junk'. Alexeyev advised Mitya to specialize in literature and languages – another segment of humanities that Bolshevik 'science' had still not decided upon. This decision triggered a scandal. Sergei Likhachev warned his son that he should be trained as an engineer, otherwise he would never be able to support himself and his family. 'You would remain a pauper!' These words would resonate in Dmitry's memory for the next 20 years, when his father's prophecy seemed to become a reality.

Still, ever a doting father, Sergei relented, and with his customary pragmatism began to dig up the connections required to make an exception for Mitya, as a child of a 'personal nobleman', to enter the university. It was not easy as Bolshevik commissions ruthlessly weeded out the children of 'former people' from the student body in favour of young people with a 'proletarian' background. Resourceful Sergei obtained letters of recommendation from important people (Ionov was probably one of them). The teachers from Lentovka wrote a glowing recommendation letter to the admission board, praising Mitya's outstanding philological talents. The admission office must have been duly impressed, and in the fall of 1923 Dmitry Likhachev matriculated as a student of social sciences, with a focus on ethnology and linguistics. He was only 16 years old.[11]

## At the University

The Petrograd university was in the midst of Bolshevik *Gleichschaltung* – not as rapid as the Nazi policy at German universities in 1933, yet painful for the faculty and some students.[12] The 'old-style' professors co-existed uneasily with the 'red professors' who were loyal to the new regime. The Bolsheviks and 'red professors' wanted to break the authority of the former: they abolished the system of scholarly titles and degrees, and aggressively promoted new appointees. Dmitry quickly discovered the divide between the two groups: in one, professors called students 'colleagues' and addressed each other as 'gentlemen' and 'ladies'; in another group 'comrades' called on 'comrades'. The old-professors were courteous and polite, cowed and marginalized by the political pressure, yet still seeking to protect the best standards of academic integrity and educational quality. They preferred to invite their students to seminars in their private apartments, away from the eyes of 'comrades'.[13]

Still, the spirit of creativity appeared not to be ebbing, due to the tremendous energy and hopes of post-revolutionary youth. Lidia Ginzburg, who studied in those years at the Institute of Art History in Petrograd, recalled that the collapse of the old world made 'the youthful intelligentsia youth go in droves into music, theatre, literature and journalism, converting their family talents and hobbies into professions ... Earning their bread in science and art appeared to be a merry pastime.'[14] In the famously long university corridor young men and women engaged in endless conversations and shared cultural news, still without looking over their shoulder, without inhibition or fear of snitches. Some of them came from the Russian intelligentsia with deep traditions of culture and learning. Walking through the famous corridor one day, Dmitry met celebrated writer Victor Shklovsky – students spoke admiringly about his life of adventure and risk in revolution and war, his travel to Persia in 1918, and his escape from the Cheka in 1921. He also found a new language to describe his experience. Bored by bourgeois Europe after a brief emigration, Shklovsky returned to Soviet Russia to become a cultural and intellectual provocateur.[15] He stopped Dmitry and asked what his age was. He was still 16. 'It is then high time to become a hooligan,' Shklovsky advised. He used the word as a synonym for a cultural rebellion. Dmitry, however, did not want to become a cultural provocateur; he still had to find himself and to gain self-confidence.[16]

Petrograd was a great bazaar of culture and education for him, with countless opportunities. As Dmitry walked from his new apartment on Vassilievsky Island to the university, he passed the Academy of Sciences and its famous library, the Institute of Russian Literature ('The Pushkin House'). Beyond them stood the Asiatic Museum and the famous Kunstkammer, the first Russian museum opened by Peter the Great. In the evening the Likhachevs crossed the Neva's majestic bridges to its southern bank, where all artistic and theatre life was located. In 1921 the Philharmonia reopened its doors for devotees of classical music, and Mitya soon became one of them.[17] The southern bank teemed with cultural iconoclasts. Dmitry dashed there from the university, where he attended lectures by Professor Zhirmunsky, to see and hear rebellious Formalists at the Zubov House. Next to Zubov was the Myatlev House and the State Institute of Artistic Culture (*Ginkhuk*), where Kazimir Malevich congregated with his Suprematist and Constructivist friends.[18]

Young Dmitry decided to spread his net of learning wide and took a double degree: Roman-German languages and Slavonic-Russian literature. In the class of Professor Zhirmunsky he read Byron, Shelley, Keats, Wordsworth and Coleridge. He studied Shakespeare with Professor Vladimir Mueller, old French literature with Aleksandr Smirnov, and English poetry with Semen Boyanus. Simultaneously, he took a course on the history of Russian journalism by Vladislav Evgeniev-Maximov, learned Church Slavonic from Sergei Obnorsky, and analysed Pushkin texts with Lev Shcherba. Textology, the art of 'slow reading' of many semiotic layers, attracted him. As if this were not enough, he went to evening seminars on Dostoyevsky in the apartment of Professor Vassily Komarovich. And on Wednesdays he went to Helfernak.[19]

Sergei and Vera worried when Mitya was not at home. The city remained crime-ridden. At the same time Dmitry could not invite too many friends to his apartment: they needed a special permit to enter the guarded Publishing House. As a result, during his first years at the university, he did not really have the social life of a student. 'I stayed at home, and studied rare books.' And there was a lot to read. Sergei Likhachev could get hold of almost any book in print.[20] In 1926–1928 Dmitry had a real windfall – access to Bolshevik Ionov's great collection. After Stalin defeated Zinoviev and the 'Leningrad opposition', Ionov was sent abroad and asked Sergei Likhachev to store in his apartment thousands of rare books and art objects. Most of this collection Ionov apparently requisitioned from the mansions of aristocrats. Dmitry discovered in this collection precious prints from the sixteenth century: perfect Renaissance *in folio* books published by Aldus Pius Manutius; precious Elsevier volumes; the Bible with elaborate etchings, in the translation of Johannes Piskator; the etchings of Rubens and Rembrandt. There were first editions of early Russian writers, and the only existing death mask of Aleksandr Blok, Mitya's favourite poet.[21]

University years are often the time when individual identity becomes articulated, and student Likhachev was no exception. His adolescent patriotism was galvanized by the renewed opera performances in the Mariinsky Theatre, especially by Mussorgsky's *Khovanshchina* and Rimsky-Korsakov's *Tale of the Invisible City of Kitezh*. In the former, Feodor Shaklovityi, brutal careerist who organized the rebellion in Moscow, sang a moving aria, bemoaning 'a deplorable destiny of Russia', the long-sufferance of the Russian people. Famous singer Pavel Andreev, who played this part, turned to the hall with a prayer: 'Oh Lord, hear the sin of the world, do not allow Holy Russia to perish from cruel mercenaries.' The audience stood up in tears and demanded encores. In Rimsky's opera Dmitry was struck by another character, Grishka Kuterma, a Russian without any honour and conscience, who led the Tatar army to the City of Kitezh. Likhachev later recalled: 'Similar Grishkas, who destroyed churches and betrayed their country, filled the land.' When Dmitry and his parents returned from the Mariinsky across the Neva bridge, they passed an absolutely dark and deserted city. 'It seemed that subjects like Grishka lurked behind every corner, people who drank and sold everything away.' University student Likhachev decided to study the historical origins of the Russian national character.[22]

Bolshevik cultural and ideological policies also galvanized Dmitry's idea of Russia. Bolsheviks and 'comrades' at the university did not tolerate expressions of Russian patriotism. Likhachev quickly came into conflict with one of the 'red professors' during an examination. The professor, a disciple of Mikhail Pokrovsky, wanted Likhachev to admit that Peter the Great was a syphilitic and degenerate. When Dmitry refused, he received a fail grade; the indignant professor reported up the line of authority about Likhachev's 'monarchist sympathies'. This was an omen of future troubles.[23] The meaning of being a Russian, the idea of Russia, troubled and confused many people during the 1920s. Private letters and diaries provide insights into the currents of national consciousness. One intellectual wrote in his private letter in December 1924: 'Old Russia has been slowly dying, and a new, robust, energetic and young Russia is growing in the form of the USSR ... A young Russian man today is a completely new creature ... with a transplanted soul.'[24] Others continued to believe that Russians betrayed their national roots and destroyed their chance to become a modern nation.[25] Two Russian émigrés in Prague, Nikolai Ustrialov and Yuri Kliuchnikov published in July 1921 a pamphlet called *Smena Vekh* (Change of Landmarks). They wrote that the Bolshevik dictatorship would be gradually 'dissolved' in the 'Russian sea', and Russia would become a nation state again. However, this required massive 'cultural work', and the return of those who emigrated during the revolution. Spurred on by this manifesto, hundreds of thousands of Russians returned from emigration to the USSR. The Bolsheviks cautiously promoted this movement, in order to weaken the political forces of the emigration. The Politburo even authorized Lunacharsky to establish the 'non-partisan journal' *Rossiya*, to attract the new collaborationists. Many nationalist writers, among them Mikhail Bulgakov, worked for *Rossiya*. Historian Mikhail Agursky later called this 'the first articulate programme of Russian national-Bolshevism.'[26]

Also in 1921 Nikolai Trubetskoy published another seminal pamphlet in Sofia, Bulgaria. He argued that Europe had let Russia down, and the future destiny of the Russian nation would be in 'Eurasia', building its own civilization in the confines conquered by Genghis Khan. Émigré intellectuals Peter Savitsky, Georgy Florovsky, Georgy Vernadsky, Lev Karsavin and many others joined the Eurasian movement. Eurasianists praised the Bolsheviks for restoring old Russia's imperial realm, subduing Ukrainian, Georgian and other separatist nationalisms. Some of the Eurasianist thinkers considered the legacy of Peter the Great 'alien' for the Russians.[27]

In emigration, Peter Struve opposed these new ideologies. The Russian liberal refused to turn against Europe, and he refused to consider the Soviet Union a *Russian* state. He believed that one day a liberal and European Russia would re-emerge from the ashes of the Russian Revolution. Russian intellectuals, he argued, would play a vital role in this 'return to Europe' on condition that they found ways to develop and preserve their national patriotic identity. A few émigré intellectuals followed this guideline, among them Mikhail Karpovich, who became professor of Russian history at Harvard University and taught a remarkable number of American historians of imperial Russia.[28]

Echoes of debates about the future of Russia reached Petrograd. The ideas of Ustyalov and Kliuchnikov resonated among professionals, including engineers. They believed that the widely trumpeted Bolshevik plans for electrification and industrialization would serve Russia's long-term interests.[29] Dmitry and other students attended public talks by Kliuchnikov, who returned to the Soviet Union. Rummaging through Ionov's collection, Likhachev found there a brochure by Lev Karsavin with his reflections on a post-revolutionary Russian identity.[30] Dmitry, however, never accepted the ideas of Change of Landmarks and Eurasianism. Instead of looking at the Bolshevik state with false hopes, young Likhachev learned to treasure the memories of Holy Russia etched in his early childhood and family trips.

### 'We Wept and Prayed'

For Dmitry Likhachev the most painful aspect of his student years was to witness 'the destruction of Russia and the Russian Church'. Looking back across 70 years of his life, Dmitry recalled: 'This destruction took place before our eyes, with bestial cruelty, and seemed to leave no hope of resurrection.' He was more and more lured by the thought of studying Old Russia. 'I wanted to have Russia on my mind, as do children sitting at the bed of a dying mother. Like them I wanted to collect the Motherland's images, show them to my friends, tell the tale of her sufferings.' This feeling, he emphasized, was very different from any forms of Russian patriotism or nationalism he had encountered before or since. 'Our love for Russia was the opposite of pride in victories and conquests. Today many would find it incomprehensible. We did not sing patriotic songs; instead we wept and prayed.'[31]

After the revolution, the old Orthodox Church, often known for its Black Hundred bent, began to change. In November 1917 the All-Russian Church

Council in Moscow freely elected the first patriarch since the times of Peter the Great, Tikhon Belavin.[32] The Bolsheviks viewed an independent Church as a grave threat and unleashed a campaign of anti-religious terror. The Cheka and Red Guards broke into churches, closed monasteries, looted and killed. Following the French Jacobins, the Bolsheviks ordered the 'opening and liquidation of holy relics' and confiscation of all ecclesiastical possessions.[33] Another devious tactic was the backing of a fifth column within the Church, the so-called Living Church or 'renovationists'. They were that part of the clergy who believed that collaboration with Bolshevism would enable them to create a kind of Russian Protestantism.[34]

In May 1922, when Mitya was still studying at the Lentovskaia, the Bolsheviks arrested the Patriarch in order to bring 'red priests' to the top of the hierarchy. Petrograd became the centre of this struggle. When the city's Metropolitan Veniamin excommunicated Aleksandr Vvedensky, the head of the Living Church, the Bolsheviks arrested him and 86 priests and parish activists. Their trial lasted for several weeks inside the Philharmonic Hall. A silent crowd of believers stood in front of the building, and prayed for the accused. Metropolitan Veniamin and three other priests were found guilty and on 12 August they were executed by firing squad.[35] Mitya saw that crowd of praying believers. Later he was also a witness of a public debate on religion with Vvedensky, in a large hall at the State Printing House. The enraged believers waited for the 'red priest' in front of the main entrance, prepared to beat him up. The party organizers asked Sergei Likhachev to usher Vvedensky from the hall to a backdoor exit via Likhachev's apartment.[36]

In 1925 the Patriarch died after several imprisonments, unbroken under the pressure. Two years later came a decisive turn in the history of Russian Christianity: the Bolshevik rulers began to shut dozens of churches, ignoring the protests of the believers. In daylight, trucks with Komsomol activists began to disrupt church services; orchestras and Komsomol choirs harassed and overwhelmed religious singing. Likhachev recalled their crude atheistic chants: 'Chase out the monks, chase out the priests; beat the speculators, down with the kulaks.' It was the start of the so-called Cultural Revolution. Metropolitan Sergius Stragorodsky, one of the Patriarch's caretakers, decided to strike a bargain with the regime. On 29 July 1927 Soviet newspapers published his 'Epistle to pastors and parishes' urging them 'to demonstrate with deeds their loyalty to the Soviet state, which he called "our motherland in a civic sense"'. He denounced 'any deed against the Soviet Union, such as war, boycott, or assassination'.[37]

This was a complicated moment for the Bolsheviks: the United Kingdom broke diplomatic relations with the USSR and Soviet trade representative Pavel Voikov was assassinated in Poland. The assassin Boris Koverda, the

19-year-old son of a school teacher with socialist beliefs, explained his act to the press: 'I avenged for Russia.' Soviet propaganda portrayed him as a White terrorist, and in retaliation, OGPU arrested hundreds of young men and women from the Russian nobility, and shot some of them. Among the victims was a cousin of Igor Anichkov, a family friend of the Likhachevs.[38] 'Everyone, both Russians and non-Russians, perceived Sergius's declaration 'against the background of persecutions', recalled Likhachev. Metropolitan Joseph in Leningrad renounced Sergius and stopped praying for him in his liturgy. Some Russian intellectuals, including the members of the Academy of Sciences showed their solidarity. The protest spread to Novgorod, Pskov, Tver, Vologda, and Vitebsk. Liturgies at that time 'proceeded with special intensity,' Likhachev wrote in his recollections. 'Choirs sang beautifully; and many professional singers, some of them from the Mariinsky Theatre, came to sing there. The entire clergy served with extraordinary deep feelings.' At Helfernak, pianist Maria Yudina and Likhachev's classmate Misha Shapiro, both from Jewish families, began to come to the Orthodox liturgy. Eduard Rozenberg, Dmitry's friend, switched from Lutheranism to Orthodoxy and was baptized under the new name of Feodor. Likhachev helped with the service.[39]

In December 1927, Andreyevsky went to Moscow with other members of the clergy from Leningrad: they met with Metropolitan Sergius and pleaded with him to rescind his declaration. The Church, they suggested, should go underground, taking the example of the ancient Christians in Rome, who prayed in the catacombs. Sergius refused, arguing that the only chance to save the Church as a structure was to stay legal, in collaboration with the Soviet regime. Young Dmitry rejected this rationale with all his heart. 'We were not politicians ... We just wanted the truth in everything and loathed political tactics, programmes, calculated and dubious formulas.'[40]

Gatherings at Andreyevsky's apartment became focused on religious matters, and atheists stopped coming. Alexeyev proposed to rename the *kruzhok* as the Brotherhood of St Seraphim of Sarov, choosing this revered monk as the group's patron saint. On 1 August 1927, the Brotherhood congregated in the apartment of Liuda Skuratova, Mitya's classmate from Lentovka, to commemorate the day of acceptance of St Seraphim's remains. The priest's elevated mood 'translated to everyone in some special indefinable way'. Young women praying with him, bright sunlight streaming through the windows, added to his epiphany. 'It was joy, and we had the sensation that our life would change from that day onward.' After the service, everyone left the apartment with caution, evading possible spies.[41] Dmitry suspected one young member of the Brotherhood of being a spy. This man, Sergei Ionkin, acted with unnatural piety, and provoked discussions on political issues.

Likhachev shared his suspicions with Andreyevsky. At the next meeting, Andreyevsky performed a little act: with a sombre face he informed everyone that the 'Brotherhood' was disbanded and bid everyone farewell. The trick worked: when assemblies resumed, Ionkin never showed up again. Still, the Brotherhood decided to bury a heavy logbook with protocols of their meetings in a distant park on Krestovsky island. In 1992, when Likhachev got access to his OGPU dossier, he found that his suspicions were correct: OGPU did have an informer in the Brotherhood, under the alias 'Ivan Ivanovsky'.[42]

The Brotherhood experience left Dmitry forever suspicious of those in the Church who collaborated with the communist authorities. His idea of a 'parish life' was when several families would be united by common traditions, spiritual and cultural habits, and would travel together, with their children.[43] And he became confirmed in his early identity founded on the foundations of Holy Russia and Russian culture.[44] Only shortly before his death Dmitry Likhachev revealed a secret that he shared with Igor Anichkov and his family. From Anichkov he received and kept in his home office the relics of Prince Daniel, the founder of the Moscow Ryurik dynasty. At a moment of danger, Likhachev decided to send the relics to St Vladimir Seminary in the United States. In 1995, after the fall of communism, the Seminary returned the relics to Moscow.[45]

## Merry Science and Secret Police

During the 1920s, the 'former people' could still hope to preserve their values and culture in the private sphere. They protected their children and preserved their cultural spaces.[46] At one of the last sessions of Helfernak Dmitry recalled Mikhail Bakhtin sombrely saying: 'Now, the time of dialogue has come to an end. The time of the monologue has arrived.' Bakhtin, in his studies of Francois Rabelais and Feodor Dostoyevsky described *a polyphony* of cultures, with their reversals of 'the top' and 'the bottom'.[47] Young Likhachev and his friends decided to defy the inevitable, and live in their owned imagined community.[48]

In the spring of 1926 Eduard Rozenberg founded a mock association called the Space Academy of Sciences (*Kosmicheskaia akademiia nauk* – KAN), and invited five of his friends, students from Leningrad University and the Institute of Civil Engineering. In early 1927 Dmitry Likhachev became the seventh member of KAN. Its mission was to celebrate 'happy science' and to search for 'merry truth'. Likhachev later recalled: 'When free philosophy and religion were gradually banned, we played some kind of masquerade ... Meetings of a facetious nature appeared to us a more risk-free thing to do. We assumed that it would not enter anyone's mind to persecute people who gather for a careless, nonchalant pastime.'⁴⁹ Every 'academician' had a Chair according to his talents and beliefs. Volodia Rakov, artistic and light-spirited, was in charge of 'apologetic theology'. Arkady Selivanov became the Chair of 'fine theology'. Anatoly Terekhovko, an atheist, was in charge of 'fine psychology', and the oldest of the group, Peter Mashkov, was responsible for 'fine chemistry'. Likhachev, in accordance with his temperament, became the Chair of melancholic philology. Rozenberg had a remarkable gift for mystifications: he invented a plethora of rituals and an entire code of behaviour. 'Academicians' greeted each other with the Greek word Χαῖρε! They sang *Gaudeamus* as an anthem, and wore on their clothing a coat-of-arms and other special insignias. They also undertook field trips. In the summer of 1926 KAN members travelled across the Caucasus, from Vladikavkaz to Sukhumi. Closer to home, the 'Academy' had a mock residence in Tsarskoe Selo, in its aristocratic old park, where Pushkin and his friends, the future Decembrists, had walked, played and flirted. Rakov, a talented artist, created albums of drawings, where 'academicians' and their female companions posed and acted in the costumes of the Napoleonic era.⁵⁰

Then there were 'scientific' presentations. Unfortunately, we know nothing of Dmitry Likhachev's report which won him KAN membership. His last presentation, delivered on 3 February 1928, became widely known and was later published. He called it 'In defence of the old Russian orthography, trampled and distorted by the enemy of the Christian church and Russian people'. It this paper, young Dmitry criticized the reform prepared by the Russian Academy of Sciences in 1917 – among the authors was, ironically, Alexei Shakhmatov (1864–1920), the man Likhachev would later consider his 'teacher'. In 1928, however, young Likhachev castigated the changes in the Russian alphabet which the Bolshevik government implemented after it came to power. The enemies of Russian people, 'whose name is legion', wanted to destroy 'the link that used to exist between the Byzantine Empire and historic Russia'. After a number of arguments (logical, formal, aesthetic, etc.) against the reform, Likhachev made a startling conclusion: 'The new orthography has been imposed by the power of anti-Christ.'⁵¹

In 1992 this paper struck Likhachev's granddaughter Vera with its 'remarkably strong anti-Soviet slant'. Likhachev simply refused to see it this way. In his mind, his paper was 'full of irony, in the spirit of carnival'. Perhaps he and the 'academicians' did not want to admit they were playing a dangerous game. Even more experienced old intellectuals still believed that they could criticize the Bolsheviks in private, while conforming to Soviet regulations in public.⁵² Yet the secret police thought otherwise. On the eve of 1928, one of the 'academicians' sent a mock telegram to members of the association from the KAN 'headquarters' in Tsarskoe Selo. He signed the telegram 'The Pope of Rome'. It immediately attracted the attention of the secret police. In January 1928, OGPU officers arrested two students: Dmitry Kalistov and Boris Ivanov. The former knew the members of KAN, and the latter was a member of the Brotherhood of St Seraphim.[53]

In early February the old standing clock in Likhachev's spacious apartment suddenly chimed eight times. Dmitry was home alone, and felt a chill down his spine. Fear gripped him. He knew that his father had switched off the chiming mechanism many years ago, before his birthday. 'Why did these clocks decide to chime solemnly for me – the first time in twenty-one years of my life?' It was not just the omen alone: about a week earlier one of his Lentovskaia classmates, a fan of Nietzsche, called him to say he worked in OGPU. He warned Dmitry that he could be arrested soon. Indeed, on 8 February, at dawn, OGPU officers came to the apartment of the Likhachevs. Dmitry observed his own arrest as if from a distance, and for him it was like another carnival scene. The only strong feeling was a sense of pity for his father. He would never forget that Sergei, so brave with the Bolsheviks, turned pale when he saw the arrest warrant for his son. He sank into a leather armchair and began to cry. Almost automatically, Dmitry muttered: 'It must be a misunderstanding. I will come back soon.' The black Ford with a chauffeur and three police officers transported him to the other side of the Neva, to the secret police headquarters on the Shpalernaya. Once in prison, jailers took away his Orthodox cross, silver watch, and pocket money.[54]

OGPU was very busy that month in Leningrad, liquidating many intelligentsia *kruzhki*.[55] The first year of Stalin's revolution from above had begun, and secret police informers reported that 'the intelligentsia in general has not shifted to the Soviet tracks'. The targeted associations ranged from literary to religious, from Josephite to Masonic. Among the most exotic were the 'Russian Martinists', the 'Russian Autonomous Masonry', 'The Order of Knighthood of the Holy Grail', and the student associations 'Societé' and 'Rophilak'.[56] Many students were released after a brief interrogation. The Space Academy, however, came in for special scrutiny. The main investigator, Albrecht Heller, whose OPGU name was 'Albert Stromin', saw the potential for linking KAN and the Brotherhood in an imagined counter-revolutionary plot of 'former people'. Born in Leipzig, with five classes of school education that he got in Russia, Heller 'specialized' in Russian intellectuals. The mock telegram from the Pope augured a successful case in his eyes. He immediately found what he was searching for: evidence of Monarchist sympathies and, even more, evidence of anti-Semitic attitudes. At the end of the 1920s, OGPU still considered fighting anti-Semitism a priority.[57]

During a very brief search in the Likhachev apartment, an officer went straight to one of the bookshelves and pulled out *The International Jew* by

Henry Ford – one of the books from Ionov's collection. This pamphlet by an anti-Semitic American genius was loosely based on the Protocols of the Elders of Zion. Apparently one of Dmitry's visitors tipped OGPU off about it.[58] Even more incriminating was the diary of Kalistov, seized by OGPU and replete with sympathy for the Whites and expressions of anti-Semitic nationalism. At one point Kalistov wrote: 'Jews ... shamelessly sat down on the neck of the revolutionary people.' They 'keep arriving from the West and the South, and a host of them settled down in Russian cities, occupying the best Russian lands'.[59] In 1992, Likhachev, the only surviving member of the Space Academy, obtained access to its file from the secret police archives. This file also became available to historian Victor Brachev, conspiracy theorist and Russian nationalist. Brachev took all the reports of secret police informers at face value. According to these informers, Rozenberg, Mashkov and Likhachev allegedly made anti-Semitic presentations. Likhachev published a rejoinder: KAN was never anti-Semitic, he protested, and Brachev's allegation smeared the reputation of his friends.[60]

In fact, many among the Leningrad Russian intellectuals viewed the role of Jews in the Russian Revolution with venom. Numerous diaries testify to strong anti-Semitism among 'former people'.[61] During the 1920s, Jews were highly visible among the Bolsheviks, as well as in OGPU. Soviet spheres of culture and propaganda were full of zealots who originated from the Jewish Pale of Settlement in Ukraine and Belarus. Greek writer Nikos Kazantsakis, who visited Soviet Russia in 1925, admired 'an explosive people who hid and trembled for centuries, but who now joined the struggle, armed to the teeth and thirsting for vengeance and justice'. Mikhail Agursky wrote ruefully: 'Jews became in the eyes of the population a considerable part of the ruling class, the elite of this class.' Those Jews, of course, rebelled against traditional Judaic faith and culture and yearned for assimilation through revolution.[62]

Russian highbrow anti-Semitism in Petersburg and Moscow during the NEP years was linked to a defensive Russian nationalism. Writer Mikhail Prishvin wrote in his diary in September 1922: 'The domination of Jews will come to an end. The growth of national feeling will little by little bring all of us to treat Jews with enmity.' At a public debate about anti-Semitism, in December 1926, Professor Yuri Kliuchnikov controversially argued that this was a new phenomenon that resulted from 'the growth of national discontent' among the Russians, a defensive reaction against the energetic rise of Jews.[63] In emigrating to Prague, Lev Karsavin admonished Russian intellectuals to spurn anti-Semitism: 'One must put an end to the silly fairy-tale ... that the Jews dreamt up and carried out the Russian Revolution. One needs to be a very uneducated person historically and full of contempt for the Russian people, to believe that the Jews could destroy the Russian state.'

Russia's national rebirth, he prophesied, would not threaten Jews, their religion and culture.[64] Karsavin's admonition fell on deaf years. By that time, the Bolsheviks had stopped flirting with the Change Landmark ideology, shut down the journal (*Novaia*) *Rossiya* and began to charge increasing numbers of 'counter-revolutionaries' with anti-Semitism, often real and sometimes invented by the investigators. *Leningradskaia Pravda* reported regularly on the arrests of 'anti-Semites'. Those who read about these arrests only became convinced that the Bolshevik regime and the Jews were one and the same.

Stromin decided to present KAN and the Brotherhood of St Seraphim as two 'organizations' of anti-Semitic and Monarchist counter-revolutionaries. He linked Likhachev and his young friends to the White Russian emigration and to the 'conspiracy' in the Academy of Sciences. Another representative of the 'former people' was added to the case: Avenir P. Obnovlensky, chairman of the All-Russian Union of Christian Youth and a member of the international YMCA. On 14 June 1928, *Leningradskaia Pravda* published an essay 'Ashes of Oaks'. The title alluded to the impotent remains of the once-powerful White Russian movement. The essay claimed that KAN was 'almost a real academy' which allegedly had a chair on the topic 'Jews [*zhidy*] in Russia', and studied tracts by the world-renowned anti-Semitic authors, Henry Ford, Chamberlain, and the Protocols of the Elders of Zion.[65]

The authors of the article were Leonid Tubelskyi and Peter Ryzhei; Likhachev wrote of them as 'specialists in denouncing *kruzhki*, on the payroll of OGPU'. 'It was outrageous: [they] depicted us as adults, some kind of senators or generals, and then anti-Semites.'[66] The OGPU factory of slander worked: Russian émigré newspapers took this article at face value; one of these newspapers wrote: 'The Space Academy was quite an active, deeply conspiratorial organization of monarchists, about to evolve into a monarchist conspiracy.'[67] Likhachev was not mentioned by name, but his presentation on the old Russian orthography was cited as a proof of the monarchist sympathies of the arrested. This would remain a permanent sword hanging over Dmitry's career and reputation.

'Academicians' and Brotherhood members, along with other arrested intellectuals and students remained for half a year in a cell in the macabre Shpalernaya prison. Likhachev recalled that those months were 'the most trying period of my life'. His inmates, however, represented a rich selection of 'former people': aristocrats, intellectuals, students, Orthodox priests and Baptists, members of underground Masonic associations, 'Satanist' sects and 'Theosophists', NEP businessmen, Chinese migrants, and professional thieves. Criminals still treated intellectuals with respect, and one of them instructed Dmitry how to behave during interrogation. When Stromin called in Likhachev to interrogate him for the first time, Dmitry covered himself with a warm winter coat, and explained that he was sick with flu. Stromin was afraid of infection and after a brief overview sent him back to his prison cell. The text of this interrogation, in the police file, has Likhachev admitting he had been a member of KAN since 'September or October 1927' and had made two presentations there: 'on the influence of the Mongols on Russian literature and language', and 'on the philosophy of *comme il faut* of the 1840s'. Stromin, however, focused on the anti-Semitic tract by Henry Ford: Dmitry denied he shared the book with anyone; yet other KAN members testified the opposite under pressure.[68]

After Likhachev's interrogations ended, he was moved to a larger cell, to wait for his verdict. There he joined the energetic Jewish businessman Kotlyar: together they cleaned the walls, the floor and the latrine in the cell. After this, it became easy to breathe. He also found there great partners for conversations: one prisoner was Karsavin's relative; another was count Vladimir Shuvalov, who studied the logic of Edmund Husserl and had chaired the Petrograd Boy Scout society before the revolution. Dmitry was favourably impressed with him and other aristocrats: they behaved in adversity with great tact and dignity. 'Our jailers accomplished a bizarre thing,' he recalled 65 years later. 'They arrested us for meeting just once a week with a few others for common discussions of the issues of philosophy, art, and religion. And then they united all of us, first in the general prison cell, and then in the camps, combining us with other people ... interested in such issues.'[69]

The wheels of Soviet jurisprudence turned slowly at the end of the 1920s. The investigation of the Brotherhood of St Seraphim and the Space Academy ended in April 1928, yet the sentence from the Commissariat of Justice came only three months later. In this sentence, the Space Academy was called an 'illegal anti-Soviet organization', 'a political *kruzhok* that discussed issues regarding the February and October revolutions, the activities of the Soviet government [and] of OGPU'. Dmitry Likhachev's file designated him a 'son of a former nobleman' indicted for 'procuring materials about world Jewry' and 'OGPU atrocities'. He was sentenced to five years in a concentration camp after which he would not be able to live in the 12 major cities of the Soviet Union, including Leningrad.[70]

Other members of the Space Academy also received five years in the camps.[71] Andreyevsky, as the main organizer of the Brotherhood, got away with five years, citing his early revolutionary credentials. Sergei Likhachev was appalled by the sentence and furious at Andreyevsky, whom he viewed as a manipulator of naive young people. Sergei tried through his connections to reduce Dmitry's sentence from five to three years, but achieved nothing. One day in early autumn of 1928, the prison director fetched the Brotherhood–KAN members and solemnly read them their sentences. The 'academicians' regarded the procedure as another scene in the Soviet carnival: the formality had nothing to do with real law and courts. Igor Anichkov had a 'superb' attitude of stoicism and nonchalance. Anichkov listened to the sentence without a trace of emotion and then asked: 'Is that all? Can we now leave?' He exited, followed by his friends, to the dismay of the armed guards. Likhachev would later recall this episode with great admiration.[72]

Two weeks later black police cars ('black ravens') brought the arrested 'academicians' from the Shpalernaya to the railway station. The guards pushed them into 'Stolypin-style' train carriages built in 1907–1911 to transport political prisoners. By Soviet standards they were almost comfortable. Friends and relatives gathered at the station, as was the custom in Tsarist times, to bid farewell to the arrested. At that time people were not afraid of showing their sympathy and solidarity with victims of the Soviet regime: they brought warm clothing and food. University librarians bought Dmitry Likhachev a large cake from the best confectioner on the Nevsky Prospect. The head of the guards spoke to the arrested students with a touch of apology: 'Do not hold it against us. We are just doing our job!'[73] The era of the Great Terror still lay ahead: the times of hysterical fear, mutual betrayals and pathological sadism had still not destroyed the moral tissue of society.

When the prison doors closed on Dmitry Likhachev, he was only 21. Just before his arrest he completed two graduation theses: one on the adaptation of Shakespeare in Russian culture under Catherine II and Aleksandr I; another about the Russian tales of Patriarch Nikon's times. His professors informed him that he had passed. This was the end of Dmitry's formal education. Later in his life he regarded the Silver Age as a continuum that lasted beyond the revolution. The bulk of the intelligentsia, he wrote later, 'was exterminated in the war of 1914–17, in the revolution, in the first years of terror'. Still he 'managed to catch the last glimpse of [*zakhvatit chut-chut*] the people of the Silver Age'. Student Dmitry Likhachev, who started with modest cultural baggage, consciously chose to stay among 'former people', to learn from them the art of intellectualism and to emulate their values.[74]

The decade of studies and religious-philosophical 'dissent' in *kruzhki* prepared young Likhachev for future life. He developed a stoic approach to realities. He liked to quote a dialogue from Shakespeare's *Julius Caesar*:

Brutus: O Cassius, I am sick of many griefs.
Cassius: Of your philosophy you make no use,
If you give place to accidental evils.[75]

Likhachev's 'philosophy' was influenced by Alexeyev (Askoldov), as well as Lossky, Karsavin, and Bergson. Its ethical core was in the idea of continuity between the past and the present. He grew to believe that even God has no power over time. The past is 'the only immutable part' of the 'timeless monolith created by God'. He also became convinced that life was a mystery that resisted rational understanding and schematic conceptualization. Luck, contingency and fortuitous events played an extraordinary role in his life. His father tried hard to commute Dmitry's sentence from five to three years, and was crestfallen when he failed. Yet Likhachev's prison inmates who returned from the camps in 1931, at the peak of the Stalinist revolution, were caught 'in an awful bind'. They were not allowed to return to Moscow, Leningrad and other major cities. They ended up in the provinces, with their intellectual careers finished or suppressed. Many of them would be re-arrested, sent back to the gulag, and executed there at the peak of the Great Terror. In contrast, Likhachev's five years turned out to be a perfect time out. He would be liberated as a 'shock-worker' on the construction of Stalin's canal and even allowed back to his home city. Likhachev summed it up stoically: 'If my parents had succeeded in reducing my sentence – I would have perished. It was a pure stroke of luck.'[76]

# CHAPTER 3

# THROUGH THE GULAG AND GREAT TERROR, 1928–1941

> Life, freedom, dignity, convictions, faith, customs, the possibility of studying, sustenance for life, food, housing, clothing – everything is now in the hands of the state. The ordinary individual is reduced to complete submission. Ladies and gentlemen ... such a state is doomed to perish from within.
>
> *Nobel Prize winner Ivan Pavlov, physiologist, December 1929*[1]

In 1928 Joseph Stalin and his Bolshevik associates abrogated the NEP and unleashed a 'revolution from above'. This policy destroyed the peasantry and produced an artificial famine. Millions died, were deported to Siberia with their families, and joined the armies of slave labour to build giant steel mills, dams, coal-mines, and machine-building factories. The regime's justification was the need to modernize the country and prepare for a future war. Decades later many Russian nationalists argued whether this 'revolution' was a tragic necessity or national genocide. Dmitry Likhachev had a firm opinion; in 1987 he wrote:

> It is immoral to view the crimes of a few paranoid politicians as a "law of history". One has to be blind to historical facts, to miss the factor of contingency and personal will ... In our times it is absurd to ... regard people who gained power by accident as extraordinary wizards of leadership.

He concluded: 'Tyranny has no system.'[2]

Some people survived in those years by sacrificing their cultural milieu, fleeing from Leningrad and Moscow to distant provinces, where nobody could denounce them and report on them to the secret police.[3] At first, Likhachev was lucky to discover a deep cultural milieu in the very place that was designed to destroy it – in the gulag. Remarkably, the ex-prisoner happened to be 'invisible' in Leningrad later, when the machinery of terror exterminated whole groups of suspects with statistical frequency. After such an experience, how could anyone believe in sociological determinism and deny the importance of individuality and pure chance?

### 'Russian Conversations' in Solovki

In late November 1928, a special train with armed guards brought Dmitry and his friends to the camp of Kem, near the White Sea. The guards unlocked the train doors and the 'academicians' saw a dreary landscape already covered with heavy snow. Shrill voices barked: 'Take your things – and out! Out!! Out!!!' Shivering in the morning cold, the prisoners lined up before an OGPU official in a long grey military coat. 'It is not Soviet power for you here,' the official shrieked. 'It is Solovetsky power.' He spoke about the Solovetsky Camp of Special Designation, better known as 'Solovki'. Prisoners also used the Russian acronym – SLON. Dmitry saw a quick demonstration of this power: a guard kicked him in the face, chasing him off the train, and his nose bled profusely. K.S. Beloozerov, the sadistic official, continued with a barrage of threats and humiliations. His aim was to break the prisoners' will, to destroy their dignity.[4]

'I could not believe that this nightmare was really happening before my eyes,' Likhachev wrote in the secret diary he started in the camp.[5] The first night in the barracks was awful: Dmitry's friends had to stay awake, and all bunks were occupied. Andreyevsky, however, found priests in the barracks, and introduced the Brotherhood members to them. They gave them names of priests to contact once they arrived at the camp. Dmitry received a good piece of advice from an experienced criminal he met in the barracks: when the cargo ship *Gleb Boky* carried prisoners to the Archipelago across the White Sea, he should stay on the upper deck, never go inside. This advice saved Likhachev's life next morning: many prisoners who chose to go inside the ship died there en route, from congestion and lack of air.[6]

When the ancient walls and towers of Solovetsky monastery appeared through thick fog, Dmitry instinctively crossed himself. He saw Holy Russia rising from the sea. In 1436 the monks Zosima, Savvaty and German arrived here and founded a '*skit*' – a place of hermitage and prayer. Soon Solovetsky monastery gained national fame. Its Superior, Philip Kolychev, became Metropolitan of Moscow, refused to bow to Tsar Ivan the Terrible and later met his death as a martyr. During the Church schism, Solovki monks sided with the Old Belief and rebelled against Moscow. Government troops took the monastery after a long and difficult siege. In 1923, on Lenin's decree, the monastery was closed and became the site of the first political concentration camp in the Soviet Union.[7] By the end of 1928 the prison population of the Main Island, where the Solovki kremlin stood, was already ten times larger than the entire number of monks before the revolution.

After 'delousing' procedures in the cold bath, Dmitry, his friends and other newly arrived prisoners marched, flanked by armed guards, to the former Trinity Cathedral, where thousands of men lived without heat and electricity for months. The altar of the cathedral served as a toilet. This was one of many crazy conversions of the 'superior' into the 'profane' on the Archipelago. 'Profane' words and deeds were the norm, while acting 'normally' was penalized. Likhachev would later comment that Solovki was a testing ground for the future. Stalinist society, particularly in big cities, mimicked camp stratification, practices and profanities.[8]

The camp had a complicated hierarchy, with 'bosses' at the top, who wielded absolute power over the lives of the camp inmates – with extraordinary autonomy from any central authority. Most OGPU officials were sent to work in Solovki as a form of punishment, for various deviations or because of their sadistic, neurotic character. Wanton torture and wilful executions were everyday occurrences. Just below the 'Chekists' stood 'internal guards' recruited from the lowest ranks of OGPU, as well as criminals, murderers, rapists and thieves, whom the Bolsheviks considered their social 'ally' in the 'class struggle'. For all this hierarchy, the boundary between victims and executioners in Solovki was blurred. 'If prisoners in these conditions had even a small amount of power over other prisoners,' Likhachev recalled, 'they began to harass and torture them, to demonstrate this power.' The dynamics of terror was created by the system from above, yet it involved everyone, from top to bottom. 'Solovki was a laboratory for running and improving social methods that would later invade the entire country.'[9]

The camp was stratified in a military way: it consisted of 15 'companies'. The First Company were the bosses (*nachalniki*). The Thirteenth, Fourteenth and Fifteenth Companies consisted of prisoners who did all kinds of slave labour. 'Normal' social roles and functions remained in this militarized mini-society in a residual way. For instance, many priests and monks were in a company that dealt with logistics and distribution, warehouses and the parcelling – because those jobs required integrity and honesty. The topography of Solovki compounded its stratification. Each island was a separate zone with its own regime and degree of severity. From the Main Island prisoners could be sent to smaller islands – often it was a one-way 'ticket'. The abandoned *skits* (hermit sites) on Anzer and Muksalma reminded one of Kafka's penal colony. The dark humour was that going there was 'a trip to the Moon' – ending with starvation, cold, torture and execution.

Almost at once Dmitry was offered a transfer to a 'better' job in exchange for becoming an informer. He refused. The Brotherhood members started to work at the bottom of this hierarchy, in one of the 'labour' companies, where life expectancy was extremely low. He, Rakov and Rozenberg cut wood, collected turf in peat bogs, and pushed carts. They also hauled heavy sleds. In addition, Dmitry, as the son of an electrical engineer, helped electricians and specialists at an animal farm. It was vital, however, to avoid being sent to the smaller islands.[10] After that, the only way to avoid untimely death was through connections, and bribes. Likhachev knew it and on his first night in Solovki gave one rouble to the head of his company. The bribe worked a miracle: he got a decent bunk, far from the toilet, and next morning stayed in bed, while the rest of the company went to work. In the morning, he found the church empty – and saw an old priest, mending his clothing. By coincidence, the man was Rev. Nikolai Piskanovsky, a Josephite priest. 'A miracle!' – wrote Likhachev in his camp notes. Piskanovsky and another priest Viktor Ostrovidov would effect two months later, without any begging on Dmitry's part, his transfer to a privileged company where he could work in tolerable conditions.[11] This was *blat*, the system of connections and mutual assistance that mitigated the camp horrors.

One never knows what Likhachev's fate would have been, but at some point he contracted typhus and was hospitalized. When he was released two months later, he was transferred, with the help of the priests, to the privileged Third Company. Still weak from typhus, he came to report to the head of the company, Baron Pritwitz, a resident of the Peter and Paul fortress in Petersburg. The company consisted of 'former people' and was one of the greatest paradoxes of Solovki.[12] The Cultural Revolution proclaimed that all camp prisoners must be 're-educated' and returned to society as 'Soviet people'. The authorities, responding to this slogan, created a prison theatre and a museum, and published a Solovki newspaper and a Solovki journal. In this way, they obtained resources from Moscow, and got promotions and decorations. In camp slang, this was called *tufta*. A former Tsarist official, Aleksandr Kolosov, persuaded the bosses to start a centre for the study of criminals, with an alleged mission of re-educating them in a socialist way. The centre became known as the Criminal Cabinet or *Krimkab*. Tipped off by the priests, who secretly ministered confessions of prisoners, Kolosov transferred to Krimkab a number of intellectuals from labour companies and penal colonies.

Kolosov's assignment to Dmitry was to do research on the lifestyle, motivation and language of orphaned children. The bosses of Solovki realized that a youth colony would be to their benefit, a great *tufta*. Boris Lindener, an imprisoned scientist from Petersburg, became a 'manager' of the new colony for young delinquents.[13] One of Dmitry's first shocks of Solovki was seeing in Trinity Cathedral many naked boys hiding under the bunks, their arms reaching out, their voices begging for food. Those 'flea boys', orphans and young delinquents who ended up in the camp, gave away all their possessions for drugs. The authorities ignored their existence, considered them 'dead souls' and did not provide them with food rations. They died quickly from hunger, cold and disease.[14] His new job gave Likhachev a chance to save the 'flea-boys', and he also began to study the children's argot, criminal habits and their card games.

One prisoner with high connections in the camp was Aleksandr Melnikov, a former follower of Aleksandr Kerensky, who knew Vera Konyaev. From him, Dmitry obtained a priceless pass 'to go everywhere'; he gained freedom to travel around the Archipelago and discover its natural habitat. 'I was able to preserve my health because of the nature of Solovki,' he recalled. Seasonal changes and the enormous vitality of northern fauna revealed to him the 'fragility and brevity of life' and 'the presence of the Lord Creator'. The arctic night ended in late March 1929 – and a fantastic flurry of colour covered rocks and stones. Also, Likhachev could explore the remarkably resourceful civilization that the generations of monks had built – in harmony with nature. Every nook and cranny of the islands preserved the signs of creative and patient labour: far-away hermit *skits*, stone crosses, elaborate waterworks, animal farms, and fisheries.[15]

Krimkab was free from informers and became 'a club' of the camp intelligentsia. The bosses of Solovki, barely literate, could not even understand what intellectuals did or talked about. They did resourceful imitation of work (*tufta*), and used the time to discuss philosophy, literature, sociology, history and art. In Krimkab, Likhachev met new young friends, among them Vladimir Kimensky-Sveshnikov who returned to Soviet Russia from emigration as a Change of Landmark adept; the Polish-Ukrainian noble Vladimir Razdolsky; and Vladimir Korolenko, whose uncle, a human rights defender and writer, was a friend of Leo Tolstoy. Dmitry also fell under the spell of the beautiful poet Lada Mogilianska, arrested for 'Ukrainian nationalism'. Krimkab attracted other poetic talents: Aleksandr Peshkovsky and Yuri Kazarnovsky recited their poetry, as well as the poetry of Mandelstam and Pasternak.[16]

Fifty-five year old Aleksandr Meyer arrived at Solovki in the spring of 1929 and quickly became an intellectual guru of Krimkab.[17] A mystical anarchist and Social Democrat in his early life, he evolved towards a philosophy of Christian Socialism, participated in the elections of the Patriarch and became an activist in Volfila discussions. After the latter was closed, he convened a philosophical *kruzhok* in his apartment which met every Sunday. Its name (*Voskresenie*) meant both 'Sunday' and 'Resurrection'.[18] According to their OGPU file, Meyer and his wife Xenia Polovtsova dreamed of a 'socialist' religious renaissance and believed that the Russian revolution could indeed produce a new society, if 'May Day would meet with Easter Sunday'. Stromin and the Leningrad OGPU added 'Sunday' to the list of counter-revolutionary associations allegedly preparing for the restoration of the monarchy. Meyer was condemned to death, but this verdict was changed to ten years in the camps.[19]

Meyer was 'a man of Russian conversational culture,' recalled Likhachev. 'His views emerged from endless Russian conversations.' In Krimkab he immediately started a 'conversation' about what 'Solovetsky power' was about. Intellectuals argued on the respective weight of three factors: an evil ideology, mischievous institutions and implementation, and evil human nature. Meyer, loyal to socialist ideals, defended the ideology and blamed everything on institutions. Still, he acknowledged the power of myth over rationalism, and recognized the role of language as a form of power.[20] All this was a revelation for young Dmitry. He was especially taken by Meyer's interpretation of *Faust*. The protagonist of Goethe's work, Meyer said, was a European Christian mind, who spurned religion and turned to the triple replacement of faith: naturalism, humanism, and social moralism. A Faustian mind worshipped 'progress', and dreamed of conquering nature itself, as well as eradicating the roots of inequality and poverty. Yet the Faustian hero inevitably ended up in a spiritual crisis, searching for lost certainties and meanings. This crisis, Meyer concluded, could be resolved only through personalized faith, 'the return to Christ'.[21] 'With the assistance of Lossky, and with Meyer's help in Solovki,' Likhachev wrote at the end of his life, 'I formed the idea that "the Whole" always precedes "the Particular". Logos, word, idea, precedes its material manifestations.' This meant seeing humanity and culture as a whole; it also meant that the destruction of any cultural artefacts was a crime against 'the whole'.[22]

Someone else who vanished in Krimkab was aristocratic Yulia Danzas. Her ancestor was an aristocrat, a friend of Pushkin, who took part in the Decembrist rebellion against the Tsar in 1825. A graduate of the Sorbonne, she served as lady-in-waiting for the last Tsarina and helped in her charity projects. She also tried and failed to talk Alexandra out of her habit of turning to sorcerers and magi, including Rasputin. She volunteered to fight in the Great War and later joined the Volfila. Disillusioned with Orthodoxy, she returned to Catholicism, the religion of her French ancestors. The Leningrad OGPU arrested her along with other active Catholics.

Danzas helped Dmitry understand the great role of the aristocracy in Russian history and culture. From Danzas, he learned about the intrigues and political idiocy of the court. Yet destroying the aristocracy meant decapitating Russian culture.[23]

The Solovki museum, another masterpiece of *tufta* activities, was a centre of ancient Russian culture on the island. It exhibited a wonderful collection of medieval art, especially rare sixteenth-century icons from the Solovetsky monastery and other northern churches, a gilded iconostasis made in Peter the Great's times, adorned with 200 precious icons, and much more. The museum's curator, Nikolai Vinogradov, was arrested 'for theft' of museum objects. Cleverly, he rebranded the Annunciation church as an 'anti-religious branch of the museum', and protected it from destruction. He also brought several artists from the penal colonies: they restored and catalogued ancient art. At the museum, Dmitry helped to catalogue icons and watched how the artists freed them from centuries of soot and dirt.[24] His sense of joy at seeing the 'liberated beauty' of ancient Russian art would guide him through the rest of his life.

## Epiphany and Liberation

In his camp notes, Likhachev wrote that the example of Solovki monks emancipated them from the sense of horror the camp instilled. 'Looking at these skies, one wanted to burn down like the Old Believers' to escape from anti-Christ, the conqueror of the world. Another strategy for emancipation was through humour and laughter. 'Humour and irony suggested to us: this life is not real. Real life would start when you returned to liberty.' Some of Krimkab's youth, poets Yuri Kazarnovsky, Dmitry Shipchinsky, and others wrote humorous essays for the journal *Solovetskie Islands*, published by the camp authorities, and attended the Solovki theatre which staged comedies and goofy satire.[25]

Suddenly, in the middle of the polar summer of 1929, the first tangible sign of a real emancipation arrived in the Archipelago. The prisoners learned that Maxim Gorky, the celebrated Russian writer, would come to Solovki as a visitor. Many remembered him as a critic of Bolshevik terror against the intelligentsia, and a humanist. People rejoiced: 'Gorky will see everything, he will not be fooled.' In reality, Gorky's visit had a different agenda. Earlier, several prisoners had managed to escape from the Archipelago to Europe; their stories provoked outrage, and the British Anti-Slavery Society called for a boycott of Soviet exports. Gorky's tour of Solovki was meant to dispel the 'misinformation in the capitalist press', not to emancipate the camp slaves.[26] Gorky arrived on 20 June 1929, accompanied by his daughter-in-law

Nadezhda ('Timosha'), in the company of high-placed OGPU officials. His visit was carefully arranged: OGPU even made a propaganda film about Solovki: this film was briefly shown around the Soviet Union and abroad. The Soviet newspaper that covered Gorky's tour proclaimed Solovki a 'picturesque and comfortable place, populated by healthy, robust people. Their days pass in labour, rest, and entertainment, just like the days of anybody who lives in freedom. Not a single oppressed face. Not a single harassed personality.'[27] The praise for slave labour as a 're-forging experience' (*perekovka*) would soon grow into an all-Union campaign with international outreach, to deceive the world.[28]

After Gorky's visit the Solovki authorities became nervous to the point of hysteria. They feared that the great success of this operation might be ruined by another flight of prisoners or some other accident. Indeed, before long a disaster struck. Innokenty Kozhevnikov, Lindener's successor in charge of the youth colony, staged a dramatic escape from the camp. He was a Red commander during the Civil War, and probably a psychopath. After disappearing with his young assistant, he sent a 'manifesto' proclaiming himself emperor of all Russia, with an amnesty for all prisoners. The manifesto urged seizing boats, landing on the mainland and marching towards Petrograd. The camp bosses went berserk. They declared a state of emergency, in view of the 'insurrection'. An orgy of arrests followed, and people were seized for even minor breaches of rules, for attending secret religious services, or just for getting together. After ferocious interrogations and torture, most of these people were shot.[29]

The camp intelligentsia faced mortal danger. Kozhevnikov sent a copy of his 'manifesto' to Krimkab. Kolosov immediately reported to the authorities, yet they could, at a whim, arrest all Krimkab employees. Likhachev worked with Kozhevnikov and his young assistant Shepchinsky in his project on young delinquents. Once Dmitry walked across the kremlin's courtyard and saw a group of prisoners running, followed by the armed guards, their bayonets gleaming. Among the prisoners was a young man with whom Likhachev had worked at the Solovki museum. Dmitry instinctively took off his hat and nodded to him. Somebody reported this little gesture of sympathy, and in Likhachev's file a potentially fatal line appeared: 'communicated with the insurgents.' As the value of life in Solovki approached zero, this could be an invitation to an execution squad.[30]

As if this were not enough, Vera and Sergei Likhachev came to Solovki to visit their son, with a group of other relatives of political prisoners. They rented a room from one of the camp guards and stayed for two weeks. Dmitry, with the assistance of his father's few roubles, was allowed to stay there overnight. It was at this moment that the authorities decided to execute a particularly large 'quota' of prisoners – 300 more men and women. One evening Dmitry heard a knock on the door. The man said: 'They came looking for you!' Likhachev understood what it meant: they had come to his company's premises to arrest him. His first thought was that this should not happen again in front of his parents. Without telling Sergei and Vera anything, he ran to hide. Finally he found a hiding place in giant wood-stacks prepared for winter heating. He stayed there through the night, praying and thinking. At a distance he could hear the sound of shots: people were being executed. It was a night, it turned out, when the 'quota' of 300 prisoners was short. Instead of Dmitry, somebody else was taken to death row. When dawn came, Likhachev mingled with the crowd of prisoners going to work. Nobody asked where he had been. And he did not tell his parents what had happened to him.[31]

It was a night of epiphany for the young philosopher. He understood that 'every day was a gift from God. I have to live today, glad that another day is granted to me. Therefore, I should not be afraid of anything.' He also decided to 'live for two, so that the other, who was taken instead of me, would not be ashamed!'[32] Among those 300 victims was a Krimkab socialite Georgy Osorgin, a 36-year-old from a prodigiously talented clan of the Russian nobility. Some weeks before the execution night, he was sent to a penal colony on Anzer for attending secret Josephite liturgies. He was brought back to the Main Island, because his wife Alevtina (Lina) arrived to see him, along with the Likhachevs. This brought his name to the bosses' attention again; he was put on the list of those to be executed. He pleaded to be granted free time to see Lina, pledging to return to the camp. He said nothing to his wife during their last meeting, and later went calmly to receive a bullet in his head.[33]

In 1930 the oases of intellectual life in Solovki began to dry up. After mass executions came another epidemic of typhus – 3,600 of the prisoners died without any medical assistance, locked in their 'sick' barracks. The new waves of terror on the mainland sent thousands of new prisoners to Solovki, yet there were few 'former people' among them.[34] In May 1930 Stalin decided to build a canal to connect the White Sea and the Baltic Sea, and OGPU suggested using 'free' slave labour from the gulag. In total, about 100,000 prisoners, among them 'former people' with education and intellectual skills, joined the construction of 'Bel-Balt' with the promise: Through Work – To Liberation![35] Gradually, all Dmitry's friends from the Space Academy joined in the construction of the canal. Kolosov, Danzas and Meyer also left. Eduard Rozenberg began to work for the Bel-Balt administration: he repeatedly sent requests to Solovki to commandeer Dmitry Likhachev from the Archipelago. OGPU did not grant these requests: Likhachev was on the black list. After several months, in the autumn of 1931, somebody in the system shifted gears:

the order came to transfer Dmitry to a huge prison camp near Lake Onega, where the main Bel-Balt administration worked. The same *Gleb Boky* took him south. A polar night blanketed the Archipelago, yet when the ship crossed the White Sea southwards, dawn came and the sun lurked above the horizon. 'It was a moment when I had a feeling of true emancipation,' Likhachev recalled.[36]

In the new camp, a woman called to him across the street: 'Dima Likhachev!' She was an assistant of Rozenberg's, who was expecting him in his office. *Blat*, the power of connections, snatched Likhachev, once again, from the crowd of prisoners and provided him with another 'good' job. Soon his parents came to visit him again. In December 1931 Dmitry Kalistov sent a request 'to hire' him as his assistant, to administer trains at the major transport junction of Zvanka. This place was within a day's trip of Leningrad. His new job was called 'a GPU associate to supervise special cargo trains'.[37] After several months in Zvanka, resourceful Kalistov got them transferred to the ancient Russian city of Tikhvin. Likhachev felt almost free, no guards watched him. He even went to Leningrad twice, in violation of the rules, to see his parents; once he even managed to see a ballet at the Mariinsky! Only tremendous luck saved him from being denounced – then he would almost certainly have been sent back to Solovki.

In July 1932, Sergei, Vera and Yura came to Tikhvin for a summer holiday. They rented a house, and Dmitry moved there. On 9 July they attended the celebration of the Mother of God of Tikhvin, a holy icon that had 'appeared' in the city six centuries ago. Tsar Ivan the Terrible paid homage to this icon before going on to conquer Kazan. Now, thousands of pilgrims prayed to the holy icon, and the ecstatic mood of the worshippers passed on to Dmitry as well. Another moment to remember was 'a business trip' with Kalistov to another ancient town, Old Ladoga. The friends toured twelfth-century cathedrals and went to a local diner to eat their dinner. The place was in the best pre-revolutionary traditions: sparkling clean, it served no alcohol, but tea in big teapots, accompanied by crunchy chunks of sugar-beet. Excellent home-baked rye and wheat bread was there aplenty. The friends stayed there and talked into the night, watching peaceful scenes of fishing on the lake.[38]

This was one of the last glimpses of Old Russia for Likhachev. The Soviet regime was already moving at full speed to erase all the traditional foundations of Russian life. On orders from the Kremlin, local authorities blew up cathedrals, dropped huge medieval church-bells from bell-towers, and destroyed old icons. In Moscow, repeated explosions of dynamite reduced to dust the famous Cathedral of Christ the Saviour, the monument to Russian victory over Napoleon and the place where the Patriarch was elected. At the same time, while Likhachev prayed to the icon in Tikhvin, a special commission from Moscow ordered the liquidation of the Solovki museum. Its valuable medieval icons, gilded iconostasis, and a unique wood-carved baldachin were burnt – everything that had inspired young Dmitry to fall in love with Russian art was gone.[39]

The Cultural Revolution prepared the ground for collectivization of the peasantry.[40] One day, still in Zvanka, Likhachev and Kalistov saw the unfolding of this historic tragedy. Kalistov rushed into their apartment, carrying two big buckets full of warm milk. He brought this milk from the station where a huge, endless train stood, waiting to be sent further north and east. Every car of the train was filled with cows confiscated from the repressed peasants. The few young women who were attending the cows did not know what to do with their milk; they gave it away for free. Likhachev recalled that it was a moment of realization: 'They are destroying agriculture, they are destroying the peasantry. The cows are doomed. It is not accidental that grocery stores have become empty.' A meal the friends had in a diner in Old Ladoga became an impossible dream.[41] In every city and town food became rationed and was distributed by the authorities, who could now decide who was worthy to eat and who was not.

In July 1932 the Bel-Balt Canal was completed ahead of time. Stalin was pleased, and allowed OGPU to release all the prisoners who had worked on the construction, with their rights restored. Sergei Likhachev sent several appeals to the Leningrad secret police, pleading with them to release his son who had 'completely mended his ways'. One of his letters read: 'With unshakeable faith that Soviet power does not punish, but rather re-educates, I am begging you to return my son to Leningrad before the end of his term, to give him freedom without restrictions, and thereby grant him an opportunity to become a wholesome worker in the construction of socialism under my personal supervision.' Sergei conveniently 'forgot' about his personal nobility, and called himself 'a worker's son'. Dmitry's liberation, he concluded, would help to increase the productivity of his socialist labour. On 8 August 1932, Dmitry received a document that as a 'shock-worker of the White Sea-Baltic canal construction', he was now free to live in any part of the USSR. This rescinded the earlier ban on residence in big cities. Dmitry decided to return to Leningrad and claim his new status. He knew that Soviet fortune was extremely capricious and convinced his reluctant parents to pack and return to Leningrad immediately.[42]

Camp life taught young Likhachev what life for dissidents in Russian history, the Old Believers and other individuals mercilessly prosecuted by the state, was like. He never forgot those who allowed him to survive. When he was a nationally famous scholar, he wrote and published essays about those people. When he discovered that Ksenia, daughter of Rev.

Nikolai Piskanovsky, continued to live in the Russian North, he began to send her money on a regular basis. And a small portrait of Rev. Viktor Ostrovidov always decorated Likhachev's work office.[43] As a gulag survivor, Likhachev returned to his home city morally unbroken, but with scars, both physical and spiritual. He could be harsh and suspicious of people whom he did not trust. He could test their loyalty and did not forgive them when they failed this test.[44] In 1988 Likhachev agreed to be consultant to a group of filmmakers who produced the first documentary about Solovki. He told them: 'Show in this film that I did not sell out to them.' He meant Soviet authorities.[45]

## Leningrad in Terror

By that time the family had lost their spacious 'business' apartment and had to move to a smaller flat, where they shared a kitchen and other facilities with other families in a typical Soviet way. Still, the Likhachevs kept their old furniture and other possessions. Sergei Likhachev managed to find his son a job in a publishing business. Yet soon Dmitry collapsed at his office desk and dark blood poured out of his open mouth. It was the start of an ulcer, a lasting 'gift' from the gulag. Experimental blood transfusion saved his life – a miracle again![46] Sergei and Vera struggled to feed their sick son and restore his failing stamina, which was a challenge in the year of great famine. Vera made regular visits to the state-run company Torgsin ('Trade with Foreigners'), where people could exchange their family valuables for quality food. Without this food, Dmitry would probably have not survived.[47] When he checked out of hospital, he could not find a new job. Everyone was afraid to hire a former prisoner.

The Leningrad which Likhachev saw in 1933 had changed beyond recognition. 'The real impoverishment of intellect began after I returned from the camps,' wrote Likhachev in the 1990s. *Kruzhki* and the intelligentsia's associations – all this was gone. There were agents and snitches everywhere. Any incautious conversation could lead to a denunciation and an arrest. 'People got scattered around the country. Some died, some began to drink and became degraded. Everyone lived on their own, afraid to speak and even to think ... The fortunate few managed to go abroad.' Among those was Yulia Danzas, who had obtained, with Maxim Gorky's help, a passport to leave the Soviet Union. Her relative, living in France, paid a large amount in hard currency to 'buy her out'.[48]

The corporate solidarity among Russian intellectuals was victim of the 'Academic Affair' of 1929–1931. The secret police framed academicians Platonov, Evgeny Tarle, Mikhail Liubavsky, Yuri Got'e and many others as organizers and participants of 'The National Union of Struggle for

Resurrection of a Free Russia'. The main architect of the case was Heller (Stromin), who had investigated the Brotherhood of St Seraphim and KAN.[49] Two thirds of the Academy's members and employees lost their jobs, were arrested and sent to the gulag.[50] Likhachev found that some of his professors crossed to the opposite side of the street, to avoid contact with him. One historian confessed, after the years of terror were over, that fear of arrest remained an 'oppressive yoke hanging over me for almost quarter of a century'.[51] Dmitry felt no fear: his fatalistic philosophy helped, and his recurrent brush with death from an ulcer put life in a different perspective.

Still, he remained unemployed. Desperate not to depend on his parents, he even went to Dmitrovlag, a big concentration camp near Moscow, where Kalistov worked, to seek a 'freeman' job there. There he met with Meyer and other Solovki acquaintances, yet immediately noticed that 'nobody wanted to speak about big issues, fearing complications and possibly a new sentence'. His employment there did not work out either. There was nothing to do but wait for better times.[52] In the meantime, Dmitry ruefully witnessed the tragedy of the peasantry: thousands of them managed to migrate to Leningrad, despite police and army cordons. The authorities ignored them completely, they were considered 'non-persons'. In the winter of 1933, when cold struck, peasant women with children tried to hide in the upper staircases and attics of buildings. The authorities ordered the locking of the entryways for the night. Dmitry once returned home on a bitterly cold night and saw a group of peasant women standing in a courtyard, in front of the locked entrance. With their bodies and blankets they circled their children, swaddled in rags and 'packed' in the centre, protecting them against the freezing wind. Dmitry could never forget this scene, and for many years was stung by remorse. 'Why I did not return and bring them some food?' Dmitry's family, like many others, took home a peasant woman, who escaped from famine in the countryside with an internal passport. Tamara Mikhailova, half-literate, but tough and resourceful, from a village near Smolensk, became de facto a new family member and later a nanny (*nyanya*) for Dmitry's children.[53]

Likhachev preserved his Solovki diary (he passed it to his father during one of the parental visits), yet he decided not to write a diary when he was free. It was a time when many destroyed their private albums and journals to erase their past. The Cultural Revolution made even staunch critics of the Soviet regime admit their isolation and alienation from the social mainstream. Some Russian intellectuals, such as scientists Sergei Vavilov and Vladimir Vernadsky believed that, 'with cultural genius' added to it, communism would indeed become a road to modernization and scientific progress.[54] Still, there were many people, old and young, who saw the tragedy without varnish. One of them was Arkady Mankov, seven years younger than Dmitry, from a professional family with traditional Russian roots.[55] In the spring of 1933 Mankov wrote in his diary: 'The current social structure in Russia experiences impoverishment and degradation. ... The state, represented by a handful of fanatical "socialists", implements its allegedly Marxist policies. This state marches on, stomping on entire peoples and generations that sink into misery and famine.' Mankov observed that the destruction of religious cults and traditional culture left a vacuum that the Bolshevik government was unable to fill. Among people he met, Mankov cherished above all the time spent with 'former people', who still 'possessed the gift' of culture and speech. When, after the fall of the Soviet Union, this diary was published, Likhachev called Mankov's diary 'the best available account of the spirit of those times'. This diary, Likhachev admitted, brought back painful memories of what his family had to cope with in the early 1930s. He wrote to Mankov: 'I am astonished by your courage. A diary like yours, if discovered, could have meant a death sentence for you.'[56]

During 1934 a precarious 'normalization' came to Leningrad. The Bolshevik elite congratulated themselves on their victory over the peasantry. The Famine began to subside, and Stalin aborted the Cultural Revolution. He, with the help of Maxim Gorky, formed a new system of 'creative unions' which was meant to regularize and control the 'new Soviet intelligentsia'. In August 1934, with great pomp and circumstance, the Congress of Soviet Writers was held in Moscow, with the participation of famous European literary figures. It was the peak of *tufta* in the sphere of culture.[57] The 'normalization' had an immediate impact on Dmitry's life, as he finally found employment. He became a proofreader at the Comintern publishing house, then moved to do similar work at the Academy of Sciences. There he met the same kind of people as in Krimkab – 'former people' of the old aristocracy and imperial bureaucracy. Despite many purges, such people were still allowed to work at academic institutions, because of their knowledge of foreign languages, high level of literacy and erudition.[58] The informal leader of the collective was Lev Feodorov, one the 'best educated people' Likhachev recalled meeting in his entire life. Later he regretted that his bouts of sickness prevented him from joining informal tours of Tsarist palaces around Leningrad which Feodorov organized for his co-workers. At that time, the old personnel still worked in those palaces and shared unique stories with the visitors – this oral history would be completely lost later. Likhachev's co-workers also toured ancient Russian cities and monasteries.[59]

The lull ended on 1 December 1934 with the assassination of Leningrad's party boss Sergei Kirov. On Stalin's order, an enormous new wave of arrests targeted 'former people' and, for the first time, the party elite, the 'untouchable' Old Bolsheviks.[60] In February 1935, the Leningrad NKVD (yet another new name for the secret police) launched 'Operation Former People' aimed at clearing Leningrad of the former nobles and other socially undesirable people. One day in February, Dmitry bumped into a young woman at work called Rorka, a secretary in the sector of staff management (*kadry*). She mentioned that she had compiled a list of nobility and put him there. Tall, handsome, with a look of suffering, Likhachev must have evoked Rorka's sympathy, hence her tipping him off. Dmitry objected that he had never been a noble, only his father had been. Rorka shrugged her shoulders: retyping would be extra work for her. In Dmitry, his gulag reflexes were alerted: he immediately offered to pay for the job, to remove him from the dangerous list. A couple of weeks later, Likhachev came to work and discovered that many desks were empty, and only a few people were leaning over their daily proofreading work. Feodorov was still there. Likhachev approached him and asked in a half-whisper: 'Where are the rest? At a meeting?' Feodorov responded in a low voice, without raising his eyes from the galleys: 'Can't you understand that all of them have been arrested?' Likhachev returned to his place speechless. About 60,000 'former people' shared this fate in those days and were deported from Leningrad.[61]

During the Great Terror, the NKVD recruited thousands of informers – some of them collaborated to save their skins, but many others out of sadistic, psychotic impulses. The corporate trust and solidarity among intellectuals was under enormous strain: discussing, not to mention writing about terror became an absolute taboo and severe self-censorship became the norm. Likhachev recalled a colleague who said around 1935–1936: 'If tomorrow St Isaac's Cathedral disappears, everybody will pretend that it has always been like that.' Likhachev commented: 'True! Nobody noticed anything, or at least appeared not to.' In reality, the terror dealt a huge blow to culture. Their deportations devastated the staff of Leningrad's museums, and particularly its suburbs and suburban palaces. 'Palace personnel were people of integrity and preserved every trifle. The new "cadres" that came to replace them concealed, stole, and wrote off the lists many objects of art – without understanding their value.' Priceless objects and data, traditions of genius loci disappeared. Even the crowd in Leningrad's streets changed. It consisted of dull and subdued faces, monotonous and automated bodies.[62]

Another blow to culture was the system of totalitarian publicity, the collective participation in the sessions of hatred against 'people's enemies' and of love for Joseph Stalin and the party leadership. Eminent Russian intellectuals, including Mandelshtam, Akhmatova and Bulgakov, had to participate in the ghastly rituals of Soviet conformism; they wrote words of praise and adoration about Stalin. Even writer Mikhail Prishvin, who tried to stay away from public life in Moscow 'to study nature' in the countryside, was obliged to attend a meeting to celebrate 'the Stalinist Constitution'. 'The entire evening I was forced to applaud ... Everyone sought with extreme eloquence to squash and smother the voice of individuality. Something menacing and unprecedented for humanity appeared to manifest itself in those marionettes, yelling and clapping.'[63] Young Dmitry managed to escape the crime of duplicity and conformism many Russian intellectuals committed. Proofreading was a flexible job, and Dmitry could take his work home; he also spent weeks in hospitals. His unassuming job and sickness gave him a perfect excuse not to appear at collective sessions at work, kept him 'invisible'. To the end of his days he was proud that he never 'voted' at public meetings for executions.

In 1933 the Soviet state introduced internal passports – a crucial instrument of population control and social engineering. Every city-dweller had to register with a local police office or face deportation. 'The period of passportization,' reminisced Likhachev, 'was one of the most terrible periods in the life of big cities. The population of Moscow and Leningrad lived in tension.' Likhachev missed the first round of registration: he was in the jaws of death in a hospital. When the Great Terror started, the next round of passportization came: this denial of registration meant automatic loss of civic and political rights, and possibly an arrest. Dmitry's friends Rozenberg, Rakov and Terekhovko failed to obtain passport registration in Leningrad, because of their 'counterrevolutionary record', and had to find a residence and work in the provinces. Dmitry was again in hospital, yet he learned he would be deported anyway if he failed to register. His father Sergei's pleas to his acquaintances among the party officials only helped to get an extension 'for medical reasons'.[64]

Suddenly, just as in Solovki, two guardian angels came to Dmitry's rescue, but this time they took the guise of women. Zina Makarova, who worked with Dmitry at the academic publishing house, fell in love with him. The feeling was mutual, and they decided to get married. The prospect of deportation put their love to a test. Then the head of the proofreading section Ekaterina Mostyko said she could help. Before the revolution she had known Nikolai Krylenko, now the feared People's Commissar of Justice, an influential actor in the system of state terror. She wrote to Krylenko's office, reminded him of their old days, and even went to Moscow and solicited for Dmitry. It was a perilous enterprise: nobody could predict how Stalin's henchman would react. Yet the Commissar agreed to help 'her daughter's fiancé' (as Mostyko presented Dmitry). Then Mostyko arranged with her female friends that the President of the Academy of Sciences Aleksandr Karpinsky would sign an affidavit letter for Dmitry.

In late March 1936, Dmitry went to the Soviet capital on the cheapest train ticket – he still depended on his father's allowance. The Academy by Stalin's order had moved from Leningrad to Moscow. Dmitry went to Karpinsky's apartment: in the lobby he met his daughter who worked as a secretary, kissed her hand, and she immediately typed up the required affidavit and got her father's signature. All this took only 10–15 minutes. Dmitry realized that he was being helped by the network of 'former people' again: it was 'absolutely necessary' to show old-fashioned manners and kiss the hand of Karpinsky's daughter! The affidavit stated that 'during his stay in the camps,' Likhachev

> started very interesting linguistic studies ... Now he is undertaking a big study on the basis of the materials he collected about the language and ideology of delinquents and about their successful re-forging. This work, purely Soviet in nature, is politically and scientifically significant.

Only part of this was true: Likhachev published a small article on the criminal argot. The document was a piece of *tufta* necessary for Likhachev's salvation.[65]

With this precious document, Likhachev went to the Commissariat of Justice, where Krylenko's secretary, 'an old lady, approached me as if I were an old acquaintance'. The conveyor-belt of connections worked like clockwork. She instructed him to wait in front of his office and to say nothing, whatever happened. Krylenko appeared all of a sudden in the anteroom where many visitors were waiting to be received. He approached Dmitry and yelled at him, flailing both arms before his face: 'We made the revolution! Spilled our blood! The future of mankind is at stake! And you spoofed around, created the "Space Academy"! You wanted to mock us, right? There are no words for such an outrage.' After this tirade, which left Dmitry petrified, the powerful Commissar disappeared again to his office. His secretary quietly beckoned Dmitry to approach her desk and asked in a low voice, as if in a game, for his passport number, address, place of work and other data. In late July 1936, Dmitry got a call from the post office. There he received a certified letter informing him that the Presidium of the Central Executive Commission of the USSR had decided to waive his criminal record. With this letter, he went to the police and received an internal passport with residency rights in Leningrad.[66]

Why this show in front of Krylenko's office? Likhachev could only guess. Sentimental reasons could not be excluded. The Commissar had studied history and philology at Petersburg University. But only when Krylenko was arrested in 1938 and executed as a 'people's enemy', along with other

Old Bolsheviks, did Likhachev understand: Krylenko wanted to impress the public in the waiting room with his watertight credentials, as he knew his position had become precarious. Whatever the answer, Dmitry avoided the fate of thousands: the kind conspiracy of 'former people', particularly women, saved him from deportation and later allowed him to start his academic career. Even at the peak of the Great Terror, human decency, compassion and solidarity still survived even in the secretariat of the Commissariat of Justice.[67]

'Rehabilitation' by Krylenko's order did not mean safety, of course. In 1937 the NKVD issued order no. 447, which targeted whole groups of the Soviet population, and led to a second arrest for many former gulag prisoners. Dmitry's friends, who were imprisoned at the time, were executed. Among them was Vladimir Korolenko, with whom Likhachev had taken strolls in the Solovki forests.[68] Still, the waiving of his criminal record removed him from the blacklist. His employment opportunities widened. Dmitry considered it the start of a 'normal life'. He married Zina soon after he received the letter from the Commissariat. Likhachev and Zina started their family life in trying conditions. Vera, Dmitry's imperious mother, believed that he had married 'down' – a cause of considerable tension in the family.[69] The young couple decided to live separately and rented a small room in a communal apartment. Privacy there was non-existent: one bathroom and one tap with cold water served many families. Across the wall lived a prostitute who regularly received clients.[70] Likhachev, hardened by his camp life, viewed material difficulties stoically. He considered his family and his new responsibilities with complete seriousness, as his supreme responsibility. Zina also managed well. She had a strong, resilient character, and came from a common Russian family in the provincial town of Kovrov. She lost her mother early, and had to raise three younger brothers. Zina took very good care of Dmitry's health and his dietary needs.

## 'Escape' to Russian Studies

Those were times of great danger and contradictions. In 1934 the ideological campaign to destroy classical humanities and Russian historical studies ended. Instead, Stalin decreed the restoration of the teaching of Russian history. A special commission of historians, supervised by the Politburo, was appointed to write 'the history of the USSR', which started a thousand years before, with Kievan Rus. Old Russia, the role of the Church in the creation of a Russian state, the state policies of Peter the Great and Catherine the Great – all these events and developments could now be studied and even positively assessed.[71] In January 1936, the 'the historical school' of Mikhail Pokrovsky fell, and its members hastily adopted new views; some of them went to the gulag.[72] Stalin turned against 'red professors', now suspected of Trotskyism, and brought from exile and camps a few historians with pre-revolutionary credentials. Now they were allowed to create a 'new' Russian-Soviet history, teach at universities and join the Academy again. Among them was Mikhail Priselkov, whom Likhachev saw in Solovki, and also the victim of the 'Academic affair' Evgeny Tarle and some others.

Stalin's motives became clear only in retrospect. He wanted to use history to prepare the Soviet people for war.[73] In 1934–1936, however, the startling shift confounded even the brightest minds. Scientist Vladimir Vernadsky began to refer to the Soviet Union in his diaries as 'an essentially Russian state'.[74] Old-school professors, worn down by fear and life in exile, embraced Stalin's personal patronage of science and scholarship.[75] Vernadsky's son, now professor of Russian history at Yale, saw Eurasianism vindicated. Sociologist Pitirim Sorokin at Harvard believed it was a return to a Russian 'organic path'. Nikolai Timashev (Nicholas Timasheff) at Fordham University wrote later about 'a great retreat'.[76] This self-delusion lasted for years.

Dmitry was encouraged when his friend Kalistov was accepted to do graduate studies on history at the Leningrad University. During his bouts of illness, to distract himself from the nagging pain, he read voluminously, made copious notes and began to write. In 1935, Dmitry published in a scholarly journal an article about criminal argot, based on his Solovki research. Likhachev argued against 'hidden admiration' for criminals, and against the propagation of criminal lingo, profanities, songs and other folklore in wider Soviet society. Likhachev concluded: 'The criminal milieu is antithetical to the idea of the state, it is disruptive to economic life, and profoundly anti-social – and in the same way the criminal argot is destructive of syntax, morphology, language as a whole ... Criminal lingo is a disease of language.' He also warned that, 'it spreads the poison of criminal ideology, and criminal mentality.'[77] Dmitry's free-thinking essay did not go unnoticed. *Leningradskaia Pravda* responded with a harsh review, calling his essay 'pernicious balderdash'. In the climate of that time such a review could justify an arrest. Academic linguists, including Victor Zhirmunsky, liked the essay and defended its young author. Still, when Likhachev applied for graduate studies at the Institute of Speech Culture, the authorities ordered the examiner to fail him.[78]

As 1937 proceeded, Likhachev was asked to stand in for an editor-in-chief of a publishing house. In contrast to proofreading, this position was visible and dangerous: its holders disappeared one after another, arrested by the NKVD. Dmitry plucked up courage and submitted a letter of resignation.

The regional party dismissed him 'for lack of vigilance', yet at least he was out of harm's way. This time, he did not stay unemployed for long. Academician Aleksandr Orlov, son-in-law of the person of influence and connections in the scholarly establishment Alexei Krylov, offered him an academic job. Orlov was a specialist in Russian medieval chronicles, trained in Moscow by the famous Vasily Kliuchevsky. A great contrarian and a fervent Russophile, he moved from Moscow to Leningrad, when everyone else was relocating in the opposite direction. He lived alone: two of his sons died before the revolution, and his only daughter emigrated.[79] He noticed Dmitry, appreciated his skills and character, and 'adopted' him. One day, he called Likhachev and in his usual peremptory manner told him to come to his seminar at the Institute for Russian Literature (IRLI). This place, known among lovers of Russian culture as 'the Pushkin House', would become Likhachev's home institution for the rest of his life.

Aleksandr Blok once praised the 'Pushkin House' as a symbol of dignity and intellectual independence. When Dmitry Likhachev entered the place, however, it 'seemed permanently mired in filth'. Some of its best linguists and historians of literature went to prison.[80] In their stead came a gang of party hacks, careerists and informers; the administrative jobs went to unprincipled scoundrels, alien to any scholarship. The attempts by Yuli Oksman to restore the Institute's ethos during the 'normalization' in 1934 ended with his arrest and exile. In 1937 the IRLI fell so low that it even failed to complete an academic edition for the centenary of Pushkin's death.[81] Orlov's formidable personality and connections provided protection for the 'Sektor' of Ancient Russian Literature he led. He posed as 'a true Russian scholar', and criticized 'Western' influences at the Institute.[82] His indispensable assistant was Varvara Adrianova-Peretz, whose husband, an academician, was arrested and died in the gulag. She and Orlov recommended Dmitry's candidacy in writing a chapter on pre-Mongol Russian literature for a fundamental project, the 'History of ancient Russian culture' prepared by the Institute of Material Culture (later the Institute of Archaeology). Likhachev worked on this piece assiduously.[83] This project introduced Dmitry to a group of influential scholars, among them archaeologists Nikolai Voronin and Maria Tikhanova. These connections would be crucial for his survival.

Vassily Komarovich and Mikhail Steblin-Kamenski, two friends of Dmitry from the 1920s, worked at the IRLI as well and welcomed him there warmly. In July 1937 they decided to spend a holiday together, outside Leningrad. Their destination was ancient Novgorod. Likhachev had never seen Novgorod and was charmed. One thousand years ago, Novgorod was a major port, which connected Russian lands to the Baltic trade and the rest of Europe. The city's architectural gems included the 'Kremlin' and whitewashed elegant churches facing each other across the placid river Volkhov. Novgorodian churches revealed common features with Byzantine art; they stood not only inside the city, but also around it – dotting the horizon like beautiful pins on a great crown. Frescoes in their interiors were painted by Feofan the Greek and other masters of the fourteenth to fifteenth centuries. The old city was still untouched by modernity and the destructive Bolshevik campaigns.

Zina was already heavily pregnant. Komarovich advised Dmitry and Zina to rent a room in the house of 'Baronessa' Tiesenhausen (her father was an Orthodox priest, and her husband, the Baron, was in the gulag). 'Baronessa' was a warm host, cooked fish-soup for the guests, and had lovely children. It was not clear, however, what happened to her parents and children's father. Every morning, Dmitry and Zina woke up to see from their windows 'a marvellous view across the field, with the Nereditsa church and a bell-tower far away on the horizon'. Dmitry did not have a camera, and later claimed he simply did not have the money to buy one. Instead, he drew sketches in charcoal on his working pad. He drew churches and also drew Zina. Likhachev would never forget that summer: the light and colours of peaceful August days, silhouettes of swallows against the whitewashed church walls, and the reflection of moving clouds against the immaculately golden cupolas of the Cathedral of St Sophia. 'I could not stop watching those cupolas, as if it were a fragment of the sea with its waves coming one after another.' Friends made trips to the nearby village of Volotovo, where a famous fourteenth-century church stood, to Khutyn, to the St Cyril Monastery, and the gorgeous Cloister of St George with its star-spangled blue onion domes. They visited Peryn, where, according to legend, many Novgorodians underwent baptism and threw the old pagan deity Perun into the river. The graveyards there were places of Russian cultural memories: the poet Gavrila Derzhavin, Blok's sister, and many others lay there. A steamer brought them back to Novgorod: on the riverbanks they could see already collectivized, but still populous and vibrant Russian villages. One of them had once belonged to the Tsar's favourite Arakcheiev and he had tried to convert them into military settlements. Arakcheiev's buildings of elegant style could still be seen from the river. In 1825, peasants rose up in rebellion and killed Arakcheiev's beloved mistress. In the early 1930s Bolshevik collectivization, however, broke the will of the countryside to resist.[84]

Immediately after their holiday in Novgorod, Zina gave birth to twin daughters, Liudmila (Mila) and Vera. Likhachev's mother was upset: she doubted her penniless son would be able to raise the twins. She also did not make efforts to help – unlike Sergei Likhachev who secretly gave money to Zina. The young family lived in abject poverty. Yet Mikhail Barmansky, a friend of the young couple, told Dmitry and Zina: 'The Lord always provides for children.' Those words turned out to be prophetic.[85]

In 1938 Victor Zhirmunsky offered Dmitry a position in his department of Western literature at IRLI, but Likhachev politely declined. He had already decided to study ancient Russian culture and to write a dissertation about the early Novgorod chronicles. In September 1939 he published his first essay on this topic. He started with a quote from August Ludwig Schlözer, a German historian who worked in St Petersburg in the 1760s: 'Try opening the chronicles of any times and any people, and try to find any history that surpasses or even equals Russian history. The latter is superior in its infinite scale, in the number of peoples constituting its historical body ...' This theme of Old Russia's diversity and scale would become a hallmark of Likhachev's writings. Likhachev's special sense of patriotism came across in other things he wrote. He dwelt on the emergence of 'national self-awareness' (*samosoznaniie*) among the tribes of Kievan Rus and focused on the sense of honour, chivalry and empathy that Russian people had for other peoples and the tribes that surrounded the Russian lands. The chroniclers, he argued, never expressed hatred towards Russia's enemies; instead they found virtues in them, tried to understand their culture. At the same time he did not forget to mention the crimes and cruelty of Russian medieval princes. The ancient scripts, he concluded, 'speak to the contemporary reader in the same eloquent way as they spoke to the generations of Russian people who were inspired by them'.[86]

This essay appeared only a few weeks after the infamous Nazi–Soviet pact, which opened the road to World War II. Arkady Mankov wrote in his diary: 'Everyone lives in intense expectation of big events, as before a storm.' Later he expressed revulsion and disgust at the 'little dirty war' against Finland, and later the annexation of the Baltic states.[87] Likhachev kept his thoughts to himself; he remained buried in his academic studies. On 11 June 1941, he successfully defended his dissertation on the Novgorod chronicles. Eleven days later, Germany attacked the Soviet Union.

# CHAPTER 4

# THE GREAT FATHERLAND WAR, 1941–1945

> People revealed themselves, as if stripped of any kind of camouflage: some turned out to be wonderful, unparalleled heroes, others – villains, scoundrels, murderers, cannibals. There was no middle-ground.
>
> *D.S. Likhachev about the Leningrad Siege*[1]

Sometimes your life depends on the geography of your vacation. On 19 June 1941 Dmitry and Zina, with their little daughters and peasant nanny Tamara, moved to a country dacha in Vyritsa, a sleepy Russian town along a placid river 40 miles south of Leningrad. Nearby were two Russian monasteries, closed by the Bolsheviks: the Nunnery of the Assumption of the Virgin, and the Cloister of John the Baptist. Initially, however, the family had planned to move north-east to Teriyoki on the Finnish gulf; that territory, so rich in memories from Dmitry's childhood, was annexed by the Soviet Union after the bloody 'winter war' with Finland. Yet the rents in Teriyoki were beyond the means of the young family. After the war, Likhachev and his mother Vera would sail by ferry past Teriyoki, and wonder: 'If we had rented this place, would we still have been alive today?'[2]

On 22 June, Dmitry and Zina stayed on the Vyritsa beach into early afternoon. Suddenly they overheard other holiday-makers talking about some planes, which had bombed the naval fortress of Kronstadt near Leningrad. Like all towns around the Soviet Union Vyritsa had a radio 'dish', a communal transmitter in the middle of its main square. Dmitry went there to listen to Vyacheslav Molotov's announcement about the war. People listened to the news grimly, in silence. 'After Hitler's blitzkrieg successes in Europe nobody expected anything good to happen.'[3] Indeed, the war arrived soon, quick and merciless, to the Russian lands. After years of extreme militarization and propaganda slogans to justify everyday misery ('Everything for defence!'), the Soviet army was smashed by the German Blitzkrieg. Soviet Army officers were disoriented and lost the initiative to the enemy; many peasants deserted, because they had no motives to fight for the Soviet regime.[4] Educated youth, who volunteered for the army, were also disoriented: they expected a quick victorious war and believed that Hitler would be overthrown by a workers' revolution in Germany. Young writer Daniil Granin, who volunteered to fight, recalled: 'The first months of the war were the most difficult ones, and partly because we lacked any hatred for the Germans.' After just the first week of war, the Soviets abandoned the Baltic States. Ten days later German panzers captured Pskov and began to approach Novgorod. The front approached Leningrad with breath-taking rapidity.[5]

Dmitry was summoned to a local draft office and, after a quick check, rejected as unfit for service. For the first month of the war he commuted between his work in Leningrad and his family in Vyritsa. It was dangerous: the Luftwaffe bombed trains. Likhachev much preferred that Zina, Mila and Vera should stay in the countryside. He also feared bringing them to Leningrad because of the enforced evacuation of children. Without any realistic information about where the Germans were, children went southward by train – straight towards the advancing enemy. Some trains got bombed, and very small children, lacking proper paperwork, got lost – and were never found by their parents.[6] Likhachev's friend Mikhail Barmansky, however, realized what Dmitry and almost everyone in Leningrad ignored: the Germans were close. He was a veteran of the Great War, with uncanny instincts. On 19 July, when Dmitry returned to his Leningrad apartment from work, he was surprised to see the whole family there. Barmansky went to Vyritsa by himself, and ordered Zina and Tamara to pack. Within a few hours they were on the train to Leningrad. Sovinformburo reported that German troops were still hundreds of miles away. In reality, they would roll into Vyritsa within two weeks. A pure chance determined again the life of Dmitry, Zina and their children: they stayed in their home city and shared its fate – the one of unimaginable horror.

## The Siege

In July the party chief of Leningrad, Andrei Zhdanov, announced that the city would never be in danger or in need of anything. On 18 July food rationing started in the city, yet the rations were still plentiful; commercial groceries and peasant markets remained open and relatively abundant.[7]

Many Leningrad intellectuals ignored the bad tidings, continued to live in summer dachas, and did not collect supplies.[8] A former Solovki inmate, Dmitry knew immediately that Soviet official announcements were *tufta*, concealing the usual disorder and lack of preparations. Dmitry told his family that there would be a famine, and it was necessary to collect food supplies.[9] He, Zina and Tamara bought loaves of bread, cut them into small parts, dried them, and stored bags of blackbread-crackers (*sukhari*). They also purchased everything canned and storable. Still, Likhachev could not foresee total famine in a huge city. Six months later Dmitry woke up in the besieged Leningrad with the same nightmare: he tormented himself for not going again and again to the same stores, stashing even more fats and bread, cans of sardines and bottles of cod-liver oil.[10]

Stalin knew that Russians would fight for their country, not for the communist regime. On 3 July he appealed to them by radio, using the plain and moving Russian words: 'brothers and sisters, my friends, to you I am turning now.' Soviet propaganda proclaimed 'a Great Fatherland War', rehashing the propaganda themes of 1914. Reactions varied greatly. Olga Freidenberg remembered: 'Everyone said that [when Stalin made his speech] his teeth chattered against the glass; he had to drink water to calm down. People of the intelligentsia, our janitor, even passers-by in the street spoke about it with rancour.'[11] Quite a few older Russians, particularly 'former people' and peasantry were affected by defeatism. Those who continued to view the Bolsheviks as 'occupiers' wondered again, as in 1918, if German occupation might be a lesser evil. Some Russians listened to German propaganda that promised to 'liberate' them from Jews and communists. Peasants believed that the Germans would disband the collective farms and reopen churches. The Soviet Information Bureau (Sovinformburo), fearing such a reaction, began to publish fictitious stories about German atrocities against the Russian peasantry.[12]

On 16 October 1941, Moscow woke up to discover that all officials were in flight from the capital. This news produced a riot with a pogrom-like mood. Rumours spread that Jews were fleeing along with the communists, carrying people's salaries and food. The long-suppressed 'economic' anti-Semitism burst out. Russians again had a bizarre moment of liberation from their own government, a kind of suicidal anarchy. Some 'former people' calmly waited for the German troops.[13] Yet the riot stopped and order returned. Some historians credited Joseph Stalin for this change: the dictator decided to stay in Moscow and suppressed the anarchy. Others believe that the October crisis produced a shift in Russian expectations. In fact, at the time Stalin's name disappeared from the propaganda, it was replaced by 'Fatherland'. At the end of November, when the temperature unexpectedly plummeted deep below zero, the Wehrmacht's great offensive came to a halt.

In Leningrad, a similar crisis of faith brewed in late August to early September, when German armies approached the city. The city leadership began to burn the archives, and evacuate their relatives and valuables, including food supplies and cash. Archivist Georgy Kniazev recorded in his diary: 'Disorientation, if not panic, reigns in the ruling circles.' Rumours began to circulate that Leningrad, like Paris in May 1940, would be declared 'an open city' and left to the enemy without resistance. People with Jewish backgrounds were in panic. Likhachev recalled that in the IRLI the scholars of Jewish origins suddenly began to talk about his 'Russian Orthodox' lineage. Another scholar from an assimilated Jewish family came dressed as an Armenian. Olga Freidenberg, a Russified Jew, lived in a suspense that seemed unbearable: 'We expected the Germans to arrive any night, any morning, by midday ...'[14]

On 17 September, the last defence line on the Pulkovo Heights to the west of Leningrad crumbled. German troops could see the entire city lying on the plains in front of them. Daniil Granin remembered retreating across these plains with his routed platoon. The Luftwaffe bombed and strafed them, corpses lay everywhere. Granin found Leningrad completely defenceless: no sign of trenches, barricades or troops. German tanks could have rolled through the city without facing any resistance. Yet Hitler suddenly decided that the city should be left to die from starvation. The Germans began to shell and bomb the city mercilessly. This turned the mood sharply against the Germans.[15]

Yuri took a picture of Likhachev, Zina and their twin daughters on a walk in the Botanical Garden around that time. In a photo, Dmitry appears elegantly dressed, in a grey demi-season coat with large lapels. His small conical beard gave him a Chekhovian look. Lost in thought, he did not look into the camera. The children also looked anxious and focused. Seconds after this picture was taken, another air raid began.[16] One of the first bombing raids demolished a building near Likhachev's house, with the café which the poet Blok had frequented. After a while, the Likhachevs decided not to go down to the shelters: they knew they could have been buried there as well and die a slow death. When the Luftwaffe started dropping incendiary bombs on Leningrad, Dmitry and other scholars served in shifts on the roof of the Pushkin House. He sat there for hours watching the magnificent panorama around him. Leningrad was camouflaged: the golden spears of the Admiralty and the Peter and Paul fortress, St Isaac's Cathedral, and the statue of the Bronze Horseman were covered. This, however, only emphasized the stunning architectural harmony. From his roof, Dmitry fantasized on how to reconstruct the city and make it even more beautiful. His pet project was to tear down ugly warehouses in the north, and create a magnificent sequence of parks and walking zones with bike paths, various zoological and botanical gardens, and small exhibitions, free from noisy traffic. His 'imagined' Petersburg gave his patriotism an aesthetic quality. The incursions of German planes interfered with Likhachev's reveries. Once he even had a glimpse of a German pilot sitting in the Stuka's cockpit. When a firebomb fell on 'his' roof, he and other volunteers would seize it with pincers, a hissing monster, and put it into a bucket of water.[17]

We do not know Likhachev's private thoughts at that time. He remembered, however, standing next to his friend Komarovich in the autumn of 1941, reading a newspaper pasted to the wall at the Institute. 'Everyone then was convinced that Germany would win the war.' Komarovich, however, remarked: 'The British lion is old and experienced. It is not easy to get him. I believe that eventually England will win.' Most tellingly, neither of them spoke about 'Soviet victory'. From that moment on, Dmitry pinned his hope for the future on a British victory! He rejected the defeatism widespread among Leningrad intellectuals.[18] His patriotism of pity and love for Petersburg-Leningrad made him oppose those who preferred a German victory.

As the weather turned cold, Likhachev was appointed 'the head of a detachment for communications'. He walked around the city, to pass messages to the Institute's scholars who no longer came to the offices, for fear of shells and bombs, or because they had grown weak from hunger.[19] For all the trumpets of propaganda, the Leningrad authorities failed to preserve and protect huge amounts of goods under their custody. In contrast to the British authorities, they refused to give food away to the population. Instead, they shipped supplies out of the city, expecting the city to fall; the rest was stored in the giant Badayevsky warehouses. The very first Luftwaffe raid on 8 September destroyed the warehouses. Likhachev and many others watched the apocalyptic golden cloud that rose to cover half the sky. That cloud consisted of tons of butter evaporating in the firestorm. That swirling cloud was an apparition of the Apocalypse for thousands. In September–October, the food ration in Leningrad dropped to 200 grams of bread for a working individual, and less for household members and children. By December this ration had shrunk to 125 grams, and the 'bread' ration had lost almost any resemblance to the real product: it consisted of glue, paper and anything imaginable. Only the authorities continued to eat abundantly, with the help of aerial supplies: the party leadership received from Moscow caviar, salmon, chocolate, even oranges, wine and bottles of champagne for the New Year celebration. The rest of the population was doomed to gradual decay and slow death from starvation.[20]

The corrupt saleswomen of the 'co-ops' doled out grams of poor-quality bread on the scales of their primitive devices. People had to stand for many hours in lines during the night, in freezing wind, in the hope of getting their rationing cards exchanged for food; many who came too late remained empty-handed. Cheating, and stealing cards and food from the old and weak, was an everyday practice. In November–December the supplies of food in the city ran out completely. Only the black market continued to work, and entrepreneurial 'speculators' obtained food in exchange for gold and other valuables.[21]

Cold was a worse killer than hunger. Already in November the temperature dipped below zero, and stayed around -20, -35 and even -40 C for the next four months. In December electric power failed, and all city communications and services stopped, including streetcars. The authorities failed to procure heating fuel – wood, oil or kerosene. Electric stoves were banned, because of frequent fires. Temperatures in apartments fell to zero. The plumbing froze and burst. Without access to water, people had to go to the ice-covered river and the canals across the snow-bound city. People could not wash themselves, and threw their frozen faeces out onto the streets, courtyards and attics. The peasant refugees, who lived in the suburbs and in abandoned apartments in Leningrad, did not have registration and ration cards. They slaughtered all their cattle, and then began to die from cold and hunger. Next to die were the workers from the Putilov mechanical plant, relocated by the authorities from the districts facing the German lines: those people could not even take their supplies with them. In December the Grim Reaper began to carry away people by the tens of thousands a day, above all children and adult males.[22] By the end of February probably a million and a half had died of famine and cold.

In 1957, Dmitry and Zina forced each other to record what they still remembered about the Siege. Likhachev recalled in great detail what happened to his friends and relatives, their body and spirit. The human brain was the last to go: only after all other bodily functions stopped, after conscience, fear and even egotism had vanished. Dmitry saw how some people lost their humanity and others triumphed to preserve it to the end. Likhachev quoted from the Book of Revelation when he remembered the Siege: 'So, because you are lukewarm, and neither hot nor cold, I will spit you out of my mouth.'[23] He also recited the psalm:

> For my soul is full of troubles: and my life draweth nigh unto the grave. I am counted with them that go down into the pit: I am as a man that hath no strength: Free among the dead, like the slain that lie in the grave, whom thou rememberest no more: and they are cut off from thy hand. Thou hast laid me in the lowest pit, in darkness, in the deeps.[24]

Many Leningraders recited the same psalm. Boris Pasternak, who did not live through the Siege, managed to capture a moment of its catharsis: 'All things imaginable on Earth and in Heaven, this city tolerated and surpassed.'[25]

In the first months of famine, Likhachev and Zina shared their supplies with relatives and friends, among them Komarovich and the Koplan family. Sophia Shakhmatov-Koplan was the daughter of Aleksei Shakhmatov, a leading scholar of the ancient Russian chronicles. In 1920 Shakhmatov had perished from malnutrition amid the revolutionary chaos; now his daughter and grandson, an amazingly talented boy, died of famine. 'Whole families disappeared', recorded Olga Freidenberg. 'People vanished in whole apartments, buildings, blocks and streets.'[26] At the Hermitage Museum, Mikhail Glinka, a historian of art, asked in October 1942 a friend, who saw the medical statistics of Leningrad, how many people died. The friend answered: 'One million nine hundred thousand people died' in Leningrad alone.[27] Official statistics were not published.

Several relatives of the Likhachevs and the Konyaevs died from famine. Among them was his favourite uncle Vasily, with whom student Dmitry liked to talk about the 'meaning of life and truth'. On 1 March 1942 Sergei Likhachev died in great pain. On his deathbed Sergei dreamed aloud about the Volga trip on the luxury riverboat in 1913, and enumerated everything they ate in the glass-covered restaurant on board. He also constantly spoke about the sausages and bacon that his older son Yuri (by then evacuated to Moscow with his wife) would ship him one day by plane. He also suspected Dmitry and his wife of stealing food from him. When he died, Dmitry covered his eyes with two big old coins, according to family custom. With great difficulty he and Zina procured a certificate of death: the authorities refused to admit the fact of mass death from famine. The document they gave mentioned death from 'sickness'. The burial was too costly. Most people preferred to leave the corpses of their relatives near public spots where the authorities 'collected' them for free. Dmitry and his wife left Sergei's corpse at the corner of a public garden, next to a pile of other bodies, wrapped or naked. They saw lorries arriving; workers loaded corpses into them like lumber. Dmitry felt no remorse, he just thought: 'What will become of us?' Only later, fear of death invaded him: the magic effect of the Solovki epiphany was over. He wrote to a friend that the reminiscences of his father's death and burial 'still burn my brains from within'.[28]

The line between villainy and pragmatism became blurred in the dying city. Cannibalism broke out in the starving city: mothers killed children to survive; fathers killed other people to feed their families. Gangs hunted down women and children, killed and ate them or sold their flesh on the black market. The city police executed hundreds of cannibals every month,

THE GREAT FATHERLAND WAR, 1941–1945    61

but the phenomenon spread like a plague.[29] Vassily Komarovich died, after his own wife and daughter stopped feeding him and eventually dropped him in a state of progressive starvation at the doorstep of an emergency centre. A group of villains operated at the Institute for Russian Literature (Pushkin House). While the Director of the Pushkin House resided in Moscow, his deputy Kanailov (in Russian his name rhymes with 'con-man') persuaded him to cut the Institute's staff – to reduce rations and to save food for himself. Likhachev recalled: 'Kanailov watched closely: when somebody became weak, he signed the order to sack him, and literally threw a person out onto the frozen street, without heat and food.' He also looted the Institute's valuable memorabilia, items that had once belonged to Russian poets and writers. In the end, the scoundrel, with his assistant, managed to leave Leningrad with numerous bags of hoarded food and stolen museum art.[30]

Next to such villainy, acts of individual integrity and sacrifice shone like diamonds. Within the family, Zina showed an example of extraordinary self-sacrifice and humanity. When Dmitry became too weak to go to the IRLI to collect his rations, Zina went. She and resourceful nanny Tamara stood in long queues at the 'co-ops' where the ration cards sometimes helped to get some bread and even fat. And she saved what she got from thieves and from her own temptation to eat it on the way home. Zina's father Aleksandr Makarov perished – he simply stopped eating, although he still had some food. She focused on saving her husband and children, as well as her mother-in-law Vera.[31] At the IRLI, Victor Manuilov, who replaced Kanailov as the acting head of the Institute, was another person of great humanity.[32] He acted energetically to save the Institute's personnel and its archives and collections. With a group of dedicated women, in the half-dead city, he visited the dying relatives of Russian writers who donated their valuable collections of letters and other memorabilia to the Pushkin House. In April 1942, when the authorities finally set up a special hospital to feed sick scientists and scholars, Manuilov managed to find a place there for disease-stricken Dmitry Likhachev.[33]

Hot meals at the well-heated hospital began to bring him back to life: his body slowly thawed from a lethal lethargy. Outside, the most dreadful winter in the city's history finally began to give way to the first war spring. Leningrad began to show more signs of life. Trams began to run again; the authorities distributed seeds, and people began to plant them everywhere: on squares, in front of the buildings, in the flower pots and even on the dinner tables inside their apartments. After one month in the hospital Dmitry began to walk and almost immediately started to collect materials for his research. In May he completed several projects, including a chapter on Archpriest Avvakum, left unfinished by Komarovich, for the 'History of Russian Literature', and a paper on the cultural legacy of ancient Novgorod and Pskov.[34]

## Patriotic Bind

In April 1942 archaeologist Maria Tikhanova from the Institute of Material Culture approached Likhachev with a book proposal. The Leningrad party authorities requested the writing of a pamphlet describing how in ancient times Russians defended their cities from the enemy. She recommended Dmitry as her co-author. Together, they walked for several kilometres across the dying city to the party headquarters at the Smolny Institute, to learn the particulars of the assignment. The starving scholars could barely climb the white-marble stairs leading to the second floor, to get to their appointment. Dmitry could smell the odours of hot food, forgotten by the starving Leningraders, from the nearby canteen reserved for party officials.[35]

The deadline for the pamphlet was in a month. Both scholars worked at home, separately, without any communication – telephones and mail did not work. The idea was to show the continuity of Russian military valour from ancient Kiev to the besieged Leningrad. The book included episodes often used in pre-revolutionary Russia to educate children in the spirit of patriotism: among them the defence of Azov in the 1640s by the Cossacks against the Ottoman Turks, the battle for Pskov against the Polish-Lithuanian King Stefan Batory in the sixteenth century, and the famous siege of the Trinity Cloister by the Polish warlord Jan Sapieha (Yan Sapega) during the Times of Trouble in the early seventeenth century. Dmitry knew all his stories from childhood and often wrote from memory: it took too much energy in the unheated apartment to stand up and reach out an arm for a book on a shelf. This work assignment gave Dmitry another reason to live, in addition to his concern about his family. His brain worked feverishly, and his writing came out well. Official editors added a few 'required' footnotes from Marx, Engels and Stalin, and the pamphlet appeared with the title 'The Defence of Ancient Russian Cities' in the autumn of 1942. It had numerous illustrations from ancient Russian chronicles, was printed in tens of thousands of copies and disseminated among soldiers and officers at the war front. Dmitry received letters with expressions of gratitude from the frontline. Among them was his friend Arkady Selivanov who was defending Oranienbaum, about 30 miles from Leningrad.[36]

Likhachev's book responded to the new and genuine surge of patriotism – which was not so much the effect of Soviet propaganda, but rather came from the heart. At a moment when everything appeared hopeless and lost, when the state abandoned them, a new mood emerged among the people that can be called the patriotism of defiance and despair.[37] Artist Ostroumova-Lebedeva wrote in her diary on 17 November: 'With all my essence, mind, heart, and soul I realize that Leningrad must not be surrendered to the Germans. Better all of us die.' Georgy Kniazev's diary referred to the Time of Troubles of 1612, when 'the Russian state seemed to be falling, only to stay intact'. Writing in the weak light of a kerosene lamp or a church candle, Kniazev wrote: 'My ancestor might have sat and written in the same way, sitting behind the walls of a cloister besieged by the Tatars or the Poles.' He concluded that the Nazi invasion left 'no choice for us the Russians': 'either ousting of the invaders and the subjugators – or death. There is no other path.'[38]

Likhachev, when he worked on his pamphlet, discovered a new depth in his personal relationship with medieval Russia and historic Petersburg. The scale of the German assault and the scale of Leningrad's defence astounded him. The Soviet levy resembled the Russian national levies in the 1612 and 1812 wars. He looked back to the Russian past to find words and analogies to describe the scale of calamity, the enormity of human grief. The Soviet official patriotic lexicon was useless, and the state propaganda had to abandon it. Suddenly, medieval chronicles looked fresh and familiar. 'From that moment on, my narrow textological studies of ancient Russian chronicles and historical novels acquired for me a modern significance.' He concluded: 'A thousand years of Russian literature produced the words for describing foreign invasions, unprecedented sieges, crushing defeats – that ended finally in the victories of spirit and courage.'[39]

Likhachev convinced himself that Old Russia was not just the nostalgic treasure of 'former people'. It could be translated for a younger audience, with its notions of Christian love, suffering for an idea, respect for ancestors, and memories of the dead. Indeed, the divisive memories of the past seemed to be purified, became 'sacred'. Russian émigrés, who supported the Soviet Union against Germany in the war, had similar feelings in 1942–1945. Vera Sandomirsky, daughter of a Russian engineer and an American intelligence official during the war, wrote in *Russian Review* in 1944: 'In 1941 [the notion of Motherland] became the highest symbol of unification, the banner for a whole nation ... And usually *rodina* is linked with the adjective that becomes an organic part of it – *sviashchennaya* – meaning sacred or holy.'[40] Nikolai Timashev wrote in 1943 about Russia as a phenomenon that re-emerged after the Bolshevik ordeal as 'an invisible *Grad Kitezh*' from the ancient legend – from the bottom of a charmed lake. He concluded: 'Why it should not be possible for history to repeat itself and for Holy Russia not to rise once more from the baptism of blood?'[41]

The Soviet authorities felt uneasy about such rhetoric at home.[42] Soviet propaganda preferred a different version of patriotism, appealing to vengeance and hatred. Ilya Ehrenburg regularly propagated this version on the pages of newspapers to Russian soldiers: 'Kill a German!' Ehrenburg's language breathed the fire of Torah. The same litany of vengeance was in the poetry and pamphlets of Konstantin Simonov and Aleksei Tolstoy.[43] This language in 1943 began to blend with the feeling of messianic chauvinism similar to that of their German enemies. Ostroumova-Lebedeva wrote in her diary: 'Venom, vengeance, and destruction of the enemy are our main impulses. Humanist ideals must be forgotten. We must remember all the horrendous sufferings of our people, the death of millions of people of our spirit, our blood, our race.'[44] The German invasion helped to forge *Soviet-Russian* patriotism. The titanic war, losses and victories, created powerful memories of tragedy and trauma, and displaced the earlier traumatic memories of the Revolution, the Civil War, Bolshevism, and even the Great Terror. This displacement legitimized the Soviet regime and de-legitimized Russian collaborationism. The official rhetoric of the Great Fatherland War gradually became the Russian people's living experience. Historian Amir Weiner detected the emergence of a new political body – constructed and stratified according to what one did during the war. The experience of war and invasion, another historian concludes, drew people closer to their state, by creating 'a common ground of shared outrage, shared enemies, and shared hopes'.[45]

In 1943, after the victory at Stalingrad, Stalin distanced himself from communist rhetoric and fully embraced the symbols of Russian greatness. The dictator knew that the terrible war required more sacrifices; he also wanted the Soviet allies, the United States and Great Britain, to believe that the Soviet Union could now be a legitimate great power, deciding on the postwar world order.[46] On 21 May 1943 the Politburo disbanded the Comintern. And on 4 September 1943 Stalin met with Metropolitan Sergius (Stragorodsky) and his two colleagues, survivors from the Great Terror. He offered them a new deal: the Patriarchate would be restored; the persecuted Russian Orthodox Church would become a legitimate junior partner of the Soviet state. The hastily convened reunion of Metropolitans, some of them flown to Moscow from the gulag, elected Sergius as Patriarch. The enthronement ceremony took place in the main Moscow cathedral, in the presence of foreign journalists and eminent officials.[47] The Living Church crumbled overnight; its adherents returned to the 'official' church. Many Russian nationalists and Russians abroad rejoiced: they even forgot how insulted they had been by Sergius's collaboration with the Kremlin in 1927. Glorious church singing and Russian patriotic symbols blinded and deceived them. They cheered as if Stalin were an emperor of 'the third Rome'. The secret police reported that Russian intellectuals expected the dictator to be succeeded by a new crop of 'national leaders' to emerge after the war.[48]

Stalin, not susceptible to illusions and emotions, placed the new Russian church under the auspices of his secret police. A cruel irony of history ordained that Georgy Karpov, the MGB supervisor of the Patriarchy, had arrested and killed priests in Pskov during the Great Terror. Among those priests was Rev. Victor Dobronravov, friend of the Brotherhood of St Seraphim.[49] The terror regime determined who would and who would not be part of the 'national body' and 'national leadership'. Millions of Russian POWs and collaborationists with the Germans were designated as 'national traitors' – they were killed, deported, and dispatched to the gulag. The 'class cleansing' began to change into 'national cleansing'.[50]

History left Russians no room for the third choice between Hitler and Stalin. Thousands of Russian POWs in German camps, addressed by General Andrei Vlasov, captured by the Germans, succumbed to a desperate delusion: defeat Stalin first, fighting as a 'Russian Liberation army' together with the Wehrmacht; then turn against Hitler. Many Russian defeatists and collaborationists cast their lot with the Vlasov army.[51] Those who did not want to make this choice found themselves in a quandary. Ivan Andreyevsky, the founder of the 'Brotherhood of St Seraphim', as well as Likhachev's mentor Sergei Alexeyev (Askoldov) worked under the German occupation in the Pskov Mission of the Orthodox Church, preaching an idea of the third way, between the Nazis and the Bolsheviks. When the German armies retreated from Pskov, both preferred to go with them. Askoldov became a priest in the 'Russian village' in Potsdam, until the Soviets came: he died in expectation of arrest. Andreyevsky fled to West Germany and then the United States.[52]

People with a Jewish background, who used to consider themselves part of the 'internationalist' Soviet community, felt suddenly excluded from the 'national body'. Linguist and literary historian Lidia Ginzburg recorded in her notes a strong temptation 'to belong', to be part of 'the people' united against the enemy. She felt an almost irresistible pressure to fill the void left by the collapse of the humanist and internationalist promise of world communist revolution.[53] Olga Freidenberg expected the worst from a 'despicable *mélange* of Marxism and the police-state Orthodoxy that fatally accompanied the rule of any Russian power embodied by non-Russian rulers'. Freidenberg feared that this public mood could be turned on and off by the authorities, while the 'plebeian masses' remained passive and at the mercy of their masters.[54]

### Bitter Taste of Victory

In May 1942, when Likhachev was about to finish 'The Defence of Ancient Russian Cities', he was summoned to a local police office, allegedly to talk to a draft official. Instead, an NKVD officer was waiting for Dmitry; he wanted to recruit him as an informer. In Leningrad, the NKVD never stopped its terror against the population. In the spring of 1943 NKVD officers in surrounded Leningrad received from the mainland fresh cadres and plenty of food. Their guidelines stayed the same: combat 'defeatism' and 'anti-Soviet sentiments'. Also the secret police saw that the Leningrad tragedy remained covered by an impenetrable blanket of silence and denial.[55]

It was a time when many Leningraders from the institutions of culture and education succumbed and agreed to cooperate with the NKVD. In his interview in 1990 Likhachev recalled how he reacted: 'Fortunately, I had gained experience of dealing with the [Cheka] operatives in Solovki. And I knew what to do so that they would give up hope of recruiting me. From the start, I refused to sign anything.' When the official asked him to sign a paper of non-disclosure of their conversations, Dmitry responded: 'I cannot do it. I talk in my sleep.' The recruiter alternated promises and threats, but finally said: 'You agree or else!' Likhachev left the office, and then refused to respond to other summons. One day, however, he met 'his' officer on the street and was ordered to come to the next appointment, in an NKVD safe house located miles away. When he showed up, completely exhausted from the effort, the recruiter decided to break his will. He called a soldier and feigned Likhachev's arrest. He also threatened that Zina would be arrested as well, and his children would be sent to an orphanage. It took Likhachev all his strength to preserve his dignity at this moment and refused. The officer realized that his bluff was called. In anger, he ordered a police chief to bring Likhachev's file and blotted out one line: 'resides in Leningrad.' This was the official cancellation of his residence permit (*propiska*) and deportation from his city.[56] On 3 June, MGB officer Ogoltsov signed the list of people found guilty of treason. Likhachev's recruiter decided to make him pay dearly for his behaviour. The police verdict was that Likhachev 'was arrested and indicted for counter-revolutionary activities. He praises fascist Germany, denigrates the intelligentsia of the Soviet Union, and predicts [*predopredeliaet*] defeat of the Soviet system in the war against fascism. He expresses readiness to serve fascism.'[57] In wartime, this verdict could quickly lead to a death sentence, not just deportation. Why did Likhachev survive again?

The deportation from Leningrad was an ordeal as well. Many deportees did not reach the mainland alive, and died from exhaustion and fatigue. Others ended up in Siberian camps or exile. Escape from Leningrad was possible only across Lake Ladoga, on ice and later by boats. Soviet propaganda trumpeted about 'the road of life' across Ladoga; but Likhachev later called it 'the road of death'. Germans bombed the ice-road; many cars fell under the ice, and people drowned in the dark, cold water of the lake. Dmitry decided to fight for the right to stay in the city: better die at home! Yet a Soviet attorney told him it was hopeless and recommended packing and leaving. Also Likhachev learned that his cousin, an electrical engineer, was harassed by an NKVD officer and, as a result, committed suicide. Likhachev decided to take the risk of a dangerous escape, with his mother, Zina, nanny and children.

Kalistov, a friend and another Siege survivor, told Dmitry that the Academy of Sciences planned to take some of the surviving scholars out of the city. Manuilov provided all necessary papers that allowed Dmitry and his family to leave the city as 'free' evacuees, not as deportees. From that moment on, the situation began to improve. Likhachev's elder brother in Moscow finally got in touch with him and sent money for travel. It was not enough: Zina and Vera had to sell all the family furniture, including the fateful standing clock that announced Dmitry's arrest. His world of childhood, of familiar books, old chairs, mirrors and paintings went to black marketeers. Vera Likhacheva managed to preserve only her family icons, some of them still in precious silver cases. On 24 June 1942 a train departed from the Finland Station, taking Likhachev, Kalistov and their families to Lake Ladoga. Fortunately, they sailed to the other side without any adventures – German planes never appeared. On the far shore they boarded another train with boarded cars, without any compartments and seats, more suitable for carrying animals. The train was packed, yet everything else looked like a Wonderland: they ate kasha cooked in real butter! With real food, other senses began to return: the Leningraders smelled the scents of the forest, they heard birds singing, and they could even feel insect bites again. For many people, however, the promise of returning life was deceptive. While the train trundled slowly eastward, hundreds of Leningraders, including some of Dmitry's colleagues, continued to die from the after-effects of starvation. There were also other tragedies and miracles of evacuation: some people became separated in the hustle and bustle, others missed the train while stepping out to find water and food. After a month of great travails, the Likhachevs reached Kazan, the old Tatar city where most of the Soviet Academy of Sciences was located during the war.[58]

Even in Kazan the NKVD minders did not let Dmitry in peace. The local authorities at first refused to register him and his family. Meanwhile, the family had to live and sleep in a big hall of Kazan University with dozens of strangers. Just as in Solovki, Dmitry obtained beds for himself and his relatives by bribing the officials – one bed cost one loaf of bread. There was only one common bathroom. Finally, the Kazan NKVD relented and granted a *propiska* to the Likhachevs. They quickly rented their own room. Rather, it was half a room, the other being already occupied by another family. They drew the boundary of 'their' space by chalk on the floor. Zina and Vera partitioned their part with a curtain, so that nobody could see them praying in the corner where they put up their icons. All the money they had from Mikhail and the sale of furniture lasted only one month. Soon the silver cases from the icons had to be exchanged for bags of potatoes. The children, Mila and Vera, caused constant worry as well. Cold and infection killed children everywhere, but the parents decided to send the twins to the local kindergarten where regular hot meals were served. Soon Vera came home with whooping cough; this became pneumonia. It was another brush with death, yet Dmitri knocked on all doors and found a man in possession of antibiotics – they had just arrived in the Soviet Union, from Britain and the United States. Vera's life was saved.[59]

When Dmitry regained his strength, he began to work on his dissertation. Fortunately, the Kazan university library (where Vladimir Lenin had once worked) was very good. Another cold winter came: the reading hall had no heating. Likhachev wore the same sheepskin coat that had served him well in Solovki, and then during the Siege; he also had to have his winter gloves on. He was writing a book, 'The national consciousness of Old Russia'. After months of hard work he finished his second (doctoral) dissertation 'Russian Chronicles and their cultural and historical significance'.[60] 'The national consciousness' published in 1945 constructed a story of Russian national roots on the basis of ancient chronicles. Alexei Shakhmatov before the revolution, and other Russian historians, whom Stalin had returned from the gulag in 1934, had already begun to do this work. Likhachev emphasized 'the struggle for equality' with other great powers of Europe; the independence of the Russian Church from the Patriarch of Constantinople; the idea of state centralization and an apology for Novgorod's brutal conquest by Moscow. In the book, 'the Russian prince brilliantly rejected all attempts from Constantinople to deny autonomy to the Russian church and reduce the church to an agent of the empire'. Likhachev completely omitted the dispute about the origins of the first rulers of Russian lands: at that time those who believed that they were the Vikings (Varangians) could be charged for siding with Nazi propaganda. Kievan Rus, Likhachev concluded, was the cradle of 'the three brotherly Slavic nations – Russians, Ukrainians, and Belorussians'.[61]

Still, one could hear Likhachev's own unique voice in this text. In his description of old-time Russian patriotism, there was the note of love-pity: "of lyrical sorrow about the motherland's sufferings'.[62] While blaming the downfall of Russian ancient culture on the Tatar Yoke, Likhachev emphasized redemption and revival after the national catastrophe. In his chapter about the Time of Troubles, he wrote: 'When the Russian state was reduced to the last shreds, only then at last Russians ... rose up to defend their country.' In other words, out of darkness came salvation; from the depth of despair a new chance emerged.[63] These words might have come from Alexeyev (Askoldov), not from Stalinist agitprop. Likhachev's careful approach to Russian national mythology was also visible in his refutation of the view that Moscow viewed itself as a 'Third Rome' and this led to a *translatio imperii* – Russian expansionism. He contended that only a few ideologues of the Russian Church shared such views. The Russian state, he wrote, just wanted to win recognition and a decent place in the 'complicated milieu of European civilization'.[64]

While Soviet schoolchildren wrote papers on 'Why I Loathe Hitler and the Fascists', Likhachev adhered to the notions of patriotism expressed by the Russian aristocrats, the romantic nationalists of the 1820s, most famously by Aleksandr Pushkin:

Twin feelings fill our heart with meaning:
Love for parental graves.
Love for ancestral hearths.

Instead of dehumanizing the enemy, Likhachev appealed to the humanity of Russians: their heroism, suffering and perseverance. When he wrote about Leningrad, he meant Petersburg, 'the most beautiful city in the world'. The Italians Bartolomeo Rastrelli, Giacomo Quarenghi and Carlo Rossi, among others, contributed to its architectural extravaganza. Only once in a while did the editor's hand introduce into Likhachev's texts phrases like 'fascist invaders'. Likhachev's idea was not to blame the destruction of Russian cities on the Germans; instead it was to teach people to deplore their loss and preserve and love whatever remained from their ancestral heritage.

In January 1944 the Siege of Leningrad ended; German troops began to retreat. Many of Dmitry's colleagues hurried to return to the city. Likhachev had to renew his residence permit, and this meant the danger of more contacts with the NKVD. Again Victor Manuilov, acting director of the IRLI, came to his assistance. He provided Likhachev with a business pretext for travelling from Kazan to Leningrad; he was assigned to supervise valuable manuscripts shipped from their wartime site back to the Pushkin House.[65] Once back in Leningrad, Likhachev found his apartment 'occupied' by an entrepreneurial truck-driver. After much hassle, Dmitry managed to evict the occupier; then he put new glass into the windows and obtained a few pieces of basic furniture: a desk and several chairs.[66] This was, however, not the end of his travails. All his documents, including his ration cards, were stolen. He went again to Manuilov: with the help of his official recommendations, he restored all the paperwork. Finally a most inexplicable thing occurred: the local police agreed to issue him an authorization to reside in Leningrad. Thus, he could return to his home city permanently after being banished from it the second time.[67]

In May 1944 Likhachev, on the Institute's assignment, went to Novgorod, which had been liberated from German troops only a few months earlier. The contrast with his pleasant pre-war vacations and what he now saw in Novgorod was almost unbearable. Instead of populous villages, Likhachev saw from the train the remains of burnt-out houses and the hulks of destroyed tanks. Snow melted and revealed uncollected corpses. The train arrived at Novgorod station, yet Novgorod was nowhere to be seen. Only the ruined cathedral of St Sophia still stood in the vicinity. Its cupolas lay on the ground, despoiled of their beautiful golden sheen, looking like the broken eggs of a mythical giant bird. Likhachev heard gasps of amazement from the people who arrived in the city with him. There was a mournful chorus of people weeping: 'Our beloved, beautiful Novgorod, what they have done to you? What has remained of you?' Children began to cry with the adults; some women fell to the ground, as if praying on the city's grave. Dmitry's heart sank when he observed the totality of the destruction. The garland of medieval churches around the city was gone. The famous Kovalev and Volotov churches, with their twelfth–thirteenth-century frescoes, were heaps of rubble and dust. Further away, the Cloister of St George stood like a skeleton, its walls scarred by shells and covered by soldiers' graffiti. Likhachev found inscriptions in Spanish left by Franco's 'Blue Division'. Some were in Estonian, left by the Estonian cavalry that served in the Wehrmacht. The local Soviet authorities were overwhelmed with problems and completely lacked any interest in the business of saving the remaining ancient artifacts. The walls of the churches that still stood intact, with the surviving fragments of ancient frescoes, remained unprotected, exposed to snow and rain.[68]

Dmitry had lost not only the most cherished places in his memory of Old Russia – the place where Zina and he spent two happy summers. Beautiful palaces and parks around Leningrad, Likhachev's *lieux de memoir* from his childhood days, also disappeared. Peterhof, Detskoye Selo and Pavlovsk were in ruins; the rumour was that this was done not by German troops, but by Soviet planes. The Yelagin palace survived the German occupation, but was destroyed by fire after Soviet troops made their headquarters there. At the time, when Soviet radio had turned increasingly triumphalist, with more and more military victories at the front, Likhachev suffered from anguish and pity at the enormity of Russia's cultural losses. Dmitry confessed his feelings to another scholar, archaeologist Nikolai Voronin. That confession opened Voronin's heart: the two men became close friends. 'We became closer to each other at that time,' Likhachev recalled later, 'because we had a common grief – the destruction of Russian cultural monuments, on the one hand by the Germans, on the other hand by our own authorities.'[69]

The war ended for the Russians on 9 May 1945, because Stalin decided to announce it one day after the German surrender to the Western Allies. Likhachev learned about victory when he walked out in the street. Strangers laughed and embraced each other; other people stood and cried, alone, remembering all those whom the war had taken. Like everyone around him, he was overwhelmed by emotions and memories. 'If people in the entire world,' Likhachev reminisced many years later, 'preserved the living feeling of horror at their war experience, contemporary politics would be completely different.'[70]

# CHAPTER 5

# PATRIOTISM DEFILED, 1945–1955

Above all, he was a Russian person who felt sore pity for the whole Russian land.
  *D.S. Likhachev about the author of* The Lay of Igor's Campaign, *1949*

'There is a good deal of wounded *amour propre* about Leningrad, a coldly handsome and once arrogant old capital': such was the impression of a young British visitor, Isaiah Berlin, on 13 November 1945. Berlin lived in Petrograd in 1917–1920, after which his family, Jewish merchants from Riga, emigrated to the United Kingdom. He returned to the city as a British Foreign Service official, and according to the Soviet secret police, as an intelligence agent. People in Leningrad looked shabby and poor, yet Isaiah Berlin found there something Moscow had lost: 'warn and torn members of the old intelligentsia'. Berlin met Leningrad's *literati*, among them Mikhail Zoshchenko and Anna Akhmatova. He reported to the British embassy that the experience of the blockade continued to fill 'all memoirs and colours every conversation'. But the Leningrad intellectuals also felt proud of their culture and legacy; they hoped that after the war Leningrad might become once again a gateway to the West. Anna Akhmatova received Berlin as 'a guest from the future': she even invited him to her tiny apartment in the 'Fontannyi House'. He also met Lev Gumilev, son of Akhmatova and the poet executed in 1921 after 'the Tagantsev Affair'. Only three years younger than Berlin, Gumilev had already experienced the gulag, fought in the war as a volunteer, and yet was 'at least as civilized, well-read, independent and indeed fastidious ... as the most admired undergraduate intellectuals in Oxford or Cambridge'.[1]

Joseph Stalin must have been an attentive reader of Berlin's report to the British Foreign Service – courtesy of Soviet spies in London. In December 1945, as soon as the Soviet dictator returned to Moscow from his long vacations on the Black Sea, he began to prepare a crackdown on the 'laxness' that had spread among Soviet educated elites during the war. The primary focus of the Stalinist attack was Leningrad. In August 1946 Stalin's lieutenant Andrei Zhdanov came to the city to deliver a blistering attack against the literary journals *Leningrad* and *Zvezda*. Following Stalin's instructions, Zhdanov railed in particular against the 'decadent, non-Soviet writings' of Akhmatova and Zoshchenko.[2] Akhmatova's son Lev Gumilev was promptly expelled from the Institute of Oriental Studies, where he had just begun to work. Two years later he would be arrested and sent again to the gulag. The so-called *Zhdanovschina* killed the hopes of post-war liberalization and Leningrad as a gateway to the West. Instead, Stalin began to promote extreme xenophobia and cultural isolation of the Soviet Union from the world. This turn killed the dreams of a 'great retreat' back to Russian national traditions. Rather, it was new trappings for Stalin's personal dictatorship and the rule of the communist party state in the conditions of approaching confrontation with the democratic Western countries. Russian émigrés who hastened to return with their families to the Soviet Union after 1945, in a new wave of repatriation, were caught in a trap: many were sent to concentration camps, some were shot in Stalin's prisons.

## The Unexpected Career

In 1946 Dmitry Likhachev was appointed a visiting professor at Leningrad University, to teach Russian history, chronicles, palaeography and culture. The head of the Department of History, Vladimir Mavrodin, had connections with influential people, including the University Rector Aleksandr Voznesensky. The educational politics after 1945 also favoured Likhachev's appointment: Kievan Rus served now as a historical justification for the new borders of the Soviet Union; Soviet propaganda praised 'the progressive Tsars' and extolled 'the true Russian virtues'. The university desperately needed qualified professors. Among Dmitry's colleagues was historian Boris Romanov (1889–1957), another prisoner of the gulag liberated in the early 1930s as a 'shock-worker' of the Bel-Balt canal.[3]

Romanov and Dmitry shared the conviction that Russian ancient history was much more than an academic field. In 1947 Romanov published a book 'People and customs of Old Russia' which would have a great influence on Likhachev. It was a response to the crude Marxist-Stalinist sociology of history; Romanov was influenced by the Bergsonian philosophy and looked for traces of it, 'the murmurs of life', in the ancient chronicles. He also explored the patterns of Russian collective behaviour, interpreting them through the category of 'national character'. Romanov discovered, at the same time as the French *Les Annales*, the value of everyday social history and used this to construct 'historical-cultural types' of the medieval Russians that, he believed, continued to define contemporary Russians.[4] This approach appealed to Dmitry. His philosophy of love-pity for Old Russia made him look at the idea of continuity as a way of preserving the images and memories of the 'dying mother', and thereby saving them as a cultural factor that would influence his compatriots and their cultural realm.[5]

Romanov was a dedicated teacher and, despite his fear of another arrest, continued the 1920s traditions of inviting students to his apartment for intellectual conversations. In the end, Romanov brought up in his 'home seminar' an outstanding group of historians of Russia.[6] Likhachev was more reserved and did not require teaching as his vocation. Still, he became very popular, especially among female students. Two young women, Rufina Dmitrieva and Marina Salmina, fell so much under Likhachev's influence and charm, that they devoted their lives to the study of Old Russia and later joined the Department of Ancient Russian Literature.[7]

Likhachev's main career, however, proceeded in the Academy of Sciences. There, in just one decade, he became a recognized authority on Old Russia and joined a very small group of leading experts in that field. With all his talents and hard work, this would have been an impossible feat without influential sponsors. One of them was Varvara Adrianova-Peretz: her husband, the founder of the famous 'seminar' on Russian medieval literature in Kiev, then in Petrograd, was arrested in 1934 and died in exile. At the peak of the Great Terror, Varvara's brother was also arrested and executed. Adrianova became very close to Likhachev during the wartime evacuation to Kazan, when she took over from Orlov the Department's management and edited the multi-volume 'History of Russian Literature'. Likhachev became one of her key authors and assistants, and this work put him in contact with a network of leading experts on Old Russia in Leningrad and Moscow.[8] Many of them were former students of the 'Peretz seminar' and supported Varvara. Vladimir Vinogradov became the head of the Academy's philological division, and Sergei Obnorsky was a member of this division; Boris Grekov directed the Institute of History and the Academy's section of history. Historian Sigurd Shmidt recalled: 'She kept telling her friends in the Moscow academic establishment: "I need Likhachev, he is essential for the Sector ... He is a man of old Petersburg manners." Likhachev visited those people in Moscow during the war, travelling from Kazan, and left a very favourable impression, charming them.'[9]

Adrianova-Peretz protected the scholastic and moral traditions of the 'Peretz seminar' from the hostile 'Soviet world'. When Orlov died in March 1947, she assumed the role of the Department's prioress (*igumenia*).

'Mother Varvara' was childless, therefore all her energy focused on her colleagues. She felt responsible for every detail, read every manuscript, checked proofs, and religiously attended every staff meeting. She also organized field trips to ancient cities in the tradition of *rodinovedenie*, advised her younger associates on how to protect themselves from flu epidemics, and loaned her own money to them. From the late 1940s, after she had developed Alzheimer's, her apartment became the Sector's second headquarters.

At the end of the war Grekov offered Dmitry a permanent position at his Institute of History in Moscow. Moving to the privileged capital from war-ravaged Leningrad would have lured many people, yet Likhachev declined the offer. Leningrad-Petersburg was his 'small homeland', and a place of martyrdom, with the marked and unmarked graves of his father, relatives and dear friends.[10] Dmitry also felt absolute loyalty and gratitude to Adrianova; and responsible for the Department's future.

In 1947 Likhachev defended his second, doctoral dissertation on the Russian medieval chronicles, and Varvara decided to groom him as her heir apparent. This choice was not obvious: Dmitry did not belong to the 'Peretz school'; when he was a student in the 1920s, he did not find the location of the 'Peretz seminar' because it met in a private apartment. Yet his moral and intellectual baggage spoke for itself, and his Solovki imprisonment reminded 'Mother Varvara' of her husband's tragic fate. She appreciated Dmitry's loyalty, his dedication to the ethos of the Russian intelligentsia. Lastly, Dmitry was tall and handsome, with melancholic eyes and endemic health problems. Varvara's private notes reveal her mother-like care for 'Dmitry Sergeevich'.[11] She carefully edited his manuscripts, watching for any potential sources of trouble and restraining his temper in scholarly exchanges: 'Formal politeness is sometimes the sharpest weapon.' In 1943 Varvara was elected a corresponding member of the Academy of Sciences; she decided that Likhachev should also get the same position – with material benefits, but also a protected status. She wrote to Dmitry: 'The dogs attack the Academy members as well, but not as much as others.' By 'the dogs' she meant careerist and ideological hacks.[12]

It was a time when Stalin made the Academy of Sciences a vital part of the colossal scientific–military complex, capable of building the atomic bomb and competing with the United States.[13] After the pompous celebration of the 220th anniversary of the Academy in June 1945, the Kremlin dictator selected its new leader: physicist Sergei Vavilov (1891–1951). When the news of Hiroshima's atomic bombardment came in August, Stalin, Molotov and Beria received Vavilov in the Kremlin and granted him resources for many projects in fundamental science. Stalin 'recommended' creating 43 well-endowed new positions in the Academy, filled through a competitive process; he also decreed doubling the salaries of academic, professorial and senior scientific staff. As one historian concluded, 'Stalin ... created not only a privileged strata, but also a genuine elite in the post-war devastated country, where people lived in misery.'[14]

Sergei Vavilov was a remarkable person: one of the two sons of a Moscow factory-owner who worshipped Russian and European culture, and raised his children on the idea of working 'for the benefit of society and the Motherland'. Sergei defined his vocation 'somewhere between experimental physics, philosophy, and history'. The Vavilov brothers, Nikolai and Sergei, became part of the brilliant cohort of Russians who populated the Silver Age: one became a phenomenal biologist, another chose physics over his passion, literature. Sergei collected an immense library of world poetry in many languages, and studied classical music and art. His idea of science was rooted in gnostic philosophy: for him everything was part of the 'Supreme Plan'; culture and natural science were two vehicles for transforming mankind.[15]

'I could have written the most frightening "Faust" in the world,' wrote Vavilov in January 1947 about his compact with the Soviet regime. Vavilov's main moral torment was the tragic death of his beloved brother Nikolai, world-famous geneticist and Bolshevik idealist, arrested in 1940 and killed by starvation in prison. Sergei appealed repeatedly to the Politburo to release his brother; he did not know that Nikolai was already dead. Vavilov, like Vernadsky, Prishvin and other Russian intellectuals, searched for explanations of the monstrous terror and 'found' them in the Russian historical record of backwardness, despotism and violence. His generation, he reasoned, had to pay the price for the failure to raise Russian people from darkness to the light of education and culture. This conclusion made him a devoted and passionate supporter of massive cultural projects and the propagation of the humanities among the masses. At that time he was not alone in believing that the nuclear revolution gave Russian scientists and intellectuals a lever to influence the State, transform society and, ultimately, to create a modern, social democratic country. He hoped to use his high position for 'the glory of Russian culture' and turn the Academy into 'the scientific brain of Russia'.[16]

One of Vavilov's cultural projects was to establish 'The Knowledge Society', a state-sponsored national network of agencies for spreading scientific knowledge and high culture in the masses, with a multi-million budget. Vavilov brought into this project his friends and colleagues. He had special and close ties to Petrograd-Leningrad scientists and scholars: during the 1930s he directed the Institute for Physics of the Academy (FIAN) and wanted to return there after the war. He disliked Stalin's Moscow and considered Leningrad to be the 'soul of the Russian nation'. He also admired the Department of Ancient Russian Literature at IRLI. When Orlov, the academician who brought Likhachev to IRLI, died, Vavilov recorded in his diary: 'The old Moscow cynic was the last (of my friends) who understood the pungency, art, and depth of real Russian speech.'[17] Vavilov's patronage allowed Varvara Adrianova-Peretz to resume in 1947 the annual publications of 'Works of the Department of Ancient Russian Literature', which had been suspended for lack of money. This edition became the crucial nexus for historians, philologists, librarians and archivists – who created a narrative of the Russian common past. In 1947 he asked historian Boris Grekov, Varvara and her friends to annotate and publish the fifteenth-century travelogue of the Russian merchant Afanasy Nikitin, to India. The plan was to present this book to India's Prime Minister Jawaharlal Nehru, who was expected to visit the Soviet Union. Likhachev and others worked hard to publish the book. Nehru did not come, and then Vavilov had a brilliant idea: an expensive book gift became the first edition in a permanent academic series of cultural masterpieces, 'Monuments of Literature', one of the most prestigious projects of Russian cultural history in Soviet times.

Many years later Likhachev described eloquently the cultural mission that he and his colleagues shared with Vavilov: 'Nazism started the war, and nourished it with ideas of extreme chauvinism and nationalism. Nazism rejected the cultural treasures of other peoples and nations. "Monuments of Literature" opposed all kinds of ideas of national exclusivity. The series aimed at encompassing the literary treasures of the entire world, of all nations and epochs. The series aimed at reviving the idea of a peaceful cultural unity of the world, of the cultural development of mankind as an indivisible process.' In 1986, during a televised discussion in Moscow, Likhachev said: 'Introducing nations to each other through a kind of cultural summit was one way to resist nationalism.'[18]

'Monuments of Literature' and other projects allowed Likhachev and other Russian scholars to merge patriotism and cosmopolitanism. Next to the editions of the works of Julius Caesar, Cicero, Pliny and Cato, 'Monuments' published Russian medieval texts: in 1949 appeared *Military Tales in Ancient Russia*; in 1950 *The Primary Chronicles* of Kievan Rus and *The Lay of Igor's Campaign*. Dmitry was among the editors and commentators of these Russian texts. At Varvara's suggestion he, with Romanov, made the annotated compilation of *The Primary Chronicles*, using the most authoritative editions of ancient manuscripts, and translated this compilation into modern literary Russian. This publication was of paramount significance for Likhachev's professional and public career. *The Primary Chronicles* (*Povest Vremennykh Let*) was the only written record of the first five centuries of Russian history. It summed up the outcome of monumental research, conducted before the revolution under the leadership of academician Alexei Shakhmatov.

Shakhmatov believed that regional chronicles of the eleventh–twelfth centuries had served as a means of creating a common 'Great Russian realm' and a common identity from Kiev to Novgorod – a cultural-historic foundation for the later Russian state. During the 1920s the Bolshevik 'red professors' treated Shakhmatov's conclusions as 'reactionary'. With the turn to 'patriotism' in the 1930s, Shakhmatov's ideas were back; at the end of the 1940s Likhachev became their main interpreter.[19] Likhachev in his early works praised and emulated Shakhmatov's view of the ancient chronicles as 'a history of the Russian people'. He objected to historian Nikolai Rubinshtein, who believed that early Russian chronicles were just a mechanical collection of local 'stories' and anecdotes, later accumulated to justify Moscow's expansionism. Likhachev, instead, insisted that *the idea of Russian unity* preceded Moscow's conquests.[20]

Likhachev also became the most authoritative interpreter of *The Lay of Igor's Campaign*. This literary work extolled patriotism and the unity of all the lands of ancient Russia by telling the story of defeat of a local prince. Foolhardy Igor went with his force to the southern steppes in 1185 to fight the Kipchak nomads (Polovtsy), ignoring bad omens and good advice. In the end, Igor lost the battle and his army. Igor's recklessness exposed Russian frontiers to their enemies. This controversial literary monument served to Russian patriots as proof of a glorious cultural heritage, destroyed by the Mongol invasion and feuds. *The Lay*, along with *The Primary Chronicles*, inspired Russian artists, from Aleksandr Pushkin to composer Aleksandr Borodin. Many British, French and German scholars, including Karl Marx, who considered Russia backward and barbaric, acknowledged the originality of *The Lay*.

Yet the monument's authenticity remained contested from the moment of its discovery. Russian aristocrat Aleksandr Musin-Pushkin, president of the Academy of Art, as well as the procurator of the Synod, found the only surviving copy of *The Lay* in an abandoned monastery. He transliterated and edited *The Lay* for his friends, including historian Nikolai Karamzin, and presented one copy to Catherine the Great. Unfortunately, the original perished in the fire of Moscow in 1812, during Napoleon's invasion. Scholars were left with Musin's imperfect edition, riddled with ambiguities, linguistic contaminations, typos, and endless questions. Shakhmatov used this edition as the authentic, if garbled, source. Numerous sceptics believed, however, it was a fake.[21]

After 20 years of anti-Russian propaganda, the Soviet authorities included *The Lay* into the cultural pantheon. In 1938, they celebrated the anniversary of this literary monument, and several Russian authors, including poet Nikolai Zabolotsky, worked on literary adaptations. The question of authenticity, however, did not go away: in 1940, French Slavist André Mazon published a book claiming that *The Lay* was a pastiche written in the late eighteenth century. According to Mazon, the unknown author, probably educated in Kiev, was inspired by *Zadonshchina*, an old literary text about the victory of the Russians over the Tatars in 1380.

Adrianova and Likhachev devoted great efforts to the refutation of Mazon's allegations. In 1949, Dmitry wrote: 'In recent times the enemies of the Russian people (A. Mazon i.a.) have been trying to prove that "The Lay of Igor's Campaign" is a forgery and thereby to raise doubts about the creative forces of the Russian nation.'[22] Dmitry's introductory article to an academic edition of *The Lay* stated that the author 'was a Russian person (*russkim chelovekom*) who felt sore pity for the whole Russian land'. The last phrase was a strong affirmation of Dmitry's identity.[23] In February 1950 Likhachev decided to publish an adapted version of *The Lay* for elementary schools, and turned to Nikolai Zabolotsky, an avant-garde poet of the 1920s, who had recently returned from the gulag. They had an exchange about Russian medieval history.[24] Dmitry wrote: 'One should not confuse Kievan Rus with Muscovy. There was an extraordinary difference between the two.' Moscow-led Russia, he explained, lost the tradition of aristocratic autonomy and cultural closeness with Roman–Greek and European civilizations. Those features faded in the xenophobic and despotic Muscovy of the fifteenth–sixteenth centuries.[25]

Dmitry and Zabolotsky, like Vavilov, thought that it was vital to reconnect Russian culture with European civilization and its classical values. It was their reaction to the times when the Soviet Union slipped back to xenophobia, obscurantism and self-isolation. This view, however, could not be openly stated in Stalin's times: Moscow despotism was a justification for the contemporary Kremlin dictatorship. At the same time as Likhachev gained academic prominence for propagating the ancient version of Russian patriotic values, he faced a new trap: the Stalinist state used the theme of 'Russian patriotism' to undermine the values he stood for.

## The Patriotic Games

In the early morning of 26 March 1946, Soviet radio broadcast Likhachev's 'conversation about national consciousness'. Millions of workers, officials, drivers, schoolteachers and students around the Soviet Union heard Dmitry speak about Russian collective memories, the legends and songs of Russia's warriors, and 'the idea of military honour'. He said that the adoption of Christianity from the Byzantine Empire 'propelled Russians, a young nation, into the historical arena'. He commented on 'the remarkable patriotic spirit' of the anonymous authors of the chronicles. Already in the twelfth century, he argued, 'Russian literature, Russian historical thinking, Russian architecture, Russian pictorial art were dominated by one common task – affirming the equal status of the Russian people among other peoples of the world.'[26]

Vera Tolz, Likhachev's granddaughter and a scholar of Russian nationalism, believes that the mood of patriotic pride in Leningrad at that time resonated with the growing nationalism of the Russian intelligentsia in the 1870s–1880s. Stalin chose to adopt conservative nationalism from that time, preached by Mikhail Katkov, Nikolai Danilevsky, Konstantin Pobedonostsev, Feodor Dostoyevsky and Konstantin Leontiev. This was a message that was contrary to Likhachev's romantic and all-inclusive idea of Russia. Historian Victor Paneiakh, who was a student of Romanov at that time, believes that Stalin wanted to build a great empire with a direct lineage to tsarist Russia and its Black Hundred reactionary tradition.[27] Ukrainian historian Serhy Yekelchyk concludes that Stalinist policies did suppress all national narratives, such as Ukrainian, and just wanted to adapt them to his 'empire of memories'. He writes that for the intellectuals of Moscow and Leningrad this meant 'a crusade against liberalism and western influences in the arts'.[28] In his secret instruction to party officials in July 1947, Stalin lashed out against the alleged 'lack of faith in Russian people' as the abiding flaw of the Russian intelligentsia. The main task of the party, the document continued, was to re-educate the Russian intelligentsia, to eradicate its 'genuflection before the West'.[29]

Stalin's new policy was to promote ethnic Russians over the Jews, Ukrainians and others who had benefited from the Bolshevik 'affirmative actions' during the 1920s. Many career-minded Russians wanted to take advantage of it. The Leningrad scholar Aleksandr Boldyrev recorded a note in his diary in July 1945 about a session of the Pushkin Commission: 'Many of its members had "Jewish names". [Only] a few [ethnic] Russians sat in the audience.' He added with satisfaction that the situation began to change: 'At the university only Russian deans are welcome.'[30] Scholars with a Jewish background sensed growing discrimination. Lidia Ginzburg registered human resources for a pogrom in the Academy: war veterans, who came to the university with a peasant background, became the main stakeholders of the 'anti-Western' campaign.[31]

Stalin's course hit literary studies in Leningrad especially hard. The new campaign targeted the Department of Philology of Leningrad University and the Pushkin House. The instructions from the party headquarters in Moscow decreed all local party organizations to organize *prorabotki*, or sessions of 'criticism and self-criticism'. Senior, established scholars became vulnerable to denunciations for 'lack of patriotism'. During a *prorabotki* session every role was prescribed. Designated 'prosecutors' called the colleagues of an accused scholar, one after another, to the podium and invited them to denounce the victim. In the end, the targeted intellectuals confessed their sins and declared their readiness for 're-education'.

To Dmitry Likhachev these sessions were 'a system to destroy kindness' – the ethical foundation of intellectual life. This system, he argued, originated in the public trials and the sessions of 'unmasking the enemies' during the 1930s. The prosecutors wanted to force the victims to admit their guilt – which could lead to their arrest. 'The tortured intellectual was brought to a state of exhaustion; he just wanted to leave the scene and admit everything.' The victim lost his or her dignity, individual and professional credentials publicly tarnished. Fear drove the rest of the audience into collective complicity with the prosecutors. The organizers, Likhachev recalled, 'made all friends, disciples, and students of the accused person attend the trial. Their presence and collaboration affected the victims most painfully.' When friends and students one after another betrayed the accuser, 'the crowd gasped in a hushed whisper: "And this one [betrayed], too? Really?" And the halls were replete with stooges and snitches.'[32] Non-attendance of the sessions was considered a sign of disapproval, 'un-Soviet behaviour'.

The patriotic sessions in 1949 led to the destruction of a 'Formalist school' in Leningrad literary studies, which included brilliant scholars Vladimir Propp, Boris Eichenbaum and Victor Zhirmunsky. Anti-Semitism permeated the air: the audience knew that the majority of formalists were Russian intellectuals of Jewish origins.[33] As a result, all the accused scholars lost their jobs in the Academy and could no longer teach students at the university. In July 1949 Grigory Gukovsky was arrested and died in prison from cardiac failure, at the age of 47. His wife was sent to a concentration camp, and his daughter Natasha stayed in Leningrad only because a son of another professor, her friend, proposed to marry her. Gukovsky's graduate students Yuri Lotman and Ilya Serman left Leningrad for relative safety in the provinces.[34] Another casualty was the liberal concept of inclusive Russian culture, which appealed to assimilated Jews and implied cultural Europeanism. Now everything Russian, including blatant nationalism, became 'progressive', and much of a European legacy was branded as 'cosmopolitan', 'bourgeois', 'decadent', and 'reactionary'.[35]

Some victims of the *prorabotki* had been through tough times before. Yet this new trial appeared to have broken their moral and physical stamina. After one of the inquisition sessions, Boris Tomashevsky, a person of strong character, fainted. The same happened to Mark Azadovsky. Zhirmunsky and Eichenbaum suffered cardiac infarctions.[36] Lidia Ginzburg believed that it was the effect of 'mutual betrayals' that made this ordeal worse than the years of war. During the siege, famine drove some deranged people into cannibalism. Now fear and conformism forced many intellectuals to participate in some kind of moral and intellectual cannibalism – in broad daylight, in the marble halls of Leningrad University, the Institute of Literature and the city branch of the Writers' Union. Walking out or speaking up in the midst of this collective cabal was an act of supreme courage. Students who were forced to take an active part in collective humiliation of their teachers came out of this experience scarred for life.[37]

Vavilov and his academic network had no capacity to contain the ghastly flood of denunciations and *prorabotki* sessions. In January 1949 the Academy expelled all its foreign members, including some Nobel laureates and André Mazon, the main sceptic regarding *The Lay of Igor's Host*. During the same year, Stalin's policy took yet another turn. In his classic lethal balancing act, he combined elevation of the Russians with a pre-emptive strike against the danger of Russian nationalism. He got information that the leading party officials from Leningrad had been discussing the idea of creating a 'Russian communist party' within the CPSU and even speculated about having Leningrad as a capital of the 'Russian' republic within the USSR. From August to October of 1949, one by one the high-placed Leningrad officials got arrested, thrown into a special prison, and brutally tortured in search of an imaginary conspiracy. Among them was Aleksandr Voznesensky, head of Leningrad University, with his brother. They were executed in October 1950.[38] The dragnet of purges harrowed the University and other cultural and educational institutions of Leningrad: not only Jews, but also ethnic Russians, began to fear arrest. Even experienced careerists and party hacks no longer knew what the correct line to follow was; uncertainty increased their frenzied activism and denunciations in *prorabotki*.

Dmitry Likhachev was not Jewish or formalist. He extolled Russian virtues. Yet gradually he was pulled into the vortex that could end up with his persecution and arrest. In April 1948 the Leningrad party authorities staged an attack against Russian medieval historians; among them was Boris Romanov. Likhachev, who was 'invited' to lead the discussion, had a choice: to be an executioner or to become a victim. To everyone's surprise, Likhachev defended Romanov's book. He said that Romanov described 'life in ancient Russia quite differently from other authors, including my works – which was on my part a certain mistake'. Russia had not only 'a beautiful façade of frescoes and mosaics, that we are rightfully proud of,' continued Likhachev, but lived through a 'quite cruel epoch'. Then he enquired: 'Is it patriotic to emphasize the difficult aspects of life of ancient Russia? Or is it better to leave them in silence?' And he answered himself, almost in Stalin-like rhetorical style: 'Silence would have meant idealization of the past, and Soviet patriotism is incompatible with this.' In his defence of Romanov, Likhachev skilfully used the *tufta* practice he had learned in Solovki: the practice of disarming and deceiving the executioners by using their own language and bending their rules. The conclusion of his speech, however, was sincere: 'The book does have a patriotism of its own kind; a lyrical attitude towards ancient Russia ... similar to the expression of sad feeling about one's close relative in trouble. And in this sense [Romanov] is a patriot ...' This clearly was his own understanding of patriotism.[39]

The reaction of the party authorities was immediate and furious: a university propagandist leaflet accused Likhachev of 'failing to meet expectations' and derailing an 'important discussion'. There were opposite reactions: Romanov, grateful for support, privately criticized Likhachev's 'excessive emphasis on patriotic themes'. He also believed that it was wrong on Dmitry's part to criticize Rubinshtein, Romanov's friend, who was a victim of the *prorabotki* in Moscow.[40]

## On a Knife Edge

Likhachev indeed walked on a tightrope. Many of his colleagues believed, erroneously, that they should collaborate with the inquisition and admit minor 'sins' to avoid major problems. By doing this, however, they found themselves on the slippery slope towards reputational and professional downfall. Dmitry's camp experience and his 'philosophy' taught him to meet danger with a well-prepared and realistic scenario. He knew that the system of terror wanted an admission of guilt from an individual: self-indictment led to the loss of personal dignity and work, possibly of freedom and life. And he was determined never to plead guilty. At the same time he knew that any open resistance to the system was suicidal. A few scholars, who dared to defend their friends or teachers, lost their jobs and one of them, Gukovsky's student, died from cancer soon after the *prorabotki*.

He also had to define his position with regard to the growing anti-Semitism. Among Likhachev's friends were anti-Semites (Dmitry Kalistov) and some took part in the 'anti-formalist' purge (Vladislav Evgeniev-Maximov).[41] Dmitry never allowed the authorities to use his name, willingly or not, in the pogrom scenarios. He did not denounce and betray his colleagues of Jewish background: Sigizmund Valk and Solomon Lurie, Eichenbaum and Gukovsky. He continued to treat Victor Zhirmunsky, purged as a formalist in 1949, as his teacher. Once he, together with Boris Tomashevsky, read an issue of the 'wall newspaper' hanging in the entry-hall of the Pushkin House, the main propaganda leaflet of *prorabotki* at the Institute. Tomashevsky sighed and said: 'It used to be much simpler: "Beat the kikes! Save Russia!" This was an act of defiance, but also a sign of complete confidence that Likhachev shared this attitude.[42]

Tomashevsky and Dmitry teamed up to defend Pavel Berkov, philologist of 'Jewish origins' at a public meeting of 'self-criticism'. Dmitry noticed that the accusers of Berkov got Lenin's citation wrong and corrected them: this was another way to disrupt the inquisition. He and Tomashevsky hoped to give Berkov time to regain strength. To their great disappointment, the accused philologist broke down under pressure and pleaded guilty.[43] In 1950, Dmitry began to collaborate with Yakov Lurie, medievalist and son of the illustrious Jewish-Russian historian of antiquity Solomon Lurie, to work on a joint project. The Luries lost their jobs because of the anti-Semitic campaign. Yakov attended the seminar of Mikhail Priselkov on medieval Muscovy; at the invitation of Adrianova and Likhachev, he began to work on a book, *Messages of Ivan the Terrible*. This marked his return to academic science and possibly a vital protection from persecution. Stalin admired the tyrannical Russian tsar, and read everything that was published about him.[44]

Such actions were extremely risky and also required moral clarity. People with Jewish origins were not only victims, but also participants in Stalinist campaigns. At the Pushkin House and the university B.S. Meilakh and I.P. Lapitsky were the most notorious agents of *prorabotki*. Igor Lapitsky clearly suffered from psychological instability: he imagined himself an iron Bolshevik in the traditions of the 1920s and attacked his victims with almost orgiastic enthusiasm.[45] His favoured target became Likhachev: he literally became obsessed with destroying Dmitry and his co-author Lurie. He sent letters to Politburo leaders Malenkov and Beria, and tirelessly published articles containing deranged accusations of a political and ideological nature. In the climate of those years such an unstable man was a source of mortal danger.[46]

In a letter to prominent Moscow medievalist Mikhail Tikhomirov in January 1951, Likhachev wrote about the 'chilling [*strashnuiu*] atmosphere surrounding myself and Varvara Pavlovna'. This letter was probably a reaction to the news from Moscow: on 24 January 1951 Sergei Vavilov died suddenly from a heart attack. The Department lost its most powerful patron, and Lapitsky reacted immediately, sensing a vulnerable prey. At the peak of the stress, Likhachev had a renewed ulcer attack. He subdued his acute pain by repeated injections of novocaine, and finally ended up in hospital. Still, a few months later, when Lapitsky submitted his article to the celebrated 'Works' of the Department, Dmitry wrote: 'If Lapitsky manages, by hook or by crook, to get his piece published, then I categorically insist that my articles should be removed. I have no desire to be published under the same cover as him.' In November 1951 at a meeting of Leningrad writers Lapitsky used distorted citations of Likhachev's and Lurie's *Messages of Ivan the Terrible*, branding this book as 'anti-patriotic'. At that time one of the Department's colleagues, M. Skripil, a respectful scholar, succumbed to the pressure and began to collaborate with the party committee, to prepare an anti-Likhachev session in the Pushkin House.[47] Dmitry defended himself skilfully. He wrote a letter to the Institute's party organization and even to Yuri Zhdanov, Stalin's son-in-law, who was known as a sober-minded person who defended scientists.[48]

In the spring of 1952 the news came that *A History of Russian Literature*, edited by Adrianova and Likhachev, had received the Stalin prize. In the past, Stalin's name had shielded prize-winners from inquisition. Lapitsky, however, refused to halt. He even boasted that he would 'take away the Stalin prize from Mit'ka' – a pejorative version of Dmitry's first name.[49] The public meeting was scheduled for 17 May. When it started, Likhachev's teacher Evgeniev-Maximov stood up and congratulated Dmitry on the Stalin prize. This broke the ice of fear in the audience.[50] Still, the *prorabotki* meeting continued as planned. Skripil, the key speaker, said: 'It is no coincidence that Dmitry Sergeevich is sympathetic to Prince Kurbsky, traitor to the Motherland.' The correspondence between Tsar Ivan and Prince Kurbsky, who fled from Ivan's tyranny to Lithuania, was the subject in Likhachev's and Lurie's work. Likhachev, instead of exploding in emotional denial, went into a tedious line-by-line dissection of Skripil's accusations, proving them wrong. His semiotic self-defence was to deconstruct the accuser's text in its totality.[51] The session ended without a confession.

Dmitry was hospitalized again in September–October 1952, with an intestinal haemorrhage, and at that time Lapitsky brought up the same 'charges' against him and Lurie. Likhachev knew that his illness was not an excuse; he had to come to a new session and defend himself. Dmitry took the floor and repeated again a textological deconstruction of the charges. He also charged Lapitsky with misquoting Marx, Lenin and Stalin. The perplexed instructor from the party committee who chaired the session concluded: 'Could it be true that none of comrade Lapitsky's accusations are correct?' At this point Likhachev shouted: 'Yes, none!' The session again closed without a verdict.[52]

On 5 March 1953 Stalin died. For several days, all professors and students at Leningrad University had to express their great sorrow for the deceased Generalissimo Joseph Stalin. Young historian Raphail Ganelin, who attended the obligatory mourning meetings, was surprised to see Likhachev in a genuinely emotional state. 'He seemed to mourn too much.'[53] What Ganelin mistakenly took for expression of sorrow for Stalin, could have been caused by painful memories. And at first, Stalin's death seemed only to make things worse in Leningrad. Boris Grekov's sickness led to his death in

September 1953: it was another blow to the 'old boys' networks' in the studies of Old Russia. As a result of political intrigues, the Academy's Presidium issued a decree to disband the Leningrad Institute of History on 20 March 1953. Likhachev's friend Dmitry Kalistov became unemployed; some historians moved to Moscow in order to continue their professional careers. Boris Romanov wrote to Nikolai Rubinshtein: 'It would be good if our corpses provide the soil on which new grass can grow in Moscow. Yet one should believe in miracles to assume this, and I learned early in my life not to expect miracles.'[54]

On 23 October 1953, the Academy of Sciences elected Likhachev as corresponding member. He joined 'the club of immortals', and received tenure with status, prestige, and a boost to his salary. In the traditions of the Russian Academy, 'corresponding member' meant the same as 'full' academician — only the person lived outside the city where the Academy was located. After 1934, when the Academy moved from Leningrad to Moscow, 'corresponding member' began to mean something like a candidate member, similar to the Bolshevik Politburo. Still, with this title, Likhachev acquired considerable perks and privileges: a higher salary, easy access to all libraries, the ability to subscribe to foreign scholarly journals and purchase scholarly books at the Academy's expense. Likhachev later recalled that this happened 'easily, without much trouble'. He also felt guilty 'bypassing Eichenbaum, Tomashevsky and other better scholars than me'.[55] Dmitry, however, did not owe his rise to his collaboration with Soviet authorities; rather he owed it to the support of the old-vintage scholars who at that time formed an influential network in the field of Russian studies. Those people viewed Likhachev as 'one of theirs', as opposed to the new wave of careerists and hacks, 'the people of 1949'.[56]

Likhachev knew that his new status did not grant him safety and recognition by the Soviet authorities. At the end of 1953, when Likhachev came to the university to collect his professor's salary, he discovered, much to his surprise, that he was arbitrarily demoted to the rank of an adjunct. The order to do this must have come from the rector. Likhachev understood and stopped going to classes. He never taught at Leningrad University again.[57] As for Lapitsky, he continued to torment Likhachev into 1957, when his career finally ended. The psychotic enthusiast of *prorabotki* completely lost his mental balance; party authorities no longer protected him, and he was fired from his academic positions. For many years after, Likhachev celebrated the day when Lapitsky was fired — his harassments left a lasting trauma.

The echoes of *prorabotki* could be heard for many years, both in Soviet academic life and in Likhachev's personal career. Likhachev's works of the late 1940s to early 1950s would often invoke retrospective critical judgements.

Younger colleagues, who looked back at the *prorabotki*, could not understand how Likhachev could have succeeded in his career and written about Russian patriotism at the time, when the very word 'patriotism' was defiled, in a ghastly anti-Semitic purge. Likhachev's version of patriotism and his scholarly interpretations confronted the iconoclastic reactions from those younger scholars, who wanted to leave behind not only Stalinism, but also the romantic idea of Russia that Stalinism so heinously compromised.

Those older Russians who had identified themselves as victims of the 'occupying' Bolshevik regime, now saw their notions of patriotism and Russian pride defiled, misused and cruelly manipulated. At a time when Stalinist propaganda blared in high-pitched tones about 'profound love for the Motherland' and praised the Russian tsars as 'gatherers of the Russian lands', when many intellectuals were persecuted for 'un-patriotic' and 'un-Russian' deeds and thoughts, how could a person of integrity, with genuine love for Russian history and culture feel, think, and behave?

Stalin's post-war campaigns of excommunication from the state-formulated 'patriotic body' of the intellectuals with Jewish background made them hold in contempt the concept of patriotism as a whole, in whatever form and shape. This dealt another mortal blow to the idea of a Russian liberal, inclusive nationalism. For decades to come, Moscow and Leningrad intellectuals learned to react to the invocations of national identity with the saying of Samuel Johnson: 'Patriotism is the last refuge of a scoundrel.'

# CHAPTER 6

# ADVOCATE OF CULTURAL LEGACY, 1955–1965

> Remarkably, the people who still lived in ruins ... sacrificed their comfort for their future, for the sake of their Warsaw! We must think about the future, so that the cultural heritage of the Russian nation will not perish.
>
> D.S. Likhachev about the people of Warsaw who<br>voted to restore the historical core of their city

Poet Joseph Brodsky wrote in Leningrad: 'If you were born in an empire, it is better to live in a dull province by the sea.' Leningrad was certainly not a province; cultural life flourished in the city. The mood after the war was much more optimistic: survivors enjoyed normalization of life; younger people saw improvements in living standards, and eagerly responded to cultural news. In Leningrad of the 1950s lived and worked theatre directors Georgy Tovstonogov and Nikolai Akimov; poets Brodsky and Aleksandr Kushner. The Mariinsky Theatre and the Music Philharmony produced world-class ballet and music, with stars like conductors Evgeny Mravinsky and Yuri Temirkanov, and dancers Rudolf Nureyev and Mikhail Baryshnikov. Still, this life was a far cry from the 'World of Arts' and the boiling energy of the Russian avant-garde. Too many talented, creative voices died prematurely, disappeared during Stalin's terror. Literature, the leading source of Russian national identity, was muted by censorship. The brain drain also continued. Some leading institutions of science and culture never returned to Leningrad after the war; they settled in Moscow. The former capital no longer had foreign embassies and correspondents stationed there, every major international event took place in Moscow. Moscow-based *Novyi Mir* created a new Russian literature and public discussions.[1] In the aftermath of Khrushchev's historic denunciation of Stalin's crimes in 1956, the Moscow intelligentsia produced a new cultural elite with political patronage – so-called 'people of the sixties' (*Shestidesyatniki*).² Leningrad intellectuals cultivated mournful defiance and attachment to the past – in contrast to the future-oriented Moscow. In the early 1960s a young scholar was struck that his mentors, medieval scholars and classical linguists, had an 'almost exaggerated loyalty' to the legacy of old Russian scholarship. Those 'real priests of scholarship' appeared to be 'the last citizens from sunken Atlantis.'³ Likhachev belonged to this tribe.

## Almost Normal Life

At the end of 1958 Dmitry confessed to his colleague: 'My ulcer gives me severe pain. Week after week I feel this pain, pain, and pain.'⁴ For ten years after his Solovki disease returned, Dmitry spent almost a third of his life in hospitals. Otherwise, his life appeared almost normal and consistent. In his private notebook, Likhachev compared his day-to-day existence to a multi-floor structure of moral (*nravstvennyie*) commitments.⁵ One floor belonged to the family; another was taken by his close friends and colleagues; and the third belonged to the Department of the Institute of Russian Literature, which Likhachev headed after 1954.

The family consisted of his mother and two brothers, Mikhail and Yuri, his wife Zina, two daughters, Vera and Mila, and nanny Tamara (who moved to live in her own apartment in the 1950s, when the twins grew up). Zina became a housewife, devoted herself completely to the twins and her sick husband. Older brother Mikhail, who became a highly-paid expert on military electronics, became a Soviet patriot and joined the Communist Party. He lived in a good apartment in downtown Moscow, and his wife, a well-placed cosmetologist, considered Dmitry and Zina poor and below their status. Only after Dmitry got a prestigious academic title, Mikhail changed his mind. Yuri was also a party member, but preferred joys of life to political matters.⁶ Both brothers highly respected Dmitry, grateful for his efforts to save their mother during the Siege and take care of her in Kazan during the wartime evacuation.⁷ After the war every summer the entire clan holidayed in the seaside resorts of Soviet-annexed Latvia. Likhachev described the Latvian resorts in his letter to a friend as 'inexpensive, pleasant, quiet, and plenty of sightseeing'. They rented a place for mother Vera, and went to see her there, and also toured historic sites in Riga.

Later in the 1950s, Dmitry returned to his favourite place, the dacha-land along the Finnish gulf. Much changed there after the war: Finnish Kuokkala became Soviet 'Repino'; Teriyoki became Zelenogorsk. The Likhachevs spent many summers in Komarovo, former Finnish Kellomäki, and in 1968 bought a dacha there. This was a place where several members of the Academy of Sciences established a dacha community. Summer cabins had neither heating nor a kitchen; the designers assumed that communism would triumph soon, and special communal services would deliver meals to academics and their families. Communism never arrived, of course, and Zina had to cook everything in a tiny corner of the corridor.[8] The nature, however, was splendid: a canopy of pine-trees, pierced by the northern sun, dotted the green carpet of blueberries, ready to pick from June until September.[9]

Mila and Vera, twin daughters, remained the centre of Dmitry's life. He called them 'Runchiki', and spent all the free time he had with them. 'Mutual love cemented my family, created its happiness,' Likhachev recalled. 'When Zina, and then Vera and Mila showed care and love for me, I felt that I was needed, that my life was not in vain.'[10] Likhachev's dream was to repeat what his parents had done for him: give them an excellent education. There was no doubt that Runchiki should be in the humanities and arts, and learn major European and classical languages. Vera's teacher of ancient Greek was Aristid Dovatur, whom Likhachev considered to be 'the last truth-seeker from Leskov's novels, a wonderful expert on classical antiquity'. From an old noble family of French immigrants, a close friend of Kalistov, Dovatur spent ten years in the gulag – crucial credentials in Likhachev's eyes.[11] Upon graduation from the Institute for Art, Sculpture and Architecture, Vera decided to become a historian of Byzantine art and got a job at the Hermitage Museum. Mila graduated from Leningrad State University, and began to work at the Russian Museum as an expert in ancient Russian folk art.

Mila married first in 1958, to Sergei Zilitinkevich, a student of physics at Leningrad University. In the next year 'little Vera' was born, the third Vera in the family. Soon the 'second' Vera married a young architect Yuri Kurbatov, her classmate. The two young families continued to live together with Zina and Dmitry in the same modest apartment. For years Dmitry and Zina had to sleep on a pullout sofa for lack of space. At home, Dmitry had to work in a tiny room of eight square metres, where books piled up to the ceiling.[12] Yet Likhachev refused to beg the Soviet authorities to improve his living conditions. The family had to wait until 1964, when the Academy put them on a shortlist for a new apartment. In her letter to a friend, Zina was jubilant: 'We will have our own bedroom and will finally sleep on our own beds.' Two big rooms went to the young couples, yet Likhachev finally acquired a spacious home office.[13]

Close friends were the second vital commitment: in the Soviet Union they were the only real keepers of trust and memories.[14] The oldest among them were 'academicians' from KAN and The Brotherhood of St Seraphim, later comrades-in-need in Solovki: Eduard (Feodor) Rozenberg and Arkady Selivanov and Igor Anichkov. In their company Likhachev unbuttoned himself, spoke with the utmost candour about anything. There were also Mikhail Steblin-Kamensky, a university classmate and companion of the Novgorod vacations, and Dmitry Maximov, an expert on Lermontov and Blok, whose dinners resembled Petersburg *soirees*, where people of 'old manners' met writers and poets.[15] Likhachev also cultivated friendship with senior professors, among them historian Romanov, and linguists Zhirmunsky and Tomashevsky. Likhachev always remembered that Zhirmunsky in 1928 wrote to the OGPU in a futile attempt to release him from prison. He introduced Dmitry to Anna Akhmatova, the greatest living Russian poet, who dwelled in a dacha nearby in Komarovo.[16] Dmitry became close with Tomashevsky during the *prorabotki*; after his death in 1957 Likhachev and Zina stayed close to his widow, Irina Medvedeva. She was the last person to try to save Komarovich during the Siege, when he was dying from famine, abandoned by his family.[17]

The Department of Ancient Russian Literature ('the Sector') was the third major commitment in Likhachev's life. In 1954 he was elected its head; he regarded the Department as more than a group of professionals; it was a band of trusted companions that should be free from intriguers, careerists and informers. Some people, who did not want to share his principles, had to leave. Sometimes it took years.[18] Like any group of scholars, the Department had its dissenters. Yakov Lurie, whom Likhachev saved from anti-Semitic persecution in the late 1940s, was one of them.[19] In 1956, Likhachev, after laborious efforts, brought Lurie to 'the Sector' as a full-time employee. Yet Lurie was too different: he was a Jew and 'scientific atheist' who grew up dreaming about world revolution.[20] He did not share Likhachev's empathy for Old Russia. He admitted in private correspondence: 'I wasted half of my life on the study of two scoundrels – Ivan the Terrible and Joseph of Volotsk.'[21] For Lurie, Likhachev was a Russian nationalist, albeit not anti-Semitic.[22] Lurie became a close friend of Moscow-based historian Aleksandr Zimin: both were sceptical of the 'scientific' nature of Likhachev's scholarship. In early 1957, Lurie wrote to Zimin: 'I do not conceal my complete rejection of all his recent literary works, and even mocked his concepts at a Sector meeting. To his credit, this did not affect his [favourable] personal attitude to me.' In another letter Lurie referred to Likhachev with a tinge of irony as the ancient tyrant in a Greek polis.[23]

Another independent spirit in 'the Sector' was Vladimir Malyshev, a hunter for Old Belief manuscripts – they formed the nucleus of the IRLI special collection (*Drevlekhranilishche*). Malyshev's hero was Archpriest Avvakum, the fiery martyr for the Old Belief. He volunteered in the war and returned with several wounds. Unable to learn foreign languages, anarchic and disorganized, Malyshev chronically could not write his doctoral dissertation and periodically attempted to leave the Sector. Likhachev viewed him as a 'true Russian character', and tried to make him more disciplined.[24] When Malyshev successfully defended his dissertation, Dmitry sent him a note: 'Everybody likes and appreciates you. And I was always fond of you.'[25]

Likhachev remained the unchallenged head of the Department for 45 years, until his death. His colleagues called him respectfully 'D.S.' after the initials of his name. He became a true successor of Peretz and 'mother Varvara'. Even those who had reservations about his strong stewardship style knew that in case of need, he would do anything to assist and protect them. One scholar recalled: 'In the Sector I was in a safe haven.'[26] The internal archives of the Department remain closed. When they open up, it will be possible to find out how much it cost Likhachev to keep this 'haven' so safe.

### 'Future Generations Will Ask ...'

It all began with a heart-to-heart conversation with Nikolai Voronin, archaeologist and a lover of Russian antiquities. Voronin was born in 1904 in Vladimir, a city adorned by beautiful golden-domed churches from pre-Mongolian times. He welcomed the revolution yet was shocked when the Bolsheviks sacked his beloved churches. He became an archaeologist and spent years digging ancient ruins in Vladimir, Grodno, Smolensk and Moscow. When the Germans attacked in 1941, Voronin volunteered for the army and was severely injured in combat. What pained him more, however, was the merciless destruction of ancient Russian heritage.[27] He published an article that proclaimed 'the defence of Russian cultural monuments' as a task of national priority. Not only did the 'German occupiers' destroy the Russian heritage, he wrote; Soviet authorities did so as well. It was a very bold thing to write. Yet the council had no power against the vandalism of local authorities. Voronin continued to petition top Soviet leaders, including Stalin, with proposals on how to stop vandalism. He did not give up even during the most dangerous years of *prorabotki*.[28] In 1944 Likhachev came to see Voronin in his tiny Moscow flat in the historic district of Arbat, and both mourned the destruction of ancient Novgorod.[29]

Likhachev admired Voronin's courage, but it took Stalin's death for him to join his campaign to preserve the cultural legacy. On 15 January 1955, he signed Voronin's fervent appeal to save and protect the old churches of the Russian North.[30] In February 1956, the journal *Zvezda* published his proposal to create a museum of national Russian art.[31] They were greatly encouraged by the change of political and moral climate in the country, produced by

Nikita Khrushchev's 'secret speech' in February 1956 on Stalin's crimes. This was a rare moment of happiness for, as it was for millions of victims of terror. In the new climate, people began to speak out their mind; publishers could publish banned Russian classics, including F. Dostoyevsky and N. Leskov; even Soviet journals and newspapers introduced glasnost. When Likhachev, like millions of Soviet citizens, learned the content of Khrushchev's speech, he became confirmed in his belief: the Soviet tyranny was not determined by 'laws' of social development; some people established it, and now others began to dismantle it.

In the spring of 1957, Likhachev and Voronin joined forces to deal with a cultural crisis in Pskov: museum curator Leonid Tvorogov wrote to them that the Pskov authorities planned to 'develop' the historic downtown and demolish its historic grounds. Despite their efforts to stop this vandalism, the authorities proceeded with their plans; the same occurred in ancient Novgorod. Some museum activists, who protested, lost their jobs. Likhachev wrote to his crestfallen colleague: 'There is no point in living without fighting, without defending what is dear to your heart.'[32] In another letter he wrote: 'Future generations will ask about what we did or did not do – not those who are indifferent to Russian culture ... We should always keep in mind that we are Russians, and everything Russian is dear and sacred [to us].'[33] When Nikolai Voronin, after much stress, fell seriously ill Likhachev addressed him with words of friendship: 'Our goal should be: to live as long a life as possible ... It is necessary to preserve the intelligentsia. Without the intelligentsia everything will perish.'[34]

Dealing with Soviet authorities required sagacity, acumen and tactical compromises. In 1925 Vladimir Vernadsky formulated this approach in a letter to an old friend: 'The task of the intelligentsia is to save Russian culture.' He recalled a fictional story about a Chinese official who volunteered to become an advisor to Genghis Khan. The official's colleagues reviled him for that. Vernadsky concluded, however, that the compromising official, not his moral opponents, saved China from the fate of Central Asia; he ensured that the Mongols did not destroy Chinese civilization. Likhachev must have been familiar with this story. Elena Vaneieva, Likhachev's secretary in the 1970s, recalled: 'He knew how to deal with the bosses to achieve what he wanted, without compromising the norms of integrity and honour.'[35] The China analogy surfaced in Likhachev's conversations in the early 1960s with Nikolai Konrad, specialist in Japanese and Chinese cultures, who attributed the repeated resurrection of China to the preservation of its literary tradition. Old books did not allow China to perish, to splinter into different kingdoms during times of trouble before and after the Ming period.[36]

Stalin's Iron Curtain began to lift after his death. In 1956 D.S. travelled to Poland; he admired the people of Warsaw, who voted to restore the historic centre of Warsaw that had been razed to the ground by the Germans. 'The projects of restoration of historical places and monuments have been approved by popular vote, in factories and offices, at schools and universities.' Polish architects offered more 'efficient' and less expensive ways to rebuild the city, yet the people of Warsaw decided against it. Russians, Likhachev proposed, should follow this Polish example.[37] Another set of discoveries awaited him in Yugoslavia in 1964. 'I found so much of interest from my reading in the libraries of Belgrade, and even more from conversations.' He visited Korchula (Corfa), the birthplace of Marco Polo, the city from where Maxim the Greek and Sophia Paleologue went to medieval Russia to make a great impact on its identity. In Belgrade's libraries and archives, Dmitry perused the archives of the post-revolutionary Russian émigrés, including the papers of Evgeny and Anna Anichkov, parents of his eccentric friend Igor Anichkov. He pored over the books of Russian émigré thinkers: Feodor Stepun, Nikolai Lossky, Nikolai Berdiaev, and others. He also read with special attention the recently published memoirs of Aleksandr Benois, the founder of 'The World of Art', and the prose of Marina Tsvetaeva, still unknown in the Soviet Union. This was the missing link in the evolution of Russian culture and philosophy, resonating with his 'Russian conversations' in Solovki.[38]

By 1962 Likhachev had already acquired a great international reputation in the professional community. He was invited to take part in a discussion about Russian culture in the *Slavic Review*, the leading Western journal of Russian studies. Georgy Florovsky, theologian and professor of Eastern Church history at Harvard Divinity School, led the discussion by his essay.[39] Florovsky was categorically against the notion that the history and culture of Old Russia was barbaric, aggressive and primitive. He questioned the rash Westernization of Russian society. Still, the cultural patterns of the Russian mentality, Florovsky reasoned, might have contributed to the *'historic unsuccess'* of Muscovy and its successor, Petersburg-period Russia. He wrote: 'The most disquieting question in the history of Old Russian culture is this: What was the reason for what can be described as its intellectual silence? ... Surely nothing original and outstanding has been produced in the realm of ideas, theological or secular.' He continued that this was 'a tragedy of cultural aberration'. Russians, he ventured to suggest, suffered from a bizarre form of idealism, 'a search for ready solutions', from Peter the Great to the Bolshevik radicals. The philosopher concluded with praise for Old Russia's culture that inspired people from Pushkin to the artists of the Silver Age.[40]

A trenchant reply to Florovsky's essay came from young American historian James Billington. He presented his own paradigm of Russian culture. He sided with Polish, Ukrainian and some Russian historians who believed that Muscovy had little in common with Kievan Rus. For him the empire of St Petersburg was a successor to the despotic and non-European customs of Muscovy, despite all the 'Swedish–Prussian' bureaucracy and 'the patina of Polish and then French culture adopted by the ruling aristocracy'. Billington interpreted the issue of 'intellectual silence' as a consequence of Russia's geography and isolation. 'The harsh frontier conditions of Muscovy,' he wrote, privileged Russian tenacious qualities: *dolgoterpenie* (long-suffering) and *blagochestie* (ardent devotion). During the sixteenth and especially seventeenth centuries, Muscovy's political brutality, self-exclusion from the classic Greek–Roman heritage and the rest of Europe produced a culture of 'nervous religiosity and prophetic intensity', but these qualities also left a fateful legacy of 'irrational, anarchistic, and even masochistic impulses'. Billington reserved his harshest judgement for Old Russian culture. 'To the historian,' he concluded, it 'may appear only as a long since harvested and burnt-out field in which only a few splendid husks remain.'[41]

Billington's essay struck Likhachev as arrogant; it touched him to the quick. Dmitry's rejoinder appeared in the *Slavic Review* in March 1963; it revealed great synergy with Florovsky. Both men clearly shared one approach to Russian culture, a similar sense of national identity. Likhachev wrote: 'It is clear that Muscovite Rus did not simply follow Kievan traditions, but consciously cultivated them.' He also wrote about the 'external, not internal' rupture between Petersburg Russia and Old Russia, and argued that 'the flowing of Russian literature, music, and architecture in the later period has deep roots in the millennium-long development of Russian culture.'[42] Equally revealing were distinctions between Florovsky's and Likhachev's reactions to Billington's critique. Florovsky admitted that the 'lack of intellectual drive' of Old Russia was a real issue, a riddle to be solved. Likhachev rejected this thesis outright. In Old Russian culture, he argued, the philosophical and social thought 'for the most part was clothed in artistic form', represented by icons, churches and epic tales. 'It is time to cease to reproach Old Russian culture for its alleged "intellectual silence", only because its worldview was clothed in the form of art and not in the form of scientific treatises.'[43]

Likhachev believed that Russian medieval culture stopped short of 'Renaissance'. Humanists and artists in Italy found a way to liberate the individual by reconnecting Christian culture with the Greek–Roman legacy. The echoes of this synthesis reached Central and Southern Europe, and even touched medieval Russia, only to be extinguished in the sixteenth century. Under the influence of Konrad, D.S. began to think that the Italian Renaissance was epiphenomenal and could potentially be replicated in other cultural contexts – even independently from Italian cultural influences.[44] Then Old Russian culture could be considered as a vital foundation for a future synthesis; and this synthesis began during the Silver Age. Many years later, in a debate with the Italian scholar and professor at Yale, Riccardo Picchio, Likhachev referred to these ideas as 'the conception of Konrad–Likhachev'.[45]

These ideas were not convincing to Western scholars. And privately, Likhachev acknowledged the despotic state as the main reason for Russian 'intellectual silence' and 'frozen Renaissance'. He wrote to poet Nikolai Aseiev in June 1961: 'The strong state was good for defence, yet for the people and national culture it was a great evil.' Because of the Moscow despotism, he continued, Russian culture, literacy and folklore went into a drastic decline in the sixteenth century.[46] Still, Billington for him was dead wrong. His experience of Solovki and of the terrorized Leningrad, and the trauma of *prorabotki* made him aware how much of Russian spiritual wealth and cultural drama remained hidden behind the façade of 'intellectual silence' during Stalin's times. The same could be true behind the façade of Muscovite 'silence'.

## Preserving the Nevsky and Russian Speech

When Voronin and Likhachev began their battle for the cultural legacy, their enemies were overwhelmingly strong and friends were few. Nikita Khrushchev, the same man that gave hope to the victims of Stalin's tyranny and 'former people', launched a new anti-religious campaign, a part of his programme of 'construction of communism' in 20 years. Khrushchev referred to museums and the protection of antiquities as an outrageous waste of people's money. His anti-religious campaign put the surviving churches and icons in jeopardy.[47] Many people, including young scientists and engineers, looked with optimism into the future, applauded Soviet cosmonauts in space and remained indifferent to the destruction of medieval cathedrals and churches. Soviet-style industrialization and urbanization caused huge cultural losses: for instance the construction of colossal river dams and power stations across the Volga left many ancient towns, graveyards, churches and monasteries flooded and destroyed. The message of 'progress' was so powerful in the late 1950s to early 1960s, that even some grandchildren of 'former people' happily dispatched old family furniture and their grandparents' letters to municipal dumps.

Playing on these sentiments, influential Moscow architect Yakov Belopolsky urged 'internationalizing' Moscow: the Kremlin's surroundings were to be architecturally reinvented and rebuilt, reflecting modern architectural trends.[48] A big casualty of modernism was an old Moscow district, Arbat, an area with lovely old lanes, classicist mansions, cosy churches and miniature gardens. A huge avenue cut Arbat into halves, accentuated by the two ugly concrete walls of the Havana-style high-rises.[49] The modernist craze threatened Leningrad as well. Writer Daniil Granin recalls that a group of city architects, responding to modern winds from Moscow, convinced the city authorities that the Nevsky Prospect, the most famous street of the city, had to be modernized. 'It was a grandiose project aimed to glorify our architects and urban authorities who wanted to be immortalized.'[50]

By that time Likhachev had acquired first-hand experience about the ways the Soviet authorities operated. In 1961, at the height of Khrushchev's Thaw, the Pushkin House selected him as a non-party candidate to the Leningrad City Council. After he was 'elected' in the predictable Soviet fashion, he attended the meetings of the council for over a year. This brief stint in the halls of power added to his skills of how to play the Soviet system. He knew that Soviet officials not only paid lip service to public opinion, but could actually hear it, as long as it was done in a non-provocative manner. Likhachev responded to Belopolsky in *The Literary Gazette*, opposing the 'internationalist' futurism in architecture. The main task of architects, he wrote, was the 'urgent need to preserve the historical, national look of our cities'. He argued sharply against the construction of concrete ugly high-rises in Leningrad, as well as in Novgorod, Pskov and other Russian cities. This trend, he warned, 'would ... create a tasteless pastiche between the new and the old, and would make the Nevsky similar to hundreds and thousands of other streets in Europe and America'. Likhachev's article triggered an avalanche of protests against the modernization of the Nevsky from other Leningraders. At a crucial meeting of the Leningrad architectural planning commission, Likhachev used even stronger words. He said that the renovation of the Nevsky would mean a mortal blow to the culture of Leningrad, would inflict a terrible wound on the country. 'We backed Likhachev,' Granin concluded. 'The Nevsky Prospect was saved.'[51]

Likhachev not only acted to prevent architectural disasters; he also addressed the ideological foundations behind the Soviet modernist campaign. The scholar of Old Russia believed that modernism, like any phase in culture, concealed creative and destructive trends. Unlike most of Soviet modernists, Likhachev knew what modernism had been like in Russia before Stalin. On the walls of his apartment hung reproductions of Amadeo Modigliani and Kazimir Malevich, the founder of Suprematism. He was a friend of Malevich's widow Natalia and her sister Angelica Vorobyeva since 1935: they worked together as proofreaders, and vacationed together.[52] He considered Malevich,

Elena Guro, Mikhail Larionov and Natalia Goncharova, 'the first abstractionists in the world'. That remark had a patriotic ring: he regretted that those artists, admired in the West, had sunk into oblivion in the Soviet Union. And now young Russian artists looked for inspiration to American abstract art and considered any Western symbol of modernity with veneration.[53]

Gradually, the 'enlightenment' campaign by Likhachev, Voronin and other defenders of the cultural heritage gained ground. The public atmosphere began to change as well: some members of the educated elites born in Stalin's era began to combine their modernist urges with the search for historical 'roots'. In 1965, the Soviet leadership, after years of procrastination, allowed the defenders of the Russian cultural legacy to open the All-Union Society for the Protection of Monuments (VOOPIK). Likhachev and Voronin joined the board of this new organization. Unfortunately, VOOPIK proved to be impotent to stop cultural vandalism, but now Soviet party officials and economic managers could use VOOPIK as a lightning rod for the intelligentsia's discontent.

In January 1966 Dmitry received an invitation to speak on the television programme *Literary Tuesday* on the topic of 'Russian language, speech, and word'. This was a programme sponsored by the Leningrad Komsomol, and its producer Boris Firsov had studied television journalism with the BBC and was a promoter of glasnost. He hired a team of talented associates: literary editor Irina Muravieva was a direct descendant of one of the Decembrists. The anchor, Boris Vakhtin, worked as a scholar in China and gained widespread recognition through his insightful essays about the Cultural Revolution. Other participants of the programme, to which Likhachev was invited, included a group of Muscovites: Vladimir Soloukhin, literary critic Vladimir Bushin, and linguist 'Koma' Ivanov.[54] There was another man who greeted Likhachev: 'Dmitry Sergeevich!' It was Oleg Volkov, graduate of the Tenishev School in Petersburg, classmate of Vladimir Nabokov, who met Likhachev in Solovki in 1929. A witness recalled: 'Two relics of the perished culture who had survived by miracle stood next to me. Both of them had an aristocratic demeanour and a fine manner of speech and behaviour.'[55] It was a curious 'compliment' to Likhachev whose parents were merchants' children without a drop of blue blood!

Television was broadcast live across the Soviet Union. Almost at once, the audience became captivated by something very unusual: the completely un-Soviet language of the conversation and its free, improvised manner.[56] Vakhtin started: 'We rediscovered our Motherland. It began with the interest in icons, in Russian antiquity. We discovered for ourselves the magnificent art and architecture, the wonderful literary monuments.' Public protest against the destruction of churches and the vandalizing of monasteries, the burning of icons, and neglect of medieval manuscripts was a national awakening. Thousands of young people became enthusiasts of the new movement. Other speakers accused the Soviet authorities of the destruction of Russian churches and changing the historical names of Russian cities, streets, bridges, and rivers.

The conversation raised sensitive issues: the 'spoiling' of the Russian language and the destruction of old Russian culture in Soviet times. Likhachev took the lead. He said that the 'soul' of Russian speech was in the Orthodox traditions and peasant roots. At the same time, he distanced himself from narrow ethnic nationalism. Borrowing arguments from Veidle, Florovsky and other émigré intellectuals, he defined Russian culture as the process of reception and accumulation of linguistic and cultural influences. The old Russian language, he said, 'mingled with the old Bulgarian language, then it was influenced by Scandinavian and Finnish, and German, then Polish, and the French and English languages.' Russian imperial culture was 'a culture of many people', including Greeks, Finns, Bulgarians, Tatars and Western European people. 'And from the end of the nineteenth century,' Likhachev continued, 'Jewish writers and artists made a great contribution to Russian culture.'[57]

The conversation violated many Soviet taboos. The head of Soviet television watched the programme live and was furious. He called from Moscow and demanded that the broadcast be stopped for the all-Union audience and continued only in Leningrad. Firsov disobeyed, so the audience could hear the end of Likhachev's explanations. In the following weeks came reprisals. The organizers were charged with 'runaway Slavophilism' and a breach of the Soviet policy of 'the friendship of peoples'. Firsov and Muravieva lost their jobs. Even the state censor responsible for the broadcast was fired.[58] For the Leningrad party authorities and the KGB, Likhachev proved his un-Soviet colours again. Common people, however, began to recognize Likhachev in the streets. When he came to a local pharmacy for a hard-to-find medicine, a pharmacist praised him for defending the role of Jews in the creation of Russian culture, gave him the medicine and even refused to accept his money. His reputation as a scholar of Old Russia began to change into nationwide recognition.

## In the Beginning was *The Lay*

On 11 April 1963 Likhachev wrote to his American friend Roman Yakobson: 'I have just returned home after a difficult operation. They did gastrectomy, removed three-quarters of my stomach.' In the next line he turned to work:

the need to turn again to the research on *The Lay of Igor's Campaign* and *Zadonshchina*. 'It must be done, because historian A.A. Zimin made a rather frivolous presentation at our department of ancient literature ... He did not cite any new facts; instead he repeated Mazon's arguments in the crudest way.'[59] Yakobson, legendary scholar of linguistics, met Dmitry Likhachev in September 1958 at the congress of Slavic studies in Moscow. The son of a wealthy Jewish industrialist, Yakobson became a member of the Russian formalist linguistic school. After a brief romance with the Russian revolution, he emigrated and became a professor at Harvard University and MIT. Temperamental, hard on many other colleagues, Yakobson fell completely under Likhachev's charm. He liked everything about him: his phenomenal knowledge of Old Petersburg, conservative dacha life-style, and Zina's berry preserves. Above all, he marvelled how Dmitry could continue Shakhmatov's traditions and become part of his 'school' long after Shakhmatov's death.[60]

Another bond between the two was their common passion for ancient Russian literature and rejection of scepticism about its authenticity and qualities. During the 1950s André Mazon returned to the USSR to search for evidence for his new hypothesis: the 'real' author of *The Lay*, he suggested, was a Ruthenian Archimandrite Ivan (Ioil) Bykovsky, one of the literary correspondents of Count Musin-Pushkin, who discovered the manuscript. In Likhachev's Department, Vladimir Malyshev supported Mazon and helped him with research in various archives. Suddenly, a brilliant and mercurial historian of medieval Russia, Aleksandr Zimin, decided to deliver a crashing blow to the manuscript's authenticity.[61] In December 1962 Zimin buried himself in archives and libraries. His mission was ambitious: to employ every 'scientific' method available to prove that *The Lay* was an eighteenth-century pastiche. He described his state of mind as 'ecstatic' and 'frenetic' (*bezumnyi*). He shared the preliminary results of his research with no one, not even his closest friend Yakov Lurie.[62]

On 27 February 1963 Zimin appeared in the main hall of the Institute of Russian Literature; over 100 scholars, including several students from Oxford, on fellowships in Leningrad, waited for his talk. Likhachev and Adrianova-Peretz were absent, both sick. The speaker was unusually nervous, paced back and forth, and even turned his back on the audience during his speech. From outside came loud noises of construction; some foreigners could not understand what Zimin was saying. The talk lasted for almost three hours. The gist of it, however, was clear: the author of *The Lay* was Bykovsky, who composed this pastiche to praise Catherine the Great's conquests of New Russia (*Novorossiia*) and Crimea from the Ottoman Empire. The news about the groundbreaking presentation travelled fast via letters and phone calls to the international community.[63]

Zimin's biographer wrote: 'One impetus for his interest in *The Lay* was the publication in 1962 of a collection of articles, edited by Likhachev.' Zimin allegedly reacted: 'I am fed up with this mendacious blabber' (*Nadoiela brekhnia*).[64] Why such a reaction? Much younger than Likhachev, Zimin had no special philosophy to guide his scholarship. Born in Moscow in 1920 to a noble Russian family, he became a historian in the 1930s, and once admitted, semi-facetiously, that he fell in love with history from reading Aleksandr Dumas' novels and Sir Arthur Conan Doyle's detective stories. The Thaw was his first experience of cultural diversity; Zimin developed what one historian called an 'aversion to myths', and 'a quest for authenticity'.[65] In this spirit, Zimin wrote to Malyshev: 'We must resolve [the question about *The Lay*] decisively, kill it outright (*napoval*).'[66]

Zimin aimed at Likhachev's reputation; he thought the academician's recent publications were below the bar of good scholarship. Likhachev's defence of the cultural legacy did not win his admiration either.[67] Zimin had a powerful sponsor in Moscow: his classmate Ivan Udal'tsov became first the head of the Institute of Slavic Studies, and then deputy head of the powerful Ideological Committee of the CPSU. After his talk in Leningrad Zimin spread the news about his 'discovery' far and wide. In Great Britain, a new edition of the ancient text was pulled out of print. Some professors even began to remove *The Lay* from their courses on Russian literature.[68] Meanwhile, Zimin refused to show his 'work-in-progress' to anybody.

The defenders of *The Lay* felt ambushed and angry. Some scholars talked about Zimin's 'lies and falsifications', others called him and other sceptics 'traitors'. Roman Yakobson wrote to Likhachev: 'Zimin's prank is miserable. Russian philologists and literary scholars seem to have made a tactical mistake, treating too softly the imaginations of Mazon and his acolytes, evidently aimed at reducing the level of Russian culture.' Another émigré scholar wrote: 'Russian people often liked to topple authorities ... Unfortunately over here, abroad, all this has been blown out of proportion, and "Mazon's fans (*mazonisty*) [*mazoniata*] joined in jubilation.'[69] Likhachev agreed, yet controlled his emotions. Zimin's strength, he believed, was not in his arguments, but in his politics: 'many people like to be in opposition.'[70]

It would be wrong to regard Likhachev's defence of *The Lay* as an act of cultural nationalism only. His textological work on interpretations of ancient texts, and his cultural intuition made him absolutely certain that the text was authentic. In 1962 he published a monograph *Textology: on the Material of Russian Literature of the 10th to the 17th Centuries*. In this book, Dmitry argued that ancient texts must be explored and verified within their historical and cultural context, in the light of the personality and ethos of their authors. He wrote that literary monuments of disputed origins could be dated only within a broader view of literary genres and styles, ideological shifts, and the evolution of literary creativity. And his 'textology' told him that *The Lay* had the old origins.[71]

The best way to deal with Zimin's challenge, Likhachev believed, was to confront him in a public discussion and publish Zimin's work. The Soviet apparatchiks of the Academy, however, decided differently. In July 1963, academician Evgeny Zhukov called Likhachev to announce the decision of the Academy: there would be no public debates on Zimin's work; instead, there would be a closed discussion by a small group of specialists. Likhachev knew that it was a mistake. He wrote to Viktor Vinogradov and Peter Fedoseiev, vice-president of the Academy: 'The ban on publication would benefit only Zimin, making him a world-famous mysterious scholar whose "outstanding" discovery was kept under wraps.'[72] All these appeals were in vain.

The Academy bosses wanted to convene a closed session in Moscow to assess the revisionist manuscript. As Likhachev predicted, this made Zimin appear to be a persecuted dissident. Likhachev commented: 'In Leningrad, the friends of A.A. Zimin act with unprecedented energy. They turn for letters of support even to people who have no doctoral degree. It is a feverish agitation.' In the end, however, he decided to show up at the closed meeting in Moscow.[73]

On 4 May 1964 the main hall of the Institute of History in Moscow was full. Specialists, however, made up less than half of the audience. Unknown young men, possibly from the academic staff, controlled the entrance and turned back many well-known scholars and intellectuals who were not on the admission list. In another complication, Zimin did not show up, citing 'cardiac conditions'. Some wondered if it was moral to criticize the author in his absence. The defenders of *The Lay* decided to go ahead anyway. Nikolai Gudzii, a veteran graduate of the 'Peretz seminar', made an emotional introduction. 'Enormous numbers of materials' from old Russian literature did not survive because of invasions, fires and other misfortunes. 'We only possess materials that survived by chance.' It was by great luck that at least one manuscript of the *The Lay* surfaced.[74]

Then the floor went to Dmitry Likhachev as the key speaker in 'defence'. He began by calling Zimin's work 'his big scholarly failure'. This failure, he argued, occurred for two reasons. First, Zimin's thesis was 'backed by spurious arguments' instead of real evidence. Second, Zimin did not have enough training in linguistics and above all in textology. Likhachev pointed to the contradiction: on the one hand, Zimin praised *The Lay* as an extraordinary literary monument of the late eighteenth century, on the other, he could not explain how Bykovsky, an obscure author, could create this masterpiece. After an hour and a half of detailed refutations, Likhachev called for the publication of Zimin's work, to allow specialists to bring to light the 'woeful shortcomings' of his research and methods.[75] Likhachev was aware that all present and the broader scholarly public outside could compare the closed session to the infamous *prorabotki*. He never allowed any ad hominem remarks against the iconoclastic scholar. Zimin, however, refused to reciprocate, when he finally appeared at the session on 6 May. He deployed accusations of an ideological nature, straight from the late 1940s repertoire. 'The cardinal question [about the *The Lay*] can be resolved correctly only from the position of Marxism-Leninism – the only methodological foundation for all works by Soviet historians, linguists, and literary scholars.' His research, he continued, was of 'Marxist' nature and had nothing to do with André Mazon's 'bourgeois idealism'.[76] Later, Gudzii fulminated: 'How despicable he [Zimin] looked in his concluding words.' Likhachev kept his cool. His line continued as follows: We should avoid attacking Zimin personally. We should only be merciless in our evaluation of his book and its methods.[77]

For all Likhachev's carefulness, the 'Zimin affair' tarnished his reputation among many younger Soviet intellectuals in Leningrad and Moscow. A collective view treated Zimin as a victim of the regime: when he was not elected to the Academy, this opinion grew even stronger. The same public opinion believed it was shameful for Likhachev to continue to polemicize with Zimin while the latter was banned from responding. Critics of Likhachev did not know that he repeatedly tried to publish op-ed pieces in Soviet newspapers in favour of publishing Zimin's work; all of them were rejected. The personal relationship between the two opponents remained strained for years. When Zimin met with D.S., he refused to talk to him. 'There was something boyish about Zimin,' wrote Likhachev in his recollections. As time went by, Dmitry received a word of reconciliation from his bitter opponent. In 1977 Zimin wrote: 'Today I reached a stage in my life when I want to reassess so much ... There is much common in our characters and thinking – yet people can be different ... All bitterness in me abates when I think about the grandeur [*podvig*] of your life'.[78] Zimin died in 1980, and Likhachev sent a postcard to his widow with words of regret and a plea to forgive him for any wrongs he had done to her husband. He sent similar cards every year on the day of his opponent's death.[79]

The 'Zimin affair' divided scholars worldwide: many sympathized with the scholar of an iconoclastic book banned by the Soviet authorities. In the United States, younger scholars of Russia James Billington, Edward L. Keenan and Nicholas Ryazanovsky took a leaf out of Zimin's rebellious stand.[80] Dmitry, however, considered 'the Zimin affair' to be a decisive defeat of the sceptics. In a letter to Irina Medvedeva he informed her that André Mazon visited Moscow and was allowed to read Zimin's manuscript. He was clearly disappointed by its content, and as a result dropped his research on Ioil Bykovsky as a possible author of the *The Lay*. Likhachev quoted Kutuzov, the leader of the Russian army in the war against Napoleon: 'Lord be praised, we began to drive the French away from Moscow!' Likhachev, however, revealed his respect for Mazon as an honest opponent, who had the integrity to concede his defeat. 'What a brave man he is. It was not easy for him.'[81]

In 2006, long after Likhachev's death, his Department finally fulfilled its pledge and published the banned book. For the sceptics the book fell flat: Zimin indeed lacked expertise in linguistics, literature, folklore and textual analysis – the fields most relevant to his project. The leading American sceptic of the *The Lay*, Edward Keenan, summed up: 'Zimin is not convincing about everything. His book, moreover, seems to be something of a relic of late Soviet scholarship.'[82] About the same time, prominent linguist Andrei Zalizniak published the result of his analysis of *The Lay* with an authoritative conclusion: it could not possibly be a pastiche of the eighteenth century, as Mazon and Zimin claimed. In an interview, Zalizniak explained: 'Even errors in the text are precisely the same as scribes had done in the fifteenth to sixteenth centuries.'[83] In other words, the unknown scribes had copied an older text that was in their possession. This could be as close as possible to the conclusion that *The Lay* was indeed a literary work from pre-Mongol Russia. Likhachev proved to be justified in his conviction.

# CHAPTER 7

# THE MAKING OF A WISE MAN, 1966–1976

> I love Russia infinitely, at its best and even at its worst. This country gives me pain, sometimes I feel ashamed of it. Still, I want Russian culture and ideals to be appreciated.[1]
>
> D.S. Likhachev's private notes

During the 1960s, reformist winds in the Soviet bureaucracy began to wane and intellectuals in Moscow and Leningrad began to explore the past with the same fervour as their predecessors had explored the future. For many people, historical novels and discussions provided an alternative idealized territory – a new imagined community. It was not Holy Russia from the Tsarist times, but rather a space for nostalgia and a vague search for social meanings. For many who had lost faith in the radiant communist future, the past became ever more meaningful, attractive and inspiring.[2] Specialists in esoteric areas, from archaeology and folklore to the medieval chronicles, philosophers of the Renaissance, ethnographers and paleo-geographers became household names in the kitchens of Soviet intellectuals.

Historian Itzhak Brudny called this time 'Reinventing Russia', the expression of nationalism. He recognizes three types of Russian nationalists that evolved – liberal, conservative, and radical – mostly divided by their attitudes towards the West, anti-Semitism, and the Stalinist years. Dmitry Likhachev appeared in his scheme as a 'liberal-nationalist intellectual'.[3] Yet the rise of an idea of Russia in the late Soviet society reflected a more complex and dramatic process, not reducible to nationalism. And Likhachev at the time began to occupy a unique place between official propaganda and new voices of dissent. His works raised the questions: Who are Russians? What became of them during the trials of revolution, war, and terror? Could they look back at their past with dignity?

## The Solovki Ghosts

On 10 July 1966 a tall, lean and elegantly dressed man alighted from the steamboat *Tataria* onto the main Solovetski Island. Dmitry Likhachev returned to the place of his imprisonment. Dmitry was overwhelmed: 'The grandiose scale of this common grave dawned upon me – the grave of people, each of whom harboured a world of spirit, but also the grave of Russian culture, of the last men and women of the Russian Silver Age and the best people of the Russian church.'[4] A young woman was waiting for Likhachev at the station. It was Svetlana Veresh, who was a classmate of his daughter Vera, and volunteered to live and work in Solovki, to create there a historical-cultural centre. Svetlana set up a room for Likhachev inside one of the monastery's towers, which used to house the 4th labour company during the gulag times. Dmitry slept on snow-white, crisp linens, with a fresh bouquet of wild flowers on the bed-table.

Among other tourists on board the *Tataria* were A.A. Zimin and Malyshev, who demonstratively refrained from talking to Dmitry. He did not mind their indifference; he valued his loneliness. Ghosts from his past surrounded him. Veresh provided Dmitry with a car and a boat, and with her help he explored again, as in 1929–1931, the vast expanses of the archipelago.[5] He followed the topography of his memory, and was surprised how much of what he remembered had been destroyed and become dilapidated. At the peak of the Great Terror, after Likhachev had been liberated, the camp regime became even more murderous. Likhachev visited the place of a lethal prison for women on the Big Zaitsky Island; the barracks in Muksalma for the children of the 'people's enemies' – kids who did not have names, only numbers on the back of their robes, so that the guards could identify them. Many churches Dmitry saw and loved as a prisoner were now in ruins, among them the Golgotha of Anzer, and the Sekirka – the place of heinous executions. Dmitry also went to see the Krimkab building: its rooms remained in good order. A torrent of reminiscences rushed in: about Kolosov, Aleksandr Meyer, Georgy Osorgin, Yulia Danzas and others. Conversations with these people rang in his memory and the idea of many dimensions of time, the philosophical conviction of young Dima, seemed to have materialized in those abandoned rooms.[6]

The anamnesis brought up haunting questions: What should be done to memorialize Solovki? In Krimkab prisoners argued that the medieval monastery should be restored, along with its elaborate hydraulic complex, allowing the use of water from the Sacred Lake behind the kremlin. In July 1966 Likhachev suggested preserving the Solovki kremlin intact, as the only existing museum of Russian medieval technologies. Yet the 'restoration specialists' adhered to what they knew. Dmitry only managed to dissuade them from removing the beautiful moss from the medieval walls. Likhachev left Solovki with a desire to return the next summer or winter, along with his wife and daughters.[7]

In February 1967 Likhachev 'discovered' the United Kingdom, where Oxford University awarded him an honorary doctorate. The previous recipients of this honour from the Soviet Union were Dmitry Shostakovich and Anna Akhmatova, scholars of literature Mikhail Alekseev and Victor Zhirmunsky. The Oxford Russian studies faculty consisted of Sergei Konovalov, son of the minister of commerce and trade in Russia's Provisional Government in 1917, Dmitri Obolensky, John Fennell and librarian John Simmons. They greatly respected Likhachev's scholarship.[8] At Oxford University Dmitry, dressed in a red mantle, delivered the Ilchester lecture, where he spoke about the origins of *The Lay* and called again for the publication of Zimin's work.[9]

Likhachev developed a great affection for 'Britishness'; he learned about it from Igor Anichkov in the 1920s, and even in Solovki he kept with him an English dictionary. He perceived the British 'national character' as a stable source of cultural traditions, and resistant to rash innovations. This perception was important for him as a living contrast to Soviet society, where Old Russia had all but disappeared under the steamrollers of revolution, war and terror. In his travel notes he extolled British manners, dignity, simplicity and tact – no doubt reflecting bitterly on the lack of such qualities among his compatriots in the Soviet Union. Likhachev studied all manifestations of British patriotism very attentively. He also stressed in his notes that in Great Britain people of high rank or wealth never felt the need to demonstrate their superiority to others. He was particularly impressed by his visit to a castle belonging to Steven Runciman, an English author of *A History of the Crusades*, admirer of the Byzantine empire, and a man of erudition and aristocratic manners.[10]

Dmitry knew Konovalov, Obolensky and Fennell from previous conferences in Moscow and abroad. He also met other Russian émigrés, among them Sir Isaiah Berlin. Most emotional was his meeting with Sofia Osorgin, sister of Georgy, the aristocratic officer who behaved heroically during the massive executions of October 1929. Dmitry had a sad duty to tell Sofia about the last hours of her brother.[11] Most unexpectedly, in Edinburgh, Likhachev met his aunt Shura (Alexandra), his mother's sister. She came to him after his lecture and waited, with trepidation, to see if he would recognize her. It was a moving rendezvous after more than 40 years of separation. With her husband Valentin Andrealetti she had emigrated to Great Britain and now lived in Edinburgh. Likhachev spent three intense days with Shura and 'Valia' in Edinburgh, meeting their Scottish friends, but also the Puni family, who had vacationed with the Likhachevs in Kuokkala before the revolution. Happiness was mixed with sadness: from Dmitry, Alexandra learned about the death of relatives, including Sergei Likhachev. In her letter to Vera, she wrote: 'I looked at infinitely gentle Mitya and saw you, my love. Our extraordinary nephew ... conquered all Scottish and non-Scottish hearts.'[12] Back home, Likhachev kept this meeting in secrecy; in all Soviet forms he wrote that he 'has no relatives abroad'.

These encounters brought back again the ghosts of Old Russia and Solovki: Dmitry was haunted by the idea that, if something happened to him, these ghosts would sink into obscurity. In October 1966 he began to record on paper his reminiscences about 'the people of Solovki'; he continued to write after his return to the United Kingdom.[13] These recollections attracted the attention of Aleksandr Solzhenitsyn. A world celebrity after his publication about Stalin's gulag in *Novyi Mir*, Solzhenitsyn secretly collected evidence for his monumental study on the Soviet system of terror, concentration camps and slave labour. Hundreds of former prisoners shared their stories with Solzhenitsyn.[14] Likhachev admired both the content and the language of Solzhenitsyn's writings: they both mourned the disappearance of peasant culture, of traditional sources of Russian speech.[15]

Solzhenitsyn met Likhachev for the first time when he came to his dacha in Komarovo in 1963. He wanted to learn about Solovki, and Likhachev showed him the secret diary he wrote in the camp. In 1967, the writer came to Leningrad and saw the scholar again. 'In the midst of his work on the history of the camps [Solzhenitsyn] came to see me. We worked together for three days. I gave him my notes on the history of Solovki and told him about Degtyarev, the main executioner of the Solovki camp. Degtyarev did not trust anyone, and preferred to shoot camp inmates personally, drawing great satisfaction from these acts. In the camp he had the nickname "chief surgeon", and he liked to give himself the title of "The Commander-in-Chief of the Solovki Archipelago". Aleksandr Isaievich exclaimed: "This is what I need!" Thus, here in my home office, the title of his book was born: *The Gulag Archipelago*.'[16] Dmitry had Solzhenitsyn listen to the tapes with records of *vorovskie pesni* – the songs criminals sang in the camp. He told the writer that political and common criminals in the camps were not enemies, and often helped each other. Solzhenitsyn interrupted him: 'How is this possible? Criminals are not humans, they are beasts.' In his times in the gulag, the camp administration encouraged the dons of organized crime to run the daily business in the camps; the criminals humiliated the political criminals, gambled with their lives and routinely murdered them.[17]

Likhachev, like many others, noticed that Solzhenitsyn overlooked the world of culture that was indispensable to many prisoners' survival. He was a principled enemy of the intellectuals; he blamed them for being the main conduit for Western ideas that contaminated the 'true Russia' and opened the gates to modern ideological obsessions, of which Bolshevism was the most terrible. Likhachev, much as he tried, could not make Solzhenitsyn share his anguish at the tragic fate of the intelligentsia who perished in the gulag. The writer was only mildly interested in Krimkab intellectuals and their conversations. Still, Likhachev was conquered by Solzhenitsyn's immense energy and talent, and above all by his determination to reveal the Russian tragedy to the world. They began to correspond and meet every time the writer came to Leningrad. In March 1968 Likhachev wrote to Solovki, to Svetlana Veresh: 'Solzhenitsyn is planning to come to see you this summer.'[18]

Meanwhile, the political and cultural climate began to grow worse. In September 1965 the KGB arrested writers Yuli Daniel and Andrei Sinyavsky for publishing their books abroad under pseudonyms. At the request of Daniel's wife Larisa Bogoraz, Dmitry sent a letter to the court and the investigator. After the court sentenced Daniel and Sinyavsky to several years in the camps, Likhachev sent letters to the authorities, arguing in favour of their pardon.[19] The Sinyavsky–Daniel affair was a signal that the Kremlin leaders were against the liberalization of cultural life. Gradually, Solzhenitsyn's official status began to decline: from famous and acclaimed Soviet writer to a *persona non grata*, and finally 'the enemy of the state'.[20]

In April 1968 Likhachev expressed dark forebodings in his notebook. He recalled a story, when a scholar in Nazi Germany wrote a book denying that New Guineans practised cannibalism. They 'added maize flour to human flesh,' the scholar wrote, therefore they were not cannibals. 'At our own cannibal rituals of *prorabotki*,' Likhachev continued, 'a pogrom organizer started with praise for his victim. This was also a kind of maize flour.'[21] Under Brezhnev, the Soviet party-state put more 'maize' on the tables of Soviet citizens, yet the cannibal approach to human lives, freedom and dignity remained its essence. Likhachev's entry also may have referred to the dramatic events unfolding in Eastern Europe. In Poland the communist leaders launched an anti-Semitic campaign of purges among students, to quell their yearning for truth. In Czechoslovakia, the reform-minded Aleksandr Dubcek liberated the press from censorship, unleashing 'the Prague Spring', but the Kremlin masters threatened to strangle it with force. On 26 June, *The Literary Gazette* lashed out against Solzhenitsyn. A few days later *Pravda* denounced 'the anti-socialist call for counterrevolution' in Czechoslovakia.[22]

When the Soviet troops moved to occupy Czechoslovakia, Solzhenitsyn was in his dacha, south of Moscow, working feverishly on *The Gulag Archipelago*. 'I believed that *our authorities* were not completely insane; I thought they would not dare to occupy ... And then they *entered* and successfully crushed the protest.' Solzhenitsyn wanted to go to Moscow, to speak to foreign journalists, to take part in some kind of a demonstration. Yet in the end he decided that writing his monumental novel was more important than ending up in a KGB prison. From that moment on, he felt the stain of guilt and shame for his non-action.[23] During the first week of August 1968 Dmitry and Zina travelled to Prague, to attend the international conference for Slavic studies. Soviet troops staged menacing exercises, and Prague lived in tense anticipation of what the Kremlin would do next. Dmitry and Zina returned home from Czechoslovakia six days before the invasion. They learned the crushing news in Komarovo, from Western radio reports. Twenty-three years later, in a speech to students at Charles University in Prague, Likhachev said: 'The entrance of tanks was so terrible that fear disappeared. On the commuter trains and on the buses, in the customary lines in front of stores people expressed their indignation.' He continued: 'We all felt boundless shame. Although we had nothing to do with this tyranny, we were ourselves the victims of this tyranny. Still we felt ashamed that this tyranny had its nest in our land, in our capital.'[24]

This sharp division between the Russian intellectuals and the Soviet State might have raised sceptical eyebrows among the Czechs. Yet Likhachev always considered Russia as 'occupied' by the Bolshevik regime and, unlike Solzhenitsyn, never identified with communism. His sense of shock was great, but different. The Soviet tanks in Prague killed the century-long Russophile spirit among the Czechs. After 1918, Czechoslovakia was one of the most important centres of Russian cultural life abroad. After August 1968 this place of sympathies and cultural affinity was defiled and destroyed.[25] In September 1968 he wrote to Svetlana Veresh: neither he nor Solzhenitsyn would now be able to come on a visit to Solovki. He could not conceal his melancholy: 'It is very sad for us now to recall the 1960s.'[26]

## Sad Farewells, Dangerous Encounters

On 16 December 1970 his mother Vera Konyaeva died in her sleep at the age of 90. On her grave, Dmitry erected a cross of grey marble, on which he inscribed her name and the name of Sergei, his father – whose remains vanished in one of the giant mass graves during the Leningrad Siege. Older mentors of Likhachev, his teachers, friends and cherished colleagues died one after another: the leader of Russian linguistics Victor Vinogradov, Nikolai

Konrad, Victor Zhirmunsky and Varvara Adrianova-Peretz Dmitry arranged for 'Mother Varvara' to be buried in the same cemetery in Komarovo as his mother, in a nearby grave. He designed a special cross for her grave, modelled in the ancient tradition of Novgorod.

The Grim Reaper took the survivors of the Petrograd-Leningrad *kruzhki* of the 1920s, among them pianist Maria Yudina and Mikhail Bakhtin. Far away from Likhachev, in the United States, Ivan Andreievsky died in 1976 after a long period of mental illness, having destroyed all his personal papers and letters. A dear and beloved friend, Nikolai Voronin passed away in the same year. A generational shift was taking place: contemporaries felt a sense of irreplaceable cultural and intellectual loss.[27] Likhachev attended the funerals, consoled the relatives and wrote obituaries, where he summarized the people's life mission and human qualities. In one of these obituaries he summed up the ideals he applied to himself: 'He was not only a decent scholar, but also a decent person, who could act against his own interests, defend scholarship, justice, people.' He admitted with regret that 'it does not happen often today. Independent people are rare.' On another occasion he wrote: 'We are getting smaller. Who knows what will happen?'[28]

The remaining bright spot for him was Solzhenitsyn, who was making great advances in researching and writing *The Gulag Archipelago*. In September 1968 Likhachev wrote to his friend Irina Medvedeva: 'I have news that our common beloved friend feels very well. They even say that his health is excellent. I have just heard about it only today and am eager to share my joy with you.'[29] 'Our mutual friend has visited us,' wrote Dmitry again to Irina at the end of 1969. 'He is happy, vigorous, and awfully business-like. He lives according to a plan. This time we embraced and kissed each other.' Likhachev made extensive notes and corrections to the draft of *The Gulag Archipelago*, where Solzhenitsyn described the realities of Solovki. The writer also showed Likhachev the draft of his other book, *August 1914*, a saga about the war and revolution. Dmitry went through the manuscript line by line and sent the writer a long list of errors, historical and linguistic. He also referred Solzhenitsyn to Vladislav Glinka, a unique expert on imperial Russia's everyday life, etiquette and military regalia.[30] When in October 1970 Solzhenitsyn was awarded the Nobel Prize for literature, Likhachev was happy and proud.[31] For him, the prize was testimony that Russian culture could still surprise the world with literary creativity and moral grandeur.

In 1971 Dmitry became a full member of the Academy. He modestly remarked to his friend Voronin: 'I am just on an elevator that carries me up.' Voronin replied that this elevator 'has been put in motion by the force of your talent and heroic energy'.[32] This did not come to him easily. He was balloted during two elections, yet each time did not receive enough votes.

Mikhail Khrapchenko, a 'red professor' and party careerist, ran against Likhachev and won. By that time the Academy, especially in the humanities and social sciences, no longer had the 'old boys networks' with whom Likhachev could identify. As a full academician, he now had the capacity to help young talented scholars and better defend objects of the cultural legacy.[33] Yet this status could not make him immune in the climate of growing ideological and political reaction. In 1969, Likhachev's privilege to travel outside the Soviet Union was suddenly revoked. He was denied permission to travel to Edinburgh, to receive another doctoral degree from the university there.[34] And his daughter Vera, now a young scholar of Byzantine art, was also told she could not travel to Western countries. One Soviet official said to Vera that her father was the reason for this restriction. Likhachev wrote to the Academy's powerful vice-president Peter Fedoseiev. 'I do not understand,' he wrote, 'why it is necessary to make me into some kind of an opposition figure in the eyes of my colleagues and foreigners.' Perhaps it would be better if he ceased all contacts with foreigners and resigned from all his public academic positions. He concluded on a note of defiance: 'The only thing I cannot entirely resign from, as a Russian person, is my participation in the defence of Russian cultural monuments, including the monuments of Leningrad.'[35] We do not know what Fedoseiev's response was, but the ban on Dmitry's and Vera's travel to the West remained in force.

In the summer of 1973 the epic struggle of Solzhenitsyn against the Soviet regime began to ricochet against Likhachev and his circle of friends. In August 1973 the KGB in Leningrad searched the apartment of Solzhenitsyn's secretary and typist Elizaveta Voronianskaia. After several days of interrogation, Voronianskaia revealed to the KGB a hiding place for the manuscript of *The Gulag Archipelago*. Unable to cope with the shock and sense of moral guilt, Voronianskaia committed suicide. When Solzhenitsyn learned about this, he ordered the publication of a Russian version of *The Gulag Archipelago*. He also publicized a letter to 'The Leaders of the Soviet Union', proposing that they should get rid of communism and restore Russia as a historic national state.[36]

When Voronianskaia was arrested, she was returning from Crimea where she was a guest of Irina Medvedeva, Likhachev's friend. After Western radios broadcasted the arrest and death of Voronianskaia, Irina chased all her relatives and friends out of her house, and refused to communicate with them – presumably to keep them out of harm's way. In October 1973 she succumbed to stress and illness, and died in her house, completely alone and without medical assistance.[37] Dmitry and Zina learned about this tragedy later, but they had other reasons to feel in danger. The KGB investigators, as it turned out, already knew that 'D.S.' was a major source for the writer: they had in their possession the manuscript of *The Gulag Archipelago*, and saw on it Dmitry's handwritten comments and corrections. The Leningrad KGB shadowed 'D.S.', controlled his visits and visitors, and even tapped his home phone. And Solzhenitsyn unwittingly continued to provide the KGB with other clues on his connections with Likhachev. When the second volume of *The Gulag Archipelago* appeared in the West, it cited 'D.S.L-v' as 'an old campmate' who told Solzhenitsyn the story of his miraculous survival during the mass executions of 1929.[38]

In the summer of 1973 the writer offered Likhachev the possibility of writing under a pseudonym a contribution for his collection *From Under the Rubble*, with a series of scathing attacks against the Soviet intelligentsia as 'the dabblers' who collaborated with the Soviet regime in search of privilege and comfort. Dmitry refused, and Solzhenitsyn did not forgive him that. In February 1974 Solzhenitsyn was deported from the Soviet Union to the West and published the book. There he wrote: 'In our collection we planned the participation of one extraordinary man, who has meanwhile obtained all kinds of titles and ranks. In private conversations his heart is aching – about the irremediable demise of the Russian people. He knows our history and culture from its deepest roots. And he refused. "Why all this? This would lead to nothing . . . ." The usual talk of the dabblers.'[39] With his moral absolutism, Solzhenitsyn had no qualms about passing such an unfair judgement on the old political prisoner and survivor of the Leningrad Siege. His implication was that the academician at some point decided to accept the privileged and comfortable life that the Soviet authorities created for the Academy members. In any case, all well-informed readers, including the KGB investigators, had no doubt who the 'extraordinary man' from Solzhenitsyn's essay was. And the regional KGB acted in a much more heavy-handed way than in Moscow.[40]

Likhachev decided to act pre-emptively. He asked for a personal appointment with the top party boss of Leningrad, Grigory Romanov. The meeting took place in Romanov's cavernous office at the Smolny Institute, the same place where in 1942 the famished Likhachev came to receive his writing assignment. We do not know what arguments Likhachev presented to Romanov. In response, the head of the Leningrad communists made a sinister remark: 'Your friends are our enemies.' He meant not only Solzhenitsyn, but also his Western friends, such as Roman Yakobson, and friends who helped the human rights movement. Still, after this meeting Vera Likhachev was allowed to travel to international conferences abroad.[41]

In October 1975 the academician Mikhail Khrapchenko called Dmitry. He informed him that he and other members of the Academy's Presidium were preparing a collective letter against Andrei Sakharov's 'activities'. The physicist and human rights defender had just received the Nobel Peace Prize.

Khrapchenko said: 'If you sign this letter, all problems in your life will go away.' Dmitry flatly refused, and the academic boss responded: '*Nu, na net i suda net*' – the Russian idiom that could be translated: 'You have just blown your last chance.' A few days later Likhachev left his apartment to go to the Institute for a workshop on *The Lay of Igor's Campaign*. He closed the door of his flat and was about to enter the lift. All of a sudden an athletic man in a balaclava attacked him and punched him hard in the chest. This could have ended fatally for Likhachev: after all, he was almost 70. Yet, by pure chance, he was dressed in a thick overcoat, and was holding a folder with his lecture notes against his chest. The coat and the folder softened the blow. This was not a robbery: the attacker ran down the staircase and disappeared. Dmitry had enough stamina to go to the Institute to deliver his talk. Next morning, however, he felt acute pain and discovered he could hardly breathe. A medical survey revealed that the attacker had broken two of his ribs.[42]

Likhachev was certain that it was a signal from the KGB. At the end of 1975 the Academy celebrated its 250th anniversary, and all its members received awards and memorial gifts. Only three members were excluded from the award list: Sakharov, Trofim Lysenko and Likhachev. Being in the same company as the famous dissident and Stalin's infamous agronomist was bizarre; it meant, however, that Likhachev was dangerously close to becoming a *persona non grata* for the Soviet authorities. He expected something worse to come, perhaps another and fatal attack. In April 1976 he learned chilling news that a son of his old friend, scholar Peter Bogatyrev, was found unconscious at the door of his apartment, with severe damage to his skull; he died two months later. Konstantin Bogatyrev spent years in Stalin's gulag, became a translator of German literature, and earned the ire of the authorities as their fearless critic. His murder was never solved.[43]

In May 1976 the Likhachev family had a close brush with disaster. They left their Leningrad apartment to go to their dacha in Komarovo. Early in the night two strangers attempted to set their apartment on fire. They brought canisters with inflammable liquid and tried to pump it through a hose under the apartment's door. Fortunately, while doing this, they prised the front door open with an iron bar to insert the hose, and triggered the sound alarm. The sound of the alarm woke all the neighbours in the multi-storeyed house. The arsonists ran away, leaving all their equipment behind. The police showed up and behaved strangely. They took the equipment with them and broke the balcony door, apparently looking for signs of fire and possible corpses. When later in the day Dmitry, Zina and the rest of the family arrived, they saw a police official inside their apartment waiting for them. His first words were 'not to worry'. Likhachev's brother Yuri, an engineer who dealt professionally with inflammable liquids, found that the arsonists planned to use a mixture of

**Plate 1**  Likhachev's parents, Sergei Likhachev and Vera Konyaeva, around 1900.

**Plate 2**  *Dachniki* (summer-folk) from St Petersburg on a Finnish gulf beach before the revolution.

**Plate 3**  Sergei Alexeyev (Askoldov) influenced Likhachev's philosophy and educational choices.

**Plate** 4    Likhachev in 1927, on the eve of his arrest.

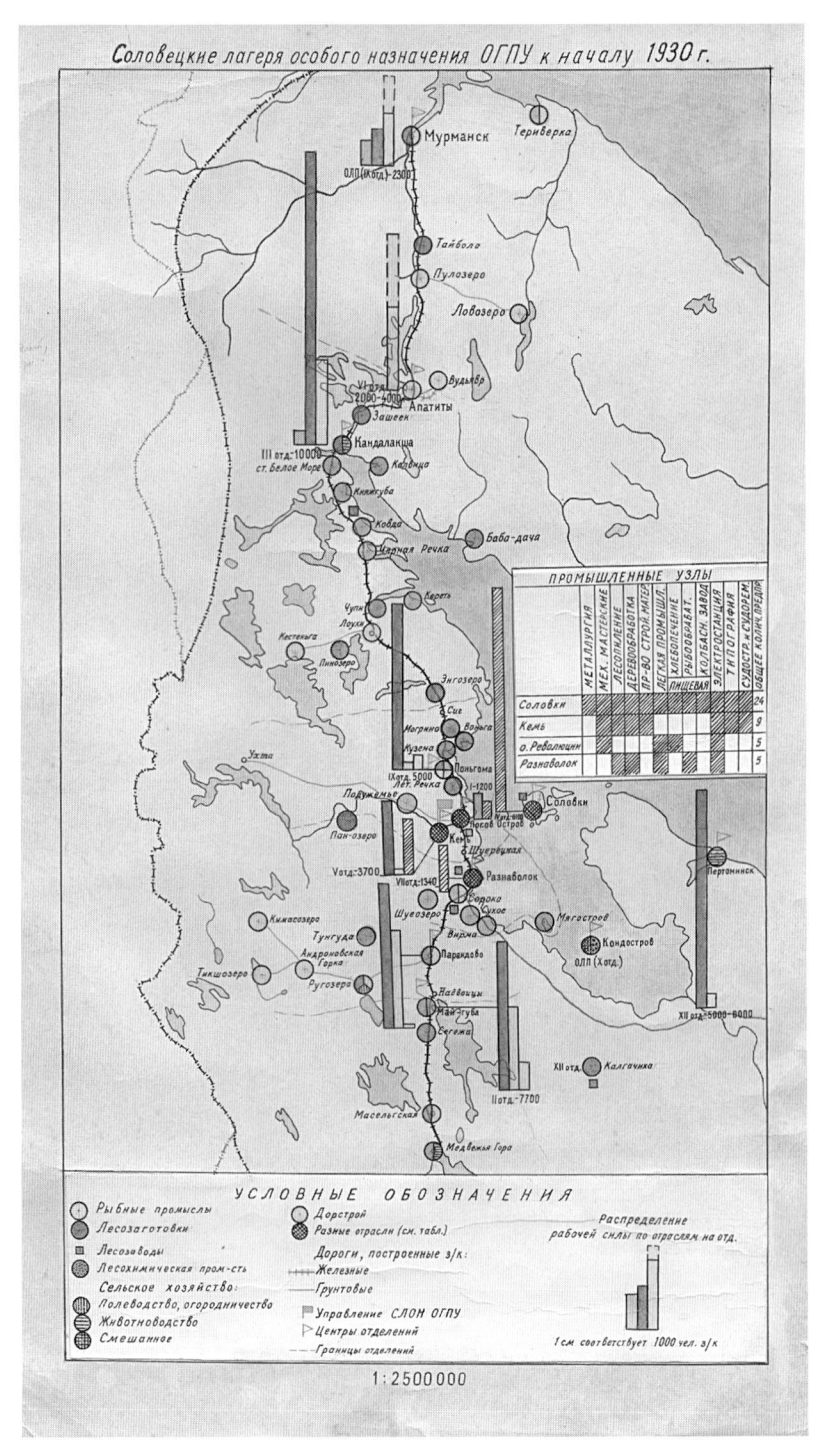

**Plate 5** Map of Solovki concentration camp.

**Plate 6** A sketch of the Solovki kremlin. The dots mark the path that Likhachev took every day to and from his work in Krimkab for three years between 1929 and 1931.

**Plate 7**  Likhachev's pass that allowed him to move around Solovki.

**Plate 8**  Reverend Nikolai Piskanovsky, who saved Dmitry's life.

**Plate 9**  Likhachev with his father and mother, on their visit to Solovki, after the night of executions, November 1929.

**Plate 10**  Likhachev and his friend, Ukrainian poet Vladimir Korolenko, incised their names on a boulder in Solovki. Korolenko was executed in 1937.

**Plate 11** Likhachev during his illness with ulcers works at home proofreading, after 1933.

**Plate 12** Likhachev and Zina Makarova, married with twins in Leningrad, 1938.

**Plate 13**  Carrying corpses in Leningrad during the Siege, 1942.

**Plate 14**  Likhachev and his students at Leningrad University, 1953. Two of the students in the picture would later join his department.

**Plate 15** Three generations of the Pushkin House. Likhachev is in the middle in the second row, 1955.

**Plate 16** Likhachev and Nikolai Voronin, who launched the movement to preserve old Russian legacy, late 1950s.

**Plate 17** Likhachev with his wife and department colleagues on a field trip to an old Russian city, around 1967.

**Plate 18** Likhachev in the department; Lurie and others mentioned in the text are in the picture, 1967. During this time Likhachev helped A.I. Solzhenitsyn to write *The Gulag Archipelago*.

**Plate 19**  Likhachev, honorary doctor of Oxford University, 1967.

**Plate 20**  Likhachev with his family, including his brothers, daughters, cousins, and wife.

**Plate 21** Likhachev on a trip, possibly in Solovki in 1966. He explored the archipelago by boat, travelling to the Big Zaitsky Islands, Muksalma, and Anze.

**Plate 22** Likhachev, full member of the Academy of Sciences, with friend Dmitry Kalistov, and granddaughter Vera, in Komarovo around 1971.

**Plate 23** Likhachev and Raisa Gorbacheva at the Cultural Foundation, Moscow, c. 1986.

**Plate 24** Likhachev and Yeltsin at the funeral of Andrei Sakharov, 1989.

**Plate 25**  Likhachev and Nicky Oppenheimer, 1992. Oppenheimer sponsored a cultural programme to collect and preserve Russian manuscripts.

**Plate 26**  Likhachev and Prince Charles, 1994.

Plate 27   Likhachev and George Soros (on right), c. 1995.

Plate 28   Likhachev dictates his memoirs.

kerosene and acetone. If the plot had worked, the entire apartment, with people, family albums, books, manuscripts and archives would have gone up in smoke within minutes.[44]

This story made it to *A Chronicle of Current Events*, the Samizdat bulletin founded by human rights activist Natalia Gorbanevskaia. At the end of 1976, when Likhachev had his 70th birthday, he received hundreds of private congratulations from his friends and colleagues. The newspaper of old Russian émigrés in France warmly congratulated Likhachev, naming him 'a man who suffers [*stradalets*] for the Russian land' and citing a line from his recent book: 'Courageous is his mind, who resides in truth.'[45]

## 'Inner Freedom'

For all his dangerous encounters, Likhachev managed to avoid the stark dilemma: preservation of dignity or loss of profession and forced emigration. He refused to become a dissident, remained prudent and did not provoke authorities. Age and experience, of course, mattered. To put it simply, he had seen enough death, suffering and grief to act heroically. And he remained loyal to his strategy: he believed he could do more for Russian culture as 'an adviser to Genghis Khan' than as an open adversary of the Soviet authorities. At the same time, he never compromised on what he considered most important, and never paid for his peace and comfort with the coin of public collaborationism. Too many of his contemporaries and older colleagues, people of great intellectual and artistic distinction, did not manage to do it. Just like during the Great Terror, 'D.S.' again performed a rare act.[46]

In his recollections, Likhachev compared the dissent of the late 1960s to 1970s with his experience of Petrograd *kruzhki* and the Solovki intellectuals. 'All of us, including Meyer, Andreyevsky, ... felt oppressed by the regime. We felt so only because each of us had to spend a great deal of our life defending our right to think ... We argued, resisted, felt outraged, etc. We were the dissidents of those years.' He remembered a Solovki prisoner whose name was Bardygin. He was a kind of thinker for himself, and he did not participate in Krimkab discussions. 'Nothing concerned Bardygin. He was fully immersed in his own philosophical and religious world. He dismissed external circumstances and those who attempted to intrude into his world.' Likhachev concluded: 'Anyone who fights for his independence, is already dependent.' Because Bardygin lived with his inner freedom intact, 'he was invincible, and this seemed to make him the man most dangerous to the authorities.'[47]

One of Likhachev's ideal literary characters was Mr Dick in Charles Dickens's *David Copperfield*. Because of his mental illness, Mr Dick was outside the British social hierarchy; as a result, he had social flexibility and the freedom to interact with the people he liked and avoid the people he disliked.[48] Likhachev learned to value this kind of freedom. He summed it up as follows: 'The most crucial thing in my personal life was always the need to defend my independence from the "currents of the time", fashion, dominant ideas, never enter into any unions and groups, to oppose ideological schemes. This stand made me appear a solitary figure, especially when friends from my youth began to pass away.'[49]

While admiring the leading thinkers of Soviet dissent, he had serious disagreements with them. This included Solzhenitsyn, the person Likhachev felt close to, and whose human and literary greatness he admired. He begged to disagree with the author of *The Gulag Archipelago* on the meaning and content of Russian history and culture. Solzhenitsyn blindly idealized the Old Belief and medieval Russian culture before Peter the Great. He considered the modern West organically and culturally alien to a 'true Russia' of his imagination. Likhachev rejected this strange concept. He was convinced that this way was a suicidal self-isolation and cultural death for Russia. And he objected when Solzhenitsyn lumped together the revolutionaries and the Russian intelligentsia, making all Russia's educated classes responsible for the revolutionary tragedy, while exempting 'the people'. Finally, Solzhenitsyn's view of Russian people was dangerously ethnic: he rejected any capacity for 'others' to contribute to Russian culture in a positive way – and he was highly negative on the assimilated Jews. Likhachev's view, as we have seen, was just the opposite.[50]

It rankled Likhachev when he heard 'anti-Semitism in reverse' from those whose parents had supported the Bolsheviks, and who now lacked empathy for the destroyed Russia. In June 1975 Likhachev heard on Radio Liberty an interview with émigré physicist Aleksandr Voronel, publisher of the Samizdat journal *Jews in the USSR*. Voronel passionately loved Russian high culture, yet could not identify himself with Russian people and customs. After years of struggle for permission to emigrate, Voronel and his wife left for Israel.[51] In his notebook, Likhachev wrote down the main points of Voronel's interview: 'Jews constitute in Russia the main part of the intelligentsia. Russian people have not grown up to appreciate Western culture. Jews are the only Westernizers in Russia. . . . Therefore the struggle in Russia for Western cultural principles is premature.' Likhachev's reaction was: 'Where does this arrogance come from? What culture do Jews in Russia have, if not Russian? Do they [Russified Jews] have Westernism in their blood?'[52]

Likhachev was not only offended. He also felt that this elitist 'Westernism' was hostile to his idea of homeland, his idea of Russia. Similar feelings can be found in the observations of Rev. Aleksandr Shmeman. A Russian émigré, Shmeman was married to a niece of Georgy Osorgin whom Likhachev met in Solovki; he taught Orthodox theology in the United States; Likhachev, Solzhenitsyn, and thousands of others admired his talks on Radio Liberty. When 'the people of the Sixties', deported from the Soviet Union, began to arrive, Shmeman was struck by their phobia of Russian patriotism. 'In Russia,' wrote Shmeman, 'they love only the "intelligentsia" and everything related to this notion.' He also wrote: 'Subconsciously, they wanted to defend themselves from pogroms. Russia [for them] is pogroms. Of course, there is some truth in this notion of Russia. Yet it is not the whole truth, and Russia is so much more than pogroms.'[53]

Likhachev could have agreed with every line. In fact, towards the end of the 1970s he felt he had to say this publicly, not to the narrow Samizdat audience, not to foreign journalists, but in the most famous and widely read of Russian literary journals.

## Russians between Good and Evil

In March 1980 *Novyi Mir* published Likhachev's essay, 'Notes on the Russian Way'. In this essay, he wrote, he wanted to counter the perception 'extremely widespread in this country and in the West' that the Russians were prone to extremism and aggression, and that the Russian national character was 'mean' (*nedobryi*).[54] From ancient times, he continued, the 'Russian way' could be best expressed by several notions: *prostor* (space) and *volya* (sense of liberty), *dobrota* (kindness or goodness) and *radost* (cheerfulness). *Dobrota* was linked to the nature of Russia and reflected in the 'sacral cheerfulness' of Russian churches, most famously in St Basil Cathedral.[55] Likhachev even found kind words for 'holy fools' – a symbol for Russian irrationality and fanaticism. Sitting close to the Tsar, a holy fool was a fearless truth-teller and prankster. In Russian fairy-tales Ivan the Fool would be inevitably transformed into 'Ivan the Tsarevich', a symbol of goodness.[56] At the peak of the terror, in the reign of Ivan the Terrible, 'there were good people, humane and fearless.'[57]

'Notes on the Russian Way' was not a programmatic manifesto. Likhachev wanted to start a 'conversation' as a way of reaching hearts and minds. For argumentation, he turned to Feodor Dostoyevsky, genius and nationalist, whom the Soviet reading public began to rediscover and discuss during the 1970s. What about Mitya Karamazov? – Likhachev wondered. Could this protagonist of Dostoyevsky's famous novel, one of the most unbalanced, irascible, and extremist of people, be considered a typical 'Russian'? And what about Smerdyakov, murderous bastard in that infamous family? Many intellectuals abroad and in the Soviet Union thought so. Likhachev disagreed.

'For Dostoyevsky the [ideal] Russian is a person of high intellect, with sublime spirit, understanding all the cultures of Europe, the whole of European history, and not at all torn and enigmatic inside.' He concluded: 'In Russian people, there was not only a lot of goodness, but also much evil, yet people were not always the cause of this evil. It came from the Smerdyakovs who changed into state leaders ...'[58]

The essay evoked ridicule among many intellectuals in Moscow and Leningrad. Westernizers among medievalists were appalled as well. Likhachev's long-time friend Mikhail Steblin-Kamensky, scholar of medieval Scandinavia, wrote in his diary: 'Why it is not evident [for Likhachev] that sixty-three years of Soviet totalitarianism put a strange imprint on the Russian people? And why it is not evident for him that this totalitarianism is a "Russian" phenomenon.' Perhaps, reflected Steblin-Kamensky, his own friend began to emulate the reactionary conservatism of Dostoyevsky or, even worse, fell to temptation to please the authorities and common fashion. Cultural historian Boris Yegorov, who admired 'D.S.' wrote down his impressions: 'The entire piece oozes with idealization and wishful thinking ... Tragedy, rudeness, irrational tomfoolery have been entirely overlooked.' Yegorov asked Likhachev about the reasons for such one-sidedness. 'He replied, I have done it on purpose, self-consciously. All our enemies would like to present the Russian people as aggressive and cruel. It is important to come up with something to counter this [image].'[59]

Most obviously, Likhachev continued his polemics with American James Billington about Russian culture, the debate he had started in the 1960s on the pages of *Slavic Review*. Billington's book *The Icon and the Axe*, much advertised in the West, vexed the Russian scholar. The icon and the axe, Billington wrote, 'were traditionally hung together on the wall of the peasant hut in the wooded Russian north'. D.S. protested against this metaphor – he believed this promoted the image of Russians as aggressive and barbaric.[60] Another opponent in the West was Harvard professor Edward Keenan who made the point of backing old claims by Polish and Ukrainian historians that 'Muscovy' had no continuity at all with Kievan Rus – was always barbaric and anti-European. In 1971 he published a book claiming that the correspondence between Ivan the Terrible and his prince Andrei Kurbsky was a seventeenth-century forgery. This time even Zimin and Lurie sided with Likhachev in rejecting Keenan's conclusions as unproven and unpersuasive.[61] Keenan did not stop at this: he decided to continue the revisionist undertaking of André Mazon, to prove that *The Lay of Igor's Campaign* was a literary artefact written in the eighteenth century.

For the contemporaries, Likhachev's essay was in blatant contradiction with reality: just a few months before the essay was published, the Soviet military occupied Afghanistan. The Western media depicted the Soviet

Union as an aggressor, 'the Russian bear' on the prowl. Even the Left in the West slipped into Russophobia: back in vogue was the travelogue of Astolphe de Custine's *Russia in 1839*, in which a nervous French nobleman warned European civilization about the threat from the East.[62] Likhachev, however, wrote his essay before the Soviet invasion: it was timed for another event from another era – the battle of Kulikovo in 1380, when Muscovy for the first time ran a gauntlet to the Golden Horde. A larger and more important target audience for Likhachev's 'Notes' was the Soviet intelligentsia, where the interest in Old Russia continued to grow.[63]

Some intellectuals, educated in Soviet times, began to see the Bolshevik revolution as a catastrophe for Russian history. The reaction of many to this news was frustrated, xenophobic, ethnic nationalism. Among new nationalists were talented 'village writers' Victor Astafiev, Valentin Rasputin, Vasily Belov, and many others. Anguished nationalist *ressentiment* spread in the ranks of the ruling party and even in the KGB.[64] Georg Myasnikov, a communist official from Penza, became a passionate sponsor of cultural preservation. In 1979 he lamented: 'Russian people are being reduced before our eyes, they live worse than anybody else. All kinds of Armenians, Azeris, Ossetians take advantage of the Russians ... Russia [*Rus'*] is getting empty.' The priority for Myasnikov was 'the revival of national dignity among the Russians', by which he above all meant ethnic solidarity against 'others'.[65] Likhachev wanted to stop this trend. He reiterated that Russia has never been 'a special civilization' separated from others. And Old Russia, he wrote with authority, was always a multi-ethnic realm, where population and ruling class did not develop racist ideas – as was the case in Western European countries. In the best part of Russian literature, Likhachev concluded, the aversion to nationalism 'became ideologically entrenched, became a conscious principle'.[66]

Nikolai Lossky's philosophical writings provided an apparent inspiration for 'Notes'. His 'Christian personalism' deeply influenced young Mitya in the 1920s. According to this philosophy, each and every individual had freedom 'to embark on the path of absolute goodness', for example 'to realize its *nomen*' independently of any historical time or material circumstances, by making ethical choices. In 1957 Lossky published in the émigré journal *Possev* a remarkable essay, 'Russian national character'. He also referred to Russian literature and concluded that, for all the horrors of the revolution and tyranny, 'goodness is one of the supreme qualities of the Russian people; therefore even the inhuman Soviet regime could not eviscerate this quality.' Lossky hoped to see a rebirth of the 'Christian foundations of Russian culture after the fall of the Soviet regime'.[67] Likhachev, like Lossky, posited his belief in the regenerative power of Russian culture. After the revolution, he wrote in his essay, all pine trees north of Petrograd had been cut down, to procure wood for heating. The beautiful natural habitat seemed to be lost forever – replaced by wild, ungainly woods. Yet after two decades majestic new pines rose from the underbrush again. This metaphor was utterly explicit – and underlined the rationale for cultural preservationism. It was also part of a broader concept that cropped up in Likhachev's thinking and writing at the time – the concept of 'ecology of culture'.[68]

The Russian forest depended on the kindness of 'others' and a better environment in its regeneration. Russian culture could not be revived without those who had been part of imperial Russia, and now were part of the Soviet Union, above all the Ukrainians and the Belorussians, the ethnic groups in the Volga region, many Georgians, Armenians, and other people of the Caucasus. These reflections harked back to the ideas expressed by Peter Struve, yet Likhachev emphasized preservation of cultural diversity more than cultural assimilation. 'A great nation with its own great culture and national traditions,' he wrote, *'ought* to be good, particularly if its life is linked to the life of a smaller nation. A great nation *ought* to help a smaller nation to preserve itself, its culture and language.'[69]

Likhachev's scholarship and academic authority was supposed to give hope to the Russians who zig-zagged between nationalist *ressentiment* and self-loathing. People who came to talk to him went away deeply impressed by his long-term visionary look. One of them was Feodor Abramov, who had been one of the 'people of 1949', a participant of the infamous *prorabotki*. Likhachev met him again in 1966 en route to Solovki with a group of academic and literary intellectuals. By that time Abramov became one of the 'village writers' who wrote with great gift about the tragedy of the Russian peasantry during and after the collectivization. They started a conversation. Abramov was surprised: 'I thought you would not even speak with me.' They became friends, and Likhachev offered him assistance and advice.[70] Abramov wrote in his diary on 17 February 1981 after meeting 'D.S.' in Komarovo. The writer felt completely transported. 'We sat together for three and a half hours, and what a conversation! About Peter the Great, ... about the peculiarities of Russian history, about our own Russian roots of Bolshevism, etc.' Abramov saw in Likhachev's essays and books an elevated way of feeling and acting as a 'good Russian'. By 'revealing' Russian spiritual roots from the darkness of time, Abramov concluded, the scholar committed an act of selfless heroism (*podvig*). 'He says that Russia started again and again anew. A wise man, a patriot, and all currents of contemporary culture go through him.'[71]

# CHAPTER 8

# RECOGNITION, 1976–1988

> [He] became the central figure in science, the person to whom everyone turned for his opinion and resolution of complex issues ... because he had a remarkable moral authority.
>
> *D.S. Likhachev about Alexei Shakhmatov*

In October 1987, Mikhail Gorbachev came to Leningrad to meet with the city elites in the former Smolny Institute for Noble Maidens. Italian architect Giacomo Quarenghi had designed a glorious white marble hall for royalty and aristocracy; now it was filled with communist nomenklatura. The new leader's charm began to wear off; he was too long-winded; perestroika had failed to produce improvements in the Soviet economy and living standards.[1] In the back rows of the hall sat an old man with a remarkably pensive expression and sad eyes. Dmitry Sergeevich Likhachev clearly did not belong in this audience. At the end of the meeting Gorbachev stepped from the podium down to the hall. His wife Raisa joined him, and the first Soviet couple began to move down the central aisle towards the exit. They greeted people without stopping. Suddenly he stopped at the row where Likhachev sat. The crowd of Soviet dignitaries gathered behind Gorbachev, blocked by the security guards and waiting for him. Likhachev recalled: 'They could not blame it on Gorbachev. So they blamed it on me. Somebody decided that my mental abilities had to be checked.' Likhachev was examined by a neurologist at the privileged party clinic. Soviet dissidents lived in danger of incarceration in mental asylums. 'I could have ended up there myself,' he recalled.[2]

D.S. did not crash a party in a state of senile dementia. Gorbachev invited him, because he considered him a wise man. 'My acquaintance with Dmitry Likhachev occurred at first through his books,' Gorbachev recalled. Every summer he and his wife Raisa vacationed in Crimea and, as was their habit, brought with them something to read on culture, art, sociology and history. At some point Gorbachev read a book by Likhachev, then another. Raisa in turn became interested. 'His reflections on Russia's ways, on the problems of Russian and world culture made a strong impression on both of us ... I wrote Dmitry Sergeevich a letter. Soon we met in person.'[3]

Who brought the books of the Leningrad scholar to the attention of the General Secretary? The most likely suspect is Yegor Ligachev, the Politburo member in charge of ideology and culture, a man with Siberian roots and other personal reasons to be interested in the Russian past. In 1982 Ligachev became the powerful deputy of Yuri Andropov in the Party Secretariat and helped to secure Gorbachev's smooth ascent to supreme power. The Gorbachevs first approached the scholar in May 1985. A black sedan stopped in front of his dacha in Komarovo, and a sprightly KGB officer handed to him a letter from Gorbacheva. The Soviet First Lady thanked him for his book, and enquired on his plans to mark the 800th anniversary of *The Lay of Igor's Campaign*.[4] Likhachev at first did not know what to think. Dmitry Chukovsky, his friend from Moscow, who happened to be next to him at that moment, explained: it meant that the Leningrad authorities would no longer mistreat him. Also it would likely mean the end of his travel restrictions. Dmitry's face brightened up. He moved his lips as if saying to someone invisible: 'Gotcha!'[5] D.S. became one of the most influential intellectuals in the Soviet Union, with the ability to send his appeals and requests directly to 'the first couple'. He could now act truly as 'a Chinese adviser to Genghis Khan' – without compromising his dignity.

## Belated Fame

Likhachev's scholarship struck many then and later as outmoded and 'romantic'. His model was Alexei Shakhmatov: at the event marking 50 years of his death in 1921, D.S. spoke about his deeply-held commitment 'to the enlightenment of people, to the Russian language, cultural monuments and the cultural legacy'. Shakhmatov loved Russia without being nationalist: he defended the cultural rights of Ukrainians, Latvians, Lithuanians and Belorussians; he was among those who supported the idea of translating the Bible into Ukrainian. And he turned the Academy's linguistic section 'into the centre of Russian culture ...'.[6] This was Likhachev's agenda as well.

As it happened, he articulated this agenda first in correspondence with Bulgarian intellectuals. In June 1978 he wrote to young Bulgarian historians that scholarship without ethical and social goals becomes a vanity fair, a tool of self-promotion. In May 1980, Likhachev said: 'It may seem bizarre, but I consider morality to be the most important quality of a scholar.'[7] In Bulgaria

Dmitry found what he lacked at home: recognition. Likhachev wrote that medieval Bulgarians lost their statehood to the Ottomans at the same time as the Russians regained theirs from the Mongol Horde. Bulgarian and Greek monks fled to Muscovy, where they were the agents of European influences. Those people brought the new religious ethics of Hesychasm, and echoes of the Renaissance to Muscovy in the fourteenth to sixteenth centuries. This inspired the artistic genius of Andrei Rublev, Feofan the Greek, Epiphanius the Wise, and others. Bulgaria as a state vanished, defeated by the Ottomans, but Bulgarian monks and priests formed 'a realm of spirit' (*gosudarstvo dukha*); they preserved written culture and pictorial art. And the Bulgarian state could emerge again after 1877, when Russian troops defeated the Ottoman Empire in the Balkans. No doubt, Likhachev applied this lesson of history to 'vanished Russia' and his own intellectual mission inside the Soviet Union.

In the 1970s, Bulgaria remained the only foreign country where Dmitry Likhachev could go without hassle. Todor Zhivkov, the Bulgarian communist leader, cited Likhachev's 'realm of spirit' in his speeches, and Liudmila Zhivkova, the leader's daughter and 'cultural Tsarina' of Bulgaria, studied art at Moscow State University and liked Likhachev's works.[8] Likhachev's 'reflections' about his life and scholarship appeared in Bulgaria first, and then were published in the Soviet Union in 1985 under the title *Letters on the Good and Beautiful*, intended for school children. They encountered a cold reception among Likhachev's colleagues. Even in the Department of Ancient Russian History at IRLI, Likhachev's 'ethical' scholarship – linked to the old intelligentsia's ethos[9] – inspired some and exasperated others. Among the enthusiasts were Lev Dmitriev, his wife Rufina, and Aleksandr Panchenko: they considered the studies of Old Russia to be more than just scholarship – a spiritual mission.[10] On the opposite flank was Yakov Lurie, who was sceptical about Bulgarian 'influence' on Russia and many other things D.S. wrote about. He wrote to Zimin to describe the Department's conference in Tbilisi in 1977 as 'a circus-like parade with D.S. at the helm'. A year later he expressed 'irritation at the created myth about a beautiful Old Russia, that we have been so assiduously promoting and enjoying'. Another Department member Gelian Prokhorov admired neo-Eurasian geographer Lev Gumilev, the author of sweeping fantasies about Russia's ties with Turkic Asia; he was not impressed by Likhachev's ideas.[11]

In 1976 Likhachev and Panchenko co-authored the book *The World of Laughter in Old Russia*. The book endorsed the works of Mikhail Bakhtin on the carnival medieval culture of Europe; Likhachev wrote that 'democratic literature' of the sixteenth century used the language of absurdity and 'counter-culture' to react to the abominations of Ivan the Terrible; this literature allowed Russians to recover from the 'real world' of the despotic state. All defeats and misfortunes that could not be amended in the 'real world' were redeemed and compensated for in the 'world of laughter'. On this dichotomy a Russian national character was formed.[12] The book received favourable attention from Western scholars. *Slavic Review* praised Likhachev as 'an original thinker in his own right', and commended him for using Mikhail Bakhtin's methods. The book, the review continued, 'should spawn a series of ... studies in an area which has been rather neglected until the last few years'.[13] In Soviet academic circles, in contrast, the book met with incomprehension. The exception was a group of 'semiotic' linguists in Tartu, led by Yuri Lotman.[14]

Meanwhile, another series of tragic events shook Likhachev's life. In 1979, after Likhachev returned from another trip to Bulgaria, he found that Mila's husband, physicist Sergei Zilitinkevich was under arrest. D.S. and everyone around him took this arrest as an attack by the Leningrad KGB against Likhachev himself. In March 1980 Likhachev's younger brother Yuri died from a heart attack at the age of 65: he was the dearest of the two brothers, and the last who saw Dmitry in Solovki, Tikhvin, and at other important moments of his life. Two dear friends, Igor Anichkov and Mikhail Steblin-Kamensky, also passed away.[15]

On 11 September 1981, when Dmitry and Zinaida travelled to Pushkin's memorial places in the Pskov region, terrible news came: their daughter Vera had died in an accident, hit by a bus. She was only 44. Likhachev had a lifelong nightmare of traffic deaths: when he was a child, he happened to see how a little boy was dragged under a streetcar in Petersburg. For years he could not forget the expression on his face. And now the nightmare came true. Elena Vaneieva recalls that Likhachev called her several days after the tragedy and invited her to come to see him at home. An advance copy of Vera's new book about Byzantine art had just arrived, and he wanted to add a new preface to it. Elena came fearful of what awaited her. She found D.S lying on his sofa, reading his daughter's book. He said that he had just drawn a new bookplate, to commemorate Vera's life. Elena was impressed by his stamina and strong will: 'In the hardest circumstances he continued to work.' Among other things, he was writing a book about gardens and parks – a semantic analysis of European art styles as a synthetic whole developing in time. The book *Poetics of Gardens* came out at the year's end. Likhachev dedicated it to the memory of 'ever cheerful and energetic' Vera.[16]

Inwardly, he was shattered. To an old friend he wrote: 'Vera's death nestles inside me, inside my heart, like some kind of shrapnel. I hoped so much that she would inherit my library, my papers, diaries, and photographs.' Likhachev kept seeing Vera in his dreams; sometimes he imagined that her soul was somewhere near him, in the form of a bird. At one moment, when the family were having dinner in the dacha, a bird tried to fly in and smashed against the windowpane. He shuddered from a sudden recognition. Then the bird came back to life and flew away.[17] His hope was 'little Vera', Mila's daughter, who revealed early scholarly talents. About 1980 she met and later married Volodya Tolz, a historian active in the dissident network and who was a friend of Yakov Lurie's son Lev and another philologist and dissident Arseny Roginsky; those young men were heavily involved in *Samizdat* and *Tamizdat* activities and were on the KGB's blacklist. Likhachev feared for the future of his granddaughter.[18] Indeed, in the summer of 1982 Volodya and Vera, who already had a little son, received an order from the KGB to choose between Volodya's arrest and an immediate emigration to the West. On 10 September, Likhachev had to bid farewell to his granddaughter. With his ban on travel to the West, he did not even know if he would ever see her again.[19]

The depression after these losses may explain a sad episode that happened in early 1982: the authorities of the IRLI demanded that the Department should dismiss Yakov Lurie, who had reached his retirement age. His wife recalled that 'D.S. consciously played the role of Pontius Pilate', washed his hands and did nothing. In 1950 Likhachev took a great risk in inviting Yakov as a co-author, and in 1956 worked hard to bring him to the Department. Yet after many years mutual incomprehension alienated them. In the end, Likhachev lost both granddaughter and Lurie; and some 'opposition-minded' intellectuals spread rumours about Likhachev's anti-Semitism and vindictiveness against the only Jew in his Department.[20]

Health problems overlapped with his depression. In the autumn of 1984, during a serious operation, he contracted a kidney infection that kept him in hospital for weeks. In addition to the ulcer, the kidney disease continued to torment Likhachev for the rest of his life.[21] This was a time when even his stoic philosophy began to give in to the blows of life. And it happened to be the time when his recognition in the Soviet Union began to grow exponentially. The main reason behind it was the moral vacuum at the end of Brezhnev's long tenure. Anatoly Chernyaev, Brezhnev's speechwriter and a future Gorbachev assistant, observed in his diary in May 1980: 'Hideous degradation, even worse than under the tsar, because today there are no more notions of aristocratism, nobility, officer's "honour" that somehow, at least in part, constrained the authorities within certain boundaries of decency.'[22] Likhachev suddenly came to be viewed as an embodiment of those lost notions. Popular magazines with multi-million circulations began to publish interviews with him. In 1983 Central Television featured him on the first channel after the primetime news. Millions watched the programme; this event ranked Likhachev among the top cultural figures in the Soviet Union.[23]

Likhachev had fans among Moscow cultural intellectuals, among them Mark Barinov, Yuri Rost and Vladimir Yenisherlov. Barinov was crucial:

20 years younger than Dmitry Likhachev, he passionately believed in ethical intellectualism, the virtues of Old Russia, and 'ecology of culture'.[24] Another Moscow admirer was Dmitry Chukovsky, grandson of a famous Russian literary critic and a classic of children's literature. As a head of the literature and art section of Soviet Television, he persuaded Likhachev to video-record an interview and managed to release it on air, without consulting Leningrad's bosses. 'This breakthrough on the television screen,' Chukovsky recalled, 'brought Dmitry Sergeevich uncanny popularity.'[25]

In 1984 Likhachev apologized to Yuri Mann, scholar of Russian literature, for delay in responding to his letter: 'After I began to speak on TV, I was simply buried by letters and requests. In 90 per cent of cases I write to respond, because people ask for assistance. I reply to such letters in the first place ... And my eyes have been weakening catastrophically. My time runs out, not much of life is left in me.'[26] Yet the public attention clearly invigorated him. Sigurd Shmidt, a younger friend of D.S., believes that 'as a true scholar and educated person, he began to create his own image'. This was the image of a public intellectual, with a language understandable to all educated classes.[27]

At home, sick and in agony over the loss of his daughter, Likhachev used a different language, the one of religious philosophy he had learned during the 1920s. At every moment, he wrote, 'here and now', we face the choice between the 'Kingdom of Christ' and the Apocalypse. 'We cannot shirk from responsibility for our every step!'[28] The 'Christian personalism' espoused by Likhachev was incomprehensible for atheists Mikhail and Gorbacheva. They did feel, however, something unusual and different in his books. Members of the optimistic postwar generation, the Gorbachevs felt a basic faith in 'enlightenment' and humanist values, and the sense of Soviet global cultural mission. When they 'discovered' Likhachev, they decided that a man of such intellectual calibre could help their perestroika.

## Conciliation through Culture

Gorbachev was fond of the old academician for yet another reason. Likhachev's works offered a Russian identity different from ethnic nationalism, dangerous for the unity of the Soviet realm. The Soviet leader was culturally Russian, his grandfather Gopkalo was an ethnic Ukrainian from the Kuban region, and Raisa's grandparents were Ukrainians and Russians from Siberia. In his memoirs, Gorbachev wrote that his 'small homeland' of Kuban Cossacks shaped his patriotism, 'not bookish, but a real one, rooted in the home soil'. In his own words, he was shaped by the 'multi-ethnic milieu, in a remarkable poly-linguist, multi-faceted, poly-populous environment'. His idea of Russia was formed by 'the centuries of Russian culture' and 'the democratic traditions of Russian higher school'.[29] He believed that Likhachev would be a perfect impersonation of such a broad cultural identity.

Not many in the Soviet intelligentsia shared these views. The cultural elites of Moscow and Leningrad became increasingly partisan and ridden by nationalist animosities. In Moscow's creative unions, 'liberals' and 'Russian patriots' grouped around different journals, hostile to each other. Quite a few 'liberals' were of Jewish descent, and many 'Russian patriots' were anti-Semitic. Likhachev was neither 'liberal' nor a 'Russian patriot' in the sense of the early 1980s. He was friendly with village prose writers – whom many 'liberals' disliked as nationalists. His essays and interviews appeared in the journals of the opposite camps. The uniqueness of Likhachev's position was obvious to thousands of his readers; people of Jewish descent wrote to him as an authority, to alert him to the rise of anti-Semitism.[30]

From 1971 on Likhachev headed the academic publishing project 'Literary Monuments'. Sergei Vavilov established it in 1947. Solzhenitsyn considered Vavilov 'a lackey-president' of Stalin. Likhachev, in contrast, greatly respected him and continued his legacy. The mission of the project, as he defined it, was to create a common cultural canon for the Russian-speaking audience, which would transcend the division between 'liberals' and 'Russian patriots', Westernizers and Slavophiles.[31] During the 1970s the editorship of 'Monuments' occupied Likhachev not less than his Department and his books. The project's volumes demonstrated that the Russian cultural legacy was the product of many civilizational influences. Likhachev maintained a delicate balance: he argued with Westernizers on the editorial board, who believed that Russian sagas and fairy-tales were too primitive to be included in the series.[32] He insisted on publication of the Byzantine 'lives of saints', camouflaging this edition under the title 'Byzantine legends'. At the same time, the series published main literary works of European culture: the works of Schiller, Heine, Goethe, E.T.A. Hoffmann, and Adam Mickiewicz. Likhachev had a special affection for English and Scottish literature: he studied it at university in the 1920s, in Zhirmunsky's seminar. To explore further the impact of Europe on the formation of Russian national-cultural identity, Likhachev published travelogues of the early eighteenth century, such as *Letters about Spain* by V.P. Botkin and *Letters of a Russian Traveller* by N.M. Karamzin.[33] And he got outstanding scholars to write introductions to all these volumes. For instance, Yury Lotman and Boris Uspensky, scholars from Tartu's 'school of structural linguistics', edited and annotated Karamzin's volume.[34]

His other priority editions were the *Memoirs* of Aleksandr Benois (1980) and *Petersburg* by Andrei Belyi (1981). Those books introduced the

Soviet-Russian reader to the world of Petersburg's Silver Age – a phenomenon which Likhachev considered crucial for modern Russian culture and identity. While Benois was not harsh on the Bolsheviks, his reminiscences conflicted with Soviet revolutionary mythology. To overcome this problem, Likhachev and his editorial board contacted influential Soviet diplomat Vladimir Kemenov, who had a lifelong passion for Russian art and met with many cultural figures of the Russian immigration, including Benois. His patronage helped overcome the bureaucratic resistance to the publication of *Memoirs*.[35] For this edition, D.S. found an old photograph of the school of Karl Mai where both Benois and Likhachev had studied. After the publication, he wrote to a colleague: 'Benois is now protected.'[36]

'Monuments' under Likhachev did not publish the works of Soviet writers. 'On anything contemporary,' he wrote to his trusted ally on the board A.M. Samsonov, 'we, with our weak backing, only get into trouble.' The only exception to this rule was Tvardovsky's *Vasily Tyorkin*, published in the series in 1976. Likhachev wrote to an editor of this project: 'This is, after all, the only genuine people's poem, unique in its kind ... And the poem is patriotic in a true sense of the word. This is the most meaningful literary event of the war years, and not only the war years.'[37] For Likhachev, *Tyorkin* was as valuable as *The Lay of Igor's Campaign* – while the former immortalized Russian peasant patriotism under Soviet rule, the latter was the only surviving example of aristocratic patriotism from pre-Mongol Russia.

His sudden popularity in the mass media and the direct connection with the Gorbachevs opened up for the old scholar entirely different horizons. In the summer of 1985 the leading 'theoretical journal' of the party, *Kommunist*, appeared with a section on *The Lay of Igor's Campaign*. Likhachev's preface opened the section. Among the contributors were Byzantine religious scholar Sergei Averintsev and Kazakh writer Oljas Suleymenov. The latter caused a mini-storm in 1976 when he claimed that *The Lay* was in reality a masterpiece of Turkic literature, contaminated by later Russian plagiarists. He was accused of 'anti-Russian Kazakh nationalism', and Likhachev was among his critics. His presence in the section was a sign of reconciliation, an invitation for a cultural dialogue.[38]

When Likhachev turned 80 on 28 November 1986 the Soviet government appointed him a Hero of Socialist Labour and awarded him the Order of Lenin. Even earlier, 'Likhachev mania' swept through the Soviet media. He featured on Soviet television in prime time.[39] He received letters from people in all walks of life. A metalworker from Donbass wrote: 'We are fortunate that in a war for Russian culture ... an old *intelligent* from Petersburg has survived and remained strong.' The great-granddaughter of

Russian industrialist and philanthropist Savva Mamontov wrote: 'You are today our Russian conscience, our hope for better times.'[40] Anastasia Tsvetaeva, 91-year-old sister of the great Russian poet, intoned: 'I feel as if you became my intimate friend. How much dignity you showed. Every one of your opinions emanated from irrefutable and fundamental ideas and feelings. Thank you. Let the Lord protect you!'[41] Journalist Yuri Rost in *Komsomolskaia Pravda* called 'the protector of our culture, our protector'. And literary critic Marietta Chudakova called him 'intelligentsia's conscience'.[42]

Lidia Lotman, a cultural historian, defined 'Likhachev mania' as follows: 'Specific features of [his] personality became an important factor in our social life at a delicate moment. D.S. became an ethical authority, when the question of historical choices became central in social debates, when people looked for moral authority, for the people they could absolutely trust.' At that time, Likhachev's moral authority was greater among the Soviet public than the authority of Andrei Sakharov, whom Gorbachev returned from his exile in Gorky in November 1986.[43]

When his ban on foreign travel ended, Likhachev began to go abroad. He met again with 'little Vera' – in Rome, Barcelona, and even in Munich, where she and Volodya Tolz worked for Radio Liberty. He attended both professional conferences and international events of Soviet 'cultural diplomacy', where intellectuals rubbed shoulders with diplomats and politicians. In October 1985 he was at 'the European cultural forum' in Budapest, where he met Soviet diplomat Sergei Zotov, fluent in three European languages and a fan of Likhachev's writings. In a conversation, they came up with the idea of 'a foundation for culture' – a non-government institution, that would perform tasks that Soviet institutions had so far failed to do. Likhachev suggested that Gorbacheva should be involved, and Zotov offered to send this proposal to Moscow right away, using diplomatic channels.[44] This was a brilliant move. Wives of the Soviet leaders lived in obscurity and appeared only at their husbands' funerals. Raisa wanted to break with this tradition, and strongly liked the proposal: she only added the adjective 'Soviet' to the foundation's title.

Early in 1986 Likhachev received a note from the Party Secretariat, the top arbiter of Soviet bureaucracy, that his idea was approved. In April the Council of Ministers passed a decree to create the Soviet Cultural Foundation (Sovetskii Fond Kultury/SFC). This 'non-government organization' was sponsored at a founding conference by *all* public and cultural institutions of the Soviet Union, from the creative Unions (of writers, artists, architects, cinema, journalists, etc.) to the trade unions, Academy of Art, all the top museums of Moscow and Leningrad, the agencies of Soviet cultural diplomacy abroad, VOOPIK, the society of book-lovers, and even Komsomol. The most prominent 'public organization' *not* listed was the Communist Party, the only real sponsor of the new foundation. Two months later the founding conference elected the foundation's board and leadership. To everyone's surprise, Gorbacheva refused to become head of the foundation and proposed instead Likhachev's candidacy. He accepted on two conditions: he would not move to Moscow from Leningrad, and he would not receive any salary for his job. Likhachev fully realized that his new project would totally depend on Raisa and the party sponsorship. He sent a letter to Yegor Ligachev, proposing Georg Myasnikov, an experienced party apparatchik, as his deputy. Myasnikov had many friends among Moscow 'liberals' and 'patriots', yet he detested the factionalism of the Soviet intelligentsia and vowed in his diary to work 'for the glory of Russia'.[45]

Officially, the foundation had a mission 'to enhance the awareness of the homeland and the world's culture, the aesthetical, patriotic, and internationalist education of Soviet people, especially the youth'.[46] Likhachev had a different idea. In June 1986 he spoke at the congress of Soviet writers in Moscow calling for 'repentance' and for 'return' of the repressed and forgotten cultural figures – among them Marina Tsvetaeva and Andrei Platonov, Nikolai Gumilev, Osip Mandelstam, Boris Pasternak, Mikhail Zoschenko, Vladimir Nabokov, and many others.[47] The Silver Age culture was gone, just as was the Old Russia – yet its legacy could be used to create a new Russian culture. In January 1987 at the first the session of the SFC board ('presidium'), with Gorbacheva present, Likhachev formulated the foundation's task as 'preserving the old culture and creating a new culture – as one process'. In July, at the next board meeting, he said he wanted the restoration of the 'moral sphere of society', bringing back 'the notions of kindness, justice, a sense of decency, honour', love for nature, and pride in one's land. Likhachev's address was drafted in part by the staff, but its remarkable messianic spirit was clearly his own. He said that the foundation's cultural activities should reach out to 'millions'.[48]

D.S. also pioneered a proposal to reach out to the Russian emigration for their collections, to publish the diaries and memoirs of the best thinkers who had left Russia after 1917. SFC scored an immediate success, acquiring many foreign 'friends' and benefactors. Many of them were attracted by the prospect of access to Gorbacheva. Yet Likhachev's reputation was also a crucial factor. Many Russian émigrés donated their family manuscripts, correspondence and valuables to the foundation, only because they trusted Likhachev.[49] In Moscow, he had supported an idea to create a museum of private collections, to house a collection of Ilya Zilbershtein, Georgy Kostaki and other remarkable art connoisseurs.[50] In July 1987 Likhachev said to the foundation's board: 'We should aim at seeing such museums created in every city and every town.' Many private art collectors, he asserted, would be happy to display their art to the general public, provided there were legal guarantees and recognition that those collections would not be confiscated by the State.[51]

Even more ambitious was the task of reaching out to Soviet society, finding recipients for the legacy of the Silver Age, and setting in motion the forces to invent a new national culture. For Likhachev this task equalled the creation of a new intelligentsia. He said to the board: 'We are the foundation of the intelligentsia's culture.'[52] His dream was to legalize and support all kinds of public associations, and *kruzhki*. Their specialization could include the protection of historic parks, the study of classical music, propaganda for classical literature, etc.[53] As a man of the 1920s, D.S. hoped that such associations could spring up by themselves, and only needed legal backing from above, to avoid local harrassment. In December 1988, Likhachev tried to persuade Gorbacheva to create a club of 'creative intelligentsia' as a transnational institution that would develop a dialogue with intellectuals abroad. This would mean a break with the Soviet practice of clearing all 'foreign contacts' through the KGB. Raisa, however, objected on legal grounds. The foundation, she said, had no legal authority to spawn other non-government associations. All of them would have to be sactioned separately by the state authorities.[54]

Youth should be the main target of the SFC's programmes, according to Likhachev's vision. Educated inside the Soviet cultural bubble, young people did not rebel against it, but escaped from its limitations into the 'underground', and became fans of rock and other Western music, Western films, and mass culture.[55] Russian nationalists and village-prose writers had been warning for years about this as a threat and demanded to ban Western culture. Likhachev also believed that the youth rock culture was 'aggressive', yet he knew that banning it would be counterproductive and stupid. And he did not support the nationalists when they promoted folkloric kitsch; he found tacky baby-dolls and professionals dancing in peasant garb artificial and morally revolting.

His proposal for the young was to create a nationwide network of high school and college clubs focused on college students, with the focus on humanities. His ideal was the school of Karl Mai and Lentovka, where the study of classical heritage was combined with creative handicraft, field trips and a patriotic democratic spirit.[56] He also hoped to reach out to Soviet youth through a cultural preservation movement. In March 1987 Leningrad authorities decided to demolish the hotel Angleterre, where poet Sergei Yesenin committed suicide in 1925. Suddenly, a grass-roots protest sprang up among high school and university students: they picketed the hotel, blocking the way for demolition workers. Likhachev immediately intervened on the side of the young. He wrote to Gorbacheva, that the 'informals' were actually 'genuinely patriotic youth'. In the end, while the old Angleterre was demolished, none of the protesters was arrested and harrassed.[57]

A child of the early twentieth century, Likhachev believed that printed media could be the main means of 'enlightenment'. He poured his heart into the foundation's bi-monthly journal *Nashe Naslediie* ('Our Heritage'). The prototypes of 'Our Heritage' were grand art journals of the Silver Age; nothing of this kind had ever existed in the Soviet Union. Raisa and D.S. negotiated with British publisher Robert Maxwell to publish the journal abroad. With Gorbacheva's assistance, the Soviet state provided foreign currency.[58] The first issues appeared in 1988 and made a big impression on the readers. All state museums, archives, and even private collections were allowed to photograph the finest exhibits from their vaults – most of them never displayed publicly since the revolution. The artifacts of Old Russia reappeared in all their colourful splendour in glitzy illustrations. Every issue contained a selection of philosophy, poetry and prose, banned in Soviet times and kept under lock and key in major libraries.

In retrospect, it is all too easy to conclude that Likhachev's vision was doomed. His idea of *kruzhki*, free associations, reconnection with 'Russian in emigration', and many others came several decades too late. Cynicism, collaborationism, greed and indifference to 'big words' were rampant in late Soviet society. Still, such were the early illusions of perestroika, and so authoritative was the figure of Likhachev, combined with the presence of Gorbachev's wife, that SFC seemed to many to become a hugely successful enlightenment project.[59] In 1988, the foundation grew into a sprawling all-Soviet network. The foundation's offshoots sprang up in every major city from Kaliningrad to Vladivostok, across Siberia and even as far as Kamchatka. The staff of all those branches numbered 650, including 78 in the central headquarters. The real estate and funds for their activities came from the party and the Soviet state. Mikhail Gorbachev provided an example of 'voluntary private donation': he donated honoraria from foreign editions of his books to the SFC.[60]

## About Glasnost and Conscience

In 1987 Gorbachev authorized glasnost – liberalization of public speech, reduced state censorship and more benign cultural policies. Revelations of Stalinist crimes and reassessment of Bolshevism, the unfinished business of The Thaw, returned to the pages of Soviet journals. The leading voices in glasnost belonged to the postwar writers and the 'people of the sixties'.

Likhachev welcomed glasnost, yet his view of history and Russia differed greatly from the mainstream of glasnost 'liberals'. Their main mission was to reveal 'the truth' about Stalinist times, to denounce those who had killed or exiled their parents and relatives, and betrayed their young idealism. Likhachev had a much longer view of the past, rooted in his own experience and also his studies of Old Russia. Soviet archival documents, when they began to appear, revealed not only 'the truth', but also *tufta*, falsifications and outrageous lies. He also understood that many people would not be ready to accept 'revelations' from a select group of writers, journalists and artists, who only a few years ago had been conformist Soviet citizens. One such person was Likhachev's older brother Mikhail, a high-placed Soviet military engineer. Early in 1987 D.S. invited him to watch the film *Repentance* by Tengiz Abuladze. It was a poignant saga of Stalinist crimes, murder, spiritual corruption and betrayal. The main character continued to shirk his responsibility for the past, until this past caught up with him, compelling his son to commit suicide. Mikhail watched the movie with a stony face and left the theatre before it ended. He refused to accept Abuladze's ethical message. He died later that year, without sharing his remorse or regrets to his brother.[61]

In 1987 *Novyi Mir* asked D.S. to peer-review an essay by Moscow philosopher Igor Klyamkin about the origins of Stalinism. In this essay Klyamkin expressed an old thesis about the responsibility of the Russian intelligentsia for the revolution and claimed that the peasantry was 'reconciled to collectivization', because peasants lacked the European tradition of property and individualism.[62] Instead of a review, Likhachev sent a letter to Zalygin, *Novyi Mir*'s editor, expressing 'intense disagreement' with Klyamkin's interpretation of history. 'The author apparently did not live a conscious life at the beginning of the 1930s; he writes about what he never saw, and did not even learn from others.' In reality, peasants fiercely resisted collectivization: it took terror and famine to crush them. Likhachev continued: 'I know personally what was the destruction of millions of peasants – children, old men, robust men. I know about famine in Russia and Ukraine. I saw a train car passing by full of frozen bodies of children and old men. I saw with my own eyes women who threw their babes off the trains with written notes, such as: "Good people, have mercy, save the toddler. Her name is Maria."' Likhachev felt pity for peasants who did not write any diaries to defend themselves against intellectuals who held them responsible for their own tragedy![63] Also Klyamkin's schematic view of the past was inimical to the 'Christian personalism' of Likhachev. His letter ended in an emotional crescendo: 'No to historical determinism and the justification of crimes against humanity! There was no "system" – only the chaos of tyranny.'

For Likhachev, an example of approaching the tragic Russian past was Boris Pasternak's *Doctor Zhivago*. In his novel Pasternak sought to break the spell of 'a dead letter' – of social abstractions of progress, revolutionary necessity, laws of history and the like, that paved the road to Soviet crimes against humanity. In 1983 Likhachev sponsored the first edition of Pasternak's prose. When glasnost started, he and Pasternak's son began to lobby quietly for *Zhivago*. In the spring of 1987 Evgeny Pasternak wrote to D.S. 'with affection and respect' about 'many promising developments'.[64] In January 1988 *Novyi Mir* began to serialize the controversial novel, with Likhachev's preface. Yuri Zhivago, he wrote, was 'one of the Russian intelligentsia, who – with doubts and spiritual losses – accepted the revolution'. Yet this acceptance was not a moral individual choice. Yuri as a Christian believer regarded 'the revolution as a natural phenomenon', yet followed his own moral compass.[65]

In 1987 Dmitry Likhachev read a memoir about Solovki by Oleg Volkov, published in Paris. He was upset by its biases and errors, particularly in the description of the people he knew. He was also convinced that describing 'the horrors of the gulag' – tortures, executions, and sufferings – would do less service to Russian culture than preserving each and every example of individual defiance, spiritual fortitude, and honourable behaviour. He wrote to Volkov's ex-wife, Sofia Mamontova, that he felt again the necessity of recording properly his memories, especially the memories of Krimkab, with 'many renowned figures of Russian culture, who attracted the youth'.[66] He did not think it was possible to divide society into victims and executioners. In 1988, when D.S. worked with a group of filmmakers on the documentary *Solovki Power*, they were able to locate Uspensky, the camp's most heinous executioner. They even filmed him secretly when he walked in the streets of Moscow as an old man. Suddenly, Likhachev baulked at the idea of identifying Uspensky by name in the documentary. 'If you can imagine the scale of Stalinist repressions, can you imagine how many [executioners] still live among us? Why then should I name only one of them?'[67] In the same year, Andrei Sakharov and other human rights activists founded the Memorial Society to commemorate the victims of Soviet crimes. Some proposed erecting a monument with the names of some victims engraved. Likhachev publicly supported the monument, yet spoke against the idea of names. 'Many of those who perished were responsible in turn for the death of thousands ... Trust me, we can end up commemorating people who themselves were often guilty of repressions.'[68]

Glasnost made possible the emergence of a civil society, a space where people could discuss, question, and demand corrections of state policies. In addition to many projects on 'ecology of culture', D.S. also backed the rapidly growing ecological movement. At the end of 1985 the Academy of

Sciences, under strong pressure, gave its approval to a colossal project to turn Siberian rivers southwards. Environmentalists and scientists immediately saw this project – the child of powerful economic lobbies under the aegis of the Ministry of Water Economy – as a scam and a potential ecological disaster. Likhachev sent protesting letters to Gorbachev. In August 1986 the Politburo stopped the project. Likhachev was also a vocal enemy of another ecologically dangerous project, the construction of a dam across the Finnish gulf, to the west of Leningrad. The official reason for the construction that began in 1979 was to prevent recurring and ruinous floods of the Neva. D.S., however, believed that the dam would cause ecological ruin to the city's environment.

Just as much as freedom of speech, Likhachev cared about freedom of conscience. At home, Dmitry and Zinaida observed the Orthodox religious calendar, with fasting and holidays, particularly for Easter. Yet for a while, he felt reluctant to speak publicly on religious matters.[69] His personal experience made him avoid the official Church and sympathize with small communities of people who practised Christianity as a choice of their way of life.[70] Religious experience as a personal choice remained part of his vision of 'a national-cultural intelligentsia' and a new Russian culture. In an interview in 1988 Likhachev said: 'We are raising patriotism, yet we do not know the wealth of Old Russian [patriotic] literature, because it cannot be accessed without a knowledge of Christian exegesis.'[71] Two years later, in a talk at Columbia University, he said: 'It is impossible to develop a culture without religion. The same concerns morality, ethics, and even economics. This has become absolutely clear now.'[72]

In 1988, Gorbachev decided to celebrate the Millennium of the baptizing of Russia. Likhachev was one of very few people who influenced this decision: he told Gorbacheva that the Millennium celebration could be a pretext for 'a dialogue between civilizations'. Gorbacheva listened attentively and promised to talk with her husband.[73] Above all, D.S. wanted to put an end to the systematic anti-religious campaigns that had continued in the Soviet Union from the first day of Bolshevik rule. In February 1988 he sent a letter to Gorbacheva, where he called these campaigns 'a civil war'. 'Do we need such a civil war now, at a time when it would be much more useful [for perestroika] to conslidate all the forces of our citizens, believers and non-believers?'[74] A month later, he appealed through a newspaper to repeal the Soviet ban on religious charity. This charity, he wrote, 'is a natural need of the church. The demonstration of compassion within the walls of hospitals, rehabs and houses of assisted living would help revive such human feelings as kindness, compassion, and mercy.'[75]

Gorbachev had a different agenda. He wanted to use the Millennium for his campaign of public diplomacy; and he dismissed religion, but wanted to use it for improving relationships with the West. In April 1988 Gorbachev received Patriarch Pimen and the Synod in St Catherine Hall of the Kremlin. He asked them: 'What can be done to resurrect the Church?' The communist state began to return to the Russian Orthodox Church some of its confiscated relics, the ruined Optina monastery, parts of the ancient Kiev-Pechersk Lavra. On 5–12 June the Soviet state celebrated the Millennium of Christianity in Russia on an international scale. Leaders of many Christian churches came, and a spectacular liturgy service took place in the Kremlin's main cathedral. An All-Orthodox assembly of churches gathered in the Trinity Cloister. The Patriarch moved into the Danilov Cloister, named after Aleksandr Nevsky's son, the first prince of Moscow. American historian of Russian culture Suzanne Massie managed to attend those events with the help of her contacts in the KGB: this organization organized and monitored the Millennium pageantry. Gorbacheva was in the centre of the events.[76]

The Gorbachevs intended to use Likhachev for public diplomacy as well. In June 1988 Gorbachev asked D.S. to join a group of Soviet dignitaries at his summit with Ronald Reagan in Moscow. Then he joined a smaller group that accompanied Nancy Reagan to Leningrad.[77] At the same time, D.S. found an excuse not to be present at the Millennium pageantry. The tragic memories of his youth, about the destruction of historic Russia and the Russian Church by the Bolsheviks, the travesty of the Church's reconstitution by Stalin – all this prevented him from making public speeches at official Soviet ceremonies. He did not like the politicized nature of the celebration and the public diplomacy role assigned to the Foundation.

Instead, he published in *Novyi Mir* in June a programmatic essay on the cultural significance of Christianity in Russian history. There he argued against a thesis of imposition of Christianity on the pagan Slav population, that resulted in the 'dual faith', Christianity and paganism, for many centuries. Such a view was popular among sceptical scholars of Russia in the West. Christianity, Likhachev wrote, 'did not turn into a conquest act against people', but rather absorbed pre-Christian traditions in a kind of centuries-long 'peaceful transfiguration of national life'. Russians 'needed universal, world religion' in order to be connected to other cultures. The beautiful liturgy of Constantinople defined the aestheticism of Russian culture. Bulgarian literature in translation into vernacular Russian provided a ready foundation for the 'highly organized literary language'. This language enabled Russians to record their national history, think philosophically about their 'national experience' and create a literature – the main vehicle of their culture for the next ten centuries. He concluded by citing Aleksandr Pushkin that the modern history of Russia 'is the history of Christianity'.[78] The continuity of this essay with Likhachev's early beliefs is striking.

The soaring of Likhachev's public status, visibility and influence in the 1980s was as miraculous and amazing as the episodes of his survival and epiphany in his earlier life. He listened to these trumpets of fame without vanity, but also as his due. He knew how to exercise and project authority, and his modest demeanour concealed high ambitions.[79] One of his favourite stories from Old Russian literature was *The Tale about Woe and Grief*. In this story, originating in the seventeenth century, a Russian prodigal son became saddled by Fate, which kept bringing him one grief after another. This Fate became an alter ego of the man, his shadow, and persecuted him. In 1987, when his life changed from despair to widespread recognition and fame, he recalled this story. He compared Fate from the story to the Devil that persecuted Ivan in *The Brothers Karamazov*. Ivan went insane. The man in the story overwhelmed his Fate by turning to faith and reconnecting with tradition, becoming a monk. Likhachev broke loose from his Fate by dedicating himself to his scholarship, public intellectualism and nationwide cultural projects. French scholar of Russian culture, Georges Nivat put it best: 'The mission of Dmitry [Likhachev] ... can be boiled down to one thing: How to regenerate Russia.'[80]

# CHAPTER 9

# PREPARING FOR COLLAPSE, 1988–1991

> I remember the revolution very clearly, and I know where people's emotions could lead. Today our country is in the grip of emotions.
> 
> D.S. Likhachev to the Congress of People's Deputies of the USSR, 13 March 1990

In Moscow, an emergency session of the People's Congress convened on 12 March 1990 to repeal the Communist Party's monopoly on political power and to institute a new executive post – president of the Soviet Union. Five years after Mikhail Gorbachev began his perestroika, the Soviet Union found itself in deep trouble. Conservatives hated Gorbachev, and radical-minded delegates did not consider him their leader anymore. The father of perestroika discovered that he no longer had an assured majority even at the Congress.

Anatoly Sobchak, a reform-minded delegate from Leningrad was worried. In May 1989 he visited communist China as a guest lecturer, and saw the democratic movement of students brutally suppressed by the army. Could it happen in the Soviet Union? In Sobchak's view, Gorbachev was the best guarantor of peaceful liberalization, and it would be madness not to elect him the president. If Gorbachev suddenly failed to be elected, this could mean a sudden collapse of central authority with disastrous consequences, just like in 1917 after the Tsar's abdication.[1] Sobchak approached Dmitry Likhachev, the oldest and most well respected delegate at the Congress, and asked him to intervene. When D.S. raised his hand, Gorbachev immediately acknowledged him: 'Dmitry Sergeevich Likhachev has a word.' The intervention was brief. Likhachev reminded the Congress that he was the only witness of the Russian Revolution in the hall: 'In the current situation, direct elections of the president will lead in effect to a civil war. Trust me. Trust my experience.

We should make a choice [of the president] here and now, without delay.' Sobchak was convinced: 'Gorbachev owed his Presidency to Dmitry Sergeevich.' The Congress elected Gorbachev by a slight majority.[2]

Likhachev's support for Gorbachev was conditional and stemmed from the knowledge of Russian history and people. He chose between the imperfect and the awful. Above all, he feared disintegration of the State, the rise of aggressive nationalism, human casualties and the damage to culture.

## Time of Troubles?

Long before the start of Gorbachev's perestroika, the 'brotherhood of the people' in the Soviet Union revealed itself as a rotten façade. Opposition-minded intellectuals in the Baltics, Caucasus, and even in Ukraine linked their future to liberation from 'Russian domination'. Xenophobic and anti-Semitic nationalists created their association called 'Memory' (*Pamyat*), and many Soviet Jews began to fear imminent pogroms.[3]

Likhachev began to worry about the rise of nationalism in the Soviet Union during the 1970s. As the editor-in-chief of 'Literary Monuments', he sought to make the series as representative of all nationalities as possible, but realized that any publication of the old work could wake up demons of nationalism. For this reason, in 1976 he strenuously objected to the publication of a complete version of Taras Shevchenko's epic poem *Kobzar* with its strong Ukrainian themes, as well as anti-Semitic and anti-Moscow sentiments. Likhachev warned the board about the 'extremely sensitive situation' in Ukraine and wrote to his colleague Samsonov: 'We cannot seek a resolution for the complex political issue before the Ukrainians in Kiev offer us a decision.'[4] Fear of triggering a nationalist avalanche haunted him in all his trips from the Baltics to Georgia.

In July 1987 Likhachev spoke at an SFC board meeting on the danger of Russian nationalism. Russian national identity, he said, was always weak in the empire, and this worked well for great Russian culture and literature. The situation, however, had changed in recent times. It was imperative to prepare an alternative agenda for the likely mobilization of Russian national feelings – cultural venues for national self-expression. Aggressive and xenophobic nationalism must be opposed not by the ideology of 'internationalism' and 'cosmopolitanism' but by cultivation of an inclusive concept of patriotism based on Russian culture.[5] 'The idiots from Pamyat,' Likhachev said about the Russian nationalists, did not understand that a national culture, 'cannot exist within one nation. It must be defined through dialogue and co-existence with other peoples and cultures.'[6]

The future of Russian identity, Likhachev argued, should be defined by the treatment of ethnic and cultural minorities. At the end of 1988, Likhachev appealed to the Commission on the Census to expand the list of registered nationalities to include the smallest ethnic groups registered by Russian ethnographers, but then removed in 1936. 'This is a highly important issue,' Likhachev wrote to the commission. 'The ethnic diversity of our country is our capital asset. If the census cannot be postponed, we must issue additional forms defining all nationalities of our country.' The census of 1989 included the ethnographic register of the 1920s and became the most comprehensive in Soviet history.[7]

In October 1988, the *Literary Gazette*, a newspaper that reached at that moment a staggering circulation of 27 million copies, published Likhachev's essay titled 'Russia' (*Rossiya*). Many Russian nationalists considered the Soviet Union as 'Russia in disguise' – a state that included both the 'alien' Balts and the 'fraternal' Belarusians and Ukrainians. This perception was chauvinist self-delusion. The Soviet rulers, guided by internationalist ideology and Machiavellian needs, deconstructed this Great Russian identity and in the 1970s–1980s national separatism was already too strong to be suppressed by force.[8] Likhachev's idea of Russia was not about preserving the empire against the will of national minorities, but rather about a commonwealth of culture, a 'realm of spirit', based on the past. 'Petersburg and Moscow remained centres of culture for Georgia and Armenia,' he wrote. 'People of Polish and Finnish cultures always found their friends there. The study of the languages of the Siberian people originated there as well.' He also defined the intelligentsia, whose language of culture was Russian, as a factor of unity: 'I believe that the Russian intelligentsia will still play its role in the pacification of nationalist enmities in our country, as well as abroad. This is one of the intelligentsia's historical missions.'[9]

Likhachev's idealistic appeal ran into a wall of incomprehension. Russian nationalists believed that 'a realm of spirit' was a spurious dream. Yuri Bondarev, a highly placed Soviet writer who sympathized with Russian nationalism, scoffed during the SFC board meeting at the notion that, 'any amount of love for the [Russian culture of the past centuries] could save us'. The Baltic and Georgian intellectuals also rejected the message. One Georgian writer, a member of SFC, called Likhachev's proposal to defend minorities as an insult: Georgian nationalists did not recognize rights of any minorities on the territory of their republic.[10] And when, a year later, D.S. came up with an idea of a Baltic university in Riga that could teach both in Baltic and Russian languages, Latvian poet Imant Ziedonis denounced it as a future tool of neocolonialism in the hands of the Kremlin. He refused to believe that Likhachev could come out with this idea. His signature on the proposal, Ziedonis said, was obtained from him by deceit.[11]

At the end of 1988 Gorbachev took a decisive step towards political liberalization when he authorized the constitutional overhaul of Soviet statehood. The supreme power, according to this reform, would become vested in the Congress of People's Deputies. Gorbachev hoped that the Congress would grant him legitimacy for further reforms and remain under control: one third of its delegates were to be appointed by the Party, the Academy of Sciences, and other Soviet organizations. The board of the Cultural Foundation convened to nominate delegates for the Congress, and Myasnikov suggested Dmitry Likhachev. The 82-year-old scholar objected. 'I have a granddaughter who lives in the Federal Republic of Germany. I met with her in the past and continue to see her.' After a momentary confusion, Gorbacheva backed Likhachev's candidacy. His new parliamentary career was in the making.[12]

He campaigned, predictably, on the theme of the decline of Russian culture and the need to preserve it. His focus was on the moral damage caused by the communist period. He recalled: 'During collectivization, many officers and military cadets refused to obey the orders to open fire at peasants; they chose instead to go to the gulag. How many Russians today would chose dignity and honour over their comfort, not to mention freedom and life?'[13] He also publicized the recent cultural disaster – the destruction by fire of the Leningrad library of the Academy of Sciences, the oldest library in Russia. Established by Peter the Great and conserved during the war and the Siege, it fell victim to an accidental fire. Hundreds of thousands of books were gone, including the personal library of Peter the Great. The authorities of Leningrad and the Academy sought to cover up the disaster. On camera, D.S. called the accident 'our cultural Chernobyl'.[14] He appealed to UNESCO for assistance, and contacted James Billington to obtain the copies of lost books from the Library of Congress. Finally, he demanded that the Academy could serve as a new and safer location for the valuable archives of the Pushkin House. He feared that another accident would demolish these archives which stored the manuscripts of Pushkin, Gogol, Turgenev, Blok, and many other Russian writers and poets. If that happened, he warned, then, 'Russian culture would be finished.' He publicly threatened to resign from the Academy if its presidium would ignore his request.[15]

On 25 May 1989 the People's Congress opened in Moscow and lasted for two weeks. Life as usual stopped in the Soviet Union. In the country where people had forgotten about free speech or public politics, the Congress was a sensational experience. Passions flared up when a group of deputies from Georgia demanded that the political leadership explain the use of troops to disperse an anti-communist and nationalist rally in Tbilisi where over 20 demonstrators died and hundreds were injured. Delegates from the Baltics and Georgia viewed it as a case of Russian imperialism. The Congress created a commission to investigate the case, with a number of well-known intellectuals and people of culture, among them Sakharov and Likhachev.

Dmitry watched the Congress with a mixture of fascination and concern. He said to the journalists: 'I had such an impression in the thirties and forties that nothing could be reborn; individuality was killed, only the yes-reflexes remained ... And it turned out that we, our people, preserved this sense of liberty. I am proud of it as a citizen and a scholar.' 'The Congress,' he said in another interview, 'liberated us from fear and taught us to speak the truth.' At the same time he remembered well that the sudden feeling of liberty in March 1917 led soon to anarchy and the spread of violence that ultimately ended with the Bolshevik coup and civil war.[16] Was the Congress an introduction to another Time of Troubles?

## 'The Fate of the Homeland is in Danger'

Likhachev took the floor only on the sixth day of the Congress. He repeated the main theme of his campaign: cultural decline was the most important source of the problems that plagued the Soviet Union. He warned the delegates that any reforms or attempts to improve the situation would fail. 'Without elementary morality and trust, social laws do not act and economic laws cannot be implemented.' He connected a low level of culture to the spread of nationalist aggression that poisons international relations. The Congress must take urgent measures to support major cultural projects and pour more funds into education and culture. He concluded with an appeal: 'The fate of the Homeland is in your hands, and it is in danger.'[17] Speaking to journalists, D.S. repeated his message even more forcefully: 'In the conditions of cultural degradation economic laws and regulations do not act, because people dodge them all the time and often succeed. Social laws and regulations fail, too. Therefore, one possible scenario would be a state of chaos – cultural and moral.'[18]

Only very few at the Congress, mostly writers and cultural figures, understood what he meant. The majority were in the grip of anger and political passions. The independent and assertive behaviour of the deputies from the Baltics and Georgia generated a political backlash. The majority focused their hatred on Sakharov, who was Russian and yet backed by 'aliens'. Sergei Chervonopisky, veteran of the war in Afghanistan (where he lost his legs), accused the Nobel Prize dissident of a lack of patriotism and disrespect for the Soviet army. His vitriolic speech ended with a triple slogan:

'Great Power. Homeland. Communism.' Sobchak compared this moment to a political earthquake: as if some kind of powerful spring yanked him from his seat – thousands of deputies stood up applauding furiously. Sakharov walked to the podium and attempted to explain his stance, yet was overwhelmed by the storm of collective venom.[19]

Likhachev saw the scene of Sakharov's maltreatment as another illustration of moral and cultural disease. 'Andrei Dmitrievich appeared at the Congress as the Visitor from the story about the Great Inquisitor. They shouted: "Crucify him! Crucify!" And he was befuddled, with his naive blue eyes, almost like a child. He looked at everything around him and simply did not understand what was happening. They did not listen to him – listened to the myth about him.'[20] The Congress divided the Soviet intelligentsia, instead of uniting it. Although all delegates spoke in Russian, they expressed incompatible, often nationalist visions. The Georgian and Baltic delegates voiced their anti-Russian sentiments. And Russians began to respond in kind. Village prose writer Valentin Rasputin turned to the Baltic and Georgian delegates and reproached them for their Russophobic views. If you wanted, 'to bid farewell to this country,' Rasputin said, then

> perhaps Russia should leave the Union as well? After all, you all blame her for all your troubles, ... her backwardness and clumsiness thwart your progressive strivings ... Perhaps it would be better this way? By the way, it would help the Russians to turn inward and resolve their own problems. We still have some resources, natural and human, and our hands can still do some work. Then we would be able to utter the word 'Russkyi', to discuss national consciousness, without fear of being portrayed as nationalists.[21]

When asked by journalists about this episode, Likhachev said that he understood Rasputin's anger. The communist regime, he explained, 'humiliated and robbed Russia so much, that Russians can hardly breathe'. He wanted to have a dialogue with the Russian writers and moderate nationalists.[22]

In his Congress delegate's form Likhachev wrote: '[I] do not belong to any party; do not join any social organizations and movements (i.e. groups, parties, and organizations of a political nature).'[23] He wanted to represent the interests of thousands of librarians, museum curators, archival workers, and defenders of cultural monuments.[24] During 1989, he established good relations with Nikolai Gubenko, Soviet actor and a man with a tragic life, who became the first minister of culture approved by the Congress. With Gubenko's assistance, Likhachev and other intellectuals obtained money for the main Moscow public libraries. In Leningrad, he continued to lobby for restoration of the destroyed collections at the library of the Academy of Sciences. His support helped to create a museum of Anna Akhmatova in the famous Fontanny Dom, the apartment where the poet received Isaiah Berlin in December 1945. D.S. solicited the restoration of cultural zones in the centres of Novgorod and Pskov. In Crimea, Likhachev lobbied for state funding to maintain and restore the unique constellation of museums and palaces so important for the history of Russian culture.[25]

Likhachev's name was also under the petitions to reinstitute to the Church ruined and misused complexes linked to the history of Russian Christianity. Among them was Trinity Court in Moscow, where Patriarch Tikhon (Belavin) waited for his tragic end, defying Bolshevik terror. With a group of philosophers, D.S. managed to lift the official ban on the name and works of Lev Karsavin, a Russian religious philosopher who had influenced him in the 1920s. Karsavin was arrested in Latvia by the NKVD in 1944 and perished in the gulag in 1952.[26]

On 14 December 1989, after an acrimonious debate at the Congress, Andrei Sakharov died from a heart attack. His funeral became a big event: hundreds of thousands went out in the bitter cold to bid farewell to the great dissident. Sakharov's body lay in state in the Presidium of the Academy, yet embarrassingly the Academy could not find an appropriate speaker for the funeral, because so many academicians had signed official letters to denounce Sakharov as a dissident. Gorbachev called Likhachev and asked him to speak at the funeral.[27] Likhachev, bareheaded in the freezing temperature, was the first to take a microphone. He stood next to Sakharov's widow Elena Bonner, Boris Yeltsin, Galina Starovoitova, and veterans of the human rights movement. The crowd of about 200,000 people gathered under the overcast skies. He opened his funeral words with a paraphrase from the Bible: 'One man who says truth can justify the existence of an entire people.' If Andrei Sakharov had not existed, then

> we the Russians would have remained forever steeped in shame. He was the only one that spoke on behalf of all of us. He rescued and preserved our honour and dignity when he gave his voice to defend the people persecuted by authorities. Sakharov defended human values, and his figure would be prominent in the history of humanity. He had no fear of power and thereby he revolutionized our perceptions of power.[28]

After Sakharov was gone, D.S. became the only one with immense moral authority at the Congress. One liberal delegate recalled: 'Likhachev was indispensable'. 'There was no other person like him in this land!'[29]

He shuttled more often between Leningrad and Moscow by night trains to participate in the legislative deliberations. When he could not come, for reasons of health, he still participated in legislative work from a distance.

In the spring of 1990, Gorbachev's ability to control the process he started began to fade. Boris Yeltsin, in an act of great political intuition, ran as a representative from the Ural district in the elections to another massive assembly, the Congress of the Russian Federation, the largest of 15 constituent republics in the Soviet Union. In Moscow and Leningrad volunteer activity by the liberal intelligentsia reached its peak: civic associations functioned at the Academy of Sciences and in the Writers' Union. Several younger members from Likhachev's Sector took part in electoral politics.[30] On 12 June, the Russian Congress declared itself a second seat of legitimate power next to the Soviet assembly and approved, almost unanimously, the Declaration of Sovereignty. The question Dmitry Likhachev raised in his essay in December 1988 suddenly became the touchstone of Soviet politics. What is a 'democratic, sovereign Russia' about? Would Russia replace the Union, reuniting other republics, such as Ukraine and Belarus, around itself? Would it just shed its empire? Many Russians believed that writer Rasputin had a point – 'Russia' could live better without other republics.[31]

In May 1990 Raisa Gorbacheva invited Likhachev to join the Soviet delegation that accompanied her husband for the Soviet–American summit in Washington DC. It was difficult for the octogenarian academician to make a trans-Atlantic trip, and he did not like to be part of Gorbachev's cultural diplomacy. Yet Likhachev had an important cultural commitment in Washington: an exhibition dedicated to a Millennium of Russian Christianity was being prepared for opening at the Library of Congress. The exhibition title was, 'Living Traditions of the Russian Faith: Books and Manuscripts of the Old Believers'. It featured exhibits from the library's own depositaries, but mainly from the Old Collection of the Pushkin House.[32] On 31 May, the exhibition opened with great pomp in the presence of Barbara Bush and a big retinue of American and Soviet visitors around the exhibition. Raisa opened the exhibition, Billington spoke next. 'When the name of Dmitryi Sergeevich Likhachev was announced,' recalled a Russian witness, he could not even get to the microphone, which was 'blocked by the crowd of Congressmen'.[33] Likhachev did not like the ceremony. Raisa regarded the exhibition as just another chance to praise her husband's policies. He was very upset when some people suggested that the Gorbachevs just used him and Russian culture to gain political legitimacy in the West.[34]

The blossom of freedoms in the Soviet Union also affected his attitudes. In April 1990 received an Easter card from Arkady Selivanov, his last living friend from the Space Academy. 'Christ is risen indeed, my dear friend and

comrade Dima! Greetings to You and all Yours on this Luminous Holiday...
Thank you for your memories and attention...'[35] In 1928 Arkady and Dima
had been arrested for their religious beliefs, and now, 70 years later, they could
finally send and receive an Easter card by regular mail. In his speech at
Sakharov's funeral D.S. spoke about how the Nobel prize dissident changed
Soviet perceptions of power. And what about his own relationship with the
Gorbachevs? What about his role as 'a Chinese adviser' in what appeared to be
the Spring of Liberation in the Soviet Union?

On the eve of his trip to Washington, Likhachev wrote for *Izvestia*, one of
the leading glasnost newspapers, an essay with a remarkably critical
assessment of SFC work. The article appeared when the Gorbachevs and D.S.
stayed in Washington. He came up with an idea of the Cultural Foundation,
Likhachev wrote, as a non-government institution, a national club for the
intelligentsia and the best elements of society. But gradually he became
frustrated by lack of progress and the bureaucratic style of work. 'How much
remains unfulfilled!' he lamented. 'How many incipient programmes went
nowhere!'[36] Likhachev proposed to restructure the SFC into a truly public
association and to lean on volunteer scientists and local associations of
intelligentsia.[37] Some intelligentsia-style activists shared this attitude.
Kataeva-Lytkina, curator of the Tsvetaeva museum, believed that Raisa and
party apparatchiks were the main obstacles in the foundation's work.[38]
Georg Myasnikov worried that D.S. took a wrong turn. He had long
believed that the academician 'plays god and hovers above clouds'. The
intelligentsia activists, Myasnikov argued, had no practical skills to
implement any of their ideas and projects. 'Is it really possible to count
seriously on a bunch of loud-mouthed intellectuals?'[39] Raisa Gorbacheva
believed that by his criticism of the SFC at this moment, Likhachev did
damage to her husband. As Myasnikov recorded in his diary, she felt insulted
and planned to discuss the article at a special board meeting. For an
unknown reason, the discussion never took place.[40] The relationship
between Gorbacheva and Likhachev remained decorous, yet Lytkina recalls
one episode when Likhachev at the SFC board meeting urged that the
museum of private collections should be opened immediately. There was a
mass exodus of intellectuals and artists from the USSR emigrating to the
West and to Israel. Private collections and artists' works were sold on the
black market and lost to the public domain. Raisa appeared not to listen to
these arguments. It reminded Lytkina of December 1989 when Mikhail
Gorbachev treated Sakharov dismissively at the Congress of People's
Deputies. 'Dmitry Sergeyevich lost patience. He wanted to leave, stood up,
and walking with difficulty, moved to the exit.' Then he regained his
composure and returned to his seat.[41]

## How to Save the Patrimony?

At the peak of glasnost, the journal 'Our Heritage', among other publications, revealed to the Russian public the full extent of cultural destruction under the Bolsheviks. The journal published the diaries of Zinaida Gippius about the revolution and the private journal of Mikhail Prishvin who agonized over 'our awful, barbaric communism', and wondered what caused Russia's rapid self-destruction.[42] Soviet journals serialized Solzhenitsyn's novel, *Red Wheel*, about the origins of the Russian revolution.[43] In another article an art historian lamented: 'The total destruction of Russian country estates ... is one of the gravest tragedies of Russian culture.' Russian peasants and demobilized soldiers pillaged and smashed to pieces everything they did not understand or value.[44]

Could the Russians learn these bitter lessons from the past and refrain from another self-destructive cycle? In April 1990, Likhachev returned again to the issue of Russian national character. He wrote in a leading philosophical journal that the Russians, 'have always been distinguished by a subconscious striving to sacrifice themselves to a sacred cause'. What cause would they embrace now as the old authoritarian system was crumbling? Could the dark, anarchic, violent aspects of Russian character prevail again as they did in 1917? Likhachev was fully aware of the danger: he claimed publicly that it 'must be deflected'.[45] In late September 1990 Likhachev read a new essay by Aleksandr Solzhenitsyn entitled, 'How We Can Rebuild Russia'. From remote Vermont, the famous writer warned his compatriots: 'The clocks of communism chimed their last hour. Yet the edifice of concrete has not yet collapsed. The danger is that instead of becoming free, we will end up crushed under the rubble.' Solzhenitsyn warned his compatriots against the temptation to keep the empire. He believed, however, that Ukraine and Belorussia would form a common state with the Russian Federation. The writer appealed to the Ukrainians: 'Brothers! Avoid a harsh separation! This is a folly of communist years.'[46]

Likhachev shared many of Solzhenitsyn's assumptions and evaluated the essay as an extraordinary document. Yet he was also sceptical about the practicality of Solzhenitsyn's advice on a union of Slavic states. The author, he noted, should come and see the changes that had happened in the country since he left it. 'The problems of relations among nations stand out more starkly and more tragically' than Solzhenitsyn remembered them.[47] A peaceful divorce of republics from the centre appeared increasingly unlikely, and bloodshed seemed to be inevitable. In October 1990, Likhachev, composer Georgyi Sviridov, writer Sergei Zalygin, and the patriarch of the Russian Orthodox Church Alexyi II (Ridiger) addressed national leaders of the Soviet Union, where Russians were in the minority, with an appeal for tolerance and reason. The text, published in *Izvestia*, raised poignant questions: 'Why is it necessary to turn away from the Russian language, which is historically common for many people of the former empire? Why are Russian books in libraries destroyed and teachers of Russian persecuted? Is it prudent to antagonize Russians by treating them as second-class citizens and urge them to go home?' The article ended in an appeal to the republics, as well as the Eastern European countries, to make a distinction between Russian language and de-communization.[48]

The fear of Soviet collapse grew. On 2 October, the President of the Soviet Union met with the creative intelligentsia, a meeting that Likhachev attended. All participants spoke about the grave crisis and compared it with 1917. Sergei Zalygin regretted that the intelligentsia, through speeches, articles, films and plays contributed to radical politics and runaway nationalism. Theatre director Mark Zakharov, who in June 1989 publicly proposed to remove Lenin from his Red Square mausoleum, now called for an emergency rule to prevent anarchy and violence. Another topic at the meeting was an imminent transition to a market economy. All cultural figures appealed to Gorbachev to prevent a cultural catastrophe by providing state funds and increasing state subsidies.[49]

When Likhachev took the floor, he proposed to develop legal guarantees for the survival of culture. In his speech, he compared culture in the USSR to a bird. Finally, the bird was released from its cage, yet outside there was no food, and the bird still had to learn to fly in this freedom. It was a moment of, 'colossal importance; not for today, but rather for centuries to come'. After that Likhachev passed to a puzzled Gorbachev a typed-up document ponderously titled, 'The Declaration on the Defence of the Rights of Culture'. It was the duty of the State, he said, to ensure that during the painful transition to a market economy the fruits of culture would remain accessible to everyone. 'Companies and business enterprises,' he continued, 'should make obligatory donations to support cultural activities and to maintain cultural monuments and other undertakings. There should be a strong regime for the protection of art; attempts to export collections under the guise of leases to Western museums must be stopped.' Likhachev urged Gorbachev again to raise the salaries of librarians, archivists, educators, artists, musicians, 'and all the people of creative work'.[50] Gorbachev promised to look at the draft of the 'Declaration', but in reality the Soviet leader had no more time or money for cultural policies. The 'Declaration' ended up on the desks of Gorbachev's assistants.[51]

There was another special danger to the Russian cultural legacy on Likhachev's mind: the restitution of church property. In June 1990, the

Russian Orthodox Church elected its new patriarch Alexyi II (Ridiger), with close ties to Boris Yeltsin and the Russian parliamentarians. The Church began to claim back what had been taken away by the Bolsheviks; in fact, it acted as the first big corporation on the new privatization market.[52] The problem was that in Imperial Russia, the Church had no unconditional property rights; from the mid-nineteenth century the State began to transfer ancient and artistic religious objects, such as icons, wood-carvings and metalworks to museums, to preserve them as a national cultural patrimony. The imperial preservationists continued to be active even under the Bolshevik rule, acting 'on behalf of workers and peasants'. Among the objects they saved were the superb Cathedral of Intercession on the Nerl, and the Assumption Cathedral in Zvenigorod – the place where Rublev's icons were discovered, restored, and placed in the Tretyakov gallery of art. In 1990 the restored treasures were under the custody of the Ministry of Culture, and cared for in special conditions in museums, libraries and educational institutions. And the Church now demanded that all this should be 'returned' to monasteries and cathedrals. Meeting those demands would have meant rolling back the preservation of ancient Russian art to the conditions of the eighteenth century. Some monks and priests had already caused irreparable damage to valuable ancient frescoes and buildings that had survived the calamities of revolutions and wars.

Alarmed, activists from Soviet cultural institutions and the Minister of Culture Gubenko wrote to the Supreme Soviet and Gorbachev with a protest against the absolutist demands of the Patriarchy. His main thesis was that, 'the total return of all monuments of religious art to the Church may ... cause giant damage to the national patrimony of the Russian state.'[53] Likhachev wholeheartedly supported the Soviet cultural institutions against the Church. He learned from the letters of Svetlana Veresh that the Church took hold of Solovki and began to 'renovate' the cloister, obliterating the remains of the political prison and effacing traces of its medieval past.[54] The long struggle for Russian cultural patrimony against the obscurantism of religious neophytes was only beginning. Irina Lobakova, Likhachev's secretary, recalled an episode from the late 1990s: at a meeting with government officials Likhachev complained about the fading ancient frescoes in the Cathedral of Assumption in Vladimir recently returned to the Church. One Russian official remarked: 'Perhaps the Lord wishes these frescoes to disappear.' Likhachev's face darkened. He said: 'Then shut your eyes and try to cross traffic on the Nevsky – this would be a similar way to find out if the Lord wishes your disappearance from this world.'[55]

The worsening political situation, however, remained the source of his most immediate anxiety. In November he attended a big conference in Rome on the topic: 'National Question in the USSR: Renewal or Civil War?' And on 20 December the Congress of People's Deputies Likhachev saw how Eduard Shevardnadze, stuttering from strong emotion, announced his resignation, protesting against 'the coming dictatorship'. The Minister of Foreign Affairs concluded: 'The future belongs to democracy and freedom!' Likhachev immediately took the floor, asking Shevardnadze to change his mind. In January 1991 more chilling news came from Lithuania: the Soviet paramilitary units clashed with the pro-independence civilian rally; armoured vehicles were used – 17 protestors died and hundreds were injured. Likhachev sent a telegram to Gorbachev protesting against the use of force in Lithuania.[56]

Against this menacing background, the scholar of Old Russia developed a new project: to create a databank of Russian ancient literary heritage somewhere in a safe place outside the Soviet Union. During his trip to Washington, the Library of Congress made a great impact on D.S. It was a cultural centre like this that he dreamed about for Russia. The library purchased innumerable cultural valuables in the Soviet Union and from Russian émigrés. And he was fascinated by the new techniques of microfilming and scanning the documents. Likhachev came up with an idea of an initiative for the salvation of Russian manuscripts. He had in mind the collection from the IRLI and other Leningrad museums, but also the medieval collections of Old Belief manuscripts preserved in various places across the Soviet Union.[57] In November 1990, Likhachev flew across the ocean again at the invitation of Billington, to lobby this idea with him. He also spoke about this project with Rev. Ioann Meyendorff, the priest of the St Vladimir Seminary in New York, and a scholar of medieval Russia.[58]

This idea was vintage Likhachev. The main American library as a place for a databank of Russian medieval manuscripts and all other major cultural collections was quite extraordinary. Neither Russian nationalists, nor Nikolai Gubenko, Likhachev's ally on many initiatives, could support it. Yet D.S. considered national cultural patrimony as a spiritual 'realm' that existed separately from the State and territory. It was good to have Russian texts microfilmed and safe in the Library of Congress. In this way, like in medieval China or in the old Bulgaria, the collapse of the State would not affect the empire of the spirit – manuscripts would not burn, and would later become the foundation for Russian resurrection.

On 21 February Likhachev wrote to Billington again under the impression of grave news from Moscow. Two days before, Yeltsin gave a speech on national television and radio: he demanded Gorbachev's resignation. D.S. urged the Librarian of Congress to accelerate the talks on the manuscript salvation project. He also asked if it would be possible to raise money for producing facsimile editions of the preserved manuscripts. Billington wrote back with a more limited proposal, approving the idea of the microfilming of Russian religious manuscripts 'of unique historical significance'. 'Our first priority must be the preservation of Russia's religious heritage ... The [Library of Congress] is glad to be able to offer its support for this important undertaking. I believe however that the project must be managed with maximum efficiency and with persistent attention to its primary goal of preservation.' Billington demanded exclusive control over the collection and 'institutional access' to the depositaries of the major libraries and cultural institutions of Leningrad.[59] And on 20 May, he informed D.S.: 'I have received a promise for some private funding to get the project started. As soon as the grant is confirmed, I would like to convene the first meeting of the advisory committee for the project and arrange a trip to negotiate direct institutional arrangements between the LC and the Leningrad curatorial bodies that control the manuscripts.'[60]

In Moscow, Raisa Gorbacheva did not like the idea of Americans dictating how and what to do, and paying for the programme. British billionaire Robert Maxwell stepped in to cover the costs, as he always did with the projects where the Soviet First Lady was involved. With an eye on formal parity, the foundation reached an agreement with the Library of Congress.[61] However, political events overtook the progress of the project, and it would begin to function only after the collapse of the Soviet Union.

In July 1991, at the Byzantine studies congress Likhachev spoke again with Rev. Ioann Meyendorff. He had a very special request: to take to the United States the relics of Prince Daniel, the founder of the Moscow dynasty, for safe-keeping. D.S. had kept the relics since the late 1970s in his apartment, in a small box covered by books and several small icons. Meyendorff took the box with him to St Vladimir Seminary. In a special note, written several months before his death and sent to the Patriarchy, Likhachev explained what he did but without giving the exact date. Moreover, he implied that this had happened before Gorbachev's perestroika, as a result of his harassment by Leningrad authorities and the KGB. Yet the note contains a key to the real date: it says 'during the *last* coming of Reverend Ioann Meyendorff to Leningrad ...'[62] This was in July 1991, shortly before Meyendorff died. If this is true, this case speaks volumes about Likhachev's fear of the violent explosion at the end of the Soviet Union's existence.

## The Miracle of Transfiguration

Seven years after the Soviet collapse, Likhachev, during a television interview, said that Mikhail Gorbachev had something in common with 'Ivan the Fool', a very popular hero of Russian fairy-tales. He hastened to explain he did not mean to insult the Soviet leader and diminish his place in history. 'Ivan the Fool always thinks about people, not about himself,' he explained. People should be grateful to Gorbachev, he said, for the gift of freedom of speech and conscience. 'I believed we would come to freedom [only] after the civil war, after the rebellion of the countries subservient to us. And Gorbachev liberated in a bloodless revolution Eastern Germany, Hungary, Poland, and Czechoslovakia! Without a single drop of blood!' Gorbachev did all this exactly because he unintentionally started the process 'a really smart dictator would not have started'. At some point, Likhachev concluded, Gorbachev, 'should have left power like Cincinnatus, should have started growing flowers. It was impossible to achieve more than he had already achieved.'[63]

Indeed, in the spring of 1991, millions of Russians had had enough of Gorbachev. Political ratings showed him trailing badly behind Yeltsin in popularity. The Soviet President clearly lost control over the economic and financial levers of the sovereign republics.[64] In June 1991 Yeltsin won the presidential elections in the Russian Federation. Thus he, not Gorbachev, became a legitimate leader for all Russians in the multi-ethnic Soviet Union. Gorbachev, ruefully observed his assistant, 'feared that the Russian people would never forgive him for renouncing the empire. But it turned out to be that the Russian people could not care less.'[65] Yeltsin staged his inauguration as President on 10 July inside the historic Kremlin. All television channels broadcasted the ceremony live. Yeltsin took an oath of allegiance to the Russian constitution. The ceremony continued to the music of Mikhail Glinka's 'Hail Russian Tsar, hail our Orthodox Lord!'[66]

Then Patriarch Alexyi addressed Yeltsin. 'You assumed responsibility for the deeply sick country.' Seventy years of communism destroyed the 'spiritual order and integrity'; destroyed the habits of three generations to pray, think, and work. The patriarch called on the Russian president to be an 'anthropological realist', as the recovery of society would be very long, difficult, and painful. It would be wrong 'to rebuild life in Russia while keeping only bad things before our eyes. So omnipotent and pervasive was evil, and yet we survived and preserved not a small amount of faith, humanism, goodness, and light. And it means that goodness [*dobro*] did exist and exists now in our hearts, in our Russia. I am convinced that it is more important for us to acknowledge and understand this goodness, rather than evil.'[67]

Alexyi's words resonated with what Likhachev believed in and wrote for decades. Two days before the Yeltsin inauguration ceremony, Likhachev attended the World Congress of Byzantine Studies in Moscow. He sat next to his younger colleague Averintsev, now the head of the Biblical Society, and philosopher Vladimir Bibikhin. The patriarch attended the congress as well and spoke about Russia's choice of religion and culture made a thousand years ago. D.S. commented aside: 'Joining Europe so early was a great fortune for Russia.' European culture is uniquely vibrant and self-inventing, and 'we all depend on it'. He mused: 'As a historian of literature, I would say that in Medieval Russia even Oriental stories came from the West.' He then said that Dostoyevsky was wrong in his famous speech at the unveiling of Pushkin's statue in Moscow in 1881, when he called Russians the unique bearers of 'universal humanism'. In fact, it was a European quality. Bibikhin noted that Likhachev's face was anxious, almost tragic. The 'death of Russian culture, the result of violence and coercion, is irreversible [*nasilstvennaia smert russkoi kultury neobratima*]' he said. 'Now we should start building a new, open, European culture.' This would be the task for young Russians, he concluded. 'I live by this hope.'[68]

What kind of culture Likhachev had in mind, he explained in his remarks in Rome, when he attended a workshop in La Sapienza University in April 1991. European culture, he said, was unique among world cultures, because it centres on the idea of the individual (*lichnost*); it is universal in its attempt to embrace all other cultures, but nonetheless stems from the freedom of individual creativity.

> All three principles of European culture are inseparable from one another. To remove one means that two others will be destroyed. To remove universalism and acknowledge only one's own national culture means that freedom will be destroyed, and vice versa. National Socialism, fascism, and Stalinism demonstrated this terrible danger. Freedom of expression is a foundation of individuality. Only freedom creates human dignity ... The supreme mission of European culture, its supreme meaning is to preserve in itself, in its science, and its emotional understanding all cultures of humanity – both existing and those that used to exist.[69]

Still, Likhachev remained pessimistic and expected the worst. The antipodes of Russian 'goodness' triumphed in the epochs of Ivan the Terrible, Peter the Great and Stalin. And who would come after Gorbachev? 'Russian people are a people of extremes, of rapid and unexpected shifts from one state to another,' Likhachev posited. 'Therefore they are a people with an unpredictable history.'[70]

The day of 19 August 1991 was the Transfiguration Day (*Preobrazhenie*) in the Julian Orthodox calendar observed by Russian believers. On that day, Likhachev with his family stayed in their dacha in Komarovo. They had no television, but foreign radio broadcasts brought scary news: a State Committee for Emergency Situations (GKChP) seized power in the Kremlin; Gorbachev's whereabouts were unknown. The academic settlement turned into a beehive of rumours. It was the long-expected coup of which Shevardnadze had warned the nation. Yet nobody knew how far the coup-makers would go in establishing their diktat. Western radio stations reported that Yeltsin was not arrested, stood on top of a tank near the Supreme Soviet of the Russian Federation and called for an all-Russian political strike against the GKChP. Radio also informed listeners that Anatoly Sobchak, the mayor of Saint Petersburg, called for an all-city meeting of solidarity with Yeltsin and resistance against those, 'who want to put us again under the yoke of a totalitarian regime'. The meeting was scheduled for 10 a.m. next morning in front of the Winter Palace.

Likhachev woke up early, determined to go to Leningrad and join the opposition rally. He called for his car from the academic garage, as he had done so for many years. He was startled to hear that there would be no transport for him anymore. The octogenarian academician decided to take a commuter train from Komarovo to the Finland station; he was even going to hitchhike his way to the city. Zinaida had terrible fear. After Vera's death she became manic-depressive, and when Dmitry failed to come home in time, she was convinced that he was arrested. This time the danger was real and acute. Luckily, before leaving the dacha, D.S. decided to dial the telephone number of the city mayor. Anatoly Sobchak was elected as mayor on the same day as Yeltsin was elected president. Sobchak picked up the phone and urged the old scholar to stay home and wait for a special car that would pick him up. After an hour or more of anxious waiting, the car came with armed people to escort the 86-year-old intellectual. A kaleidoscope of stunning events continued: an hour and a half later D.S. stood on the podium near the Winter Palace facing the enormous square. It was the same place where in July 1914 Nicholas II had faced a Russian patriotic rally at the outbreak of World War I. Around 300,000 people showed up, including students, state employees, and also many workers from the major industrial plants. Afghan veterans were especially active, offering protection and defence against a possible attack.[71]

Sobchak opened the meeting at 10 a.m. The crowd chanted: 'Stop fascism!' Likhachev spoke next. 'Do not be seduced by the duplicitous talk of the coup leaders,' he said. 'Those who seize power always invoke national interests. Do not trust this! They had a chance to defend national interests a long time before, when they were responsible for the country and had power in their hands.'[72] According to witnesses, the scholar, usually so reserved, measured and calm in public, suddenly showed political verve and temperament. Rafail Ganelin, historian of Russian revolution, said that Likhachev at that moment revealed, 'a genius for revolution – a truly Russian feature'.[73] The Leningrad radio under Sobchak's control broadcasted an appeal signed by D.S. Likhachev,

D.A. Granin, and other Leningrad cultural figures: the anti-constitutional coup, it read, 'was aimed above all at Russia and the Russians', it was 'the cause of honour and conscience' to support the Russian government and its president Yeltsin, 'the supreme legitimate power in the Russian state'.[74]

Nobody on the square yet knew how events would play out: people expected troops to storm the Russian parliament in Moscow that night. This was a moment when the fear and anger Likhachev harboured for most of his life was released. He was moved and inspired by the huge number of people who opposed the coup. He did not expect it. When Sobchak's car brought him back to Komarovo, the academician gathered a band of little children from the neighbourhood and led them to the seaside. Still in his suit, with a tie, he began to fly a kite with them. He celebrated freedom and the spirit of democracy that he had experienced in his childhood on the same spot 80 years ago.[75]

In Moscow the coup began to unravel. On 24 August the tricolour Russian flag appeared over the Kremlin and the White Palace. The formidable, 'edifice of concrete', communism collapsed as if demolished by a magical wand. Victory was as unexpected as it was absolute. The defeat of the August coup made Yeltsin an internationally acclaimed saviour. On 6 September 1991, Sobchak and the Leningrad city council officially renamed Leningrad into St Petersburg. Many streets regained their pre-revolutionary names, including the street where Likhachev lived. Instead of the Prospect named after Bolshevik Nikolai Shvernik, it became again the second Murinsky Prospect. Likhachev expected the fall of Bolshevism all his life, yet when it happened, it was nothing short of a miracle. It seemed the same to the 'former people' and their descendants, who lived to see that amazing change. On the eve of the coup many Russian émigrés arrived in Moscow and Leningrad to participate in the Congress of Compatriots – the first reunion of Russian émigrés with their homeland. Some of them came to Russia for the first time and by pure coincidence became witnesses to the historical turn.

Euphoria evaporated within a month. Solzhenitsyn was correct in his forebodings after all. The collapse of the communist state triggered disaster in the economy and finances. On 1 December people in Ukraine voted in favour of independence and elected communist apparatchik Leonid Kravchuk as president. Kravchuk refused to participate in any kind of federated commonwealth with Russia, not to mention speaking about a union with Moscow as the centre. The last hope for unity expired on 12 December, when Yeltsin met with Kravchuk and the head of the Belorussian Supreme Soviet Stanislav Shushkevich in the remote resort of Viskuli. Acting behind Gorbachev's back, the three politicians declared the Soviet Union dead as 'the subject of international law and geopolitical reality'. The leaders proclaimed a nebulous Commonwealth of Independent States and agreed to manage together the enormous Soviet armed forces. Russia assumed the role of legal successor of the Soviet Union and a nuclear power. On 25 December, triumphant Yeltsin evicted Gorbachev and his staff from the Kremlin, and the red flag over the ancient Russian citadel went down for the last time.

The rapid disappearance of the USSR created a sense of enormous uncertainty and anxiety among millions of Russians. Those outside the Russian Federation woke up to discover they had turned into migrants in foreign countries. Russian nationalists were in a state of total shock: the Russian Federation was the rump of a big Russia they dreamed of in their imagination. Even some Russian liberal-minded intellectuals shared the sense of shock. They were taken aback when their allies from the non-Russian republics, such as the Baltics, Georgia, and particularly Ukraine, bade farewell to them. Independent republics ambushed the 'democratic Russia' with the same demands of unconditional and harsh divorce they had presented to Gorbachev and the Soviet Union. This was the start of a profound mutual alienation and the origin of many troubles in the future.

Likhachev was better prepared than most of his countrymen for the finality of the Soviet Union's collapse. He was happily surprised that it occurred without major bloodshed and a civil war. In October 1991, when the USSR was on its last legs, he said that he did not fear the collapse of the Union. 'We know what kind of a Union it was; it does not deserve to be regretted.' Still he echoed Solzhenitsyn's warning: 'debris from the crumbled empire, pulled into the vortex of events, can take with them our spiritual ties – those ties that are less visible but more important historically.' He repeated his old credo: Russian language and culture should remain as a 'realm of spirit' after the collapse of common statehood. 'I believe that Russian language for a long time would remain a connecting element in the cultural life of our country,' he said. In the cultural sense his imagined homeland encompassed 'the entire space from the Carpathian Mountains' in Ukraine to Vladivostok, 'the country that includes Georgia, Armenia, Uzbekistan, with all the smallest and larger peoples of Russia. I do respect national independence,' he hastened to add, 'but purely emotionally as long as I live I will not be able to consider the Latvians or the Armenians as foreigners.'[76]

His granddaughter Vera summed up his attitude as follows: 'He was prepared to sacrifice the political empire in order to preserve the cultural empire.'[77] In the light of what he said and did this meant a reconstruction of a Russian-European culture on the foundations of medieval Kievan Rus, Old Belief, the Great Russian culture from the imperial period and the heritage of the Silver Age. For a man in his late eighties, this was his last and most daunting mission.

# CHAPTER 10

# THE SMOKE OF THE HOMELAND, 1991-1999

> During the last years, I have become a realist, if not a pessimist. More than one generation should pass before Russia emerges renewed and powerful from the current chaos and savagery.
>
> D.S. Likhachev, 14 April 1993

After the August coup collapsed, Dmitry Likhachev sent a letter to Boris Yeltsin. He asked him to give support to the Cultural Foundation that, he wrote, gathered, 'a large group of progressive, active intelligentsia, and what is particularly dear to my heart, many promising young people'. Now, 'when democracy and reason triumphed,' he continued, 'the foundation can do more than ever for Russian culture.' He suggested transferring the institution to Russian jurisdiction. Yeltsin responded immediately and positively.[1] When Gorbacheva learned about it, she sent her letter of resignation. D.S. sent her a farewell letter of appreciation and gratitude to her and her husband; she was courteous, but deeply offended. Likhachev, she felt, had committed an act of betrayal to her husband. Dmitry Furman, an intellectual close to the Gorbachevs, wrote: 'Picturesque, to the point of grotesque ... this [man called the] "conscience of Russian intelligentsia" dropped the defeated Gorbachev without blinking an eyelash and switched to the side of the victorious Yeltsin.'[2]

Likhachev did not consider himself bonded by loyalty to the Gorbachevs. He believed that Yeltsin's victory was the best possible scenario in the tragedy of Soviet collapse; it prevented a possible violent disintegration as it already happened in another country, communist Yugoslavia. Yeltsin wanted to build a liberal democratic Russia in partnership with Western countries, and did not want to quarrel with other post-Soviet republics over borders and territories. There was another reason why Likhachev wanted to build his relationship with Yeltsin as a future leader. He wanted to be his 'Chinese adviser', this time trying to save the Russian cultural legacy from the new destructive forces: a market revolution and commercialization of the cultural sphere. In this advisory capacity, Likhachev sought to influence Yeltsin's thinking on another question: preservation of cultural ties among the parts of the collapsed Soviet Union, based on the unique role of Russian culture and language.

Yeltsin's Russia turned out, however, to be a very traumatized and unstable place, and Likhachev increasingly became pessimistic about chances, at least in the foreseeable future, to build a strong and democratic society on the ruins of the past. Other post-Soviet countries, such as the Baltic states, refused to be in Russia's cultural orbit and moved to join the West. And Yeltsin's entourage, after an intense romance with Western democracies, began to change direction, borrowing old ideas from the arsenal of Russian nationalism and a despotic past.

## Ashes and Diamonds

In January 1992 a new economic era began in the Russian Federation. Radical economic reforms by the Gaidar government unleashed forces of the market, above all in the financial sphere. The free floating of the ruble erased people's savings in the banks, as well as the funds for the institutions of culture, academic scholarship and fundamental science. Prices soared 2,500 per cent, and continued to rise with no end in sight.[3] The reforms plunged Likhachev's 'realm of spirit' into bankruptcy. Millions of cultural workers, including librarians, museum curators, scientists, university professors and academic scholars, did not get salaries for months and lost their savings to hyperinflation. The Soviet cultural establishment crumbled; the circulation of literary and cultural journals shrank from millions to thousands; thoughtful literary and illustrated journals, the main vehicles of glasnost and cultural projects, collapsed and gave way to pulp fiction and the yellow press. Likhachev's big Soviet academic salary of 2,000 rubles was turned into dust by the new market prices. He personally did not sink into misery because of his celebrity status: he got numerous honoraria and received a grant from German academic institution. Though the academic and university libraries stopped subscribing to foreign specialized journals. The manuscript salvation project was called off for lack of funds.

The Cultural Foundation, now under Russian jurisdiction and renamed the Russian Cultural Foundation (RCF), was haemorrhaging financially as well. In Soviet years, the foundation received 50 million rubles from the state budget.[4] In January 1992 its budget consisted of a heap of valueless rubles, and only 50,000 dollars. The foundation's remaining liquidity was placed in a high-interest bank account, and this interest paid the staff's salaries. Yet it was clear that without new sources of funding any reforms would be meaningless, and the foundation would have to close its programmes.[5] Georg Myasnikov was in despair. 'We existed due to the good support of the party structures,' he wrote in his diary. 'The liquidation of the communist party destroyed this powerful base. Nobody needs us among the advisors, administrators, and emissaries of [Yeltsin].' Likhachev, in his opinion, continued to 'daydream'. Myasnikov resigned from the Cultural Foundation in February 1992, bitter and without hope.[6]

Likhachev was already 84, and the weight of old age made travel between Petersburg and Moscow more and more difficult. Nevertheless, he persevered. At its board meeting in April 1992 he admitted that without Gorbacheva the foundation had to find 'a new face' and financial independence. He dismissed the rumours of his retirement. 'I have moral commitments, and I will not leave until the foundation stands on its feet and works in the right way ...' He was adamantly against putting the foundation on a commercial track: this would kill its cultural mission. The only alterative was to find generous donors. Who would give money, Likhachev wondered, 'without demanding everyday pledges of loyalty and gratitude, like the old philanthropists did'.[7]

The new Russian government, just like Myasnikov prophesied, had no time or money for the Cultural Foundation. Yegor Gaidar and his liberal economists in Yeltsin's cabinet cut state expenditures to the minimum. The creation of wealthy entrepreneurs and a partnership with the West for them was the foundation for a Russian democracy. Likhachev considered this to be myopic. 'Democracy built on the ruins of culture is not good for anything,' he wrote in May 1992. 'It is a pity that the current leaders of Russia do not understand a simple truth: for Russia the only chance to find a decent place in the world is ... our national culture.' Without its cultural baggage, Russia in Western eyes would remain an alien country of 'occupants and semi-Tatars'.[8]

Newly minted Russian entrepreneurs also could not be counted on for generosity. They had little in common with the legendary Russian merchants and industrialists who sponsored art before the revolution, such as Pavel Tretiakov, Savva Mamontov and others. In St Petersburg Likhachev joined the board of Sobchak's foundation for the 'salvation of St Petersburg-Leningrad', where he worked with a number of Russian businessmen and liberal politicians. Yet Sobchak, desperate to find money from business ventures, legalized gambling in the city, which led to criminalization and corruption.

Finding benefactors abroad was also problematic. The foundation under Gorbacheva received substantial support from several Western billionaires and foundations. One of them was British billionaire Robert Maxwell, who helped to publish the foundation's journal, 'Our Heritage', and pledged to assist the manuscripts salvation project. In November 1991, however, Maxwell died in suspicious circumstances while sailing on his luxury yacht. After his death, the British press revealed that he had plundered the pension funds of his 30,000 employees.[9] Other helpful billionaires were Armand Hammer and George Soros: yet they had their own agenda and had no interest in helping Likhachev to preserve the Russian cultural legacy. The greatest hope of Likhachev was assistance from the Russian émigré community around the world. D.S. dreamed that some Russians, who lived for decades in Western democratic countries, would return to the Russian Federation, and would begin to invest in its economy and its culture. The Russian state, he said, should turn to these émigrés, 'just as Peter I had once turned to European countries'.[10]

Indeed, some émigré benefactors, motivated by nostalgic patriotism, continued to donate to Likhachev's projects and the Cultural Foundation. Among them were Lidia Versano, Eduard Falts-Fein and Georgy Vasilchikov. The latter was an aristocrat who lived in Switzerland and worked for the Oppenheimer Foundation. In February 1992, Likhachev received a letter from Vasilchikov with promising news: the Oppenheimer Foundation had agreed to open a grant line for the Russian International Cultural Foundation in the amount of one million US dollars. The Oppenheimer Foundation was a charitable institution of Harry Frederik Oppenheimer and his son Nicky, the major owners of the diamond company De Beers, and the heirs to a global diamond cartel. From 1977 on De Beers had exclusive rights in the Soviet Union to the uncut diamonds of Yakutia in exchange for hard currency.[11] Yet the Oppenheimers were concerned not only about profit. Harry Oppenheimer was a Jewish convert to Christianity, a graduate of Oxford, and had a great philanthropic streak. The 'diamond money' from the Oppenheimer foundation became the biggest windfall for the Cultural Foundation.[12]

Armed with the promise of 'diamond money', D.S. planned to launch a number of highly visible programmes to attract Western attention to Russian art. His favourite project was to publish an album of the unknown works of Kazimir Malevich, from the vaults of the Russian Museum and private collections. Another planned cultural initiative was an exhibition, 'Diaghilev and Russian Symbolism': the founder of the Ballets Russes was a perfect figure to introduce the diversity of Silver Age art.[13] D.S. also continued to plan a Russian museum of contemporary art, from private collections and from new acquisitions. He knew that at the time many leading artists began to sell their works to Western collections, in order to survive in harsh economic conditions. He hoped to use 'diamond money' to purchase the best works for a future museum. His favourite candidate for leading such a museum was Vasily Pushkarev, known among artists as 'a new Tretiakov'. For 25 years Pushkarev worked as the director of the Russian Museum in Leningrad and used state funds to purchase thousands of valuable works of Russian art, even when they violated the established canons of socialist realism.[14]

Unfortunately for Likhachev, the power of corruption was stronger than his idealism. Most of the 'diamond money' never materialized or disappeared without trace, through the cracks in the foundation. Month after month passed and Pushkarev remained 'a director without a museum', without any budget or space. He could not even pay the debts to the artists for their works. Likhachev was furious. Paying money to the artists for their works was a matter of honour for the foundation, he insisted, like paying a debt after a card game. 'We have to turn to the Oppenheimers to give us hard currency,' he rumbled on. 'This is my decision!'[15] It was as if the spirits of his grandfather Mikhail and another grandfather Semyon Konyaev were speaking through him at this moment. Yet he was losing his battle.

He began to think about resigning from the foundation early in 1993. Larisa Nazarova, an RCF official, recalls: 'For him it was a very painful farewell. Financial difficulties and the situation in the country affected him, but the main reason was personal.' On 23 February, Lev Dmitriev, his deputy in the Department passed away. This shook D.S. deeply; he had been grooming Dmitriev for decades as his heir-apparent. He wrote to a colleague: 'With the passing of Lev Alexandrovich, I no longer have any friends. In the autumn my last camp inmate Selivanov died. After the death of sweet, clever, simple Lev Alexandrovich, I feel completely lonely in the Pushkin House.'[16] Like the tragic death of his daughter Vera, this event reminded Likhachev of the precarious nature of all his endeavours. He desperately wanted to sort out his papers and write down his recollections about the wonderful people he had met in the 1920s and in Solovky. Many years earlier he confessed: 'Hundreds of people shimmer in my memory. When I am gone, all memory about them will expire! I do not pity me, but I pity them.'[17]

Likhachev had looked for a younger successor in the foundation, but he feared that his replacement would be a Russian nationalist, an enemy of his cause. With the financial debacle looming again, the RCF board opted for the film director Nikita Mikhalkov as the leader. Mikhalkov's father had authored the Soviet anthem; he was a national celebrity himself and seemed to have the necessary traits for successful leadership: enormous charisma, an impressive ability to open the doors of the powers-that-be to the institution, and tremendous entrepreneurial energy. He also had an extensive record of public activism in the area of preservation of Russian heritage.

Likhachev, however, objected strongly. A human rights activist commented: 'While Likhachev, a grandson of merchants, was an aristocrat of spirit, the hereditary nobleman Mikhalkov was a mouthpiece of the Soviet mentality.'[18] Mikhalkov's worldview had no room for the principles that Likhachev regarded as fundamental for the future of Russian culture: European universalism, individualism, and freedom. The filmmaker declared himself a monarchist and promoted the ideology of a powerful Russian state as the only way to support a distinct 'Russian civilization'. He became a fan of Ivan Ilyin, the most authoritarian, rhetorical, and nationalist of figures among the leading Russian thinkers expelled by the Bolsheviks in 1922. Ilyin argued that Russia faced a hostile Europe, and liberalism was alien to its mission and national interests. 'I categorically reject his ideology,' Likhachev said about Mikhalkov to the foundation's board.[19]

Yet he had to consent to the election of a new leader: 'I will be in Moscow on May 21,' he wrote to a colleague from 'The Literary Monuments', and 'will make formal my retirement from RCF. Five years are lost. All this served a few people who wanted to enrich themselves.'[20] When he, to his dismay, saw the overwhelming victory of Mikhalkov against other candidates, he just could not force himself to step down and said he would stay as an honorary chairman. Yet the new leader unceremoniously marginalized him. Eventually D.S. sent to Mikhalkov a letter of his resignation. He cut all ties with the foundation.[21] A few months later, the magnificent Tretyakov Mansion of the RCF on Gogolevsky Boulevard perished in flames; the arsonists remained unknown. Many valuables, including paintings and archives, perished and disappeared. Among them were valuable gifts, including diamonds presented by Harry and Nicky Oppenheimer.[22]

## 'Citizenship in Another Country ...'

In the early years many wondered: What would be the role of the 'new Russia' in the post-Soviet space? What should be the policy towards millions of Russians and Russian-speakers who became citizens of other post-Soviet countries? American-Ukrainian scholar Roman Szporluk, found two camps among the Russians: empire-savers and nation-builders. Both camps consisted of people with sharply different views, yet none of them could square the circle. The Russian Federation was only a truncated part of the former empire, and still it could not become a nation-state. Empire-savers advocated the re-integration of Russians, Ukrainians and Belorussians into one larger state. And nation-builders complained that the Russian Federation still had too many national republics and autonomous regions. Yeltsin adopted the term, 'multinational people of Russia' (*rossiyskii narod*), as a basis for citizenship, and the term *russkyi* ('Russian') was reserved for an ethnic majority. Yet that did not answer the problems. Szporluk concluded that liberals in the Russian Federation 'need to propose their own democratic, tolerant, and progressive model of Russia'. Otherwise they might lose the ground to the forces of xenophobic and aggressive nationalism.[23]

Likhachev waged a different campaign. His mission was to save the Russian 'realm of spirit' that the forces of national separatism threatened to destroy. On 15 February 1992, newspapers published the text of an agreement, signed in Minsk by Yeltsin and the leaders of the Commonwealth of Independent States, the entity that replaced the Soviet Union, 'about returning cultural and historical valuables to the states of their origins'. This agreement authorized each state to send national experts to the museums, libraries and archives across the post-Soviet space in order to create systematic lists of what belonged to each national culture. This agreement represented what Likhachev abhorred. Four days later he sent a telegram to Yeltsin: 'I consider [the agreement] a catastrophe, without parallel in the history of our fine arts. It will rip apart the unified cultural realm and will turn the commonwealth countries into provincial states; it will also mean disorder and chaos, and cultural losses for all independent states, not only in Russia ... I implore you to halt the execution of this barbaric, antinational document.'[24]

Yeltsin's advisers for cultural affairs clearly could not grasp the scholar's stand. What was the fuss about? Why not restore historical justice and settle at once all the problems with the restitution of cultural valuables? In early March, the president's administration sent a bill to the Supreme Soviet: 'About the museum activities and museum organizations on the territory of the Russian Federation.' This bill incorporated word for word the idea of a re-division of cultural heritage according to its national provenance and obligated all museums to return all items they had ever received from other museums, universities, libraries and other institutions now located on the territory of other states. During the twentieth century many massive transfers of cultural valuables, organized and chaotic, forced and voluntary, took place on the territory of the former Russian empire. World War I led to the relocation of museums and libraries from the Western borderlands occupied by the enemy to the East. During the early Soviet period, the Bolsheviks also reallocated art from Leningrad and Moscow to the capitals of national republics as part of their affirmative action and enlightenment policies. World War II left behind an even more catastrophic landscape: valuable art disappeared without trace and great collections vacillated as wartime trophies from one side to the other. In a word, the parliamentary bill of March 1992 opened a true Pandora's box.

Museum officials gathered in St Petersburg urged Yeltsin to withdraw the museum bill: 'We are convinced this bill will lead to ... a sellout and pillage of [our] invaluable national heritage,' they wrote. 'In effect it will destroy Russian museums.' Likhachev's protest was the most relentless. He defined the bill as an act of, 'the conscious elimination of Russian culture'. Yeltsin's inept advisers who drafted the bill should be brought to the international court. 'If this policy with regard to culture persists,' Likhachev went on, 'one should ask for citizenship in another country. It is an indignity to live in a country whose government treats culture in such a way. I will appeal to the world's public opinion and UNESCO through the media, to rein in the antinational policy of the government in the area of culture.'[25]

Such a declaration startled many and triggered an emotional discussion. Some commentators in Ukraine and other post-Soviet countries believed that Likhachev sided with 'great Russian chauvinism'. It was dishonest, they reasoned, to refuse to return to the newly independent states the valuables that 'Russian imperialism' had taken away from Ukraine and other 'colonies'. Likhachev's old-time enemies among Russian nationalists attacked him from the opposite angle, arguing that he did not want to return the art that had been sent by the Bolsheviks to the museums in non-Russian borderlands. An op-ed piece signed by cellist Mstislav Rostropovich and writer Andrei Bitov, Nikita Mikhalkov and others, mused: 'While we do not share [Dmitry Likhachev's] readiness to apply for foreign citizenship, we understand it is a gesture of despair. Does this government have any sense of shame, to allow, with renunciation of Russian citizenship by the academician Likhachev, a new tide of forced cultural emigration?'[26] Yuri Lotman reminded readers that the historian Karamzin in the early nineteenth century had threatened 'to leave for Turkey with his wife and children', if the Tsar introduced a parliament in Russia. Unlike Karamzin, however, Likhachev was not a fan of empire. 'His words stem from his conviction,' Lotman explained, 'that freedom should be earned by the level of culture, not only by laws written on paper. It is painfully apparent today, that many aspects of the country's future are being determined by culturally ignorant people.'[27]

Likhachev patiently explained his position. He was against 'returning' to Russia all Russian art. And it was impossible to return to the Hermitage museum the masterpieces of Rembrandt, Raphael, and other artists of the Flemish and Italian schools, sold by Stalin's officials to the Americans.[28] The result of the redistribution of culture according to the national-territorial principle, argued Likhachev, would be chaos and net loss for all countries involved. Scythian gold exhibited at the Hermitage was found on the territory of Soviet Ukraine. To what national habitus should it be returned? In Ukraine, the Museum of Russian Art consisted of works loaned by the Tretyakov Gallery in Moscow. Should this art be sent back, leaving Ukraine with only Ukrainian art? And should many great artists who lived and created in Petersburg and Moscow be also 'nationalized' according to their countries of origins? Should Gogol, Bulgakov, Akhmatova and Malevich be considered Ukrainians?

In his letter to Yeltsin on 25 May, D.S. presented another convincing argument:

> For your eyes only. Russia has a colossal advantage over other republics. It is *culture*. If we preserve this culture, we would keep in a good-natured and honest way our advantages in the whole region of Eastern Europe. Only we possess the technical and scientific terminology. Science entirely belongs to us. Among the academies of science *only* the Armenian and the Georgian academies have real achievements; the rest of them are purely decorative. The Baltics aside, Russian language will remain everywhere in the textbooks for higher education and science. Preserving Russia's culture means to preserve us as a Great Power. This is the only way ... Thus our supreme task is to preserve culture, language, libraries, and museums.[29]

The entire biography of Likhachev proves that he was quite indifferent to geopolitics and the greatness of the Russian state. In May 1991 he wrote: 'There is no greater shame for a nation than seizing foreign territories, a violation of the sovereignty of another people under the pretext, mostly dubious, of restoring "historical rights".'[30] He was glad that Yeltsin refused to raise the issue of Russia's borders with Ukraine and other republics when the Union was dissolved. The letter was the only recorded evidence when he used in explicit language the concept of Russia's cultural dominance in Eastern Europe. Perhaps the scholar hoped to find a common language with Yeltsin, who did want the rebirth of Russia as a great European country. In any case, Yeltsin listened, and distanced himself from the idea of redistribution of culture within the Commonwealth. He inserted into the amended bill a paragraph sent to him by Likhachev and formulated by academician N.N. Pokrovsky. According to this paragraph, cultural artifacts from libraries, archives and museums could not be alienated from their cultural habitus by any government agency. Exchange of collections, 'transferred during the Second World War', could happen only, 'on the basis of parity, each time by a specific decision of the president of Russia'.[31] It was a success.

In 1993 political instability and social dislocation, unleashed by the sudden Soviet collapse, reached dangerous proportions. The Russian communist party re-emerged as a major force that capitalized on the mass misery caused by economic reforms, the nostalgia for Great Power, and the reactionary nationalism. Many liberals also changed their views, lamenting the 'dismemberment of Russia'.[32] Among Likhachev's younger colleagues this type of reaction was palpable as well. A member of his Department Gelian Prokhorov argued that 'new Eurasianism', based on the writings of Lev Gumilev, was a better concept for Russia than Western-inspired liberal reforms. Russia, according to the adepts of 'new Eurasianism', was destined to be a strong power, distinct and separate from Europe. Of course, Prokhorov argued with Likhachev, Russian culture is European. Yet what would the Russians do when others take advantage of their weakness? It is not enough to build an empire of culture. Without a strong state, 'Russian culture would be trampled. You need real force to defend culture.' Likhachev did not reply, recalled Prokhorov, but 'stern disapproval' was in his eyes. In his interviews and publications D.S. called 'new Eurasianism' a reactionary idea that erected mental barriers between the Russians and a 'universalist' European cultural legacy.[33]

In 1993, Likhachev was invited to lecture in Tallinn, Estonia. The Baltic countries belonged to Likhachev's Russian 'cultural realm'. The Baltic Germans for two centuries belonged to the imperial Russian elite. Riga and other Baltic cities were places where Russian thinkers, writers and poets could live in greater freedom than in their homeland, before and even after Soviet annexation. Likhachev liked to spend his holidays in Latvia after World War II; he met with many Baltic writers and intellectuals, including future Estonian president Lennart Meri. And in 1990–1991 he supported the Baltics' movement towards independence. At the same time, in his interview with an Estonian journalist, he asked Estonians not to blame Russians for their tragic experience after the annexation. Russians, he said, had 'suffered enormous, multimillion casualties at Stalin's hands, especially among the intelligentsia and peasantry'. On top of that, they ended up being blamed for other people's tragedies.[34]

In the crowd that came to meet Likhachev in Tallinn, Russians were in the majority. They bitterly complained about their precarious situation and their status as migrants. Likhachev decided to write a letter to the liberal mayor of St Petersburg Sobchak about this situation. 'Forty-eight thousand Russians,' Likhachev wrote to Sobchak, 'have no legal status and can be expelled any day in an unknown direction (they have no relatives and close friends in Russia).' In high school and universities the language of education was only Estonian. 'Russian books in the libraries are destroyed. Russian history in Estonian texbooks consists of one paragraph.' Cultural politics trampled on pragmatic interests: the Balts rejected Russian manuals and terminology for naval affairs and navigation in the Baltic Sea. With this, they cast away three centuries of experience and observation.[35] Likhachev's idea of a Russian 'realm of spirit' in the Baltics was in grave danger. And he hoped Sobchak would help to develop new policies to correct this situation.

'We should patiently seek to change [Estonian, Latvian, and Lithuanian] attitudes to Russians and Russian culture,' he advised Sobchak. 'And we should act vigorously.' The exchange programme should include tours by Russian theatres in the Baltics, exhibitions of Russian art, and invitations for Estonian artists to St Petersburg. Likhachev met with Moscow's ambassador in Tallinn and discussed with him his old favourite idea of a Baltic university, with a centre in Stockholm, and branches in all three Baltic capitals. This university, if established, could symbolize a continuous presence of Russian culture in the Baltic region from the Hanseatic times and would be 'accessible for Russian speakers of Estonia, Latvia and Lithuania.'[36]

Sobchak and other Russian liberal politicians, however, lacked resources and never worked out any consistent cultural policies for Russia's 'near abroad'. Instead, they regarded any discussion of this issue as the expression of aggressive Russian nationalism, even 'fascism'. As a result, as Roman Szporluk warned, they left this agenda to the Russian communists and ultra-nationalists to exploit. During 1993 the Russian Supreme Soviet, once the symbol of Russia's sovereignty and democracy, became a centre of mobilization for these rising forces. By the autumn, the Supreme Soviet and Yeltsin were in a political fight for life. On 21 September, the Russian president decided, as his biographer describes, to 'go for total victory'. By decree he abolished the Congress of People's Deputies and the Supreme Soviet. In return, the Russian parliament voted to rescind Yeltsin's presidency and elect a new leadership. The showdown was swift, bloody and decisive: on 4 October 1993 four tanks of the Taman division on Yeltsin's order shelled the Russian parliament. Yeltsin argued that his brutal actions were the only way to abort an approaching civil war.[37] He also used the situation to introduce a new constitution that gave enormous power to the presidency and created a weak new parliament.

Likhachev backed Yeltsin without hesitation. The old man added his signature to the 'Letter of Forty-Two' eminent cultural figures. This letter urged Yeltsin to ban 'all kinds of communist and nationalist parties, fronts, and assemblies'; to stop their newspapers and television programmes, and to disband the Congress of Supreme Soviets, the Supreme Soviet, and the Constitutional Court. 'History provides us again with a chance to take a leap to democracy and a civilized community. We should not miss this chance as we have already done so in the past!' The letter appeared in *Izvestia*, only on 5 October, as a retrospective justification of Yeltsin's victory.[38]

Likhachev consistently spoke against violence and aggression. In this episode, however, his fears of 'another October' of 1917 prevailed over his wisdom. He also strongly believed that force should and could be used against the enemies of liberal democracy, communist and nationalist extremists. Earlier, together with Galina Starovoitova and other liberal politicians D.S. supported a ban on the former communist nomenklatura and KGB officers from participating in politics and becoming highly placed state officials. The questionable legality of Yeltsin's actions notwithstanding, he recognized the President as the only legitimate ruler. Two weeks after the bloodshed, he addressed Yeltsin with a personal letter, expressing his sympathy.[39]

Unfortunately, 'The October Smoke' over the burning building of the Supreme Soviet caused grave political and legal damage to the young Russian liberal democracy. Already in December 1993 the party of Vladimir Zhirinovsky and the Russian communists received the largest share of the vote in the new parliamentary elections. And the Russian liberals never learned their lessons from the tragic events of that year, and never agreed what could be a 'democratic, tolerant, and progressive model of Russia' in harmony with its neighbours.

## Life's Accomplishment

On 27 May 1994, after 20 years of exile and emigration, 70-year-old Aleksandr Solzhenitsyn returned to Russia. Solzhenitsyn applauded Yeltsin for standing up to the coup, and in October 1993 he stood on his side against the opposition. Yet he was shocked by Ukraine's independence and was horrified to see how the Russian president gave away Russia's 'historic territories, access to the sea, and millions of Russians'. In his essay, 'The Russian Question at the end of the 20th century', published in *Novyi Mir* in July 1994, the writer defined what happened as the Third Smuta, comparable to the times of Boris Godunov and the Bolshevik victory. He also defined the radical economic reforms as 'the Great Russian Catastrophe', and wondered: Would Russians have the strength to survive as a people this time? Could the Russian people, culture and language be rescued after 'the dollar's blow'?

After landing in Magadan, where he gave tribute to millions of gulag victims, Solzhenitsyn flew to Vladivostok and boarded a special train car with his family and began to ride westward across Siberia. During frequent stops in provincial cities and towns along the way, the famed author met with his country's people. By the time he reached Moscow, he was firmly convinced that the Russian government, while touting political liberties and anti-communism, had failed to preserve the Russian people.[40] On 28 October 1994, when the worldwide celebrity finally addressed the State Duma, he faced a semi-empty hall. The ruling liberals dismissed him. For them, Solzhenitsyn was a prophet from another time from whom they did not want to hear. On 16 November, the President, who was rather nervous, received the writer and talked with him for over four hours. Solzhenitsyn tried, for instance, to persuade Yeltsin to return to Japan the four Kurile Islands, seized by Stalin in 1945. He also urged the President to grant independence to Chechnya in exchange for some territory. Yeltsin ignored these recommendations. On 11 December he signed a decree to crush Chechnya's separatism, and sent troops to the rebellious region of the Caucasus. For a few months, Solzhenitsyn had his own programme on the national television channel; then it was cancelled without any explanation. The writer retreated into the privacy of his new home near Moscow.[41]

Likhachev observed the drama of Solzhenitsyn's return and his one-man opposition to the post-Soviet political and media establishment. He admired the writer's personal integrity and uncompromising stance; his ability 'to tell truth to the Tsar' and to criticize the new liberal economic mantra. The media portrayal of Solzhenitsyn as an out-dated, flawed prophet offended and made him think about his own life's accomplishments. He was 20 years older than Solzhenitsyn, and his stamina had begun to diminish fast. 'My memory gives in,' he admitted in a letter to a colleague in 1994. And in early 1997, when Italian scholars invited him to lecture and receive the book prize for *The Poetics of Gardens*, he wrote to a friend: 'I do not know how I would cope with it. I've lost a great deal of strength lately ... A walk over ten minutes leaves me exhausted.'[42]

On 28 November–2 December 1996 his 90th birthday was celebrated with great pomp in St Petersburg. Yeltsin invited him to the Kremlin as well. At a gala inside the IRLI all the political elite was present, but the vast majority of the audience consisted of eminent writers, poets, actors, scholars and scientists. One observer cracked a joke: 'One can even imagine that a revolution took place, and the intelligentsia won!' The din of accolades for Likhachev, however, did not hush other voices who asked: what is the value of the hero of these celebrations? What are his life's accomplishments? Young journalist Dmitry Bykov voiced the opinion of sceptics: Likhachev, he wrote, was not a 'real *intelligent*' of the public myth. He is not a heroic dissident or a great scholar. 'There is no ground,' concluded Bykov, to revere Likhachev as, 'an idol and an icon of spirituality and culture.'[43] The young scholars of the 1990s did not know how much Likhachev's scholarship had shaped minds several decades earlier. They considered him a 'popularizer'. His love of

Old Russia and a continuing fixation on *The Lay of Igor's Campaign* appeared odd, out-dated, and not necessary anymore.[44]

Another judgement on Likhachev's accomplishments came from his younger colleague Dmitry Bulanin. Likhachev, in Bulanin's view, will be remembered for his role as a teacher of life during the 1970s–1980s, when his ethical teachings responded to the needs of millions. In this teaching, Bulanin explained, D.S. 'urges his audience to turn to Russian cultural heritage and asserts that acceptance of this heritage evokes one's national pride [and] positively influences one's moral feeling.' The roots of Likhachev's enormous popularity Bulanin found in the conservative nature of Russian culture and the country's search for moral-religious authority, going back to the Middle Ages. Bulanin argued that Likhachev was in a sense, 'the last Russian *intelligent*', the last symbol of the great conservative tradition.[45]

At the end of 1997, Likhachev responded to Bulanin, rejecting his theses, point by point. He dismissed his argument that he was an embodiment of Russian conservative culture. The Silver Age Petersburg of his childhood and Petrograd of his youth was not conservative at all. 'If conservatism was endemic to Russian culture as a whole,' he wrote, 'then how to explain the splendid Russian avant-garde, "Dyagilev seasons", in Paris?'[46] He was perplexed by Bulanin's statement that he was too young to catch the spirit of the old intelligentsia: the spirit of this intelligentsia, he argued, lasted through the 1920s. Finally, he was not a teacher of life and never had any 'ethical teaching'. He always preferred to act instead of preaching, 'according to my conscience'. He took efforts to save Nevsky Prospect in Petersburg, the Kremlin in Solovky, Novgorod and its frescoes, the parks around Petersburg; to protect the environment of Russian rivers and Lake Baikal; he published 'Literary Monuments', and helped to publish Pasternak's *Doctor Zhivago*. What *right* did Bulanin have to correct his biography?[47]

The Sector's colleagues were shocked by the rejoinder. 'What is so offensive there?' – some of them wondered. Bulanin later wrote that he actually wanted to compare Likhachev to Savonarola or Leo Tostoy.[48] Clearly, D.S. had a different idea about his life's accomplishments, which eluded even his Department colleagues. Above all, he wanted to be seen as a scholar and protector of the Old Russian legacy. And this was what attracted so many prominent personalities he met during the last decade of his life. This gave him in their eyes an aura of authority. Still, there was also his demeanour and personality that added to this authority. In May 1994, he impressed Prince Charles during his visit to the Pushkin House. The prince's foundation provided funds to scan all Pushkin's manuscripts as a form of charity. At the official ceremony Prince Charles said: 'It was worth coming to Petersburg only to get acquainted with academician Likhachev.'

On the prince's invitation, D.S. and his daughter Liudmila went to the UK and stayed on his estate at Highgrove in Gloucestershire. After Likhachev's death, Prince Charles wrote about his 'spiritual nobility'. 'Although he enjoyed incredible fame in Russia, he was not corrupted by it ... He remained an aristocrat.'[49]

Yeltsin also felt the effect of Likhachev's personality. Yeltsin's wife admitted that D.S. was the only person her husband 'was afraid of'.[50] An accident brought him and Naina Yeltsina together. During the first state visit by Elizabeth II in October 1994, the academician was invited to the Queen's farewell party on her royal yacht. It was very cold outside, he felt sick, and retreated inside the boat. The President's wife saw him there, called for a doctor, and brought a cup of tea to warm him up. Naina Girina came from a sturdy Old Belief peasant family in Orenburg; after the fall of communism, Naina became openly religious.[51] 'I was very confused,' she recalled about the meeting on the yacht, 'to find such a great man so near,' but 'soon we already chatted like old friends. Such a light was coming from him!' They began to meet in Moscow and St Petersburg; D.S. met with Tatiana, one of Yeltsin's two daughters.[52]

Yeltsin met with D.S. in November 1994 and asked him about his needs. The old scholar talked about the 'Declaration of the Rights of Culture', that Gorbachev had failed to implement in 1990. The President listened and promised his support. From that time on, D.S. could send private letters to Yeltsin with a note: 'Per agreement with Boris Nikolaevich, for the President only.'[53] This did not change the content and style of their correspondence: Likhachev's letters were courteous, discreet, factual, and always ended with a personal 'post scriptum'. In contrast to so many people writing to Yeltsin, D.S. never asked anything for himself. All his letters concerned specific actions. He urged Yeltsin to support the environmental movement. He was against the privatization of land; this, in his view, would kill the idea of the regeneration of a free peasantry, potentially a most massive group of free, autonomous citizens in Russia. Above all, he requested support for Old Russia's legacy: a museum to open, a medieval monastery to restore, or to purchase a valuable collection of manuscripts from private hands. This was a common cause that Yeltsin and he could share.

In July 1997 he explained to the President that Petersburg was the natural place for a television channel dedicated to classical culture. He lobbied for the Leningrad television company to become such a channel: it featured programmes that appealed to the middle-class educated public in and around the Russian Federation. Likhachev learned that powerful business people in Moscow wanted to replace it with another commercial channel based in Moscow. In his letter to Yeltsin, Likhachev argued that the cultural haemorrhage from Petersburg to Moscow, opened by the Bolsheviks and enforced by Stalin, must be stopped and reversed. 'Russia must not lose access to Petersburg's traditions in culture, as well as on television.' 'In the future Petersburg should influence [*okhvatit*] not only the Baltic region with its republics, but also all countries of Europe.' The cultural television channel was finally created, but in Moscow: this time D.S. lost.[54]

All failures notwithstanding, Likhachev persevered. His last letter to Yeltsin was written shortly before his death, from the hospital. 'I am now healthy again,' he wrote. He requested money from the presidential reserves to restore the classical terrace in the Monplaisir Palace in Peterhof. Mikhail Lermontov and Aleksandr Dumas admired the seaview from there. 'This is also my most favourite place, a most beautiful place. Please send my regards to Tatiana Borisovna and Naina Iosifovna.'[55]

## Burying the Romanovs

In one conversation with Bella Kurkova, a journalist from the Petersburg television company, D.S. said with confidence that Russians would see 'good times'. Kurkova wondered how soon. 'Maybe in a hundred years,' Likhachev replied without a twinkle of irony. 'Several generations should pass.' Kurkova was clearly not so patient.[56] In the 1990s, many Russians did not know what tomorrow would bring; public intellectuals competed in forecasts about the next presidential elections. The scholar of Old Russia, however, had a very different relationship with time. For him, the past was never quite the past. All past tragedies for him continued to poison and divide public consciousness in Russia, until resolved by acknowledgment, confession and repentance.

With this in mind, Likhachev got involved in the venomous politics regarding the burial of the last Tsar and his family. On 17 July 1918 the Bolsheviks in Yekaterinburg killed Nicholas II, his wife Alexandra, their five children, and their servants in an act of 'class justice'. Yakov Yurovsky, commissar of the Ural Soviet and the leader of the execution squad, did everything to hide the corpses. On his order, the Red Guard soldiers dumped the corpses into a pit dug in the middle of a marshy road near Porosenkov Log, poured sulphuric acid on them, and covered the pit with wooden ties from a nearby railroad shack. They burned the corpses of Tsarevich Alexei and one of the daughters, Maria Romanova, and buried the remains separately.[57] The Whites, when they controlled the region during the Civil War, investigated the murder of the imperial family, but did not find the place and mistakenly concluded that all of the remains were incinerated. Seventy years later, two professional Russian investigators went on a private quest and found the last Tsar's remains. Their discovery became an international sensation. British and American experts and scientists, along with Russian experts, investigated the remains using the method of DNA analysis which was still novel at the time. In Great Britain, scientists used a blood sample of the Duke of Edinburgh, the Queen's husband and grandson of Alexandra Romanova's sister. Their conclusion was unanimous: the remains belonged to Nicholas II, Alexandra Feodorovna, their daughters Olga, Tatiana and Nastasiia, physician Evgeny Botkin, chambermaid Anna Demidova, valet Aloisy Trupp, and the cook Ivan Kharitonov.[58]

In the Russian Federation, the investigation fell on hard times from the very start. Patriarch Alexyi and Church officials refused to recognize the remains as authentic. The reasons for that are not clear; some in the clergy believed in anti-Semitic tales that the Romanovs were victims of a ritual murder by Jews.[59] In 1993 President Yeltsin set up a State Commission for an official identification of the remains. The 'Romanov affair' troubled him: in 1977 he carried out the Politburo order to erase the Ipatiev house in Yekaterinburg, where the 11 victims met their terrible end. Yeltsin's patronage only made politics around the remains more divisive. The Russian communist party and Russian nationalists, who hated Yeltsin's guts, rallied behind the Orthodox Church. Still, in February 1998, the commission, now chaired by liberal politician Boris Nemtsov, accepted the scientific evidence and decided that 'Russian Emperor Nicholas II and the members of his family' would be buried in the Peter and Paul Cathedral in St Petersburg. The Holy Synod and the Patriarch stuck to their guns. As the funeral ceremony approached, scheduled for 17 July 1998, the anniversary of the terrible murder, most Russian politicians followed the Patriarch and declared they would not go to St Petersburg. Yeltsin, after two heart attacks, a poor political rating, and ferocious opposition, was reluctant to go against Alexyi, the Church, and the formidable opposition.

Likhachev followed this matter closely. He knew about the scientific details of verification; among the members of the State Commission were scholars he trusted. For him 'the Romanov affair' was very personal: he recalled his shock in 1918 when he had learned about the murder of the Tsar and his family. There was another aspect to the story: the crime in Yekaterinburg opened the gates for bloodshed, divided Russian society into those who mourned and those who reacted with glee and vengeance. D.S. agreed with Solzhenitsyn: 80 years later, Russian society continued to live in 'the atmosphere of February 1917'. 'Presentations, banquets, dancing, gambling, rich parvenus, all that had been there ... during the February revolution,' Likhachev recalled. Yeltsin's pro-Western government lacked popular support, and a new authoritarian regime could appear around the corner, under the guise of 'restoring order' and national pride.[60]

Likhachev was never a monarchist, yet many Russians at the end of the 1990s began to look with nostalgia at the old monarchy. This popular nostalgia became the object of manipulation and farcical intrigues. For many years Grand Duke Vladimir Kirillovich Romanov was the head of the purely symbolic Imperial House of the Romanovs, despite the fact that Nicholas II declared him unfit for dynastic succession. After the August coup, Vladimir corresponded with Yeltsin, 'on behalf of the Imperial Family and myself'. Sobchak invited the Grand Duke to visit St Petersburg, calling him 'Your Majesty', and 'Your Imperial Highness'.[61] In early November 1991, the Grand Duke and his wife Leonida came to Petersburg and mingled with the crowd of Russian monarchists and resurfaced aristocracy.[62] Vladimir died a year later, but Leonida began to present his grandson Georgy as an heir to the Russian throne. The rest of the Romanovs were aghast, but in Russia Leonida found a following, and the Patriarch gave her his blessing. In July 1998, Leonida refused to attend the ceremony in the Peter and Paul Cathedral. Likhachev learned about other farcical details: Georgy asked to pose for a photo on the throne in St George Hall in the Winter Palace of St Petersburg; he also planned to take an oath of allegiance to Russia in the Ipatyev Cloister, where the Romanov dynasty had started.[63]

Likhachev took it very seriously and began to act. D.S. urged Alexyi II to change his position. He also urged him, 'to acknowledge publicly the nature and extent of the Russian Orthodox hierarchy's complicity with the Soviet organs of repression so that the Church could be freed', from the past and reclaim its moral authority in the future, to 'better promote reconciliation in the society'.[64] This required a Church Sobor and a break with many prejudices and people. Alexyi, however, was unable to accomplish it.

Eduard Falts-Fein, one of Likhachev's admirers among the Russian émigrés, advised him to write to Yeltsin about Leonida and Georgy, a new pretender. According to Falts-Fein, D.S. persuaded the President to reject the request for a special status of 'the Imperial House' in Russia and thereby put to rest the monarchist pipe-dream. In September 1997 a liberal journalist asked Likhachev incredulously if there was any chance for Georgy to become the Tsar. D.S. calmly responded: 'He could have.' Impostors and pretenders often played on the gullibility of Russians in the past. 'Everything depends on a chance ... Some people may have followed [Georgy], taken faith in him.'[65]

The surviving Romanovs, including Nicholas, great-great-grandson of Nicholas I, and Prince Michael of Kent, a cousin of Elizabeth II, planned to attend the funeral. If Yeltsin did not attend, Falts-Fein told Likhachev, 'Russia would be disgraced in front of the whole world.' D.S. wrote to Yeltsin to convince him to come. The President's assistant mentions that Yeltsin received three letters from the old academician.[66] In one of them, written on 6 July, Likhachev wrote: 'I came to a firm conclusion: you must be present at the funeral. The Patriarch decided not to attend, and he is right *for himself* and *for the Church*: this requires a decision of the Church Sobor.' The remains, he continued, were certified with almost 100 per cent certainty. In a world where people are bitterly divided, 'one should have confidence in science, scientists, and professionals'. As for the speech at the funeral, Likhachev advised Yeltsin to say what he recently said to the mothers of Russian soldiers, killed in Chechnya: ask for forgiveness. 'With this, you will confirm that you are the leader of the nation.' Naina Yeltsina later confirmed that D.S. indeed convinced her husband with his letters.[67]

On the morning of 17 July, the day of the ceremony, Likhachev came to the Peter and Paul Cathedral with his daughter Liudmila. Daniil Granin, writer and friend, found him in good shape, robust and fresh. Upon his entry to the cathedral, Yeltsin greeted Nikolai Romanov, the head of the former royal clan. Then he opened the ceremony. Facing the coffins, the Russian president enunciated every word clearly, firmly, and with great empathy:

> It is a historic day for Russia. Eighty years have passed since the slaying of the last Russian emperor and his family. We have long been silent about this monstrous crime. We must say the truth: The Yekaterinburg massacre has become one of the most shameful episodes in our history ... Those who committed this crime are as guilty as are those who approved of it for decades. We are all guilty.

The murder, the Russian president said, was 'the result of an uncompromising split in Russian society into an "us" and "them" mentality. The results of this split can be seen even now.' This funeral, he said, should become 'a symbol of unity for the nation, an atonement of common guilt'. The President solemnly concluded: 'We must do it for the sake of our generation and those to come. Let's remember those innocent victims who have fallen to hatred and violence.'[68]

A long and beautiful Orthodox requiem service began. The priests, on instructions from the Holy Synod, did not mention the victims by name. Instead, they mourned, 'those who died in the years of ferocious persecutions, whose names, Lord, only Thou knowest'. Behind the President, stood the Romanovs, cellist Mstislav Rostropovich and his wife Galina Vishnevskaia, liberal politicians Boris Nemtsov and Galina Starovoitova, and other eminent figures. Immediately behind Yeltsin, closest to him stood Dmitry Likhachev. He held a candle in his hand, and his face was calm and solemn.

'All turned out well,' he wrote to a colleague. 'The trouble-makers were absent' and the boycott of the funeral by many politicians and nationalists was a kind of 'self-purification'. Fortunately, there was no money to convert the funeral into a staged event. In a newspaper interview, he expressed great satisfaction: 'The century began with the murder and ends with the burial of its victims. This is an event of moral order, and it would definitely affect the future of Russia.'[69]

He probably meant distant times. Meanwhile, Russian society remained divided and poisoned by politics. In August 1998, Yeltsin awarded Likhachev the Order of St Andrew, established by Peter the Great and abolished after the fall of monarchy. D.S. was the first cavalier to receive this decoration since 1917. The next one was Mikhail Kalashnikov, the designer of the world-famous semi-automatic weapon. Liberal critics were indignant: 'This is our new identity: with Pushkin in one arm and with the Kalashnikov gun in another.' In December of the same year, Aleksandr Solzhenitsyn was awarded the same decoration. At that time, however, the writer published his essay, 'Russia in Collapse'. All the years of Yeltsin's rule, he wrote, were catastrophic for Russia. He blamed the United States for building a new *cordon sanitaire* against Russia. Therefore, he refused to accept the Order of St Andrew from Yeltsin's hands. This time, the Duma and the Patriarchy applauded the writer.[70]

Likhachev sharply disagreed; he rebuked the writer for 'elementary lack of culture'.[71] As always, Likhachev went against the grain of the public opinion. And for all the criticisms of Yeltsin, he did not see any good successor to the Russian president. 'It is a tragic situation,' he said to a journalist. 'I fear very much there will be denial of freedom of speech and the press.' He feared that the next leader would take Russia back to authoritarian rule.[72]

# CONCLUSION

# DEATH AND BEYOND

At dawn on 26 March 1998, half-awake in bed, he heard a voice: 'Soon we will move forward.' He wrote later: 'The voice was loud, as if inside me. I did not understand immediately what it meant. Then it dawned upon me.'[1] Even in his teens, Mitya began to think about a fleeting gift of life, and many times only a chance and his guardian angels snatched him from the jaws of death: in Solovki, in Leningrad during the Great Terror, in the winter of the Siege, on the operating table in 1963, and in 1976, when he was attacked. His philosophy and concerns for a bigger cause pushed the imminence of his end to the back of his mind. After Vera's accidental death, however, he never stopped thinking about it.

Religious faith, Christianity, helped him to face the inevitable. 'Science that had once alienated us from God,' Likhachev wrote, 'now begins to bring us close to God.' Geneticists, physicists, and astronomers 'caught a glimpse of God's presence'.[2] He referred to scholars of literature as those who are responsible for 'opening minds' of people to the aesthetical and ethical Absolute.[3] He argued with the teaching of Nikolai Fedorov, late-nineteenth-century thinker, who famously argued that in the future science would be able to resurrect the dead. 'One should not resurrect individuals naked,' wrote Likhachev in his notes, 'without the milieu that surrounded them, without culture and knowledge.' He believed that instead the goal of science should be 'to resurrect human culture of all centuries in its integrity', to find ways for the preservation of memories. In this way, the problem of time would be resolved: everything would remain as if written by a needle on an eternal hard drive.[4] This was an echo of Mitya's reflections of the 1920s that gave meaning to all his activities later in his life.[5]

Old age, he commented, 'is a vortex of unforeseen, chaotic, and destructive forces. This is a powerful play of elements. This vortex drags you in. It is necessary to swim away from it, keep a distance, and resist its pull.'[6] Living to the end with dignity, avoiding helplessness and pain preoccupied Likhachev. He corresponded with Victor Zorza, a British journalist and a founder of hospices around the world. Victor's family of Polish Jews perished in Belsec after the Nazi–Soviet partition of Poland; he joined the Polish Home Army and ended up in the United Kingdom. In 1975 his daughter Jane died from cancer, and this changed his life and vocation. In 1991 he set up the first hospice in Leningrad-Petersburg, under the Russian British Hospice Society. In search of funds, Zorza turned to Western dignitaries and ambassadors, as well as Russian politicians. And four years later he approached Likhachev with a request to help him solicit support for hospices from Yeltsin and the Patriarch: 'I beg you, Dmitry, to call Alexyi personally.' When D.S. learned that Zorza became ill and wanted to retire, he wrote to him: 'My dear Victor! Without you, the hospices that you successfully organized in this country may become an easy prey for corrupt individuals. I have already learned that there are attempts to create commercial hospices in Petersburg. It is imperative to preserve the purity of the movement you have created ... I am very hopeful that you will respond to my prayer and would not abandon suffering people.'[7]

In one of his notebooks Likhachev recorded: 'From a moral viewpoint, you should live as if every day is the last one. And you should work as if you were immortal.' This is exactly how it happened to him. Almost until the last moment, he stayed with a clear mind, wrote, travelled and gave interviews. Until finally the problems caused by his ulcer, an old 'gift from Solovki' caught up with him. He was hospitalized with colon cancer and brought to the Botkin Hospital. It was the medical institution founded by Sergei Botkin, father of the physician murdered together with the Tsar. The doctors operated on him, but nothing could be done to save his life. His last words were about his wife Zina. 'I did not say goodbye to her,' he repeated. He died on 30 September 1999, two months before his 93rd birthday.[8]

His body lay in state in the Taurida Palace, with the military guards standing to attention. The palace, the eighteenth-century residence built by Prince Potemkin after Russia had annexed Crimea, saw the rise and fall of the first Russian Duma and the one-day drama of the Constitutional Assembly disbanded by the Bolsheviks in 1918. Thousands of people came to bid farewell to the scholar of Old Russia. The Academy of Sciences, many foreign consulates, the government of Lithuania and the Armenian and Jewish communities of St Petersburg sent their condolences and flowers. An Orthodox requiem service took place at the Prince Vladimir Cathedral, where Dmitry Likhachev had mourned his father in 1942. The Sector scholars attended the service; on the previous evening they read the psalms over the coffin of their longtime leader. Dmitry's remains, according to his wish, were buried in the familial grave next to his mother, daughter and brother Yuri at the Komarovo cemetery. His cross of light grey granite was in the vicinity of another cross on the grave of Anna Akhmatova. Naina Yeltsina attended all ceremonies, including the wake at the Pushkin House and the Orthodox service.[9] His death left his wife and daughter devastated. Zina died in April 2001; Mila passed away three and a half months later.

All Russian television channels interrupted their programmes to announce Likhachev's death. One announcer said: 'Now the century has really ended for Russia.' Sergei Averintsev, one of Likhachev's younger friends, compared the deceased to a *mystagogue* in ancient Greece. Mystery and charisma cannot be fully explained. 'We are bidding farewell to the cultural type that cannot be resurrected,' he wrote. 'We shall never see such people again. In these days we must recall with gratitude that he defended the values of the cultural tradition that he embodied, against the power of fear and indifference during the Soviet decades. He was often alone.'[10] Outside Russia those who admired him summed up his scholarly impact. Robin Milner-Gulland wrote in his essay that Likhachev was 'less a miner of hidden depth than a maker of maps' across centuries and cultures. He was, the British scholar continued, always fascinated with the dynamics, transitions, metamorphosis, movement. 'This hunger for dynamism', very modern by nature, remained anchored in 'his continual, and evidently growing, preoccupation with the great constants of European culture'.[11]

His life and works became a part of dynamic Russian culture. He left behind an immense collection of works and publications; his books continue to be published and read; the Department of Ancient Russian Literature still publishes its 'Works'; his monumental 'Literary Monuments' remain the hallmark of academic editions. He also managed to edit and annotate 12 volumes of 'Monuments of Old Russian Literature' (1978–1994), and in 1997 launched the 20-volume 'Library of Old Russian literature', the most comprehensive collection on this subject that had ever existed.[12] Yet his last mission: the translation of Russian 'realm of spirit' into an open and humanist Russian culture, remained unfinished, contested, and, by many indications, undermined. There is nobody of Likhachev's stature on the horizon who could continue his mission; instead of 'foxes' and 'hedgehogs' in Isaiah Berlin's taxonomy, there is a tendency to relativize and trivialize any kind of truth. 'Cultural elites' in Russia have other, more down-to-earth and mercenary concerns. Under Vladimir Putin, the discussions about an idea of Russia turned again to the illiberal and xenophobic 'Eurasianism'; conservative nationalism from Ivan Ilyin to Aleksandr Solzhenitsyn became fashionable. With this new turn, Russian intellectuals fell again into a twin trap: some of them began to express loathing for 'Russia and Russian people' who failed to live up to their expectations; others began to praise a 'special Russian civilization', based on Orthodoxy and European conservative values that the liberals in Europe allegedly betrayed. This is the trap that D.S. had avoided and consistently opposed.

In the West, too many people began to treat Russia again as an eternal source of trouble. Likhachev, in his bouts of pessimism, envisaged this development. In 1992 he wrote to his classmate in the School of Karl Mai: 'Everything will indeed disappear when we pass away. Nobody will remember real Russia. Instead, they will think that Russia has always been a dirty, dark country that retarded civilization. Nobody will believe that Russia had once been wealthy and cultured. And those would know it will be called "nationalists" and "Black Hundreds".'[13]

Yet there is always hope. The grand idea of a Russia in a 'concert of national cultures', as mentioned in the preface of this book, may no longer look as utopian and marginal as it was twenty, even ten years ago. One of many things that 'the Russian fox' from Petersburg learned well was patience and perseverance, combined with a gift of looking ahead, across many years beyond the confines of an individual life. Likhachev demonstrated with his own life that a Russian idea could overcome the temptations of nationalism and move, across many trials and frustrations, to the idea of supranational humanity, based on European values. His intellectual biography can serve as an inspiration for generations of open-minded Russians and Western students of Russia in the decades to come.

# NOTES

## Preface   A Russian Fox

1. Nikolai Riazanovsky, 'Dmitry Likhachev i Rossiia: kriticheskaia otsenka', http://likhachev.lfond.spb.ru/Memoirs/rjazanovskii.htm.
2. http://www.britannica.com/biography/Dmitry-Sergeyevich-Likhachev.
3. D.S. Likhachev, *Vospominaniia. Razdumia. Raboty Raznykh Let* (St Petersburg: Ars, 2006), vol. 1, pp. 122, 124.
4. D.S. Likhachev to A.L. Grishunin, 12 September 1996, T.L. Latypova, V.I. Bronnikova, eds, 'Iz epistoliarnogo naslediia D.S. Likhacheva'. This is an unpublished collection of Likhachev's correspondence with scholars, literary figures and artists (Moscow, 2008). The author thanks Vera Zilitinkevich-Tolz for providing a copy.

## Chapter 1   Vanishing Russia, 1906–1921

1. D.S. Likhachev, *Vospominaniia. Razdumia. Raboty Raznykh Let* (hereafter: *VRL*) vol. 1 (St Petersburg: Ars, 2006), pp. 19–22, 24–29. 'Vstrecha v Kontsertnoi studii Ostankino 12 marta 1986 g', E.V. Galperina, ed., *Ostankinskie vechera* (Moscow: Iskusstvo, 1989), pp. 111–132.
2. D.S. Likhachev, *VRL*, vol. 1, p. 33.
3. D.S. Likhachev, the introduction to: S.S. Bychkov, ed., *Sviataia Rus. Zhizneopisaniia dostopamiatnykh liudei zemly Russkoi (X–XX vv)* (Moscow: Moskovsky Rabochii), pp. 6–7.
4. D.S. Likhachev, *VRL*, vol. 1, p. 33.
5. Wayne Dowler, *Russia in 1913* (DeKalb, IL: Northern Illinois University Press, 2010), p. 90; Likhachev admitted in the 1980s that his parents, while influenced by the ethos of the intelligentsia, were not quite part of it. Interview by Urmas Ott with Dmitry Sergeevich Likhachev, early fall 1989, http://www.youtube.com/watch?vj1Lpsny1hKE.
6. B.I. Kolonitsky, 'Intelligentsiia v kontse XIX – nachale XX veka: Samosoznaniie sovremennikov i issledovatelskiie podkhody', p. 182.
7. D.S. Likhachev's letter to Prof. Agerton, in: D.S. Likhachev, *VRL*, vol. 3, p. 488.
8. On the origins of a holistic cultural nationalism among Russian liberal intellectuals, see Vera Tolz, *Russia's Own Orient: The Politics of Identity and Oriental Studies in the Late Imperial and Early Soviet Periods* (London: Oxford University Press, 2011), pp. 34–38; Emily D. Johnson. *How St Petersburg Learned to Study Itself: The Russian Idea of Kraevedenie*

(University Park, PA: Pennsylvania State University Press, 2006); on the missing English notion see Eric Hobsbawm, *Interesting Times* (London: Time Warner books, 2002), p. 20.

9. Richard S. Wortman, *Scenarios of Power. Myth and Ceremony in Russian Monarchy*. Vol. 1: *From Peter the Great to the Death of Nicholas I* (Princeton, NJ: Princeton University Press, 1995).
10. D.S. Likhachev, 'V.M. Zhirmunsky – svidetel i uchastnik literaturnogo protsessa pervoi poloviny XX v.', in: V.M. Zhirmunsky, *Teoriia literatury. Poetika. Stilistika* (Leningrad: Nauka Yazyk, 1977), pp. 5–14.
11. Emily D. Johnson, *How St Petersburg Learned to Study Itself*, pp. 40–41, 46–48.
12. D.S. Likhachev, 'Schastie i neschastia v moei zhizni (vmesto avtobiografii)' *Mansarda* 1 (1996), p. 47; Interview of Urmas Ott with Dmitry Sergeevich Likhachev, early autumn 1989, http://www.youtube.com/watch?v=j1Lpsny1hKE.
13. On the life of the Russian aristocracy on the eve of the revolution see: Douglas Smith, *The Former People. The Final Days of the Russian Aristocracy* (New York: Farrar, Straus, Giroux, 2012); D.S. Likhachev, *VRL*, vol. 1, p. 53.
14. Dmitry Likhachev, *Poeziia sadov. K semantike sadovo-parkovykh stilei* (Leningrad: Nauka, 1982).
15. See Likhachev's comments in his television talk at Ostankino, on 12 March 1986, E.V. Galperina, ed., *Ostankinskiie vechera* (Moscow: 1989), pp. 111–132.
16. D.S. Likhachev, *VRL*, vol. 2, p. 270.
17. D.S. Likhachev, *Vospominaniia*, pp. 93–94. On Russian Populism, see Franco Venturi, *Roots of Revolution. A History of Populist and Socialist Movements in Nineteenth Century Russia* (Chicago: University of Chicago Press, 1983) (originally published in 1960).
18. Historians, not quite logically, emphasize the rapid development of non-Russian national identities, ignoring the rise of the Great Russian identity. See Ronald Suny, ed., *Cambridge History of Russia* (New York/London: Cambridge University Press, 2008).
19. Vladimir Nabokov, *Speak Memory: An Autobiography Revisited* (New York: G.P. Putnam's Sons, 1966), p. 244.
20. D.S. Likhachev, *Zametki i nabliudeniia. Iz zapisnykh knizhek raznykh let* (Leningrad: Sovetskii pisatel, 1989), p. 223.
21. D.S. Likhachev, *VRL*, vol. 1, pp. 88–93.
22. Stephen Lovell, *Summerfolk: A History of the Dacha, 1710–2000* (Ithaca, NY: Cornell University Press, 2003); also see Olga Malinova-Tziafeta, *Iz goroda na dachu. Sotsiokulturnyie faktory osvoieniia dachnogo prostranstva vokrug Peterburga (1860–1914)* (St Petersburg: European University, 2013).
23. D.S. Likhachev, *VRL*, pp. 70–82; see also Likhachev's interview by Urmas Ott, October 1990, http://www.youtube.com/watch?v=j1Lpsny1hKE.
24. D.S. Likhachev, letter to B.V. Shklovsky, 20 April 1982, *Iz epistoliarnogo naslediia D.S. Likhacheva*, an unpublished collection of letters (Moscow 2008), courtesy of Vera Zilitinkevich-Tolz; Likhachev's personal notebook, 1972–1975, from the personal archive of Vera Zilitinkevich-Tolz.
25. Mark D. Steinberg, *Petersburg Fin de Siecle* (New Haven: Yale University Press, 2011), pp. 12–13; John E. Bowlt, *Moscow and St Petersburg, 1900–1920: Art, Life, and Culture of the Russian Silver Age* (London: Vendome Press, 2008), pp. 11–13, 374; also his: *The Silver Age: Russian Art of the Early Twentieth Century and the 'World of Art' Group* (Newtonville, MA: Oriental Research Partners, 1979); Vladimir Veidle, *Zimnee solntse. Iz rannikh vospominanii* (Washington: Viktor Kamkin Inc, 1976), http://lib.rus.ec/b/356411/read.

26. Vera Tolz, *Russian Academicians and the Revolution*, p. 25; also her: *Russia's Own Orient*. For other bearers of this type of identity see: 'V.D. Nabokov, Liberal i patriot', *Zvezda* 7 (2009); Michael Karpovich, 'Two Types of Russian Liberalism: Maklakov and Miliukov', in *Continuity and Change in Russian and Soviet Thought*, E.J. Simmons, ed. (Cambridge, MA: Harvard University Press, 1955), pp. 129–143.
27. Peter Struve, 'Intelligentsia i natsionalnoie litso', *Slovo* 10 March (1911), http://www.angelfire.com/nt/oboguev/images/struve.htm. See also: Richard Pipes, *Struve: Liberal on the Right, 1905–1944* (Cambridge, MA: Harvard University Press, 1980); Olga Yu. Malinova, *Liberalnyi natsionalizm (seredina XIX – nachalo XX veka)* (Moscow: RIK Rusanova, 2000); Olga Zhukova, 'Edinstvo kultury i politiki: liberalno-konservativnyi proekt P.B. Struve v sozdanii Rossii', in: O.A. Zhukova, V.K. Kantor, eds, *Petr Berngardovich Struve* (Moscow: ROSSPEN, 2012), esp. pp. 105–115.
28. Mark von Hagen, 'The Great War and the Mobilization of Ethnicity', in: *Post-Soviet Political Order: Conflict and State-Building*, Barnett R. Rubin and Jack L. Snyder, eds (London: Routledge, 1998), pp. 34–57; Eric Lohr, *Nationalizing the Russian Empire: The Campaign against Enemy Aliens during World War I* (Cambridge, MA: Harvard University Press, 2003); Joshua Sanborn, *Drafting the Russian Nation: Military Conscription, Total War, and Mass Politics, 1905–1925* (DeKalb, IL: Northern Illinois University Press, 2003).
29. Igor Arkhipov, 'Patriotizm v period krizisa 1914–1917 godov', *Zvezda* 9 (2009); V.A. Obolenskii, *Moia zhizn, moii sovremenniki* (Paris, 1988), pp. 258–459; Struve blamed his fellow liberals from the Kadet party for the inability to come to terms with Russian nationalism and demanded the annexation and Russification of Galicia. Pipes, *Struve*, pp. 216–217.
30. Peter Holquist, 'The Role of Personality in the First (1914–1915) Russian Occupation of Galicia and Bukovina', in: John Klier, ed., *Anti-Jewish Violence: Rethinking the Pogrom in European History* (Bloomington, IN: Indiana University Press, 2010), pp. 52–73; also see M.M. Prishvin, *Dnevniki, 1914–1917* (St Petersburg: Rostok, 2007), pp. 103–117.
31. Boris Kolonitsky, 'Slukhi ob imperatritse Aleksandre Fedorovne i massovaia kultura (1914–1917), in: *Vestnik istorii, literatury, iskusstva. Otdeleniie istoriko-filologicheskikh nauk RAN* (Moscow: Nauka, 2005) pp. 362–378; Prishvin, *Dnevniki 1914–1917*, p. 221.
32. F.A. Gaida, *Liberal'naia oppozitsiia na putiakh k vlasti (1914–vesna 1917 g.)* (Moscow: ROSSPEN, 2003).
33. There were 135,000 school and university students in St Petersburg in 1917. M.A. Orlov, ed., *Leningrad. Putevoditel, tom 1. Istoria, ekonomika, kultura* (Moscow-Leningrad: OGIS, 1933), p. 398.
34. N.V. Blagovo, *Shkola na Vasilevskom ostrove. Istoricheskaia khronika*, part 1 (St Petersburg: Nauka, 2005); Likhachev, 'Schastie i neschastia'; http://www.karlmay.spb.ru/index.par; R.Sh. Ganelin, ed., *Iz Istorii Russkoi Intelligentsii. Sbornik materialov i statei k 100-letiiu so dnia rozhdeniia V.R. Leikinoi-Svirskoi* (St Petersburg: Dmitrii Bulanin, 2003).
35. D.S. Likhachev, *VRL*, vol. 1, p. 123. For similar feelings see B.N. Lossky, 'Nasha semia v poru likholetia 1914–1922 godov' in: *Minuvshee. Istoricheskii Almanakh*, Vol. 11 (Moscow: Atheneum Feniks, 1992), pp. 134–135.
36. B.N. Lossky, op cit., p. 172. Another witness wrote about 'light-mindedness' and 'frivolity' at the start of the revolution: S.B. Veselovsky, *Semeinaia khronika. Tri pokoleniia Russkoi zhizni* (Moscow: AIRO-XXI, 2010), p. 386.
37. Douglas Smith, *Former People*, pp. 134–156, 236.
38. Interview with D.S. Likhachev in the TV programme *Nochnoi polet* (*Night Flight*), September 1998, https://www.youtube.com/watch?v=gBnV0M8wwg8, accessed on 16 August 2014; D.S. Likhachev, *VRL*, vol. 1, pp. 121–124.

39. Natalia Lebina, Andrei Chistikov, *Obyvateli i reformy. Kartiny povsednevnoi zhizni gorozhan v gody NEPa i khrushchevskogo desiatiletiia* (St Petersburg: Dmitrii Bulanin, 2003).
40. Interview of Urmas Ott with Likhachev, October 1990, at http://www.youtube.com/watch?v=j1Lpsny1hKE; Likhachev, 'Schastie i neschastia', pp. 47–48.
41. D.S. Likhachev, 'Schastie i neschastia v moei zhizni', *Mansarda*, pp. 47–48, at: http://www.lihachev.ru/pic/site/files/fulltext/schsteineschstevmoeyjizni.pdf); Interview of Urmas Ott with Likhachev, October 1990, at http://www.youtube.com/watch?v=j1Lpsny1hKE
42. D.S. Likhachev, Interview with Lev Smirnov, *Connaissance des arts*, #495 (Fevrier, 1993) in: D.S. Likhachev, *VRL*, vol. 2, p. 250.
43. Gippius, *Dnevniki*, 2 December 1918, at: http://www.bibliotekar.ru/gippius-zinaida/10.htm, p. 454; S.E. Trubetskoi, *Minuvshchee* (Moscow: DEM, 1991), at: http://www.sakharov-center.ru/asfcd/auth/?t=book&num=1687.
44. Vera Tolz, *Inventing the Nation. Russia* (New York: Oxford University Press, 2001), pp. 13, 218.
45. B.E. Nolde, 'Itogi 1917 goda. Brestskie peregovory i Brestskii mir', *Vestnik Evropy*, Petrograd (January–April 1918), pp. 357–373; Boris Kaganovich, *Evgeny Victorovich Tarle. Istorik i vremia* (St Petersburg: Evropeiskii universitet, 2014), p. 91.
46. Oleg Budnitskii, 'The Jews and revolution: Russian perspectives, 1881–1918', *East European Jewish Affairs*, 38: 3 (2008), p. 331; M.M. Prishvin, *Dnevniki 1918–1919* (St Petersburg: Rostok, 2008), p. 39; *Dnevniki 1920–22* (Moscow: Moskovskii Rabochii, 1995).
47. D.S. Likhachev, *VRL*, vol. 1, p. 123.
48. Likhachev's interview on television programmes of 1995 and 1997, https://www.youtube.com/watch?v = 92H6U2fs0XY and https://www.youtube.com/watch?v = gBnV0M8wwg8.
49. D.S. Likhachev, *VRL*, vol. 1, pp. 105–106.
50. Vladimir V. Veidle, *Zimnee solntse. Iz rannikh vospominanii* (Washington: Viktor Kamkin Inc, 1976), accessible at: http: lib.rus.ec/b/356411/read.
51. D.S. Likhachev, *VRL*, vol. 1, pp. 107–108.
52. Emily D. Johnson, *How Petersburg Learned to Study Itself*, pp. 124–135; I.A. Golubeva, 'I.F. Grevs i N.P. Antsiferov: Ot Italii k Peterburgu (k voprosu stanovleniia urbanistiki kak nauchnoi distsypliny)' in: *Istoriograficheskii sbornik*, Vyp. 23 (Saratov: SGU, 2008), pp. 24–34.
53. B.N. Lossky, op. cit., *Minuvshee*, vol. 12, p. 67.
54. D.S. Likhachev, '*Russkii sever*', http://likhachev.lfond.spb.ru/articl100/Russia/rus_sever.pdf.
55. Likhachev, '*Russkii sever*', http://likhachev.lfond.spb.ru/articl100/Russia/rus_sever.pdf.

# Chapter 2  Patriotism of Pity, 1921–1928

1. Lidia Ginzburg, *Zapisnye knizhki, vospominaniia, esse* (St Petersburg: Isskustvo-SPb, 2002), p. 380.
2. Sheila Fitzpatrick, *The Cultural Front: Power and Culture in Revolutionary Russia* (Cornell, NY: Cornell University Press, 1992); also her: *The Commissariat of Enlightenment: Soviet Organization of Education and the Arts under Lunacharsky* (Cambridge University Press, 2002).
3. On Helfernak see D.S. Likhachev, *VRL*, vol. 1, pp. 132–133.
4. The group of linguists also included Grigory Gukovsky, Lev Scherba, Victor Vinogradov and others. Lidia Ginzburg, *Zapisnyie knizhki, vospominaniia, esse*, pp. 447–448; D.V. Ustinov, ed., 'Lidia Ginzburg. Pisma k B.Ia. Bukhshtabu', *NLO*, no. 49 (2001), accessed at http://magazines.russ.ru/nlo/2001/49/pismgin.html; V.P. Zubov, *Stradnye gody*

*Rossii: Vospominaniia o Revolutsii, 1917–1927* (Munich: Wilhelm Fink Verlag, 1968), reprinted in Russia in Moscow by the publisher Indrik in 2004. Available at http://kn.sobaka.ru/n86/03.html, accessed on 6 October 2012.

5. Vladimir Belous, 'Volfila (Petrogradskaia Volnaia Assotsiatsiia) 1919–1924', in: Modest Kolerov, ed., *Issledovania po Istorii Russkoi Mysli*, vol. 11, books 1 and 2 (Moscow: Modest Kolerov i 'Tri Kvadrata' 2005).
6. See more in: Stuart Finkel, *On the Ideological Front: The Russian Intelligentsia and the Making of the Soviet Public Sphere* (Yale University Press, 2007), pp. 13–15.
7. V. Goncharov, V. Nekhotin, eds, *Delo 'Petrogradskoi Boevoi Organizatsii' (PBO) (1921). Prosim osvobodit iz tiuremnogo zakliuchenia* (Moscow: Sovremennyi pisatel, 1998); V.Yu. Cherniaev, 'Delo "Petrogradskoi boegoi organizatsii V.N. Tagantseva"', in: L.P. Beliakov, V.M. Zablotskyi, eds, *Repressirovannye geologi* (Moscow and St Petersburg: MPR RF, VSEGEI, RosGeo, 1999), pp. 391–395.
8. In Petrograd the list of deportees included philosophers Leonid Karsavin, Nikolai Lossky, economists Alexei Ugrimov and Boris Brutskus, sociologist Pitirim Sorokin and editorialist Boris Khariton, in: A.N. Artizov, Z.K. Vodopianova, E.V. Domracheva, et al., *'Ochistim Rossiiu Nadolgo ...' Repressii protiv inakomyslaschikh. Konets 1921 – nachalo 1923* (Moscow: Mezhdunarodnyi fond 'Demokratiia' – Materik, 2008), pp. 473–474.
9. S.A. Alexeyev-Askoldov, 'Religioznyi smysl russkoi revoliutsii', *Iz Glubiny. Sbornik Statei o Russkoi Revoliutsii* (Moscow-Petrograd: Russkaia Mysl, 1918), pp. 1–45.
10. On Askoldov's teaching see N.O. Lossky, *Istoriia russkoi filosofii*, http://www.runivers.ru/philosophy/lib/authors/author64156/.
11. D.S. Likhachev, 'Zametki k vospominaniiam o Vere', http://www.nasledie-rus.ru/podshivka/7907.php_; information from Alexei L. Dmitrenko who did research in the papers of the Lentovskaia school, in his communication to the author on 31 December 2015.
12. M.B. Rabinovich, *Vospominaniia dolgoi zhizni* (St Petersburg: Evropeiskii dom, 1996), p. 85; Peter Konecny, 'Conflict and Community at Leningrad University, 1917–1941' (PhD diss., University of Toronto, 1992).
13. D.S. Likhachev, *VRL*, vol. 1, pp. 113–114.
14. Lidia Ginzburg, 'Zapisi 1920–1930-kh godov (1932)', in: Lidia Ginzburg, *Zapisnye knizhki. vospominaniia, esse* (St Petersburg: Isskustvo-SPb, 2002), pp. 101, 192.
15. Viktor Shklovsky, *The Sentimental Journey*; Veniamin Kaverin, 'Zasada', in his: *Epilog. Memuary* (Moscow: Agraf, 1997), pp. 9–30.
16. Recollections by D.S. Likhachev on this episode in: B.F. Yegorov, *Vospominaniia* (St Petersburg: Nestor, 2004), p. 467; also Likhachev's letters to V.B. Shklovsky on 19 January 1973 and 20 April 1982, *Iz epistoliarnogo naslediia D.S. Likhacheva*.
17. Likhachev's recollections on 5 February 1992 in: B.F. Yegorov, *Vospominania-2* (St Petersburg: Rostok, 2013), p. 177; B.N. Lossky, op. cit., *Minuvshee*, vol. 12, pp. 51, 62, 83–84, 96.
18. D.S. Likhachev, 'Ob intellektualnoi topografii Peterburga v pervoi chetverti dvadtsatogo veka' in his: *Vospominaniia* (St Petersburg: Logos, 1995), pp. 49–50; Natalia Murray, *The Unsung Hero of the Russian Avant-Garde: The Life and Times of Nikolay Punin* (Boston, MA: Brill, 2012), pp. 149–151.
19. D.S. Likhachev, *Vospominaniia*, pp. 111–113.
20. Likhachev's recollections on 5 February 1992, in: B.F. Yegorov, *Vospominania-2* (St Petersburg: Rostok, 2013), p. 177; Interview of Ivan Tolstoi with Dmitry Likhachev in 1998, posted on 2 October 1999, http://www.svobodanews.ru/content/transcript/24200559.html.; D.S. Likhachev, *Vospominaniia*, pp. 112–113.

21. D.S. Likhachev, *Vospominaniia*, p. 97; more detailed discussion of this library and Ionov is in the letter of Dmitry Likhachev to Ilya Zilberstein, 15 June 1984, IRLI, fond 769, fail 34; *Dmitry Likhachev i ego epokha*, p. 358.
22. D.S. Likhachev, *VRL*, vol. 1, p. 100.
23. Interview with Likhachev by S. Bychkov, *Druzhba narodov* 6 (1988), reproduced in: D.S. Likhachev, *Kniga bespokoistv. Statyi, besedy, vospominaniia* (Moscow: Novosti, 1991), p. 317.
24. V.S. Izmozik, ed., 'Chastnye pisma serediny 1920-kh godov. Iz arkhiva politkontrolia OGPU', and V.S. Izmozik, 'V zerkale politkontrolia', *Nestor* 1 (2000), pp. 38–39, 41, 51, 263.
25. Stepan Veselovsky, 'Dnevniki 1915–1923', *Voprosy istorii*, 11–12 (2000), the entries of 5 and 27 May 1922, pp. 64–65, 69; O.Iu. Malinova, *Rossia i Zapad v XX veke. Transformatsiia diskursa o kollektivnoi identichnosti* (Moscow: ROSSPEN, 2009).
26. Mikhail Agursky, *Ideologiia natsional-bolshevizma*, pp. 70–89; A.F. Kiselev, ed., *Politicheskaia istoriia Russkoi emigratsii. 1920–1940 gg. Dokumenty i materialy* (Moscow: Vlados, 1999), pp. 172–218.
27. A.F. Kiselev, ed., *Politicheskaia istoriia Russkoi emigratsii, 1920–1940 gg*, pp. 236–273; Serguei Glebov, 'The Challenge of the Modern: The Eurasianist Ideology and Movement, 1920–1929' (Ph.D. diss., Rutgers University, 2004).
28. Pipes, *Struve*, pp. 301, 337–338, 412–413, 440–441; Struve, 'Dnevnik Politika', *Vozrozhdenie* 206 (25 December 1925), reproduced in A.F. Kiselev, ed., *Politicheskaia istoriia Russkoi emigratsii. 1920–1940 gg*, pp. 100–101; Norman G.O. Pereira, 'The Thought and Teachings of Michael Karpovich', *Russian History* 36 (2009), p. 266.
29. Agursky, *Ideologiia natsional–bolshevizma*, pp. 110–112, 290.
30. On Igor Anichkov, who combined monarchism with other eccentric ideas, see: V.P. Nedialkov, ed., *I.E. Anichkov. Trudy po iazykoznaniiu* (St Petersburg: Nauka, 1997); Letter of Dmitry Likhachev to Ilya Zilberstein, 15 June 1984, RO IRLI, fond 769; D.S. Likhachev, S.S. Zilitinkevich, V.P. Nedeliakov, 'I.E. Anichkov. Biograficheskii ocherk', 1997 at http://www.gup.ru/pic/site/files/fulltext/Anichkov_biogr_ocherk.pdf, accessed on 10 May 2014.
31. D.S. Likhachev, *VRL*, vol. 1, pp. 122, 124.
32. Dmitry Pospelovsky, *The Russian Church under the Soviet regime, 1917–1982*, vol. 1 (Crestwood, NY: St Vladimir's Seminary Press, 1984), pp. 28–29; Pavel G. Rogoznyi, *Tserkovnaia revoliutsiia 1917 goda* (St Petersburg: Liki Rossii, 2008).
33. On the Bolsheviks and the Russian Orthodox Church see: Anatoly Levitin and Vadim Shavrov, *Ocherki po istorii tserkovnoi smuty*, vol. 1 (Kusnacht: Glaube in der Dritten Welt, 1978).
34. Edward E. Roslof, *Red Priests: Renovationism, Russian Orthodoxy, and Revolution, 1905–1946* (Bloomington, IN: Indiana University Press, 2002), esp. p. 39. Roslof links 'renovationism' to the atmosphere of peasant socialism, but completely ignores the evidence of the role of the Bolshevik government and its secret police.
35. Dmitry Pospielovsky, *The Russian Church under the Soviet regime 1917–1982*, vol. 1, pp. 97–98; Anatoly Levitin, Vadim Shavrov, *Ocherki po istorii russkoi tserkovnoi smuty. Prilozheniie 2 k pervomu tomu*, http://krotov.info/history/20/krasnov/1_274.html.
36. D.S. Likhachev, *VRL*, vol. 1, p. 102.
37. *Izvestia*, 19 August 1927.
38. Boris Koverda, 'Pokusheniie na polpreda Voikova', http://www.rovs.atropos.spb.ru/index.php?view=publication&mode=text&id=13; http://www.xxl3.ru/kadeti/koverda.htm.

39. D.S. Likhachev, *Vospominaniia*, p. 120; M.V. Shkarovsky, *Russkaia Pravoslavnaia Tserkov v XX veke* (Moscow: Veche, 2010), pp. 218–220, 222; Letter of D.S. Likhachev to the daughters of Rev. Feodor on 16 September 1992, cited by Shkarovsky, op. cit., p. 225.
40. D.S. Likhachev, *VRL*, vol. 1, p. 135; Shkarovsky, op. cit., p. 87; Oleg Panchenko, in: E. Vodolazkin, ed., *Dmitry Likhachev i ego epokha: Vospominaniie, esse, dokumenty, fotografii* (hereafter: *DLEE*) (St Petersburg: Logos, 2002), pp. 344–345.
41. D.S. Likhachev, *VRL*, vol. 1, pp. 133, 138.
42. D.S. Likhachev, *VRL*, vol. 1, pp. 135–137.
43. Oleg Panchenko, in: *DLEE*, pp. 349–350.
44. 'M.V. Yudina. Pisma k V.S. Liublinskomu, 1956–1961', ed. by A.M. Kuz, *Zvezda* 9 (1999): 162.
45. D.S. Likhachev, 'Spravka o sudbe moshchei sviatogo blagovernogo kniazia Daniila Aleksandrovicha', *VRL*, vol. 1, pp. 394–395.
46. On the adaptation of the nobility to Soviet life see: Sofia Chuikina, *Dvorianskaia pamiat: 'byvshie' v sovetskom gorode (Leningrad, 1920–30-e gody)* (St Petersburg: Izdatelstvo Evropeiskogo universiteta, 2006), pp. 30–36, 78; Smith, *Former People*, pp. 225–245.
47. From the enormous literature on M.M. Bakhtin, see: Katerina Clark and Michael Holquist, *Mikhail Bakhtin* (Harvard University Press, 1984); V.L. Makhlin, *Mikhail Mikhailovich Bakhtin* (Moscow: ROSSPEN, 2010).
48. D.S. Likhachev, *VRL*, vol. 1, p. 141; Bakhtin's remark from Dmitry Likhachev's recollections in an interview with Ivan Tolstoy in 1998, http://www.svobodanews.ru/content/transcript/24200559.html, accessed on 22 October 2012.
49. D.S. Likhachev, *Vospominaniia*, p. 136.
50. D.S. Likhachev, *Vospominaniia*, pp. 137, 138.
51. 'Tezisy doklada o staroi orfografii, 1928'. The text of Likhachev's presentation can be accessed at http://www.lihachev.ru/pic/site/files/fulltext/tezisy_dokladov_o_staroy_orfo.pdf; D.S. Likhachev, *Vospominaniia*, p. 137.
52. The author's communication with Vera Zilitinkevich-Tolz, a telephone conversation on 23 October 2012.
53. M.V. Shkarovsky, 'Russkiie katoliki v Sankt-Peterburge (Leningrade), in: *Minuvshee: Istoricheskii almanach* 24 (St Petersburg: Atheneum – Feniks, 1998), pp. 451–452, 457–458; V.V. Antonov, *Petrograd-Leningrad 1920–1930-e. Vera protiv bezbozhiia. Istoriko-tserkovnyi sbornik* (St Petersburg: Liki Rossii), pp. 110–111. Antonov uses information from the secret police files he saw in the archive of St Petersburg FSB (former KGB).
54. The name of this friend was Sergei Neustruiev. D.S.Likhachev, *VRL*, vol. 1, p. 142; Delo no. 195 Dmitriya Likhacheva, a documentary film, https://www.youtube.com/watch?v=h6MRTF-2Uzw.
55. V.S. Izmozik, 'Nastoieniia nauchnoi i pedagogicheskoi intelligentsii v gody NEPa po materialam politicheskogo kontrolia i narrativnym istochnikam', in: *Za 'Zheleznym zanavesom'*, p. 354.
56. Brachev, 'Iz arkhiva "Kosmicheskoi akademii nauk"', p. 315; D.S. Likhachev, 'Pismo v redatsiiu', *Sankt-Peterburgskaia panorama* 6 (1992), p. 6.
57. On Stromin-Heller and his career see: http://alexanderyakovlev.org/almanah/almanah-dict-bio/57138/16.
58. D.S. Likhachev, *Vospominaniia*, p. 140.
59. V.S. Brachev, 'Iz arkhiva "Kosmicheskoi Akademii Nauk", Dnevnik D.P. Kalistova (1926–1927 gg.)', *Russian Studies. Ezhekvartalnik russkoi filologii i kultury 1996* (1998) P. 4, pp. 315–317, 323–324; the author's interview with Evgeny Lukin, 28 August 2010.

60. During the 1960s, D.S. Likhachev began to suspect that Kalistov had been recruited by the OGPU and broke his friendship with him. After reading his police file, Likhachev commented to his family members: 'Kalistov let us down.' Vera Zilitinkevich-Tolz in a telephone conversation with the author, 23 October 2012. V.S. Brachev, 'Iz arkhiva "Kosmicheskoi Akademii Nauk", Dnevnik D.P. Kalistova (1926–1927 gg.)', *Russian Studies. Ezhekvartalnik russkoi filologii i kultury 1996* (1998) P. 4, pp. 315–327, 323–324; as to the secret file on D.S. Likhachev, the author could see a copy of it in the D.S. Likhachev Foundation's archive, courtesy of Oleg Leikind.
61. The first well-documented studies of this anti-Semitism of the 1920s can be found in: N. Teptsov, 'Monarkhia pogibla, a antisemitizm ostalsia. Dokumenty Informatsionnogo otdela OGPU 20-kh godov', *Neizvestnaia Rossiia. XX vek*. Vypusk 3 (Moscow: Mosgorarkhiv, 1993); V.S. Izmozik, 'V zerkale politkontrolia. Politicheskii kontrol i rossiiskaia povsednevnost v 1918–1928 godakh', *Nestor* 2001, no. 1(5), pp. 256–259.
62. Nikos Kazantzakis, *Russia: A Chronicle of Three Journeys in the Aftermath of the Revolution*. Transl. by Michael Antonakes and Thanasis Maskaleris (Berkeley, CA: Creative Arts Book Company, 1989), pp. 40–44; Mikhail Agursky, *Ideologiia natsional-bolshevizma*, pp. 264–265; Oleg Budnitsky, *Rossiiskie evrei mezhdu krasnymi i belymi, 1917–20* (Moscow: ROSSPEN, 2005); also his, 'The Jews and revolution: Russian perspectives, 1881–1917', *Eastern European Jewish Affairs* 38, 3 (2008), pp. 321–334. See also, Yuri Slezkine, *The Jewish Century* (Princeton, NJ: Princeton University Press, 2006), pp. 204–329.
63. Vladimir Vernadsky, *Dnevniki 1941–43* (ed. by V.P. Volkov) (Moscow: ROSSPEN, 2010); L.S. Gatagova, L.P. Kosheleva, K.A. Rogovaia, G. Cadio. *TsK VKP(b) i natsionalnyi vopros. Kniga 1*, 1918–1933 (Moscow: ROSSPEN, 2005), pp. 409–412, 452–453.
64. Lev Karsavin, 'Rossiia i evrei', *Versty* 3 (Paris, 1928); Vadim Rossman, *Russian Intellectual Anti-Semitism in the Post-Soviet Era* (The University of Nebraska Press; Hebrew University of Jerusalem, 2002), pp. 30–33.
65. Tur, 'Pepel dubov', *Leningradskaia Pravda*, 14 June 1928. The same newspaper on 15 June published an article with the title 'Class enemy hides behind the back of anti-Semite', 'Anti-Semites with [Bolshevik] party card'.
66. Likhachev's interview with Ivan Tolstoy, 1998, http://www.svobodanews.ru/content/transcript/24200559.html.
67. 'Novaia kontr-revolutsionnaia organizatsiia. Soobshchenie iz Peterburga', *Slovo*, 961 (17 August 1928), Sergei Melgunov papers, HIA.
68. D.S. Likhachev, *Vospominaniia*, pp. 141–142; the record of Likhachev's interrogation is from his secret police file, the archive of the D.S. Likhachev Foundation, courtesy of Oleg Leikind.
69. D.S. Likhachev, *Vospominaniia*, pp. 142, 143.
70. The interview excerpts with Dmitry Likhachev and the fragments of the police file are found in the archive of Radio Liberty, http://www.svobodanews.ru/content/transcript/24200559.html. This data was posted on 2 October 1999 and accessed on 22 October 2012.
71. One 'member of the organization' was not sentenced: a young woman, Morozova, who was at the time only 17. She was exiled, later returned to Leningrad, and became a successful Soviet geologist. Interview with Evgeny Lukin, 28 August 2010.
72. D.S. Likhachev, *Vospominaniia*, p. 144.
73. D.S. Likhachev, *Vospominaniia*, p. 144.
74. D.S. Likhachev, *VRL*, vol. 1, p. 122.
75. William Shakespeare, *Tragedy of Julius Caesar*, Act Four, Scene Three.
76. The excerpts of Likhachev's interview to Ivan Tolstoy, at http://www.svobodanews.ru/content/transcript/24200559.html.

## Chapter 3   Through the Gulag and
Great Terror, 1928–1941

1. Quoted in Elena Ignatova, *Zapiski o Peterburge. Zhizneopisaniie goroda so vremeni ego osnovaniia do 40-kh godov XX veka* (St Petersburg: Amfora, 2005), pp. 707–708.
2. D.S. Likhachev in a letter to S.P. Zalygin, editor of *Novyi Mir*, RO IRLI, fond 769.
3. A story of escape of 'former people' to a faraway village is described in: Aleksandr Chudakov, *Lozhitsia mgla na staryie stupeni. Roman-idillia* (Moscow: Vremia, 2013).
4. D.S. Likhachev, *Vospominaniia*, pp. 155, 397–398.
5. Dmitry made these notes defying a strict ban and later managed to pass them to his father. See 'Solovetskie zapisi 1928–1930', http://www.sakharov-center.ru/asfcd/auth/?t=book&num=325.
6. D.S. Likhachev, *Vospominaniia*, pp. 147, 405.
7. Yuri Brodsky, *Solovki: Dvadtsat let Osobogo Naznacheniia* (Moscow: ROSSPEN, 2002); D.B. Pavlov, 'Solovetskiie lageria osobogo naznacheniia OGPU', and N.N. Popova, 'Repressirovannaia intelligentsia. Solovetskii izvod', in: D.B. Pavlov, ed., *Repressirovannaia intelligentsiia, 1917–1934* (Moscow: POSSPEN, 2010), pp. 320–484.
8. This viewpoint was reflected in the first Russian film about Solovki camp by Marina Goldovskaia, *Vlast Solovetskaia* (1988); also see D.B. Pavlov, 'Solovetskiie lageria osobogo naznacheniia OGPU', pp. 321–322; D.S. Likhachev, the Solovki notes, 1928, in *Vospominaniia*, p. 407.
9. Dmitry Likhachev, interview in the film *Vlast Solovetskaia* by Marina Goldovskaia (1988), http://www.youtube.com/watch?v=X5X0ToMsLrs. See more in: Anne Appelbaum, *GULAG. A History* (New York: Random House, 2003), chapter 2; I.I. Chukhina, 'Dva dokumenta komissii A.M. Shanina na Solovkakh', in: N.G. Okhotin, A.B. Roginskii, eds, *Zvenia. Istoricheskii Almanakh. Vypusk 1* (Moscow: Progress, Feniks, Atheneum, 1991), pp. 357–388.
10. D.S. Likhachev, from his Solovetsky notes, 1928; *Vospominaniia*, p. 406.
11. D.S. Likhachev, from his Solovetsky notes, pp. 176–177, 406.
12. D.S. Likhachev, from his Solovetsky notes, p. 143.
13. Boris Lindener (1884–1960) worked in the Geological-Mineralogical museum in Petrograd and taught at Petrograd University; in 1926 he was arrested and worked as a prisoner in Solovki until 1930. http://baza.vgdru.com/1/19226/.
14. D.S. Likhachev, *Vospominaniia*, pp. 156–163, 406.
15. For the description of nature and Melnikov's role see Likhachev, *Vospominaniia*, pp. 172–176; also Brodsky, *Solovki*, p. 143.
16. D.S. Likhachev at http://www.solovki.ru/history26.html, accessed on 24 November 2012 (this information later disappeared from the internet). On Mogilianska see http://www.solovki.ca/writers_023/mogiljanska.php; D.S. Likhachev, *VRL*, vol. 2, pp. 428–431, 440–441, 444–449.
17. Meyer was born in Odessa to a German-Russian Lutheran family; his father was a teacher of Latin and Greek, and an avid collector of philosophical literature. See a biographical note by S.G. Stratanovsky, http://www.nlr.ru/nlr_history/persons/info.php?id=112.
18. *Sankt-Peterburgskaia Panorama*, 6 (1994), p. 6.
19. Yuri Medvedev, '"Voskresenie". K istorii religiozno-filisofskogo kruzhka A.A. Meiera', http://marecki.ru/archive/medvosk.rtf, accessed on 3 November 2012; V.V. Antonov, '"Voskresenie" Meiera i "voskresniki" Nazarova. Dukhovnye poiski petrogradskoi intelligentsia 1920-kh godov', in: A. Kobak and V. Antonov, eds, *Nevskyi arkhiv:*

*Istoriko kraevedcheskii sbornik*, IV (St Petersburg: Izdatelstvo Chernyshova, 1999), pp. 296, 302.
20. D.S. Likhachev, *VRL*, vol. 2, pp. 418–422.
21. Alexander Meyer, 'Razmyshleniia pri chtenii "Fausta"' (1935), in: A.A. Meyer, *Oeuvres Philosophiques* (Paris: La Presse Libre, 1982).
22. D.S. Likhachev, *Vospominaniia*, pp. 227–228.
23. D.S. Likhachev, *Vospominaniia*, pp. 230–235; V.P. Stark, ed., *Dvorianskaia semia. Iz istorii dvorianskikh familii Rossii* (St Petersburg: Nabokovskii fond, 2000).
24. D.S. Likhachev, *VRL*, vol. 1, pp. 192–201.
25. D.S. Likhachev, *VRL*, vol. 1, pp. 166–170, 202.
26. Michael David Fox, *Showcasing the Great Experiment. Cultural Diplomacy and Western Visitors to the Soviet Union, 1921–1941* (New York: Oxford University Press, 2011), chapter 4.
27. *Izvestia*, 21 September 1929, cited in Brodsky, *Solovki*, p. 256.
28. Cynthia A. Ruder, *Making History for Stalin: The Story of the Belomor Canal* (University Press of Florida, 1998).
29. D.S. Likhachev, *VRL*, vol. 1, pp. 183–184.
30. Ibid., p. 184; his: *Vospominaniia*, pp. 192–194.
31. D.S. Likhachev, *VRL*, vol. 1, pp. 186–190.
32. Ibid., pp. 189–190.
33. A.M. Osorgin to her brother S.G. Trubetskoy, in: Brodsky, *Solovki*, p. 267; also Serge Schmemann, *Echoes of a Native Land: Two Centuries of a Russian Village* (New York: Vintage, 1999); Smith, *Former People*, pp. 292–294.
34. On the epidemics, see D.B. Pavlov, 'Solovetskiie lageria osobogo naznacheniia', p. 339; D.S. Likhachev, *Vospominaniia*, p. 194. In 1928 the prison population of SLON was 22, 176. By April 1930 it increased to 57, 325. D.B. Pavlov, 'Solovetskie lageria osobogo naznacheniia', p. 338.
35. Applebaum, *GULAG*, pp. 62–70; Cynthia A. Ruder, *Making History for Stalin: The Story of the Belomor Canal* (University Press of Florida, 1998); Paul R. Gregory, Valery Lazarev and V. V. Lazarev, *Economics of Forced Labor: The Soviet Gulag* (Stanford, CA: Hoover Institute Press, 2003); Brodsky, *Solovki*, p. 117; also http://www.Solovki.ca/gulag_Solovki/belo.php.
36. Likhachev, *Vospominaniia*, pp. 272–277.
37. Interview with Evgeny Lukin, 28 August 2010. Information from Vera Zilitinkevich-Tolz in a telephone conversation with the author, 15 October 2012.
38. Likhachev, *Vospominaniia*, pp. 277–282.
39. A few icons would later end up in the state museums and decades later became the glory of their medieval collections. Likhachev, *Vospominaniia*, pp. 203–207; M.V. Shkarovsky, *Russkaia Pravoslavnaia Tserkov v XX veke* (Moscow: Veche, 2010), pp. 88–91.
40. V.V. Kondrashin, *Golod 1932–1933 godov. Tragediia rossiiskoi derevni* (Moscow: ROSSPEN, 2008); Elena Osokina, *Our Daily Bread: Socialist Distribution and the Art of Survival in Stalin's Russia, 1927–1941* (New York: M.E. Scharp, 2000); V. Danilov, O. Khlevniuk, A. Vatlin, et al., *Kak lomali NEP. Stenogrammy plenumov TsK VPKB 1928–1929*. Vols 1–5 (Moscow: Fond Demokratiia, 2000) and classic Victor Danilov, Roberta Manning, Lynn Viola, eds, *Tragediia sovetskoi derevni. Kollektivizatsiia i raskulachivanie. Dokumenty i materialy v 5 tomakh* (Moscow: ROSSPEN, 1999–2004).
41. D.S. Likhachev, *VRL*, vol. 1, pp. 224–225.
42. One of these letters was in Likhachev's secret police file, the archive of D.S. Likhachev Foundation, courtesy of Oleg Leikind; D.S. Likhachev, *VRL*, vol. 1, pp. 225–226.
43. O. Panchenko in: *DLEE*, pp. 346–348.

44. The authors' interview with Victor Paneyakh on 25 June 2009, St Petersburg; conversation with Vera Zilitinkevich-Tolz on the phone, 15 October 2012.
45. 'Vospominaniia V. Listova, Solovetskii zek smotrit chekistskii film 1928 goda "Solovki"', http://www.solovki.ca/tv/listov.php.
46. Liudmila Likhacheva, in: E. Vodolazkine, ed., *Dmitry Likhachev i ego vremia*, p. 26.
47. Elena Osokina, *Zoloto dlia industrializatsii* (Moscow: ROSSPEN, 2009), pp. 70–82, 84; Likhachev to Arkady Mankov in August 1994, in A.G. Mankov, *Dnevniki tridtsatykh godov* (St Petersburg: Evropeisky Dom, 2001), p. 12.
48. Likhachev, *Vospominaniia*, p. 283; D.S. Likhachev, *VRL*, vol. 3, p. 447.
49. B.V. Ananyich, V.M. Paneiakh, A.N. Tsamutali, eds, *Akademicheskoie delo 1929–1931 gg. Dokumenty i materialy sledstvennogo dela, sfabrikovannogo OGPU*, Vypusk 1–2 (St Petersburg, 1993); Victor Paneiakh 'K sporam ob "Akademicheskom dele" 1929–1931 i drugikh sfabrikovannykh politicheskikh protestakh', *Soobscheniia Rostovskogo muzeia*, Vypusk XIII (Rostov, 2003).
50. V.P. Zakharov, M.P. Lepekhin, E.A. Fomina, eds, *Akademicheskoie delo 1929–1931 gg. Vyp. 1. Delo po ovineniiu akademika S.F. Platonova* (St Petersburg: BAN, 1993); S.K. Egorov, et al., *Akademicheskoie delo 1929–1931 gg. Vyp. 2. Delo po obvineniiu akademika E.V. Tarle* (St Petersburg: BAN, 1998), chast 1 and 2; B.V. Ananyich, V.M. Paneiakh, 'Prinuditelnoie "soavtorstvo"', http://www.ihst.ru/projects/sohist/books/inmemoriam/87-111.pdf.
51. Likhachev, *Vospominaniia*, pp. 284–285.
52. Brodsky, *Solovki*, p. 296; D.S. Likhachev, *Vospominaniia*, p. 284.
53. D.S. Likhachev, *Vospomianiia*, pp. 289–290.
54. M.M. Prishvin, *Dnevniki, 1930–1931*, the entry of 14 April 1931, p. 368; Sergei Ivanovich Vavilov, *Dnevniki 1909–1951*, Kniga 2 (Moscow: Nauka, 2012), p. 82 (the entry of 19 March 1940); V.I. Vernadsky, *Dnevniki 1941–1943* (Moscow: ROSSPEN, 2010), p. 59 (the entry of 2 November 1941).
55. Mankov's father, like Likhachev's father, had the status of 'personal' nobility and was a legal consultant at the State Senate. During the revolution the Mankov family escaped from Petrograd to the ancient city of Kalyazin on the Volga.
56. A.G. Mankov, *Dnevniki 1930-kh godov* (St Petersburg: Evropeiskii dom, 2001), pp. 31, 38, 42–43; Likhachev's note is in the preface to this publication, pp. 12–13.
57. Special information of the Secret Political Department of the GUGB NKVD of the USSR 'O khode vsesoiuznogo s'ezda Sovetskikh pisatelei', 31 August 1934, in: Andrei Artizov and Oleg Naumov, eds, *Vlast i khudozhestvennaia intelligentsiia. Dokumenty TsK RKP(b) – VKP(b), VChK – OGPU – NKVD o kulturnoi politike 1917–1953 gg.* (Moscow: Mezhdunarodnyi fond 'Demokratiia', 1999), pp. 227–228, 232–236.
58. Elena Ignatova, *Zapiski o Peterburge. Zhizneopisaniie goroda so vremeni ego osnovaniia do 40-kh godov XX veka* (St Petersburg: Amfora, 2003), pp. 596, 601–602, 603.
59. Likhachev, *Vospominaniia*, p. 298; on the destruction of museums as the nobles' 'nests' see Douglas Smith, *Former People*, pp. 259–260, 279–282.
60. On the mechanism and dynamics of terror see: Oleg Khlevniuk, *Khoziain. Stalin i utverzhdenie stalinskoi diktatury* (Moscow: ROSSPEN, 2010).
61. V.A. Ivanov, 'Operatsiia "byvshiie liudi", v Leningrade (fevral – mart 1935 g.)', *Novyi chasovoi: russkii voenno-istoricheskii zhurnal* 6–7 (1998), pp. 71–72; D.S. Likhachev, *VRL*, vol. 1, pp. 228–229.
62. D.S. Likhachev, *Vospominaniia*, p. 299; Chuikina, *Dvorianskaia pamiat: 'byvshie' v sovetskom gorode*, pp. 83–85.
63. M.M. Prishvin, *Dnevniki, 1936–1937*, the entries of 13 and 25 November 1936, pp. 354–355, 367.

64. D.S. Likhachev, *VRL*, vol. 1, pp. 235–236; Valerii Popov, 'Pasportnaia sistema sovetskogo krepostnichestva', *Novyi Mir* 6 (1996), http://magazines.russ.ru/novyi_mi/1996/6/popov.html.
65. D.S. Likhachev, *VRL*, vol. 1, pp. 236–238.
66. D.S. Likhachev, *VRL*, vol. 1, p. 237; *Dmitry Likhachev i eto epokha*, pp. 81–83.
67. On Krylenko see the Soviet-style biography: M.N. Simonyan, *Ego professiia – revoliutsiia. Dokumentalnyi ocherk o zhizni i deiatelnosti N.V. Krylenko* (Moscow: Znaniie, 1985). On the solidarity among Russians see: M.M. Prishvin, *Dnevniki 1930–1931*, pp. 104–105.
68. J. Arch Getty, '"Excesses Are Not Permitted": Mass Terror and Stalinist Governance in the Late 1930s', *Russian Review*, vol. 61, no. 1 (January 2002), pp. 128–130.
69. Reminiscences of Vera Zilitinkevich-Tolz, in 'V nem prelomilsia ves XX vek', *Novaia Gazeta*, 28 June 2013, http://novayagazeta.ru/arts/58805.html.
70. Liudmila Likhacheva in: *DLEE*, p. 31.
71. For more on this change see: David Brandenberger, *National Bolshevism: Stalinist Mass Culture and the Formation of Modern Russian National Identity, 1931–1956* (Cambridge, MA: Harvard University Press, 2002); Sergei Kudryashov, ed., 'Istoriiu – v shkolu. Sozdaniie pervykh sovetskikh uchebnikov', *Vestnik Presidenta Rossiiskoi Federatsii* (2008).
72. L.D. Berendt, 'Institut Krasnoi professury', pp. 192–195. A few 'red professors' loyal to Stalin survived the Great Terror and moved to leading positions. The division between the 'red professors' and the Russian scholars continued.
73. Brandenberger, *National Bolshevism*; Terry Martin, *The Affirmative Action Empire: Nations and Nationalism in the Soviet Union, 1923–1939* (Ithaca, NY: Cornell University Press, 2001).
74. E.I. Kolchinsky, 'V.I. Vernadsky i bolsheviki', in: Manfred Heinemann and Eduard I. Kolchinsky, *Za 'Zhelesnym Zanavesom': Mify i realii sovetskoi nauki* (St Petersburg: Dmitry Bulanin, 2002), pp. 146–147.
75. Rafail Ganelin, '"Afiny i Apokalipsis" Ya.S. Lurie o sovetskoi istoricheskoi nauke 1930-kh godov', in: N.M. Botvinnik, E.I. Vaneeva, eds, *In Memoriam. Sbornik pamiati Ya.S. Lurie* (St Petersburg: Feniks, 1997), p. 148.
76. Roman Goul, 'N.S. Timasheff 1886–1970', *Russian Review*, vol. 29, no. 3 (July 1970), pp. 363–365; David L. Hoffman, 'Was there a "Great Retreat" from Soviet Socialism?: Stalinist Culture Reconsidered', *Kritika*, vol. 5, no. 4 (Fall 2004), pp. 651–674; Matthew E. Lenoe, 'In Defense of Timasheff's Great Retreat', *Kritika*, vol. 5, no. 4 (Fall 2004) (New Series), pp. 721–730.
77. D.S. Likhachev, 'Cherty pervobytnogo primitivizma vorovskoi rechi', *Yazyk i myshlenie*, vol. 3–4 (Leningrad, 1935), pp. 47–100.
78. D.S. Likhachev, *Vospominaniia*, pp. 301–304.
79. On Orlov, http://www.ras.ru/nappelbaum/511e7b25-6f31-4bc2-b0b0-ba250ad1c400.aspx?hidetoc=1.
80. A.A. Formozov, 'Russkie arkheologi i politicheskie repressii 1920–1940-kh godov' (Moscow: Institute of Archaeology, 1998), pp. 190–206 at: www.ihst.ru/projects/sohist/papers/archeology/1998/3/191-206.pdf. 'The Slavists Affair' fabricated by the NKVD in 1936 led to the arrests of Mikhail Speransky and Vladimir Peretz, linguists Nikolai Durnovo, Vladimir Vinogradov, A.M. Selishchev, V. Sidorov, and others, who were charged with a fantastic conspiracy to create a 'Russian nationalist party'.
81. For Kniazev's recollections about the degradation of the Pushkin House, see G.A. Kniazev, *Dni velikikh ispytanii: Dnevniki 1941–1945* (St Petersburg: Nauka, 2009), the entry of 15 January 1942, pp. 402–403.

82. D.S. Likhachev, *Vospominaniia*, pp. 375–376.
83. D.S. Likhachev, *Vospominaniia*, p. 387.
84. D.S. Likhachev, *Vospominaniia*, p. 307; also his: 'Zametki k vospominaniiam o Vere', http://www.nasledie-rus.ru/podshivka/7907.php, accessed on 19 August 2011.
85. 'Zametki k vospominaniiam o Vere', http://www.nasledie-rus.ru/podshivka/7907.php, accessed on 19 August 2011.
86. D.S. Likhachev, 'Russkie letopisi', *Zvezda* 9 (1939), pp. 160–166.
87. M.M. Prishvin, *Dnevniki, 1938–1939* (St Petersburg: Rostok, 2010), the entry for 15 September 1939, p. 422; A.G. Mankov, *Dnevniki tridsatykh godov*, pp. 229, 238, 240, 245, 279–280.

## Chapter 4    The Great Fatherland War, 1941–1945

1. D.S. Likhachev, *VRL*, vol. 1, p. 286; cited in Cynthia Simmons, 'Leningrad Culture under Siege (1941–1944)', in: Helena Goscilo and Stephen Norris, eds, *Preserving Petersburg: History, Memory, Nostalgia* (Bloomington, IN: Indiana University Press, 2008), p. 173.
2. D.S. Likhachev, *VRL*, vol. 1, p. 253.
3. D.S. Likhachev, *Vospominaniia*, p. 313 (Likhachev recorded this on 29 June 1957).
4. Mark Solonin, *22 iiunia. Anatomiia katastrofy* (Moscow: Iauza-Eksmo, 2011); Georgii Alekseevich Kniazev, *Dni Velikikh Ispytanii. Dnevniki 1941–1945* (St Petersburg: Nauka, 2009), 22–23August 1941, pp. 140–141.
5. Daniil Granin, 'Vsyo bylo ne sovsem tak', *Zvezda* 4 (2010). Internet version; also Olga Freidenberg, 'Osada cheloveka' (published by K. Nevelskoy), *Minuvshee: Istoricheskii alkmanakh*, vol. 3 (Moscow: Progress-Feniks, 1991), p. 10; Michael Jones, *Leningrad: State of Siege* (London: John Murray, 2008), pp. 22–37.
6. D.S. Likhachev, *Vospominaniia*, p. 315.
7. Michael Jones, *Leningrad*, p. 93.
8. Quoted in: Natalia Murray, *The Unsung Hero of the Russian Avant-Garde. The Life and Times of Nikolay Punin* (Boston: Brill, 2012), p. 237.
9. A more typical experience, when intellectuals ignored the approaching famine, is in: V.M. Glinka, *Vospominaniia o blokade* (St Petersburg: Limbus Press, 2010), pp. 76–77.
10. D.S. Likhachev, *VRL*, vol. 1, pp. 254–258.
11. Olga Freidenberg, 'Osada cheloveka', p. 10.
12. Alexey Nazarov, 'The Transformation of the Presentation of the Enemy in the Soviet Cinematographic and Photographic Chronicles. June–December 1941', in: Lev Gudkov, ed., *Presentation of the Enemy* (Moscow: OGI, 2005), pp. 175–188; Prishvin, *Dnevnik 1940–1941* (Moscow: ROSSPEN, 2012), p. 520 (the entry of 20 July1941) and p. 563 (the entry of 3 September 1941); O. Budnitsky, *Svershilos, prishli nemtsy!: ideinyi kollaboratsionizm v SSSR v period Velikoi Otechestvennoi voiny* (Moscow: ROSSPEN, 2012).
13. Yuri Nagibin, *T'ma v kontse tunnelia* (Moscow: PIK, 1994), http://lib.ru/PROZA/NAGIBIN/tonnel.txt.
14. Kniazev, *Dni Velikikh Ispytanii*, pp. 138–139, 147, 152–153; Likhachev, *Vospominaniia*, pp. 325–326; Freidenberg, 'Osada cheloveka', p. 12. On anti-Semitism see: N. Lomagin, *Neizvestnaia blokada*, vol. 2, p. 443.
15. Granin, 'Vse bylo ne sovsem tak', *Zvezda* 4 (2010); Michael Jones, *Leningrad*, pp. 39–42; Olga Berggolts, *Olga: Zapretnyi dnevnik* (Moscow: Azbuka, 2010), p. 70.
16. Freidenberg, 'Osada cheloveka', p. 15; Likhachev, *Vospominaniia*, p. 319.
17. D.S. Likhachev, *Zametki i nabliudeniia. Iz zapisnykh knizhek raznykh let* (Leningrad: Sovetskii pisatel, 1989), pp. 462–463.
18. D.S. Likhachev, *Vospominaniia*, p. 323.

19. Prikaz no. 169 po Institutu Literatury Akademii Nauk SSSh, 24 November 1941. Signed by B.S. Meilakh. Courtesy of the Likhachev Foundation and the Museum of the Blockade, St Petersburg; D.S. Likhachev, *Vospominaniia*, p. 327.
20. Interview with Irina Sandomirskaia, 28 January 2014, at http://www.colta.ru/articles/literature/. According to her 'We cannot grasp or understand the breadth and depth of this social invention.' Also: Irina Sandomirskaia, *Blokada kriticheskoi teorii i biopolitiki iazyka* (Moscow: NLO, 2013).
21. D.S. Likhachev, *Vospominaniia*, p. 330.
22. See *Osteuropa zeitschrift*, 'Die Leningrader Blockade?Der Krieg, die Stadt und der Tod', Manfred Sapper, Volker Weichsel (Hg.) Berlin 8–9/2011; and Anna Reid, *Leningrad: the epic siege of World War II, 1941–1944* (New York: Walker, 2011).
23. The Book of Revelation, 3:16; Feodor Dostoyevsky quoted this phrase in *The Brothers Karamazov*. Likhachev commented about the psalm in his private notes in 1972.
24. Psalm 88.
25. N. Murray, *The Unsung Hero*, p. 240; Shaporina, *Dnevnik*, p. 65, the entry of 3 November 1947.
26. D.S. Likhachev, *Vospominaniia*, pp. 333, 342–343; Freidenberg, 'Osada cheloveka', p. 21.
27. Knyazev, *Dni velikikh ispytanii*, p. 388; Glinka, *Vospominaniia o blokade*, pp. 9, 212.
28. D.S. Likhachev, *VRL*, vol. 1, pp. 291–295, 311.
29. N. Lomagin, *Neizvestnaia blokada*, vol. 2, documents 62–75, inter alia; Michael Jones, *Leningrad*, pp. 216–219.
30. D.S. Likhachev, *VRL*, vol. 1, pp. 277–278, 282.
31. Ibid., pp. 290, 310.
32. On Manuilov see: http://www.pushkinskijdom.ru/Default.aspx?tabid=127; V.A. Manuilov, *Zapiski schastlivogo cheloveka* (St Petersburg: Evropeiskii Dom, 1999). He came from the family of a physician in Novocherkassk, knew many Russian poets, and backed the Institute's best philologists and historians.
33. 'Iz istorii Pushkinskogo Doma (rukopisnyi otdel v gody voiny)' at http://literary.ru/literary.ru; Likhachev, 'O Blokade', *Zvezda*, 11 (2006), p. 17.
34. The archives preserved a handwritten 'work plan' of 'senior scholar' D.S. Likhachev for the second quarter of 1942, signed on 15 June 1942. The archive of the Likhachev Foundation, courtesy of Oleg Leikind.
35. On Maria Tikhanova, see http://www.archaeology.ru/Download/Shchukin/Shchukin_1983_Pamyati_Marii.pdf; the diary of N.A. Ribkovsky, in: Natalia N. Kozlova, 'Stseny iz zhizni "osvobozhdennogo rabotnika"', *Sotsiologicheskiie issledovaniia* 2 (1998), pp. 111–112.
36. D.S. Likhachev, *VRL*, vol. 1, p. 300.
37. I borrowed the term from Serguey A. Oushakine, *The Patriotism of Despair: Nation, War, and Loss in Russia* (Cornell, NY: Cornell University Press, 2009). Lisa Kirschenbaum, 'Local Loyalties and Private Life in Soviet World War II Propaganda', *Slavic Review*, lix (2000); Geoffrey Hosking, 'The Second World War and Russian National Consciousness', *Past and Present* 175 (2002), pp. 170–172.
38. Olga Freidenberg, 'Osada cheloveka', p. 23; Lomagin, *Neizvestnaia blokada*, vol. 1, p. 239; Kniazev, *Dni Velikikh Ispytanii*, pp. 342, 344 (the entry of 9 and 10 December 1941).
39. Likhachev, 'Posleslovie k broshiure 1942 goda', *Znamia* 1 (1975); reproduced in Likhachev, *Kniga Bespokoistv*, pp. 273–281.
40. Vera Sandomirsky, 'Soviet War Poetry', *Russian Review* 4, no. 1 (Autumn 1944), pp. 47, 57.
41. N.S. Timasheff, *Religion in Soviet Russia, 1917–1942* (London: Sheed and Ward, 1943), p. 162.

42. Nikolai Tikhonov, *Pered novym pod'emom. Sovetskaia literatura v 1944–1945 gg* (Moscow: Sovetskii pisatel, 1945), p. 17, cited in Lazar Fleishman, 'Pasternak i khristianstvo'.
43. On Ehrenburg, see Boris Frezinsky; Joshua Rubenstein, *Entangled Loyalties*; and Ehrenburg's 'O nenavisti', 5 May 1942, http://bibliotekar.ru/informburo/37.htm.
44. Ostroumova-Lebedeva's diary of early 1943 cited in N. Lomagin, *Neizvestnaia blokada*, vol. 1, p. 304. Also Geoffrey Hosking, 'The Second World War and Russian National Consciousness', *Past and Present* 175 (2002), pp. 162–186.
45. Amir Weiner, 'Saving Private Ivan: From What, Why, and How?' *Kritika*, vol. 1, no. 2 (Spring 2000), pp. 305–336; Rebecca Manley, *To the Tashkent Station: Evacuation and Survival in the Soviet Union at War* (Ithaca, NY: Cornell University Press, 2009).
46. At the same time the dictator skilfully played on a motive that the Western powers could not be true and trusted 'friends of Russian people' – a motive that deeply resonated with Russian historical experience.
47. On the motives for disbanding the Comintern see: Silvio Pons, *La rivoluzione globale. Storia del comunism internazionale 1917–1991* (Torino: Einaudi, 2012), pp. 153–154. On the restoration of the Russian Orthodox Church see: O.Yu. Vasilieva, I.I. Kudryavtsev, L.A. Lykova, *Russkaia Pravoslavnaia Tserkov v gody Velikoi Otechestvennoi voiny. 1941–1945. Sbornik Dokumentov* (Moscow: Izdatelstvo Krutitskogo patriarshego podvoria, 2009).
48. See the report dated 24 July 1943 in: A. Artizov and O. Naumov, *Vlast i khudozhestvennaia intelligentsiia. Dokumenty TsK RKP(b) – VKP (b), VCHK, OGPU, NKVD o kulturnoi politike 1917–1953 gg.* (Moscow: Mezhdunarodnyi fond 'Demokratiia', 1999), pp. 487–499, particularly pp. 492 and 494.
49. In January 1945 in Leningrad the authorities staged a trial of the members of the Pskov Mission: the court sentenced many of them to 15–20 years in concentration camps. Shkarovsky, *Russkaia pravoslavnaia tserkov*, pp. 192, 208–209.
50. Alfred J. Rieber, 'Civil Wars in the Soviet Union', *Kritika*, vol. 4, no. 1 (2003), pp. 129–162; Amir Weiner, 'The Making of a Dominant Myth: The Second World War and the Construction of Political Identities within the Soviet Polity', *Russian Review* 55:4 (October 1996), pp. 638–660.
51. See D.P. Karov, 'Nemetskaia okkupatsiia i sovetskiie liudi v zapiskakh russkogo ofitsera Abvera, 1941–1943 gody', in: K.M. Aleksandrov, ed., *Pod nemtsami. Vospominaniia, svidetelstva, dokumenty* (St Petersburg: Scriptorium, 2011), pp. 407–409; Kirill Aleksandrov, *Pod Nemtsami. Vospominaniia, svidetelstva, dokumenty* (St Petersburg: Filologicheskii fakultet SpbGU, 2011); N. Lomagin, *Neizvestnaia blokada*, vol. 2, p. 474.
52. On the Pskov mission see: Shkarovsky, *Sudby iosiflianskikh pastyrei* (St Petersburg: Satis Derzhava, 2006), pp. 276, 290.
53. Andrei Zorin, 'Lidia Ginzburg: Opyt "primireniia s deistvitelnostiu"', *Novoie Literaturnoie obozreniie* 101 (2010).
54. Freidenberg, 'Osada cheloveka', pp. 34 and 35.
55. S.K. Bernev, S.V. Chernov, eds, *Blokadnyie dnevniki i dokumenty. Seria 'Arkhiv Bolshogo Doma'*, 2nd edn (St Petersburg: Evropeiskii Dom, 2007); Berggolts, *Olga: Zapretnyi dnevnik*, pp. 77–83.
56. When Likhachev told Zina about this episode, she fully approved his behaviour. Interview with Estonian journalist Urmas Ott, October 1990, http://www.youtube.com/watch?v=j1Lpsny1hKE. On the recruitment of informers see N. Lomagin, *Neizvestnaia blokada*, vol. 2, Document 24 on pp. 84–85.
57. The copy of this file from the Museum of Leningrad's Defence is in the archive of the D.S. Likhachev Foundation, courtesy of Oleg Leikind.
58. D.S. Likhachev, *VRL*, vol. 1, pp. 300–305.

59. D.S. Likhachev, 'Zapiski k vospominaniiam o Vere', http://www.nasledie-rus.ru/podshivka/7907.php.
60. D.S. Likhachev, 'Zapiski k vospominaniiam o Vere', http://www.nasledie-rus.ru/podshivka/7907.php.
61. D.S. Likhachev, *Natsionalnoie samosoznaniie drevnei Rusi. Ocherki iz oblasti Russkoi literatury XI–XVII vv.* (Moscow-Leningrad: Izdatelstvo Akademii Nauk SSSR, 1945), p. 19.
62. Ibid., p. 61.
63. Ibid., pp. 66–67, 118.
64. Ibid., pp. 95, 98–104.
65. 'Mansarda'; on the details of the evacuation see: http://www.literary.ru/literary.ru/print.php?subaction=showfull&id=1203427624&archive=1203491298&start_from=&ucat=&. Also V.A. Manuilov, *Zapiski schastlivogo cheloveka. Vospominaniia. Avtobiograficheskaia proza*, edited by N.F. Budanova (St Petersburg: Evropeiskii Dom, 1999).
66. D.S. Likhachev, 'Zapiski k vospominaniiam o Vere', http://www.nasledie-rus.ru/podshivka/7907.php.
67. D.S. Likhachev, *VRL*, vol. 1, p. 246.
68. D.S. Likhachev, *VRL*, vol. 1, pp. 249–251; D.S. Likhachev to I.M. Kudryavtsev, 28 July 1947, 'Iz epistoliarnogo naslediia D.S. Likhacheva', courtesy of Vera Zilitinkevich-Tolz.
69. D.S. Likhachev, *Vospominaniia*, p. 387.
70. D. Likhachev, *Zametki i nabliudenia: Iz zapisnykh knizhek raznykh let* (Leningrad: Sovetskii pisatel, 1989), pp. 113–115.

## Chapter 5 Patriotism Defiled, 1945–1955

1. Henry Hardy, ed., *Isaiah Berlin: Letters, 1928–1946* (New York: Cambridge University Press, 2004), pp. 601–612; see also his 'Meetings with Russian writers in 1945 and 1956' in I. Berlin, *Personal Impressions*, ed. Henry Hardy (Princeton, NJ: Princeton University Press, 2001), pp. 198–254.
2. The exploration of Zhdanovschina's main campaigns is in: G.V. Kostyrchenko, *Tainaia Politika Stalina. Vlast i Antisemitizm* (Moscow: Mezhdunarodnyie otnosheniia, 2001), pp. 276–303; P.A. Druzhinin, *Ideologiia i filologiia. Leningrad, 1940-e gody: Dokumentalnoie issledovaniie*, vol. 1 (Moscow: NLO, 2012), pp. 75–104.
3. V.M. Paneiakh, *Tvorchestvo i sudba istorika: Boris Aleksandrovich Romanov* (St Petersburg: Dmitry Bulanin, 2000).
4. Paneiakh, *Tvorchestvo i sudba istorika*, pp. 213–226, 390–395.
5. D.S. Likhachev, 'Boris Aleksandrovich Romanov i ego kniga "Liudi i nravy drevnei Rusi"', *Trudy Otdela drevnerusskoi literatury* (Moscow-Leningrad: Izdatelstvo AN SSSR, 1958), http://feb-web.ru/feb/todrl/t15/t15-486.htm.
6. Conversation with Boris Ananyich on 24 August 2010, the Institute of History, St Petersburg. This group included Boris Ananyich, Victor Paneiakh, Rafail Ganelin and Aleksandr Fursenko.
7. R.P. Dmitrieva, M.A. Salmina, 'Dmitrii Sergeevich Likhachev – prepodavatel istoricheskogo fakulteta Leningradskogo universiteta (1946–1953)', *Trudy Otdela Drevnerusskoi Literatury* {hereafter *TODL*} (St Petersburg: Nauka, 1996), vol. 50, p. 28. 'Rufina Petrovna Dmitrieva', in: *TODL* (St Petersburg: Nauka, 2003), vol. 53, p. 666; V.A. Romodanovskaia, 'Maria Salmina', in: *TODL* (St Petersburg: Nauka, 2014), vol. 61, p. 751.
8. On the 'seminar' and the network of its graduates see: 'Uchitel i ego ucheniki. Pamiati akademika V.N. Peretza', http://aej.org.ua/history/1470.html.

9. Interview with S.O. Shmidt, 8 January 2008, Moscow. The audio record and the transcript are in the author's personal archive.
10. D.S. Likhachev in: *Sergei Ivanovich Vavilov: Ocherki i vospominaniia*, 2nd edn (Moscow: Nauka, 1981), pp. 262–264.
11. Likhachev's recollections about her are in, *Vospominaniia*, pp. 378–380; Letters and notes from Adrianova-Peretz to Malyshev, RO IRLI, f. 494, op. 2, d. 106, ll. 45, 49, 62.
12. Recollections of Panchenko in: *DLEE*, p. 99.
13. See Patryk Babiracki and Kenyon Zimmer, eds, *Cold War Crossings: Travel and Exchange across the Soviet Bloc, 1940s–1960s* (College Station: Texas A&M UP, 2014).
14. P.A. Druzhinin, *Ideologiia i filologiia*, vol. 1, p. 235; on the salaries and other privileges see the same volume, pp. 211–234.
15. S.I. Vavilov, *Dnevniki. 1909–1951*, vol. 2 (Moscow: Nauka, 2013), pp. 268, 298.
16. Ibid., pp. 298–299.
17. Vavilov's diary entry for 6 January and 7 March 1947, *Dnevniki. 1909–1951*, pp. 269, 303. On Adrianova's anniversary in March 1948 he sent her a congratulating note. 'Iubilei chlena-korrespondenta AN SSSR V.P. Adrianovoi-Perets', *TODL* vol. 6 (1948), pp. 407–409; D.S. Likhachev, 'Neskolko slov o S.I. Vavilove kak initsiatore serii "Literaturnyie pamiatniki"', at: http://www.lihachev.ru/bibliografiya/by/4474/.
18. D.S. Likhachev, 'Zadachi serii "Literaturnyie pamiatniki"', *Russkaia literatura* 4 (1977), pp. 103–108; D.S. Likhachev, 'Vavilov'; Dmitry Likhachev's meeting with an audience in the Ostankino television show on 'Vstrecha v Kontsertnoi studii Ostankino 12 marta 1986 g', E.V. Galperina, ed., *Ostankinskie vechera* (Moscow: Iskusstvo, 1989), pp. 111–132.
19. D.S. Likhachev, 'Shakhmatov kak issledovatel russkogo letopisaniia', in: S.G. Obnorskii, ed., *A.A. Shakhmatov, 1964–1920: Sbornik statei i materialov* (Moscow, Leningrad: Izdatelstvo Academii Nauk, 1947), pp. 253–293.
20. D.S. Likhachev, 'O Letopisnom Periode Russkoi Istoriografii', *Voprosy Istorii* 9 (September 1948), pp. 21–40.
21. The most complete information about the history of the monument's discovery and its subsequent 'life' is in: B.L. Bogorodskii, D.S. Likhachev, O.V. Tvorogov, V.L. Vinogradov, eds, *Slovar-spravochnik 'Slova o polku Igoreve'. V 6 vypuskakh* (Leningrad: Nauka, 1965–1984).
22. Z.K. Vasilieva, 'Leonid Alekseevich Tvorogov (1900–1978). K 100-letiiu so dnia rozhdeniiia', *Pskov* 12 (2000), p. 221.
23. D.S. Likhachev, preface to *Slovo o Polku Igoreve* (Leningrad: Sovetskii pisatel, 1949), pp. 26–27.
24. 'Rabota N. Zabolotskogo nad "Slovom o Polku Igoreve". Kommentarii D. Likhachev i N. Stepanova', *Voprosy Literatury* 1 (1969), pp. 164–188.
25. D.S. Likhachev, 'Istoricheskii i politicheskii krugozor avtora "Slova o polku Igoreve"', in: V.P. Adrianova-Peretz, ed., *Slovo o Polku Igoreve. Seriia Literaturnyie Pamiatniki* (Moscow-Leningrad: AN SSSR, 1950), pp. 8, 38.
26. Tatiana M. Goriaeva, ed., *'Velikaia kniga dnia ...' Radio v SSSR. Dokumenty i materialy* (Moscow: ROSSPEN, 2007), pp. 471–473.
27. Paneiakh, *Tvorchestvo i sudba istorika*, p. 237.
28. Serhy Yekelchyk, *Stalin's Empire of Memory. Russian–Ukrainian Relations in the Soviet Historical Imagination* (Toronto: University of Toronto Press, 2004), pp. 71, 154.
29. 'Zakrytoie pismo TsK VPK(b) o dele professorov Kliuevoi i Roskina', 16 July 1947, at http://www.alexanderyakovlev.org/fond/issues-doc/69339.
30. A.N. Boldyrev, *Osadnaia Zapis (Blokadnyi dnevnik)*. Prepared by V.S. Garbuzov and I.M. Steplin-Kamenskii (St Petersburg: Evropeiskii Dom, 1998), the entry of 11 July 1945, p. 348.

31. Lidia Ginzburg, *Zapisnyie knizhki, vospominaniia, esse* (St Petersburg: Iskusstvo-SPB, 2002), pp. 353–355.
32. Likhachev, *Vospominaniia*, pp. 359–360; Efim Etkind, *Zapiski nezagovorshchika. Barselonskaia proza* (St Petersburg: Akademicheskii proekt, 2001), pp. 133–135. For the description of the sessions of the 1930s see: Sheila Fitzpatrick, *Tear off the Masks! Identity and Imposture in Twentieth-Century Russia* (Princeton University Press, 2005); also J. Curtis, *Boris Eichenbaum: ego semia, strana i russkaia literature* (St Petersburg: Akademicheskii proekt, 2004), pp. 181–183.
33. J. Curtis, *Boris Eichenbaum*, p. 142; K. Azadovsky and B. Yegorov, 'Kosmopolity', *Novoie literaturnoie obozreniie* 5 (1999), pp. 83–135; Druzhinin, *Ideologiia i filologiia*, vol. 2, p. 239.
34. V.I. Demidov, V.A. Kutuzov, eds', *'Leningradskoie delo'* (Leningrad: Lenizdat, 1990); Druzhinin, *Ideologiia i filologiia*, vol. 2, pp. 486–494.
35. Druzhinin, *Ideologiia i filologiia*, vol. 2, pp. 96, 110, 168.
36. For Eichenbaum, the loss of professional life was a terrible blow: during the war he lost a manuscript on the life of Leo Tolstoy, his last son perished in the battle of Stalingrad, then his wife died. J. Curtis, *Boris Eichenbaum*, p. 190.
37. Etkind, *Zapiski nezagovorshchika*, p. 135; Druzhinin, *Ideologiia i filologiia*, vol. 2, pp. 96, 110, 168.
38. Druzhinin, *Ideologiia i filologiia*, p. 2, pp. 473–492; David Brandenberger, 'Stalin, the Leningrad Affair, and the Limits of Postwar Russocentrism', *The Russian Review* 63 (April 2004), pp. 241–255, esp. pp. 248–252.
39. Paneiakh, *Tvorchestvo i sudba istorika*, pp. 247–249.
40. Paneiakh, *Tvorchestvo i sudba istorika*, p. 252. Likhachev's defence did not save Romanov for long; in October 1950 the latter was fired from Leningrad University. He could never again teach or publish his works.
41. Eichenbaum wrote in his diary: 'Evgeniev-Maximov behaved awfully – absolutely base, sneaky old man, who bends over backwards to procure material goods for himself.' Cited in J. Curtis, *Boris Eichenbaum*, p. 196.
42. D.S. Likhachev, *VRL*, vol. 1, pp. 313–316.
43. Likhachev, *Vospominaniia*, p. 360.
44. Irina Ganelina, 'Y.S. Lurie: istoriia zhizni', *In Memoriam. Sbornik pamiati Y. S. Lurie* (St Petersburg: Atheneum-Feniks, 1997), pp. 16–175. Likhachev's memory deceived him: in writing his memoirs, he said that in 1951–1952 he hired Lurie to the Sector. This happened, however, only in 1957.
45. Mark Azadovsky wrote to linguist Nikolai Gudzii in October 1949 about Lapitsky's activities at the University: 'He plays the clown, humiliating science and the best scientists in the past and in the present.' Constantin Azadovsky, ed., '"Udastsia li prorubit etu stenu..." Iz pisem M.K. Azadovskogo k N.K. Gudziiu 1949–1950 godov', *Russkaia literatura* 2 (2006); for more on Lapitsky's 'career' see: P.A. Druzhinin, *Ideologia i filologiia*, vol. 2, p. 535.
46. See, for example, the letter of Lapitsky to Malenkov dated 26 December 1951, published in: Petr Druzhinin, 'Pushkinskii Dom pod ognem bolshevistskoi kritiki', http://www.nlobooks.ru/node/1089.
47. Likhachev, *Vospominaniia*, pp. 366–367; D.S. Likhachev to M.N. Tikhomirov, January 1951, ARAN, f. 693, op. 4, d. 345, l. 13; D.S. Likhachev to Vladimir Malyshev, 21 June, 25 July, 31 July 1951, RO IRLI archive, f. 494, op. 2, d. 728, l. 17, 22, 23.
48. Druzhinin, *Ideologiia i filologiia*, vol. 2, p. 536.
49. Druzhinin, *Ideologiia i filologiia*, vol. 2, p. 537.

50. See Likhachev's remarks in 1983, at the 100th anniversary of Vladislav Evgeniev-Maximov, published in: 'Chernye dni Leningrada. Vospominaniia', prepared by Natalia Maximova, *Zvezda*, 2 (2011).
51. D.S. Likhachev, *VRL*, vol. 1, pp. 320–321.
52. D.S. Likhachev, *VRL*, vol. 1, p. 321. The text of Likhachev's recollections erroneously attributed this episode to 1950.
53. The author's interview with R.Sh. Ganelin, 5 September 2010, St Petersburg.
54. Paneiakh, *Tvorchestvo i sudba istorika*, pp. 315–326.
55. N.N. Pokrovsky, 'Dmitry Sergeevich Likhachev i nachalo sibirskoi arkhiografii', *Arkheograficheskii Ezhegodnik za 1999*, Sigurd Shmidt, ed (Moscow: Nauka, 2000), p. 405.
56. The author's interview with Sigurd Shmidt, 8 January 2008, Moscow; the author's interview with Vera Zilitinkevich-Tolz, 14 November 2009, Washington DC; the author's interview with Rafail Ganelin, 5 September 2010, St Petersburg.
57. D.S. Likhachev, *VRL*, vol. 1, p. 322.

## Chapter 6   Advocate of Cultural Legacy, 1955–1965

1. On the shift of cosmopolitan culture to Moscow see: Katerina Clark, *Moscow, The Fourth Rome: Stalinism, Cosmopolitanism, and the Evolution of Soviet Culture, 1931–1941* (Cambridge, MA: Harvard University Press, 2011), p. 15. On the role of *Novyi Mir* see Denis Kozlov, *The Readers of Novyi Mir: Coming to Terms with the Stalinist Past* (Cambridge, MA: Harvard University Press, 2013).
2. Vladislav Zubok, *Zhivago's Children: The Last Russian Intelligentsia* (Cambridge, MA: Harvard University Press, 2009).
3. S.S. Averintsev, 'Opyt peterburgskoi intelligentsii v sovetskie gody – po lichnym vospominaniiam', *Novyi Mir* 6 (2004); Helena Goscilo, Steven M. Norris, eds, *Preserving Petersburg: History, Memory, Nostalgia* (Bloomington, IN: Indiana University Press, 2008).
4. Likhachev to Malyshev, 30 December 1958, RO IRLI archive, f. 494, op. 2, d. 728, l. 9.
5. 'Zametki k vospominaniiam o Vere', publication by Zinaida Kurbatova, *Nashe Nasledie* 79–80 (2006).
6. Zina Kurbatova in the film *Chasnyie Khroniki* (2006), https://www.youtube.com/watch?v=92H6U2fs0XY.
7. Interview with Vera Tolz, 28 June 2013, http://www.novayagazeta.ru/arts/58805.html.
8. L.M. Arinshtein, I.Yu. Yurieva, eds, *Neizvestnyi Likhachev*, p. 273.
9. 'V nem prelomilsia XX vek', *Novaia gazeta*, 26 August 2013, at: http://www.novayagazeta.ru/arts/58805.html; D.S. Likhachev to I.M. Kudriavtsev, 23 March 1948, *Iz epistoliarnogo nasledija D.S. Likhacheva*, p. 80; D.S. Likhachev to Vladimir Malyshev, 15 July 1948 and 22 June 1950, RO IRLI, f. 494, op. 2, d. 728, ll 4, 16.
10. 'Zametki k vospominaniiam o Vere', *Nashe Nasledie* 79–80 (2006).
11. 'Zametki k vospominaniiam o Vere', *Nashe Nasledie* 79 – 80 (2006).
12. D.S. Likhachev to M.N. Tikhomirov, 27 December 1970, ARAN, f. 693, op. 4, d. 345, l. 12ob.
13. Z.A. Likhachev and D.S. Likhachev to I.N. Medvedeva-Tomashevskaia, 10 November 1964, Leningrad, in: N.V. Bogdanov, O.Yu. Efishov, A.V. Vertel, eds, *Pisma Likhachevykh I.N. Medvedevoi-Tomashevskoi v Krym (1963–1973 gg.)* (Simferopol: N. Orianda, 2013), p. 22. Mila and Vera moved to their own flats only in the 1970s.
14. See Vladimir Shlapentokh, *Strakh i druzhba v nashem totalitarnom proshlom* (St Petersburg: Zvezda, 2003).

15. In February 1928 Maximov was arrested in connection with the Brotherhood of St Seraphim, but soon released.
16. Recollections of Aleksandr Panchenko, in: E. Vodolazkin, ed., *Dmitry Likhachev i ego epokha: Vospominaniie, esse, dokumenty, fotografii* (St Petersburg: Logos, 2002), pp. 364–365.
17. Likhachev's cable to Malyshev on 30 March 1957, RO IRLI, f. 494, op. 2, d. 749, l. 1; N.V. Bogdanov, O.Yu. Efishov, A.V. Vertel, eds, *Pisma Likhachevykh I.N. Medvedevoi-Tomashevskoi v Krym (1963–1973 gg.)* (Simferopol: N. Orianda, 2013); Zoia Tomashevskaia, 'Kak i zachem pisalos "Stremia"', http://www.philol.msu.ru/~lex/td/?pid=012211&oid=01221.
18. D.S. Likhachev to Malyshev on 6 June 1955, RO IRLI, f. 494, op. 2, d. 728, l. 41.
19. I.E. Ganelina, 'Ya.S. Lurie: istoriia zhizni', in: N.M. Botvinnik, E.I. Vaneieva, eds, *IN MEMORIAM. Sbornik pamiati Ya.S. Lurie* (St Petersburg: Atheneum-Feniks, 1997), pp. 5–9; the author's conversation with Irina Yefimovna Ganelina, Lurie's widow, 29 January 2009, St Petersburg; Ya.S. Lurie, *Izbrannyie stat'i i pisma* (St Petersburg: European University of St Petersburg, 2011).
20. I. E. Ganelina, 'Ya.S. Lurie: istoriia zhizni', pp. 9–11; the author's conversation with Irina Yefimovna Ganelina, 29 January 2009.
21. Lurie in a personal letter to Aleksandr Zimin, 18 February 1960 and also April 1960, the archive of the Institute of History, St Petersburg. Joseph of Volotsk was a clerical reformer of the sixteenth century, defender of monastic landownership and the Church's dependence on the despotic state.
22. Cable from Likhachev to Vladimir Malyshev, 25 January 1956, in: Letters and cables from Likhachev to V. Malyshev, RO IRLI, f. 494, op. 2, d. 748, l. 63.
23. Lurie's letter to Aleksandr Zimin, early 1957 (undated) and 5 February 1960, the archive of the Institute of History, St Petersburg.
24. D.S. Likhachev to M.N. Tikhomirov, 7 July 1954, ARAN, f. 693, op. 4, d. 345, l. 18; D.S. Likhachev to V.I. Malyshev on 5 August 1955, RO IRLI, f. 494, op. 2, d. 728, l. 42; also another letter to Malyshev, probably April 1957, RO IRLI, f. 494, op. 2, d. 749, l. 3–4.
25. Lurie to Zimin, 19 April 1959, the archive of the Institute of History, St Petersburg.
26. I.P. Smirnov, in: Vodolazkin, *Dmitry Likhachev i ego epokha*, p. 116.
27. D.S. Likhachev, *Vospominaniia*, pp. 386–388.
28. A.A. Formozov, '"Rol" N.N. Voronina v zashchite pamiatnikov kultury Rossii', *Rossiiskaia arkheologiia*, no. 2 (2004), pp. 173–180, available at: http://www.russiancity.ru/dbooks/d04.htm
29. D.S. Likhachev, *Vospominaniia*, p. 387.
30. 'Nelzia tak otnositsia k pamiatnikam narodnogo zodchestva. Pismo v redaktsiiu', *Literaturnaia Gazeta*, 15 January 1955, p. 1.
31. D. Likhachev, 'Sozdadim muzei russkogo narodnogo iskusstva', *Zvezda*, 2 (1956), pp. 188–189.
32. Z.K. Vasilieva, 'Leonid Alekseevich Tvorogov (1900–1978). K 100-letiiu so dnia rozhdeniia', *Pskov* 12 (2000), pp. 219–220; Z.K. Vasilieva, 'Potomstvo nam ne prostit.' Perepiska L.A. Tvorogova s D.S. Likhachevym o sokhrannosti pamiatnikov stariny, 1957 g. http://museums.pskov.ru/pskovoldmodern/tvorogov/tvor3
33. D.S. Likhachev to Tvorogov, 31 May, 6 and 22 June 1957, in: Z.K. Vasilieva, 'Potomstvo nam ne prostit.'
34. D.S. Likhachev to N.N. Voronin, 5 March 1959, in: *Iz epistoliarnogo naslediia D.S. Likhacheva*, p. 226.
35. V.I. Vernadsky, 'Ia veriu v silu svobodnoi mysli. Pisma I.I. Petrunkievichu', *Novyi Mir* 12 (1989), cited in: A.A. Formozov, ' "Rol" N.N. Voronina'; the author's interview with Elena Vaneieva, 22 September 2009.

36. C.P. Fitzgerald, *China: A Short Cultural History* (Boulder, CO: Westview Press, 1985).
37. D.S. Likhachev, '"Berech" pamiatniki proshlogo', *Neva* 3 (1963), pp. 195–196.
38. D.S. Likhachev to V.B. Shklovskii, 16 November 1964, 'Iz epistoliarnogo naslediia D.S. Likhacheva', p. 217; N.V. Bogdanova, et al., eds, *Pis'ma Likhachevykh I.N. Medvedevoi-Tomashevskoi v Krym (1963–1973 gg.)* (Simferopol: N. Orianda, 2013), pp. 20–21, 24–25; D.S. Likhachev to I.S. Zilbershtein, 15 June 1984, RO IRLI, f. 769 (Letters of Likhachev).
39. Georgy Vasilievich Florovsky (1893–1979) graduated from the Novorossiia Imperial University in Odessa. After the revolution he emigrated to Czechoslovakia, then lived in Paris and Belgrade. He joined and then broke with the 'Eurasian' movement.
40. Georges Florovsky, 'The Problem of Old Russian Culture', *Slavic Review*, vol. 21, no. 1 (March 1962), pp. 1–15.
41. James H. Billington, 'Images of Muscovy', *Slavic Review*, vol. 21, no. 1 (March 1962), pp. 24–34.
42. D.S. Likhachev 'Further Remarks on the Problem of Old Russian Culture', *Slavic Review*, vol. 22, no. 1 (March 1963), pp. 115–120; Georges Florovsky, 'Reply', *Slavic Review*, vol. 21, no. 1 (March 1962), pp. 35–36, 40; D.S. Likhachev 'Further Remarks', p. 117.
43. D.S. Likhachev 'Further Remarks', pp. 117, 119, 120.
44. Nikolai Iosifovich Konrad (1891–1971) was educated in Kiev and worked at the Academy's division of Oriental Studies. He was arrested in 1938, but survived and returned to academic work in 1941. The ideas that influenced Likhachev can be found in N.I. Konrad, *Zapad i Vostok. Stat'i* (Moscow: Glavnaia Redaktsiia Vostochnoi Literatury, 1966), esp. pp. 102, 114, 120 and 254.
45. Likhachev to Picchio, 24 October 1975. RO IRLI, fond 769.
46. D.S. Likhachev to N.N. Aseiev, June 15, 1961, *Iz epistoliarnogo naslediia*; *Nikolai Aseiev: rodoslovnaia poezii. Stat'i. Vospominaniia. Pisma*, compiled by A.M. Kriukova, S.S. Lesnevskii (Moscow: Sovetskii pisatel, 1990).
47. N.S. Khrushchev. *Stroitelstvo kommunizma i razvitiie selskogo khoziaistva*, vol. 4 (Moscow: Gospolitizdat, 1963), p. 298.
48. Y. Belopolsky, 'Gorod blizkogo zavtra', *Literaturnaia gazeta* 10 June 1965.
49. Georgy Knabe, 'Final: Arbatskaia epopeia', in T. Kniazevskaia, ed., *Russkaia intelligentsia* (Moscow: Nauka, 1999), pp. 342–350; author's interview with Moscow archeographer and 'kraieved' Sigurd Shmidt, 17 January 2008, Moscow; Stephen V. Bittner, *The Many Lives of Khrushchev's Thaw: Experience and Memory in Moscow's Arbat* (Ithaca, NY: Cornell University Press, 2008).
50. D.A. Granin, 'Odin iz poslednikh', in his: *Tainyi znak Peterburga* (St Petersburg: Logos, 2002), pp. 333–339.
51. D.S. Likhachev, 'Chetvertoie izmereniie', *Literaturnaia Gazeta*, 10 June 1965, p. 2; Catriona Kelly, 'Ispravliat' li istoriiu. Spory ob okhrane pamiatnikov v Leningrade 1960–1970-kh godov', *Neprikosnovennyi zapas* 2 (64) (2009), http://nlobooks.ru/sites/default/files/old/nlobooks.ru/rus/nz-online/619/1326/1334/index.html; D.A. Granin, 'Odin iz poslednikh', pp. 333–339.
52. D.S. Likhachev in a letter to V.P. Yenisherlov, 21 April 1998, in *Iz epistoliarnogo naslediia D.S. Likhacheva*.
53. Vera Zilitinkevich-Tolz, letter of 5 May 2011 to the author; the entry of 1967 from the notebook of Dmitry Likhachev from the 1960s, courtesy of Zilitinkevich-Tolz; Robin Milner-Gulland, 'Vospominaniia o D.S.Likhacheve', http://likhachev.lfond.spb.ru/Memoirs/robin.htm; also the author's conversations with Milner-Gulland in Brighton, UK on 4 November 2013.
54. B.M. Firsov, *Raznomysliie v SSSR: 1940–1960-e gody* (St Petersburg: Evropeiskyi universitet, 2008), p. 326; Yuli Kim, 'Sudar dorogoi' *Zvezda* 8 (1998), p. 105.

55. Vyacheslav Ivanov in E. Vodolazkin, ed., *Dmitrii Likhachev i ego epokha*, p. 173.
56. Firsov, *Raznomysliie v SSSR*, p. 438.
57. 'Literaturnyi Vtornik' GARF, f. 6903, op. 1, d. 866, ll. 6–54, published in Firsov, *Raznomysliie v SSSR*, pp. 462–504.
58. Firsov, *Raznomysliie v SSSR*, pp. 439, 491–502; Ivanov in: *DLEE*, p. 173.
59. D.S. Likhachev to R.O. Yakobson, The MIT Institute Archives, Roman Jakobson Papers, 1908–1982, Box 15, folder 77, pp. 1–2.
60. Vyacheslav Ivanov and Oleg Panchenko in: *DLEE*, pp. 162–163, 363; the author's interview with Boris Uspensky, Rome, 6 April 2014.
61. There are numerous valuable recollections about A.A. Zimin. See Ya.S. Lurie, 'Iz vospominanii ob Aleksandre Aleksandroviche Zimine', in: *Odissei. Chelovek v istorii. Obraz 'drugogo' v kulture* (Moscow: Nauka, 1994); S.M. Kashtanov in G.N. Sevostianov and L.T. Milskaia, eds, *Portrety Istorikov. Vremia i sudby. Tom 1. Otechestvennaia istoriia* (Moscow – Jerusalem: Universitetskaia kniga. Geshrim, 2000), pp. 369–384; V.P. Kozlov, ed., *Istorik v Rossii mezhdu proshlym i budushchim* (Moscow: RGGU, 2012).
62. Correspondence between A.A. Zimin and Ya.S. Lurie, letters 283, 284, undated, around February 1963, from the personal collection of I.E. Ganelina, now in the archive of the Institute of History, St Petersburg (subsequently: Zimin–Lurie correspondence IH).
63. Recollections of Will Ryan in a conversation with the author, East Croydon, 20 November 2013.
64. S.M. Kashtanov in *Vremia i sudby*, p. 378; A.A. Zimin, 'Obreteniie svobody', published by V.G. Zimina, *Rodina* 8 (1990), p. 89.
65. Denis Kozlov, *The Readers of Novyi Mir Coming to Terms with the Stalinist Past* (Cambridge, MA: Harvard University Press, 2013), p. 201.
66. Zimin to Malyshev, RO IRLI, fond 494, op. 2, no. 516, ll. 41–42; cited in: L.V. Sokolova, ed., *Istoria spora o podlinnosti 'Slova o Polku Igoreve'* (St Petersburg: Pushkinskii Dom, 2010), p. 17.
67. Recollection of N.I. Pavlenko in: V.P. Kozlov, *Istorik v Rossii mezhdu proshlym i budushchim* (Moscow: RGGU, 2012), p. 32; S.N. Kisterev, 'K kharakteristike nekotorykh vospominanii ob Aleksandre Aleksandroviche Zimine', *Vestnik 'Alians-Arkheo'*, Vypusk 2 (Moscow-St Petersburg, Alians-Arkheo, 2013), p. 21.
68. L.V. Sokolova, ed., *Istoriia spora o podlinosti 'Slova o polku Igoreve'. Materialy diskussii 1960-kh godov* (St Petersburg: Pushkinskii Dom, 2010), p. 26.
69. The letters are cited in: L.V. Sokolova, ed., *Istoriia spora*, pp. 25–27, 30.
70. Likhachev to Boris Rybakov, *Russkaia Literatura*, no. 3 (1994), p. 260; Likhachev to Robinson, 2 June 1963, in: L.V. Sokolova, ed., *Istoriia spora o podlinosti 'Slova o polku Igoreve'*, p. 41.
71. D.S. Likhachev, *Tekstologiia: na materiale russkoi literatury X–XVII vv* (Moscow-Leningrad: Izdatelstvo akademii nauk, 1962). In 1967 Likhachev succinctly expressed his scientific credo to Viktor Vinogradov: 'I consider it absolutely proven textologically that "The Lay" emerged earlier than "Zadonshchina"'. Letter of D.S. Likhachev to V.V. Vinogradov, 3 October 1967, *Iz epistoliarnogo naslediia*, p. 193.
72. Letter of Likhachev to Vinogradov, in: *Istoriia spora o podlinosti 'Slova o polku Igoreve'*, p. 40; Letter of Likhachev to Fedoseev, in: L.V. Sokolova, 'K istorii spora o podlinnosti 'Slova o polku Igoreve': (Iz perepiski akademika D.S. Likhachev)', *Russkaia Literatura*, no. 2 (1994), p. 256.
73. L.V. Sokolova, ed., *Istoriia spora o podlinosti 'Slova o polku Igoreve'*, pp. 56–57, 71; also her 'Kistorii', *Russkaia Literatura*, no. 2 (1994), pp. 221–223.
74. L.V. Sokolova, ed., *Istoriia spora o podlinnosti*, p. 161.
75. L.V. Sokolova, ed., *Istoriia spora o podlinnosti*, pp. 163, 167–68, 175.

NOTES TO PAGES 103–108   203

76. L.V. Sokolova, ed., *Istoriia spora o podlinnosti*, pp. 526–527.
77. 'K istorii', *Russkaia Literatura*, no. 2 (1994), pp. 224, 234.
78. D.S. Likhachev, *Vospominaniia*, p. 389; L.V. Sokolova, ed., *Istoriia spora o podlinnosti*, p. 115.
79. On Likhachev's sending annual postcards, the author's interview with Yakov Gordin, St Petersburg, 6 January 2008.
80. On the prejudice in Western scholarship against Likhachev see: Robin Milner-Gulland, 'Natsionalnaia samobytnost Rossii: o zapadnykh issledovaniiakh, trudakh D.S. Likhacheva i kulturnom oblike Rossii', http://www.lfond.spb.ru/programs/likhachev/100/stenogrammi/gulland.html.
81. Z.A. Likhacheva and D.S. Likhachev to I.N. Medvedeva-Tomashevsky, 22 December 1964, in: N.V. Bogdanova et al., eds, *Pisma Likhachevykh I.N. Medvedevoi-Tomashevskoi v Krym*, p. 26.
82. Norman W. Ingham, 'Historians and Textology', and Edward L. Keenan, 'The Long-Awaited Book and the Bykovskii Hypothesis', *Kritika* vol. 8, no. 4 (Fall 2007), pp. 832, 833, 834, 817–830.
83. RIA Novosti, http://ria.ru/science/20071219/93148250.html#ixzz3sQtxOHPT. A.A. Zalizniak, *'Slovo o polku Igoreve': vzgliad lingvista* (Moscow: Rukopisnyie pamiatniki Drevnei Rusi, 2008).

## Chapter 7    The Making of a Wise Man, 1966–1976

1. D.S. Likhachev, 'Zametki k vospominaniiam o Vere', http://www.nasledie-rus.ru/podshivka/7907.php.
2. Catriona Kelly, 'Ispravliat li istoriiu? Spory ob okhrane pamiatnikov v Leningrade 1960-kh–1970-kh godov', *Neprikosnovennyi zapas* 2 (64) 2004, http://magazines.russ.ru/nz/2009/2/kk7-pr.html.
3. Yitzhak M. Brudny, *Reinventing Russia. Russian Nationalism and the Soviet State, 1953–1991* (Cambridge, MA: Harvard University Press, 1998), esp. pp. 9, 139, 140, 142, 174.
4. D.S. Likhachev, *Vospominaniia*, pp. 391–392.
5. Svetlana Veresh, 'Na puti k Solovkam: vospominaniia pervogo direktora Solovetskogo muzeia', *Almanakh 'Solovetskoie more'* 4 (2005), http://www.solovki.info/?action=archive&id=399; '"Milaia dobrovolnaia zatrovnitsa". Pisma D.S. Likhacheva k S.V. Veresh', *Nashe Naslediie* 79–80 (2006).
6. D.S. Likhachev, *Vospominaniia*, p. 390.
7. Ibid., pp. 390–391.; D.S. Likhachev to S.V. Veresh, 28 November 1967, in 'Milaia dobrovolnaia zatrovnitsa'.
8. Obolensky, leading Oxford Byzantologist, was son of Prince Dmitri Obolensky and Countess Maria Shuvalova; he and Fennell were 'in-laws'; they married the sisters Lopukhin; John Simmons, Konovalov's student, was the best British bibliographer of Russian literature. On their support see the letter from J.S.G. Simmons to Oxford's Vice-Chancellor, 11 January 1967, Bodleian Library, The University of Oxford, file 6/HD/2C, file 15.
9. D.S. Likhachev, 'The authenticity of *Slovo o Polku Igoreve*: a brief survey of the arguments', *Oxford Slavonic Papers*, vol. XIII (1967), pp. 33–46; on Zimin see p. 46.
10. D.S. Likhachev, *Vospominaniia*, vol. 2, pp. 355–361.
11. D.S. Likhachev, *Vospominaniia*, vol. 2, p. 263.
12. Information about Likhachev's meeting with his relatives, as well as private letters and photographs of Alexandra Andrealetti, the author received from Vera Zilitinkevich-Tolz, 15 December 2015.

13. 'Vospominaniia Likhachev. Zapisi Oseni 1966 g.' from the film 'Chastnyie khroniki (2006), http://www.youtube.com/watch?v=92H6U2fs0XY.; private notes of D.S. Likhachev on 29 August 1967 and subsequent undated pages, provided to the author by Vera Zilitinkevich-Tolz.
14. Denis Kozlov, *The Readers of Novyi Mir*, pp. 218, 221.
15. Solzhenitsyn regretted the loss of peasant culture in his polemics with academician V.V. Vinogradov in *Literaturnaia Gazeta* on 4 November 1965.
16. Liudmila Saraskina, *Aleksandr Solzhenitsyn* (Moscow: Molodaia Gvardiia, 2008), pp. 518–519; http://www.solovki.ru/history26.html, accessed on 27 January 2012.
17. D.S. Likhachev, 'Solovki 1928–1931', http://www.ruthenia.ru/folktee/CYBERSTOL/GULAG/Lichachev.html, accessed on 27 January 2012.
18. On Solzhenitsyn's ideas regarding Russia and the intelligentsia, the most perceptive observations are in: Aleksandr Shmeman, *Dnevniki: 1973–1983* (Moscow: Russkii Put, 2005), pp. 184–185; Likhachev's letter to Veresh, 26 March 1968, 'Milaia dobrovolnaia zatvornitsa'.
19. S.S. Averintsev, 'Ukhodit epokha', *Literaturnaia Gazeta*, 6–12 October (1999), pp. 1, 9; information from Vera Zilitinkevich-Tolz in her letter to the author, 5 May 2011.
20. Sergei Yursky, 'Opasnyie sviazi', http://magazines.russ.ru/october/2000/6/urski.html, accessed on 20 May 2015.
21. Private notes of D.S. Likhachev on 18 April 1968, provided to the author by Vera Zilitinkevich-Tolz.
22. Jaromir Navratil, with Malcolm Byrne, Peter Kornbluh, Mark Kramer, eds, *The Prague Spring 1968* (CEU Press, 1998); N. Tomilina, S. Karner, eds, *Prazhskaia vesna i mezhdunarodnyi krizis 1968: Stat'i, issledovaniia, vospominaniia* (Moscow: Mezhdunarodnyi fond demokratiia, 2010).
23. A. Solzhenitsyn, *Bodalsia telenok s dubom*, http://www.lib.ru/proza/solzhenicyn/telenok.txt
24. Irina Yurieva, ed., *Neizvestnyi D.S. Likhachev, Neopublikovannyie materialy iz arkhiva Rossiiskogo Fonda Kultury* (Moscow: Rossiiskii Fond Kultury, 2006), pp. 274–275.
25. D.S. Likhachev's lecture notes on 16 December 1991 in: *Neizvestnyi D.S. Likhachev*, p. 278.
26. D.S. Likhachev to Veresh, 4 September 1968. The phrase about the 1960s is omitted in the *Nashe Naslediie* publication; the author found it in: *Iz epistoliarnogo naslediia D.S. Likhacheva*, prepared by RGALI.
27. Lidia Azadovsky to A.I. Maliutin, 31 January 1971, cited in: P.A. Druzhinin, *Ideologiia i filologiia*, vol. 2, p. 524; M. Chudakova, 'Obval pokolenii', *Novoe literaturnoe obozrenie*, no. 77 (2006).
28. Z.A. Likhachev and D.S. Likhachev to I.N. Medvedeva-Tomashevskaia, 13 March 1969 and D.S. Likhachev to I.N. Medvedeva-Tomashevskaia, 18 August 1969 and 14 October 1969 in: *Pisma Likhachevykh v Krym*, pp. 58, 63, 64.
29. D.S. Likhachev to I.N. Medevedeva-Tomashevskaia, 19 September 1968, Leningrad, in: *Pisma Likhachevykh v Krym*, p. 51.
30. D.S. Likhachev to I.N. Medvedeva-Tomashevskaia, 2 November 1969, in: *Pisma Likhachevykh v Krym*, p. 65. The list of 'errors' that remained in the novel was recorded in Likhachev's notebook (around 1974), provided to the author by Vera Zilitinkevich-Tolz; M.S. Glinka, *Khranitel. K 100-letiiu so dnia rozhdeniia V.M. Glinki. Stat'i. Pisma. Proza* (St Petersburg: ARS, 2003).
31. D.S. Likhachev to I.N. Medvedeva-Tomashevskaia, 14 August and 4 October 1970, in: *Pisma Likhachevykh v Krym*, p. 73.
32. Letter from Nikolai Voronin to Likhachev, 28 May 1971, RO IRLI, fond 769.

33. Z.A. Likhacheva to I.N. Medvedeva-Tomashevskaia, 12 July 1966; D.S. Likhachev to I.N. Medvedeva-Tomashevskaia, 14 October 1970, in: *Pisma Likhachevykh v Krym*, pp. 41, 73.
34. D.S. Likhachev to P.N. Fedoseiev, 21 April 1973, RGALI, f. 2894, op. 1, delo 338, ll. 21–23, in: *Iz epistoliarnogo naslediia D.S. Likhacheva*, pp. 429–430.
35. D.S. Likhachev to P.N. Fedoseiev, 21 April 1973, RGALI, f. 2894, op. 1, delo 338, ll. 21–23 in: *Iz epistoliarnogo naslediia D.S. Likhacheva*, pp. 430–431.
36. Saraskina, *Aleksandr Solzhenitsyn*, p. 680.
37. Zoia B. Tomashevsky, 'Kak i zachem pisalos "Stremia"', http://www.philol.msu.ru/~lex/td/?pid=012211&oid=01221.
38. Telephone conversation with Vera Zilitinkevich-Tolz, 27 February 2008 and 20 September 2010; interview with Evgeny Lukin, 28 August 2010, St Petersburg.
39. A.I. Solzhenitsyn, 'Obrazovanshchina' in: *Iz-pod glyb* (Paris: IMKA-Press, 1974), http://www.vehi.net/samizdat/izpodglyb/index.html.
40. Yefim Etkind, *Zapiski nezagovorshchika. Barselonskaia proza* (St Petersburg: Akademicheskii proiekt, 2001); Sergei Yursky, 'Opasnyie sviazi', http://yurskiy.ru/069b.html.
41. Recollection of Vyacheslav Ivanov and Gelian Prokhorov in: *Dmitry Likhachev i ego epokha*, pp. 106, 110, 175.
42. On this assault: *Nedelia* 38 (1989); Likhachev's interview with Urmas Ott, November 1990, https://www.youtube.com/watch?v=PIypMiUMo0.; information from Vera Zilitinkevich-Tolz to the author in a letter of 5 May 2011.
43. Petr Bogatyrev, friend of Roman Yakobson, lived in emigration in Prague during the 1920s, and returned to the Soviet Union in 1940. On Konstantin Bogatyrev, see the programme on the BBC Russian Service, http://www.bbc.co.uk/russian/radio/2009/07/090716_archive_culture_bogatyrev.shtml. Likhachev's correspondence with P.G. Bogatyrev is in: *Iz epistoliarnogo naslediia Likhacheva*, pp. 173–181.
44. Likhachev's interview with Urmas Ott, November 1990, https://www.youtube.com/watch?v=PIycpMiUMo0; information to the author from Vera Zilitinkevich-Tolz, an email, 5 May 2011.
45. D. Bezrukikh, 'Dobryi Stradalets za Russkuiu zemliu. K 70-letiiu Akademika D.S. Likhacheva', *La Pensee Russe*, http://russianmind.eu/dobryi-stradalets-za-russkuyu-zemlyu-k-70-letiyu-akademika-d-s-likhacheva.
46. On this pragmatic side of Likhachev's public philosophy see also: V.M. Lurie, 'Kogda intelligentsia ushla ... a nauka ostalas: Razmyshleniia po povodu knigi D.M. Bulanina "Epilog k istorii russkoi intelligentsia"'. Doklad na zasedanii Sankt-Peterburgskogo Obshchestva vizantino-slavianskikh issledovanii, 2005, http://byzantinorossica.org.ru/lurie_bulanin.html.
47. D.S. Likhachev, *Vospominaniia*, p. 267.
48. D.S. Likhachev in his interview with Andrei Maksimov in the television programme *Night Flight*, St Petersburg, 1997, https://www.youtube.com/watch?v=K4J7faEHjPE, accessed on 23 May 2014.
49. D.S. Likhachev, *VRL*, vol. 2, p. 466.
50. On Solzhenitsyn's attitude towards the Jews see Aleksandr Shmeman, *Dnevniki 1973–1983* (Moscow: Russkii Put, 2005), pp. 184–185.
51. Nina Voronel, *Bez prikras. Vospominaniia* (Moscow: Zakharov, 2003), p. 331.
52. D.S. Likhachev, the notebook of 1970s, provided to the author by Vera Zilitinkevich-Tolz, the entry for 27 June 1975. Aleksander Voronel later recalled that the human rights movement in Russia 'was made up so overwhelmingly of Jews'; Alexander Voronel, 'Twenty years later', in: Noah Lewin-Epstein, Yakov Roi, Paul Rittenband, eds, *Russian Jews on Three Continents* (London: Frank Cass, 1997), pp. 422–423.

53. Aleksandr Shmeman, entry for 19 April 1977, *Dnevniki, 1973–1983* (Moscow: Russkii Put, 2005), pp. 360–362.
54. D.S. Likhachev, 'Zametki o Russkom. Priroda, rodnik, rodina, i prosto dobrota.' *Novyi Mir* 3 (1980), p. 10.
55. D.S. Likhachev, 'Zametki o Russkom. Priroda, rodnik, rodina, i prosto dobrota.', pp. 15–17.
56. D.S. Likhachev, 'Zametki o Russkom. Priroda, rodnik, rodina, i prosto dobrota.' p. 16.
57. D.S. Likhachev, 'Zametki o Russkom. Priroda, rodnik, rodina, i prosto dobrota.' pp. 15–17.
58. D.S. Likhachev, 'Zametki o Russkom. Priroda, rodnik, rodina, i prosto dobrota.' pp. 32–34.
59. From the diary of M.I. Steblin-Kamensky. The author thanks Vladimir Ryzhkovsky who had access to the original and shared his notes with him; Recollections of B.F. Yegorov in: *DLEE*, p. 200.
60. James Billington, *The Icon and the Axe. An Interpretive History of Russian Culture* (New York: Vintage Books Edition, 1970), p. VII. D.S. Likhachev, *Vospominanii*, vol. 2, p. 454. Likhachev's remarks on *The Iron and the Axe* are in: '"V Interesakh Sovremennosti". D.S. Likhachev beseduet s literaturovedom D. Moldavskim', *Literaturnaia Gazeta*, 1 October 1969.
61. E. Keenan. *The Kurbskii–Groznyi Apocrypha. The Seventeenth-Century Genesis of the 'Correspondence', Attributed to Prince A. M. Kurbskii and Tzar Ivan IV* (Cambridge, MA: 1971). D.S. Likhachev, 'Kurbskii i Groznyi – byli li oni pisatelyami?' *Russkaia Literatura* 4 (1972); A.A. Zimin, 'Pervoie poslaniie Kurbskogo Ivanu Groznomu (tekstologicheskiie problemy)' and Ya.S. Lurie, 'Pervoie poslaniie Ivana Groznogo Kurbskomu (voprosy istorii teksta)' in: *TODL*, vol. 31 (1976), pp. 176–234.
62. David Fogelsong, *The American Mission and the 'Evil Empire': the Crusade for 'a Free Russia' since 1881* (London: Cambridge University Press, 2007).
63. Jack V. Haney, 'The Revival of Interest in the Russian Past in the Soviet Union', *Slavic Review*, vol. 32, no. 1 (March 1973), pp. 1–16.
64. Fyodor Abramov, *Neuzheli po etomu puti idti vsemu chelovechestvu? Putevnye zametki. Frantsiia, Germania, Finliandiia, America* (St Petersburg: St Petersburg University, 2000), pp. 18–22, 139–143; Liah Greenfeld, *Nationalism: Five Roads to Modernity* (Cambridge, MA: Harvard University Press, 1992); Nikolai Mitrokhin, *Russkaia partiia: Dvizhenie russkikh natsionalistov v SSSR, 1953–1985 gody* (Moscow: Novoe literaturnoe obozrenie, 2003), pp. 318, 500; Zubok, *Zhivago's Children* (Cambridge, MA and London: Belknap Press of Harvard University Press, 2009), pp. 236–245.
65. Born to a family of Penza peasants in 1926, Myasnikov opened several museums dedicated to Russian artists and public figures from the pre-revolutionary era. G.V. Myasnikov, '"Dusha moia spokoina ...": Iz dnevnikov raznykh let', published by M.G. Myasnikov, *Nashe naslediie*, no. 59–60 (2001), the entry of 19 April 1980, http://www.nasledie-rus.ru/podshivka/6012.php.
66. 'Zametki o Russkom', p. 35.
67. N.O. Lossky, *Vospominaniia. Zhizn i filosofskii put* (Moscow: Russkii put, 2008), pp. 203, 225; N.O. Lossky, *Kharakter russkogo naroda* (Munchen: Possev, 1957). Likhachev took notes from this work in his notebook in 1975.
68. D.S. Likhachev, 'Zametki o Russkom', p. 18.
69. D.S. Likhachev, 'Zametki o Russkom', pp. 10, 18.
70. D.S. Likhachev, *VRL*, vol. 1, p. 322.
71. L.V. Krutikova-Abramova, 'Smerti Net ...' (Abramov's diaries), *Zvezda* 11 (2006), p. 68.

## Chapter 8 Recognition, 1976–1988

1. On Mikhail Gorbachev's rise and policies see Archie Brown, *The Gorbachev Factor: New Edition* (London: Oxford University Press, 1997); Vladislav Zubok, *A Failed Empire: The Soviet Union in the Cold War from Stalin to Gorbachev* (Chapel Hill, NC: University of North Carolina Press, 2007), pp. 278–302.
2. In 1988, 800,000 patients in the Soviet Union were registered in psychiatric hospitals for regular checkups. Leonid Mlechin, *Yuri Andropov: Posledniaia nadezhda rezhima* (Moscow: Tsentrpoligraf, 2008), pp. 176–177; D.S. Likhachev, 'Schastie i neschastia v moiei zhizni', *Mansarda* 1 (1996), pp. 47–50.
3. M.S. Gorbachev in: *DLEE*, p. 271.
4. Recollections of Zinaida Kurbatova in: *DLEE*, p. 35.
5. James Billington wrote in his book that Likhachev became a 'cultural adviser' to the Gorbachevs. The reality was more ambiguous; Likhachev's position was informal, yet extremely influential. J. Billington, 'Dmitriy Likhachev's Living Legacy: The Open World Program', 18 June 2006 at: http://www.openworld.gov/news/print.php?lang=1&id=300&view=print.
6. 'Vstupitelnoie slovo akademika D.S. Likhacheva. Soveschanie v Institute Russkoi Literatury AN SSSH posviashchennoie pamiati A.A. Shakhmatova,' *Arkheograficheskii Ezhegodnik za 1970* (Moscow: Nauka, 1971), pp. 390–394.
7. Likhachev's letter on 12 June 1979 and Kaneva's notes of May 1980 in: Kaneva, *Simetria do vremeto* (Sofia: 'Duma 2008', 2012), pp. 351, 353, 410.
8. D.S. Likhachev's recollections of Liudmila Zhivkova, written on 22 July 1981, in: Kaneva, *Simetria do vremeto*, p. 479. More on the Bulgarian trips, publications and awards in: S.O. Shmidt, 'Nravstvennyie vershiny uchenogo i pisatelia', in Addendum to: D.S. Likhachev, *Pis'ma o dobrom. Literaturnyie Pamiatniki* (Moscow: Nauka and St Petersburg: Logos, 2006), pp. 278–280.
9. Recollections of Rufina Dmitrieva, in: *DLEE*, p. 96.
10. Interview with A.M. Panchenko by Nikolai Klavdin, *Zvezda* 5 (2012), at http://magazines.russ.ru/zvezda/2012/5/p7.html.
11. Lurie's letter of 21 April 1977 and the undated letter in May 1978, Correspondence of Ya.S. Lurie and A.A. Zimin, the Archive of the Institute of History, St Petersburg. The author's interview with Elena Vaneieva, 22 September 2009, by telephone; the author's interview with Gelian Prokhorov, 22 November 2008.
12. D.S. Likhachev, A.M. Panchenko, *'Smekhovoi Mir' Drevnei Rusi* (Leningrad: Nauka, 1976), pp. 10–11, 57–62.
13. Richard W.F. Pope, 'Fools and Folly in Old Russia', *Slavic Review*, vol. 39, no. 3 (September 1980), pp. 476–481.
14. Interview with Arseny Roginsky, 15 January 2008; on Lotman's attitude to Likhachev see: Yu.M. Lotman, B.A. Uspensky, *Perepiska* (Moscow: Novoie literaturnoie obozreniie, 2008); B.F. Yegorov, et al., eds, *Yu.M. Lotman, Z.G. Mints – B.F.Yegorov: Perepiska. 1954–1965* (Tallinn: TLU, 2012).
15. From an interview with Elena Vaneieva, 22 September 2009, by phone; Vera Zilitinkevich-Tolz, Manchester, 19 April 2011. Recollections of A.V. Lavrov in: *DLEE*, p. 113.
16. 'Zametki k vospominaniiam o Vere', http://www.nasledie-rus.ru/podshivka/7907.php; 'Zametki o russkom', p. 11; Likhachev to Shklovsky, 20 April 1982, *Iz epistoliarnogo naslediia D.S. Likhacheva*; D.S. Likhachev, *Poeziia sadov. K semantike sadovo-parkovykh stilei* (Leningrad: Nauka, 1982), p. 4.

17. D.S. Likhachev to Shklovsky, April 20, 1982, *Iz epistoliarnogo naslediia*; Likhachev to Zlata Khrzhonstovskaia, around 1982, RO IRLI, fond 769.
18. Vladimir Tolz helped to collect information for *A Chronicle of Current Events*. Arseny Roginsky published and edited the Tamizdat collection *Pamyat* (Memory) in Paris, dedicated to Russian history in the twentieth century, including the history of repressions. N.M. Botvinnik, E.N. Vaneieva, eds, *In Memoriam: Sbornik pamiati Ya.S. Lurie* (St Petersburg: Atheneum-Fenix, 1997), pp. 26–27.
19. Information to the author from Vera Zilitinkevich-Tolz, 18 August 2009; the author's telephone conversation with Vladimir Tolz, 20 September 2008.
20. *In Memoriam: Sbornik pamiati Ya.S. Lurie*, pp. 28–29; interview with Irina Efimovna Ganelina, 29 December 2009, St Petersburg.
21. Information to the author from Vera Zilitinkevich-Tolz, 18 August 2009.
22. A.S. Chernyaev, *Sovmestnyi iskhod. Dnevnik dvukh epokh, 1972–1991* (Moscow: ROSSPEN, 2008), p. 405.
23. A.L. Grishunin to D.S. Likhachev, 12 November 1983, in: *Iz epistoliarnogo naslediia D.S. Likhacheva*.
24. In 1982–84 Barinov was director of the Pushkin Museum in Moscow, http://www.amr-museum.ru/russ/exibit/news2006/news733_r.htm.
25. D.N. Chukovsky in: *DLEE*, pp. 266–267.
26. Dmitry Likhachev to Yuri Mann on 4 October 1984, 'Nado speshit skazat', *Nashe Nasledie*, no. 79–80, 2006, http://www.nasledie-rus.ru/podshivka/7905.php.
27. The author's interview with S.O. Shmidt, 16 January 2008, Moscow.
28. Private notes of D.S. Likhachev (undated, 1980s and early 1990s), courtesy of Vera Zilitinkevich-Tolz.
29. Mikhail Gorbachev, *Zhizn i reformy*, kniga 1 (Moscow: Novosti, 1995), pp. 35, 61.
30. D.S. Likhachev, 'Sluzheniie pamiati', *Nash Sovremennik* 3 (1983), pp. 171–174; RO IRLI, fond 769, Letter to Likhachev from Varlen Soskin, 16 January 1987.
31. D.S. Likhachev, 'Zadachi serii "Literaturnyie pamiatniki"', in: D.V. Oznobishyn, ed., *Literaturnyie pamiatniki* (Moscow: Akademia nauk, 1978), pp. 5–20. D.S. also gave its due to his predecessor, Nikolai Konrad, who guided 'The Monuments' from 1962 until his death in 1970.
32. D.S. Likhachev's letter to A.M. Samsonov, 1 April 1976. ARAN, fond 1713, opis 3, delo 162, l. 31ob.
33. D.S. Likhachev, 'Zadachi serii "Literaturnyie pamiatniki"', in: D.V. Oznobishyn, ed., *Literaturnyie pamiatniki* (Moscow: Akademia nauk, 1978), p. 15; B.F. Egorov, 'D.S. Likhachev i "Literaturnyie pamiatniki"', *Arkheograficheskii ezhegodnik za 1999 god* (Moscow: Nauka, 2000), p. 407.
34. On the Karamzin edition, the role of Lotman and Uspensky, and the controversy around it see Likhachev's correspondence with Andrei Grishunin, *Iz epistoliarnogo naslediia*.
35. On Vladimir Semenovich Kemenov see: L.G. Kramarenko, 'Nad ego pismennym stolom visel portret Surikova', http://artist-mag.ru/index.php/2009-02-19-16-25-25/38-1-2008/93-2009-04-02-10-03-59.
36. D.S. Likhachev to A.L. Grishunin, 7 November 1978; D.S. Likhachev to I.S. Zilbershtein, 22 September 1980, *Iz epistoliarnogo naslediia*.
37. D.S. Likhachev to A.L. Grishunin, 3 July 1974, *Iz epistoliarnogo naslediia*; D.S. Likhachev's letter to A.M. Samsonov, 9 September 1974. ARAN, fond 1713, opis 3, delo 162.
38. D.S. Likhachev, 'Zolotoie slovo drevnerusskoi literatury', *Kommunist* 10 (July 1985), pp. 45–47.
39. D.S. Likhachev to N.V. Mordiukova, *Zametki i nabliudeniia*, p. 485; Recollections of D.N. Chukovsky in: *DLEE*, pp. 266–267; D.S. Likhachev, *Vospominaniia*, vol. 2, pp. 393–410.

40. Letter from N.K. Volkov to Likhachev, 19 January 1987; Letter from M.O. Volkova to D.S. Likhachev, 27 November 1986, RO IRLI, fond 769.
41. Letter from A.I. Tsvetaeva to Likhachev, 14 April 1986, RO IRLI, fond 769.
42. Yuri Rost, Marietta Chudakova in *Komsomolskaia pravda*, 28 November 1986.
43. Lidia Lotman in: *DLEE*, p. 152. Interview of Urmas Ott with D.S. Likhachev, October 1990, http://www.youtube.com/watch?v=j1Lpsny1hKE.
44. D.S. Likhachev, *Izbrannoie: mysli o zhizni, istorii i kulture* (Moscow: Rossiiskii fond kultury, 2006), p. 291.
45. G.V. Myasnikov, 'Dusha moia spokoina', the diary entry of 29 July and 1 November 1986; on Likhachev's recommendation letter for Myasnikov see Likhachev's note in September 1986, '"Khranite svoikh druzei." Pisma D.S. Likhacheva V.P. Yenisherlovu', *Nashe Naslediie*, 79–80 (2006), http://www.naslediie-rus.ru/podshivka/7906.php.
46. *Literaturnaia gazeta*, 19 November 1986, p. 1.
47. V.P. Yenisherlov, 'Trevozhnaia sovest', *Nashe Naslediie* 79–80 (2006), http://www.naslediie-rus.ru/podshivka/7905.php.
48. 'Stenogramma zasedania' on 22 January 1987 and on 1 July 1987, in: L.M. Arinshtein, I. Yu. Yurieva, eds, *Neizvestnyi D.S. Likhachev. Neopublikovannyie materialy iz arkhiva Rossiiskogo Fonda Kultury* (Moscow: RFC, 2006), pp. 16, 25.
49. *DLEE*, p. 279.
50. N.B. Volkova, T.L. Latypova, Ye.Iu. Filkina, eds, *I.S. Zilbershtein: shtrikhi k portretu: k 100-letiiu so dnia rozhdeniia* (Moscow: Nauki, 2006), pp. 7–10, 17; http://www.rusarchives.ru/evants/exhibitions/zilbersh_ab.shtml, accessed on 27 December 2014.
51. L.M. Arinshtein, I.Yu. Yurieva, eds, *Neizvestnyi D.S. Likhachev*, p. 64.
52. L.M. Arinshtein, I.Yu. Yurieva, eds, *Neizvestnyi D.S. Likhachev*, p. 58.
53. D.S. Likhachev, 'Kultura: programma na sto let (interviu)', *Literaturnaia gazeta* 32, 10 August 1988, p. 3.
54. L.M. Arinshtein, I.Yu. Yurieva, eds, *Neizvestnyi D.S. Likhachev*, pp. 107, 111; G.V. Myasnikov, 'Dusha moia spokoina ...' the entry of 27 December 1988, http://www.naslediie-rus.ru/podshivka/6012.php, accessed on 16 March 2014.
55. On the Westernism of Soviet youth and their alienation from Soviet official culture see: A. Yurchak, *Everything was Forever, until it was No More. The Last Soviet Generation* (New York: Princeton University Press, 2005); Sergei Zhuk, *Rock and Roll in the Rocket City: The West, Identity, and Ideology in Soviet Dniepropetrovsk, 1960–1985* (Baltimore, MD: Johns Hopkins University Press and Washington, DC: Woodrow Wilson Center Press, 2010).
56. L.M. Arinshtein, I.Yu. Yurieva, eds, *Neizvestnyi D.S. Likhachev*, pp. 32, 106–107; conversation with M.I. Milchik, 21 August 2008, St Petersburg.
57. Radio Liberty programme about this episode on 11 April 2007, at http://www.svobodanews.ru/content/transcript/391633.html. Likhachev's letter to the Party Secretariat on 26 March 1987, RO IRLI, fond 769.
58. D.S. Likhachev's report to the SFC on 4 February 1988, *Neizvestnyi Likhachev*, p. 59; D.S. Likhachev's letter to M.N. Poltoranin, 22 January 1992, 'Pamiat istorii sviashchenna', *Nashe Naslediie* 79–80 (2006).
59. On these mythologies see: Andrei Levandovsky, *Proshchaniie s Rossiei. Istoricheskiie ocherki* (St Petersburg: Ivan Limbakh, 2011), pp. 614–647.
60. L.M. Arinshtein, I.Yu. Yurieva, eds, *Neizvestnyi D.S. Likhachev*, p. 94; A.Ya. Kompaniets, 'Fond rabotaiet vkholostuiu, a suprugu prezidenta vvodiat v zabluzhdeniie', *Nezavisimaia gazeta*, 23 April 1991.
61. Recollections of Zinaida Kurbatova from the film *Chastnyie khroniki* (2006), https://www.youtube.com/watch?v=92H6U2fs0XY.
62. I. Klyamkin, 'Kakaya ulitsa vedyot k khramu', *Novyi Mir* 11 (1987), pp. 150–188.

63. The letter to S.P. Zalygin without a date, RO IRLI, fond 769; D.S. Likhachev, 'Nakanune ...' in his: *Zametki i nabliudeniia: Iz zapisnykh knizhek raznykh let* (Leningrad: Sovetskii pisatel, 1989), pp. 598–606, http://www.lihachev.ru/pic/site/files/interview/nakanune.pdf; the author's conversation with Igor Klyamkin, 17 February 2011, Moscow.
64. D.S. Likhachev, 'Zvezdnyi dozhd' in: Boris Pasternak, *Vozdushnyie puti: Proza raznykh let* (Moscow: Sovetskii pisatel, 1982), pp. 3–17. E.L. Pasternak to D.S. Likhachev, 29 March 1987. D.S. Likhachev to A. Banketov, 19 August 1987, RO IRLI, fond 769.
65. D.S. Likhachev, 'Razmyshleniia nad romanom B.L. Pasternaka "Doktor Zhivago"', *Novyi Mir* 1 (1988), pp. 5–22.
66. Letter from D.S. Likhachev to S.V. Volkova, 2 November 1996, *Nashe Naslediie* 87 (2008), http://nasledie-rus.ru/podshivka/8709.php.
67. D.S. Likhachev in *Vlast Solovetskaia*, by Marina Goldovskaia (1988), http://www.youtube.com/watch?v=DNvYLTvy1jI.
68. L.M. Arinshtein, I.Yu. Yurieva, eds, *Neizvestnyi D.S. Likhachev*, pp. 83–84.
69. D.S. Likhachev, 'Samoie strashnoie – eto polukulturnyi chelovek' (interview), *Rabochaia tribuna*, 16 September 1990, pp. 1–2.
70. Sergei Averintsev, 'Po povodu statii A. Zubova "Puti Rossii"', *Kontinent* 3 81 (1994), at http://magazines.russ.ru/continent/2011/148/av10.html.
71. D.S. Likhachev, 'Predvaritelnyie itogi tysiacheletnego opyta'.
72. D.S. Likhachev, 'The National Nature of Russian History', The Second Annual W. Averell Harriman Lecture, 13 November 1990 (New York: The W. Averell Harriman Institute for Advanced Study of the Soviet Union, Columbia University, 1990).
73. Sergey Deyev's blog at: http://russiaru.net/Sergei_Deev/status/25e7f000000b7/.
74. D.S. Likhachev's letter to Raisa Gorbacheva, 28 February 1989, RO IRLI, fond 769.
75. D.S. Likhachev, 'Garantii peremen', *Leningradskii rabochii*, 17 March 1989, p. 4.
76. Andrei Zubov, ed., *Istoriia Rossii. XX vek*, vol. 2 (Moscow: AST, 2009), pp. 537–539; Suzanne Massie, *Trust but Verify. Reagan, Russia and me* (Rockland, ME: Maine Authors Publishing, 2013), pp. 349–358.
77. 'US Librarian of Congress remembers Likhachev', *St Petersburg Times*, 4 December 2006, http://www.openworld.gov/article/print.php?id=221&lang=1.
78. D.S. Likhachev, 'Kreshcheniie Rusi i Gosudarstvo Rus', *Novyi Mir* 6 (1988), pp. 232, 249, 258–259.
79. Interview with Vera Zilitinkevich-Tolz, 14 November 2009, Boston.
80. D.S. Likhachev and N.I. Vaneieva, *Povest o gore-zlochastii. Literaturnyie pamiatniki* (Leningrad: Nauka, 1984); D.S. Likhachev, 'Semnadtsatyi vek v russkoi kulture', preface to *Biblioteka literatury Drevnei Rusi*, RAN. IRLI, D.S. Likhachev, L.A. Dmitrieva, N.V. Ponyrko, eds, vol. 15 (St Petersburg: Nauka, 2006), pp. 11–12; G. Nivat in: *DLEE*, p. 204.

## Chapter 9 Preparing for Collapse, 1988–1991

1. Anatoly Sobchak, *Khozhdeniie vo vlast* (Moscow: Novosti, 1991), pp. 167–184.
2. Anatoly Sobchak, Khozhdeniie vo vlast, pp. 167–184.
3. Roman Szporluk, *Russia, Ukraine, and the Breakup of the Soviet Union* (Stanford, CA: Hoover Institution Press, 2000); Ronald Grigor Suny, *The Revenge of the Past: Nationalism, Revolution, and the Collapse of the Soviet Union* (Stanford, CA: Stanford University Press, 1994); Mark R. Beissinger, *Nationalist Mobilization and the Collapse of the Soviet State* (New York: Cambridge University Press, 2002).

4. D.S. Likhachev to A.M. Samsonov, 23 April 1976, ARAN, fond 1713, delo 162, ll. 33–35.
5. L.M. Arinshtein, I.Yu. Yurieva, eds, *Neizvestnyi D.S. Likhachev*, p. 35.
6. D.S. Likhachev, 'Patriotizm protiv natsionalizma' in: G. Ivanova, V. Kanunnikova eds, *Govoria otkrovenno: Zametki pisatelei o mezhnatsionalnykh otnosheniiakh* (Moscow: Khudozhestvennaia literatura, 1989), p. 99 (Likhachev's contribution was written in 1984).
7. L.M. Arinshtein, I.Yu. Yurieva, eds, *Neizvestnyi D.S. Likhachev*, pp. 113, 115–116. On the role of imperial ethnographers and the first Soviet census see Francine Hirsch, *Empire of Nations: Ethnographic Knowledge and the Making of the Soviet Union* (Ithaca, NY: Cornell UP, 2005).
8. On this see Serhy Yekelchyk, *Stalin's Empire of Memory: Russian–Ukrainian Relations in the Soviet Historical Imagination* (Toronto: University of Toronto Press, 2004); also David Brandenberger, *Stalinist Mass Culture and the Formation of Modern Russian National Identity, 1931–1956* (Cambridge, MA: Harvard University Press, 2002).
9. D.S. Likhachev, 'Rossiia', *Literaturnaia gazeta*, 12 October 1988, pp. 5–6; D.S. Likhachev, 'Veruiu v russkuiu intelligentsiiu', *Literaturnaia gazeta*, 28 December 1988, p. 4.
10. L.M. Arinshtein, I.Yu. Yurieva, eds, *Neizvestnyi D.S. Likhachev*, p. 117.
11. 'Sovmestnoie zasedaniie pravleniia Sovetskogo fonda kultury', 25 January 1990, in: *Neizvestnyi D.S. Likhachev*, p. 131.
12. 'Sovmestnoie zasedaniie pravleniia Sovetskogo fonda kultury', 25 January 1990, in *Neizvestnyi D.S. Likhachev*, pp. 101–102.
13. Conversation of A. Mikhailovsky with D.S. Likhachev, *Nedelia* 38 (1989); D.S. Likhachev, *Kniga bespokoistv*, pp. 379, 383; D.S. Likhachev, 'Nauka bez morali pogibnet', *Izvestiia*, 25 March 1989.
14. D.S. Likhachev in *Dym Otechestva* directed by Victor Semeniuk, http://vk.com/video6047327_170739626. Conversation of A. Mikhailovsky with D.S. Likhachev, *Nedelia* 38 (1989); D.S. Likhachev, *Kniga bespokoistv*, pp. 386–387.
15. Conversation of A. Mikhailovsky with D.S. Likhachev, 'Nauka bez morali pogibnet', *Kniga bespokoistv*, p. 379.
16. 'Na S'ezde tsarstvuiet svoboda', *Uchitelskaia gazeta*, 3 June 1989; D.S. Likhachev, 'K voprosu o vlasti', *Smena*, 20 June 1989, pp. 1, 2; D.S. Likhachev, '200 slov o perestroike', *Literaturnaia gazeta*, 26 April 1989, p. 1.
17. 'Vystupleniie deputata D.S. Likhacheva', *Leningradskaia pravda*, 31 May 1989, p. 4.
18. Ibidem; 'Na S'ezde tsarstvuiet svoboda'.
19. Sobchak, *Khozhdeniie vo vlast*, pp. 43–48.
20. 'Na S'ezde tsarstvuiet svoboda'; 'K voprosu o vlasti'.
21. *Pervyi s'ezd narodnykh deputatov SSSR, 25 May–9 June 1989. Stenograficheskii otchet*, vol. 2 (Moscow: Politizdat 1989), pp. 456–459.
22. 'Na S'ezde tsarstvuiet svoboda'; 'K voprosu o vlasti'; V.P. Astafyev's recollection of their conversation during the Congress is in: *DLEE*, p. 294.
23. A note of D.S. Likhachev to Khazanov on 10 November 1989, RO IRLI, fond 769; the interview with Urmas Ott, http://www.youtube.com/watch?v=j1Lpsny1hKE&feature=related; GARF, fond R-9654, opis 3, delo 2285, ll. 6–8.
24. D.S. Likhachev, 'Garantii peremen', *Leningradskii rabochii*, 17 March 1989, p. 4.
25. 'Otchet o rabote narodnogo deputata SSSR akademika D.S. Likhacheva', by L.A. Alekseieva, SFC expert, 18 December 1989, RO IRLI, fond 769.
26. Ibidem; Likhachev's handwritten note on the memorandum about Karsavin, 22 November 1989, RO IRLI, fond 769.

27. D.A. Granin at: http://www.lfond.spb.ru/programs/likhachev/100/stenogrammi/granin.html; Yu. Rodman, 'Pokhorony Sakharova', *Vestnik* online, 22 January 2003, http://www.vestnik.com/issues/2003/0122/win/rodman.htm.
28. D.S. Likhachev, *Razdumia o Rossii* (St Petersburg: Logos, 1999), pp. 641–643.
29. O.V. Basilashvili in: *DLEE*, p. 295.
30. John B. Dunlop, *The Rise of Russia and the Fall of the Soviet Empire* (Princeton, NJ: Princeton University Press, 1993), pp. 142–143.
31. A. Chernyaev, *Sovmestnyi iskhod. Dnevnik dvukh epoch, 1972–1991 gody* (Moscow: ROSSPEN, 2010), the diary entry for 21 January 1990; also see the entry for 25 February 1990, pp. 838, 843.
32. Abby Smith, Vladimir Budaragin, *Living Traditions of Russian Faith: Books and Manuscripts of the Old Believers* (Washington, DC: Library of Congress, 1990); 'D.S. Likhachev v Biblioteke Kongressa SShA v Vashingtone na otkrytii vystavki drevnerusskikh rukopisei', *Sovetskaia kultura* no. 23 (9 June 1990), p. 9; Sergey Deyev's recollections in: http://russiaru.net/Sergei_Deev/status/25e7f000000b7/.
33. The author's interview with James Billington, the Library of Congress, Washington DC, 13 November 2008; Sergey Deyev's recollections at: http://russiaru.net/Sergei_Deev/status/25e7f000000b7/.
34. Recollection of Vyacheslav Ivanov in: *DLEE*, p. 291; the author's conversation with Daniil Granin, Moscow, 8 December 2008; and with Vittorio and Clara Strada, San Candido, 2 July 2014; Sergey Deyev's blog at: http://russiaru.net/Sergei_Deev/status/25e7f000000b7/.
35. The postcard, dated 15 April 1990, RO IRLI, fond 769.
36. The interview of D.S. Likhachev with Urmas Ott, http://www.youtube.com/watch?v=j1Lpsny1hKE&feature=related; D.S. Likhachev, 'Ne stat by nam "obkomom kultury" ...', *Izvestia* no. 154 (3 June 1990), p. 3.
37. 'Ne stat by nam "obkomom kultury"'.
38. Kataeva-Lytkina in: *DLEE*, p. 279; Z.Ya. Kompaniets, 'Fond rabotaet vkholostuyu, a suprugu prezidenta vvodyat v zabluzhdenie', *Nezavisimaia gazeta*, 23 April 1991.
39. G.V. Myasnikov, 'Dusha moia spokoina', the entry of 27 December 1988.
40. G.V. Myasnikov, 'Dusha moia spokoina', the entry of 20 January 1992.
41. Kataeva-Lytkina in: *DLEE*, p. 281.
42. *Nashe Naslediie* 5 (1990), pp. 59–83.
43. *Nashe Naslediie* 16 (1990), pp. 83, 90–93.
44. *Nashe Naslediie* 4 (1990), p. 144.
45. D.S. Likhachev, 'O natsionalnom kharaktere russkikh', *Voprosy filosofii* 4 (1990), p. 6.
46. Aleksandr Solzhenitsyn, 'Kak nam obustroit Rossiiu', pamphlet to *Komsomolskaia Pravda*, 18 September 1990.
47. *Literaturnaia gazeta*, 10 April 1991.
48. 'Perevod s russkogo. Chem oborachivaetsia iazykovaia neprimirimost', *Izvestiia*, 25 October 1990.
49. 'Vremia sovmestnykh deistvii. Vstrecha M.S. Gorbacheva s deiateliami sovetskoi kultury', *Pravda*, 3 October 1990, p. 2.
50. 'Vremia sovmestnykh deistvii. Vstrecha M.S. Gorbacheva s deiateliami sovetskoi kultury', *Pravda*, 3 October 1990, p. 1.
51. D.S. Likhachev, *Izbrannoie* (St Petersburg: Logos, 1997), edited by T. Shmakova, p. 296.
52. Nikolay Mitrokhin, 'Russkaia pravoslavnaia tserkov v 1990 godu', *Novoie literaturnoie obozreniie* 83 (2008), at: http://magazines.russ.ru/nlo/2007/83/mi21.html accessed 30 May 2015.
53. GARF, fond 9654, opis 7, delo 554, ll. 65–93.
54. GARF, fond 9654, opis 7, delo 554, ll. 90–91.

55. I.A. Lobakova in: *DLEE*, pp. 275–276.
56. E. Vodolazkin in: *DLEE*, p. 16.
57. On this idea see Billington's telegram to Likhachev on 5 March 1991, RO IRLI, fond 769; http://belaya-krinica.kiev.ua/article/a-15.html.
58. Letter to Likhachev from V. Rev. John Meyendorff, Dean of St Vladimir's Orthodox Theological Seminary, 9 February 1991, RO IRLI, fond 769.
59. James Billington to D.S. Likhachev on 5(?) March 1991, RO IRLI, fond 769.
60. James Billington to D.S. Likhachev on 20 May 1991, RO IRLI, fond 769.
61. The official information on the project is still unavailable. For the summary see: http://belaya-krinica.kiev.ua/article/a-15.html.
62. 'Spravka D.S. Likhacheva o sud'be moshchei sviatogo blagovernogo kniaza Daniila Aleksandrovicha, March 30, 1999' at: www.lihachev.ru/pic/site/files/fulltext/pazdumia_o_ros/041.pdf, accessed on 30 May 2015. The recollections about Meyendorff at the Byzantine congress in Moscow are in: I.P. Medvedev, 'Neskolko slov o moikh vstrechakh s otsom Ioannom Meiendorfom', in: A.V. Levitskyi, ed., *Svidetel istiny. Pamiati protopresvitera Ioanna Meiendorfa* (Ekaterinburg: Ifizd otdel eparkhii, 2003), p. 195; Oleg Panchenko believes this happened 'in the early 1980s', in: *DLEE*, p. 348.
63. D.S. Likhachev interviewed by Andrei Maksimov, autumn 1997 at: https://www.youtube.com/watch?v=gBnV0M8wwg8.
64. Sergei Vasiltsov, Sergei Obukhov, 'Vozrast Kharizmy', *Sovetskaia Rossiia*, no. 74 (3 June 2004); Nikolai Shchipanov, Igor Iakovenko, 'Reiting', *Dialog* 10 (1990); for the situation in Leningrad see 'Miatezhnikam poveril lish odin iz desiati leningradtsev', *Smena*, 27 August 1991.
65. Quoted in Serhii Plokhy, *The Last Empire* (New York: Basic Books, 2014), p. 40.
66. *Izvestiia*, 11 July 1991, p. 1.
67. *Izvestiia*, 11 July 1991, pp. 1–2.
68. V.V. Bibikhin, 'Sergei Sergeevich Averintsev', http://uni-persona.srcc.msu.ru/site/authors/bibihin/averincev.htm.
69. D.S. Likhachev, 'Tri osnovy evropeiskoi kultury i russkii istoricheskii opyt', theses, 15 April 1991 at: http://likhachev.lfond.spb.ru/articl100/Russia/3_osnov.pdf, accessed on 15 December 2015.
70. D.S. Likhachev, 'Tri osnovy evropeiskoi kultury i russkii istoricheskii opyt'.
71. Immediate reports on what happened in Leningrad in those hours are: *Smena*, 21 August 1991; A. Golovkov, A. Chernov, 'Anatoly Sobchak. Proryv. Interviu bez iedinogo voprosa', *Moskovskiie novosti*, 1 September 1991, p. 10.
72. Alla Repina, 'My narod, pust oni eto znaiut!' *Smena*, 21 August 1991, p. 2.
73. Historian Rafail Ganelin shared with the author these details he heard after the coup from Zinaida Kurbatova, Likhachev's granddaughter. The author's interview with Ganelin on 5 September 2010; A. Golovkov, A. Chernov, 'Anatoly Sobchak. Proryv. Interviu bez iedinogo voprosa', *Moskovskiie novosti*, 1 September 1991, p. 10.
74. Film about the August events in Leningrad by Sergei Loznitsa, *Event*, at: http://www.youtube.com/watch?v=dirBo7WeMto.
75. 'The Last Interview of Dmitry Likhachev', *Argumenty i fakty* 40, 6 October 1999, http://www.aif.ru/archive/1634024.
76. D.S. Likhachev, 'Oblomki Soiuza mogut smesti i nashi dukhovnyiie sviazi (Otvety na voprosy LG)', *Literaturnaia gazeta*, 30 October 1991, p. 13.
77. The author's conversation with Vera Zilitinkevich-Tolz on 20 November 2011, Washington DC.

## Chapter 10  The Smoke of the Homeland, 1991–1999

1. L.M. Arinshtein, I.Yu. Yurieva, eds, *Neizvestnyi D.S. Likhachev*, pp. 154–155, 172; Likhachev refers to his 'recent meeting' with Yeltsin in his letter to Mikhail Poltoranin, 22 January 1992, in: D.S. Likhachev, 'Pamiat storii sviashchenna', *Nashe Naslediie* 79–80 (2006).
2. Yenisherlov, 'Trevozhnaia sovest', *Nashe Naslediie* 79–80 (2006); Dmitry Furman, 'Gorbachev i ego epokha', *Svobodnaia mysl* 11 (1995), p. 71. Likhachev's letter to R.M. Gorbacheva on 3 October 1991, *Nashe Naslediie* 59–60 (2001), http://www.naslediie-rus.ru/podshivka/6014.php; *Raisa: Pamiati Raisy Maksimovny Gorbachovoi* (Moscow: Vagrius, 2000), pp. 92–93.
3. Steven L. Solnick, *Stealing the State. Control and Collapse in Soviet Institutions* (Cambridge, MA: Harvard University Press, 1998); Petr Aven, Alfred Kokh, *Revoliutsiia Gaidara: Istoriia reform 90-kh iz pervykh ruk* (Moscow: Alpina publisher, 2013).
4. A.Ya. Kompaniets, 'Fond rabotaet vkholostuiu, a suprugu prezidenta vvodyat v zabluzhdenie', *Nezavisimaia gazeta*, 23 April 1991.
5. Pismo pravleniia SFK M.S. Gorbachevu, 28 December 1990; 'Stenographic record of "roundtable" on the issues of culture of Russian provinces (31 January 1992) and the role of Russian international foundation of culture', RO IRLI, fond 769.
6. Myasnikov, 'Dusha moia spokoina', the diary entries of 30 January and 12 February 1992.
7. L.M. Arinshtein, I.Yu. Yurieva, eds, *Neizvestnyi D.S. Likhachev*, pp. 217, 222; D.S. Likhachev, 'Oblomki Soiuza mogut smesti i nashi kulturnyie sviazi', *Literaturnaia gazeta*, 30 October 1991.
8. *Nevskoie vremia*, 6 May 1992.
9. On Maxwell see his profile at BBC on 21 March 2001, http://news.bbc.co.uk/1/hi/business/1249739.stm; http://www.theguardian.com/media/greenslade/2011/nov/03/pressandpublishing-daily-mirror.
10. D.S. Likhachev, '"Izbavi nas ot lukavogo." O tom, shto volnuet', *Pravda*, 16 November 1991; S.A. Filatov in: *DLEE*, p. 319.
11. Diary of Jay Edward Epstein, 4 December 1978, http://www.edwardjayepstein.com/diary/opp.htm, accessed on 30 June 2015; John Tikhotsky, *Russia's Diamond Colony: the Republic of Sakha* (Amsterdam: Harwood Academic Publishers, 2000).
12. L.M. Arinshtein, I.Yu. Yurieva, eds, *Neizvestnyi D.S. Likhachev*, p. 226; the letter from G.I. Vasilchikov, 21 February 1991, RO IRLI, fond 769; Yenisherlov, 'Trevozhnaia sovest', *Nashe Naslediie* 79–80 (2006).
13. L.M. Arinshtein, I.Yu. Yurieva, eds, *Neizvestnyi D.S. Likhachev*, pp. 173, 194–195.
14. On Vassily Alekseievich Pushkarev see http://rutv.ru/brand/show/episode/250572; L.M. Arinshtein, I.Yu. Yurieva, eds, *Neizvestnyi D.S. Likhachev*, p. 176.
15. L.M. Arinshtein, I.Yu. Yurieva, eds, *Neizvestnyi D.S. Likhachev*, pp. 215–216, 218.
16. The author's interview with Vice President of the Russian Cultural Foundation L.V. Nazarova by phone, 6 July 2015; Likhachev to Grishunin, 29 April 1993, in: *Iz epistoliarnogo naslediia*, pp. 403–404.
17. D.S. Likhachev to V. Shalamov, 20 September 1979 in: V. Shalamov, *Neskolko moikh zhiznei*, edited by I. Sirotinskaia (Moscow: Eksmo, 2009), pp. 941–942.
18. The author's conversation with Arseny Roginsky, the head of Memorial Society, 15 January 2008.
19. On Ilyin see: Semen Frank, *Neprochitannoie. Statyi, pis'ma, vospominaniia* (Moscow: Moskovskaia shkola politicheskikh issledovanii, 2001), p. 509.
20. D.S. Likhachev to Grishunin, 29 April 1993, in: *Iz epistoliarnogo naslediia*, p. 404; the author's interview of Vera Zilitinkevich-Tolz, by telephone, 19 April 2001.

21. A letter from D.S.Likhachev to N.S. Mikhalkov (around the end of September 1993), RO IRLI, fond 769; the first page of his next letter to N.S. Mikhalkov (around the end of October 1993) reproduced in: *DLEE*, p. 275.
22. Interview of Andrei Sinitsyn with D.S. Likhachev, *Kommersant-daily*, 11 June 1998, p. 10; I.A. Lobakova in: *DLEE*, p. 275.
23. Roman Szporluk, *Russia, Ukraine, and the Breakup of the Soviet Union*, pp. 187–204, 219; on Yeltsin's position with regard to 'rossiyskii' and 'russkiy' see Tolz, *Inventing the Nation*, p. 252.
24. A copy of the telegram is in RO IRLI, fond 769.
25. 'Zakon surov. No eto – zakon? Stenogramma sobraniia muzeinoi obshchestvennosti', *Nezavisimaia gazeta*, 25 March 1992.
26. 'My obiazany predupredit Vas ob otvestvennosti: Pismo prezidentu Rossii B.N. Yeltsinu ot 17 marta', *Nezavisimaia gazeta*, 2 April 1992.
27. 'My obiazany predupredit Vas ob otvestvennosti: Pismo prezidentu Rossii B.N. Yeltsinu ot 17 marta', Nezavisimaia gazeta, 2 April 1992.
28. A.G. Mosyakin, 'Antikvarnyi eksportnyi fond', *Nashe Naslediie* 2–3 (1991); E.A. Osokina, 'Na Bolshoi doroge s Rembrandtami', *Rodina* 9 (2006).
29. D.S. Likhachev to Yeltsin, 25 May 1992, *Iz epistoliarnogo naslediia*, p. 498.
30. D.S. Likhachev, 'Kulturnoie odichaniie grozit nashei strane iz blizhaishego budushchego', *Izvestiia*, 29 May 1991.
31. D.S. Likhachev to Yeltsin, 6 April 1992, *Iz epistoliarnogo naslediia*, p. 499; *Neizvestnyi D.S. Likhachev*, pp. 182–183.
32. Ilya Prizel, 'The Influence of Ethnicity on Foreign Policy: The Case of Ukraine', in: Roman Szporluk, ed., *National Identity and Ethnicity in Russia and the New States of Eurasia* (Armonk, NY: M.E. Sharpe, 1994), p. 117.
33. The author's interview with Gelian Prokhorov, 22 November 2008, Philadelphia.
34. Interview with Urmas Ott, https://www.youtube.com/watch?v=PIycpMiUMo0; GARF, fond 7523, opis 145, delo 1385, ll. 4–6.
35. Copy of the letter from D.S. Likhachev to A. Sobchak is in RO IRLI, fond 769.
36. Copy of the letter from D.S. Likhachev to A. Sobchak is in RO IRLI, fond 769.
37. M.K. Gorshkov, V.V. Zhuravlev, L.N. Doprokhotov, eds, *Yeltsin–Khazbulatov: iedinstvo, kompromiss, bor'ba* (Moscow: TERRA, 1992); Timothy Colton, *Yeltsin: A Life* (New York: Basic Books, 2008), pp. 272–280.
38. 'Pisateli trebuiut ot pravitel'stva reshytelnykh deistii', *Izvestia*, 5 October 1993, p. 3.
39. D.S. Likhachev, 'Pust vysshei meroi dlia nikh budet vechnyi pozor', *Vechernii Peterburg*, 6 October 1992, p. 1; Information of I.Yu. Yurieva to the author, 19 October 2015; Likhachev's letter to Yeltsin on 19 October 1993 in: *Iz epistoliarnogo naslediia*, p. 501.
40. Liudmila Saraskina, *Aleksandr Solzhenitsyn* (Moscow: Molodaia Gvardiia, 2008), pp. 804–806, 817–828; A.I. Solzhenitsyn, 'Russkii vopros v kontse XX veka', *Novyi Mir* 7 (July 1994).
41. Saraskina, *Aleksandr Solzhenitsyn*, pp. 825–842; Roy Medvedev, 'Poet i Tsar', *Rossiiskaia gazeta*, 26 September 2000, at http://www.rg.ru/anons/arc_2000/0926/hit.shtm.
42. D.S. Likhachev to Grishunin, 20 April 1994 and 12 September 1996, *Iz epistoliarnogo naslediia*, pp. 405, 409; D.S. Likhachev to V.P. Yenisherlov, 21 October 1997, 'Pamiat istorii sviashchenna'; D.S. Likhachev to S.O. Shmidt, 20 June 1997, *Nashe naslediie* 79–80 (2006), at: http://www.naslediie-rus.ru/podshivka/6014.php.
43. Dmitry Bykov, 'Ierarkh, ili o gosudarstvennom intelligente', *Russkii Zhurnal*, 14 August 1997, at http://old.russ.ru/journal/ist_sovr/97-08-14/bykov.htm.

44. Interview with Boris Uspensky, 6 April 2014, Rome; V.M. Lurie, 'Kogda intelligentsia ushla, … a nauka ostalas', June 2005, St Petersburg Society of Byzantine-Slavic Studies, at http://byzantinorossica.org.ru/lurie_bulanin.html.
45. Dmitry Bulanin, 'Dmitry Sergeevich Likhachev i russkaia kultura kontsa dvadtsatogo veka: K 90-letiiu', *Russkaia literatura* 1 (1997), pp. 3–13, reprinted in: D.M. Bulanin, ed., *Epilog k istorii russkoi intelligentsii: Tri iubileia* (St Petersburg: Dmitry Bulanin, 2005), pp. 19–42.
46. D.S. Likhachev, 'Propoved ili postupok? (Otvet na iubileinoie privetstvie D.M. Bulanina), *Russkaia literatura* 2 (1998), pp. 212–213; reprinted in Bulanin, *Epilog k istorii*, pp. 45–46.
47. Bulanin, *Epilog k istorii*, pp. 43–45.
48. A.G. Bobrov in: *DLEE*, p. 389; Bulanin, op. cit., pp. 7–8.
49. Recollections of T.I. Krasnoborodky and the letter of Prince Charles (without the date), in: *DLEE*, pp. 127–131, 223; D.S.Likhachev in his interview by Andrei Maximov in the television programme *Night Flight*, at: https://www.youtube.com/watch?v=gBnV0M8wwg8.
50. Evgeny Vodolazkin in an interview, http://tayga.info/video/2015/04/22/~120853.
51. Colton, *Yeltsin. A Life*, pp. 14–15.
52. N.I. Yeltsina in: *DLEE*, p. 322.
53. The letter from D.S. Likhachev to Yeltsin on 17 June 1997 at: http://www.icr.su/sbt1/sbt1gl3_16.htm.
54. A.G. Bobrov in: *DLEE*, p. 393; D.S. Likhachev from St Petersburg to B.N. Yeltsin, 24 October 1993; also his letter on 18 July 1997 in: *Iz epistoliarnogo naslediia*, pp. 502–503, 505–506. Interview with S.N. Krasavchenko, October 2007, at: http://www.interun.ru/kko_bc.html; draft letter from D.S. Likhachev to S.N. Krasavchenko, RO IRLI, fond 769.
55. D.S. Likhachev to B.N.Yeltsin, August 9, 1999 in: *Iz epistoliarnogo naslediia*, pp. 509–510.
56. See this interview at: https://www.youtube.com/watch?v=92H6U2fs0XYB; also A. Kurkova in: *DLEE*, pp. 247–248.
57. The account of this murder and the concealment of remains by Yurovsky (1934) is at: http://www.alexanderpalace.org/palace/yurovmurder.html, accessed on 24 July 2015.
58. Robert K. Massie, *The Romanovs: The Final Chapter* (London: Random House, 1996); *Pokaianiie. Materialy pravitelstvennoi komissii po izucheniiu voprosov, sviazannykh s issledovaniiem i perezakhoroneniem ostankov Rossiiskogo Imperatora Nikolaia II i chlenov iego sem'i. Izbrannyie dokumenty* (Moscow: Vybor, 1998).
59. Gelii Riabov, 'Soshestviie vo Ad. Posmertnaia sud'ba tsarskoi sem'i', *Kontinent* 148 (2011) at: http://magazines.russ.ru/continent/2011/148/ri43.html.
60. D.S. Likhachev's interview in television programmes of 1995 and 1997, https://www.youtube.com/watch?v=92H6U2fs0XY and https://www.youtube.com/watch?v=gBnV0M8wwg8.
61. Correspondence of V.K. Romanov, GARF, d. 2769.
62. *Smena*, 7 November 1991.
63. D.S. Likhachev in *Night Flight*, September 1997, https://www.youtube.com/watch?v=gBnV0M8wwg8.
64. James H. Billington, *Russia in Search of Itself* (Washington DC: Woodrow Wilson Center Press, 2004), p. 62.
65. Eduard Falts-Fein, 'Kak D.S. Likhachev postavil tochku nad "i" v tsarskom dele', *Nashe nasledie* 79–80 (2006), http://www.nasledie-rus.ru/podshivka/7912.php.
66. Falts-Fein, 'Kak D.S. Likhachev postavil tochku'; recollections of S.A. Filatov in: *DLEE*, p. 321.

67. D.S. Likhachev to B.N. Yeltsin, 6 July 1998. A copy is in the archive of the D.S. Likhachev Foundation. Recollections of N.I. Yeltsina in: *DLEE*, p. 322.
68. Address by Yeltsin: 'We are all guilty', *New York Times*, 18 July 1998.
69. 'Mogut byt generaly-geroi, no ne byvaet geroicheskogo general'nogo shtaba', *Segodnia*, 6 October 1999, http://www.segodnya.ua/tenyears/843550.html.
70. A. Solzhenitsyn, *Rossiia v obvale* (Moscow: Russkii Put, 1998); Saraskina, *Aleksandr Solzhenitsyn*, p. 863.
71. Saraskina, *Aleksandr Solzhenitsyn*, pp. 864–865.
72. D.S. Likhachev in the programme *Night Flight*, September 1999, https://www.youtube.com/watch?v=K4J7faEHjPE.

## Conclusion   Death and Beyond

1. Zapisi D.S. Likhacheva, the 1990s, courtesy of Vera Zilitinkevich-Tolz.
2. O. Panchenko in: Vodolazkin, ed., *Dmitry Likhachev i ego epokha*, p. 416.
3. D.S. Likhachev, 'Ob obshchestvennoi otvetstvennosti literaturovedeniia,' in: *Kontekst. 1973. Literaturno-teoreticheskiie issledovaniia* (Moscow: Nauka, 1974). On the special role of this article D.S. wrote in his letter to Robin Milner-Gulland, 16 February 1977. The copy of the letter provided by R. Milner-Gulland.
4. D.S. Likhachev, *VRL*, vol. 2, pp. 495, 502.
5. D.S. Likhachev, *VRL*, vol. 2, p. 495.
6. D.S. Likhachev, *VRL*, vol. 2, p. 498.
7. Copy of this letter in the Manuscript Division, IRLI, fond 769.
8. D.S. Likhachev, *VRL*, vol. 2 p. 483. The author's interview with Gelian Prokhorov, 22 November 2008, Philadelphia.
9. Prokhorov in: *DLEE*, p. 411.
10. S.S. Averintsev, 'Ukhodit epokha', *Literaturnaia gazeta*, 6–12 October (1999), pp. 1, 9.
11. Robin Milner-Gulland, 'Dmitrii Sergeevich Likhachev (1906–1999),' *Slavonica*, vol. 6, no. 1 (2000), pp. 141–150.
12. See his bibliography in Russian, http://likhachev.lfond.spb.ru/search/bibliogr_likhachev.php, and http://likhachev.lfond.spb.ru/Monogr/redact_vstupl.htm.
13. D.S. Likhachev, *VRL*, vol. 1, p. 384.

# SELECT BIBLIOGRAPHY AND FURTHER READING

Alekseyeva, Liudmila, *The Thaw Generation: Coming of Age in the Post-Stalin Era* (Boston: Little, Brown, 1990)
Alexopoulos, Golfo, *Stalin's Outcasts: Aliens, Citizens and the Soviet State, 1926–1936* (Ithaca, NY: Cornell University Press, 2003)
Billington, James, *Russia in Search of Itself* (Washington DC: Woodrow Wilson Center Press, 2004)
Bittner, Stephen, *The Many Lives of Khrushchev's Thaw: Experience and Memory in Moscow's Arbat* (Ithaca, NY: Cornell University Press, 2008)
Boobbyer, Philip, *Conscience, Dissent and Reform in Soviet Russia* (London: Routledge, 2005)
Braithwaite, Rodric, *Across the Moscow River: The World Turned Upside Down* (Yale, 2002)
Brandenberger, David, *National Bolshevism: Stalinist Mass Culture and the Formation of Modern Russian National Identity, 1931–1956* (Cambridge, MA: Harvard University Press, 2002)
Brudny, Yitzhak M., *Reinventing Russia: Russian Nationalism and the Soviet State, 1953–1991* (Cambridge MA: Harvard University Press, 1998)
Bulgakov, Mikhail, *The Heart of a Dog* (London: Vintage, 2009)
Clark, Katerina, *Moscow, the Fourth Rome: Stalinism, Cosmopolitanism, and the Evolution of Soviet Culture, 1931–1941* (Cambridge, MA: Harvard University Press, 2011)
Cohen, Stephen F., *The Victims Return: Survivors of the Gulag after Stalin* (London: I.B.Tauris, 2011)
Dobrenko, Evgeny, *The Making of the State Reader: Social and Aesthetic Contexts of the Reception of Soviet Literature*, translated by Jesse M. Savage (Stanford, CA: Stanford University Press, 1998).
Dobson, Miriam, *Khrushchev's Cold Summer: Gulag Returnees, Crime, and the Fate of Reform after Stalin* (Ithaca, NY: Cornell University Press, 2009)
Dowler, Wayne, *Russia in 1913* (DeKalb: Northern Illinois University Press, 2010)
English, Robert, *Russia and the Idea of the West: Gorbachev, Intellectuals and the End of the Cold War* (New York: Columbia University Press, 2000)
Etkind, Alexander, *Warped Mourning: The Stories of the Undead in the Land of the Unburied* (Stanford, CA: Stanford University Press, 2013)
Figes, Orlando, *People's Tragedy: The Russian Revolution, 1891–1924* (London: Pimlico, 1997)
Finkel, Stuart, *On the Ideological Front: The Russian Intelligentsia and the Making of the Soviet Public Sphere* (New Haven, CT: Yale University Press, 2007)
Fitzpatrick, Sheila, *The Cultural Front: Power and Culture in Revolutionary Russia* (Ithaca, NY: Cornell University Press, 1992)
——— *Everyday Stalinism: Ordinary Life in Extraordinary Times* (Oxford: Oxford University Press, 2000)

Fitzpatrick, Sheila and Yuri Slezkine (eds), *In the Shadow of Revolution: Life Stories of Russian Women from 1917 to the Second World War* (Princeton, NJ: Princeton University Press, 2001)

Fuerst, Juliane, *Stalin's Last Generation: Soviet Post-War Youth and the Emergence of Mature Socialism* (Oxford: Oxford University Press, 2010)

Ginzburg, Eugenia, *Journey Into the Whirlwind* (Fort Washington, PA: Harvest Books, 1995)

Hellbeck, Jochen, *Revolution on My Mind: Writing a Diary under Stalin* (Cambridge, MA: Harvard University Press, 2006)

Hosking, Geoffrey, *Rulers and Victims: Russians in the Soviet Union* (Cambridge, MA: Belknap Press, 2006)

Jones, Polly, *Myth, Memory, Trauma: Rethinking the Stalinist Past in the Soviet Union, 1953–1970* (New Haven, CT: Yale University Press, 2013)

Kelly, Catriona, *St. Petersburg. Shadows of the Past* (New Haven, CT: Yale University Press, 2014)

Khlevniuk, Oleg, *Stalin: New Biography of a Dictator* (New Haven, CT: Yale University Press, 2015)

Kozlov, Denis, *The Readers of Novyi Mir: Coming to Terms with the Stalinist Past* (Cambridge, MA: Harvard University Press, 2013)

Likhachev, Dmitry S., *Reflections on the Russian Soul: A Memoir* (Budapest: CEU, 2000)

Lincoln, Bruce W., *Passage Through Armageddon: The Russians in War and Revolution, 1914–1918* (New York: Simon and Schuster, 1986)

Lourie, Richard, *Sakharov: A Biography* (New England: Brandeis University Press, 2002)

Lovell, Stephen, *Summerfolk: A History of the Dacha, 1710–2000* (Ithaca, NY: Cornell University Press, 2003)

McAuley, Mary, *Human Rights in Russia: Citizens and the State from Perestroika to Putin* (London: I.B.Tauris, 2015)

Malia, Martin, *The Soviet Tragedy: A History of Socialism in Russia* (New York: Free Press, 1995)

Manley, Rebecca, *To the Tashkent Station: Evacuation and Survival in the Soviet Union at War* (Ithaca, NY: Cornell University Press, 2009)

Merridale, Catherine, *Ivan's War: Life and Death in the Red Army, 1939–1945* (Picador, 2007)

Miner, Steven Merritt, *Stalin's Holy War: Religion, Nationalism, and Alliance politics, 1941–1945* (Chapel Hill, NC: University of North Carolina Press, 2003)

Mukhina, Lena, *The Diary of Lena Mukhina: A Girl's Life in the Siege of Leningrad* (London: Macmillan, 2015)

Murray, Natalia, *The Unsung Hero of the Russian Avant-Garde: The Life and Times of Nikolay Punin* (Boston: Brill, 2012)

Osokina, Elena, *Our Daily Bread: Socialist Distribution and the Art of Survival in Stalin's Russia, 1927–1941*, translated and edited by Kate Transchel and Greta Bucher (Armonk, NY: M.E. Sharpe, c2001)

Oushakin, Serguei, *The Patriotism of Despair: Nation, War, and Loss in Russia* (Ithaca, NY: Cornell University Press, 2009)

Overy, Richard, *Russia's War* (London: Penguin, 1999)

Paperno, Irina, *Stories of the Soviet Experience: Memoirs, Diaries, Dreams* (Ithaca, NY: Cornell University Press, 2009)

Pipes, Richard, *Struve: Liberal on the Right (1905–1944)* (New Haven, CT: Harvard University Press, 1980)

Polonsky, Rachel, *Molotov's Magic Lantern: A Journey in Russian History* (London: Faber & Faber, 2011)

Reddaway, Peter (ed.), *Uncensored Russia: Protest and Dissent in the Soviet Union* (Florida: American Heritage Press, 1972)

Reid, Anna, *Leningrad: Tragedy of a City under Siege, 1941–1944* (Bloomsbury, 2012).

Richards, Susan, *Lost and Found in Russia: Encounters in a Deep Heartland* (London: I.B.Tauris, 2009)

Ruder, Cynthia Ann, *Making History for Stalin: The Story of the Belomor Canal* (Florida: University Press of Florida, 1998)

Sakwa, Richard, *Putin and the Oligarch: The Khodorkovsky-Yukos Affair* (London: I.B.Tauris, 2014)
—— *Frontline Ukraine: Crisis in the Borderlands* (London: I.B.Tauris, 2015)
Schmemann, Serge, *Echoes of a Native Land: Two Centuries of a Russian Village* (New York: Vintage, 1999)
Shalamov, Varlam, *Kolyma Tales* (New York: W.W. Norton, c1980)
Shklovsky, Victor, *A Sentimental Journey* (London: Penguin, 2001)
Shlapentokh, Vladimir, *Soviet Intellectuals and Political Power: The Post-Stalin Era* (Princeton: Princeton University Press, 1990)
Slezkine, Yuri, *The Jewish Century* (Princeton, NJ: Princeton University Press, 2006), chapter 3, and part of chapter 4 (on Soviet society)
Smith, Douglas, *The Former People: The Final Days of the Russian Aristocracy* (New York: Farrar, Straus, Giroux, 2012)
Solzhenitsyn, Aleksandr, *The Oak and the Calf* (London: Harper Collins, 1980)
—— *One Day in Life of Ivan Denisovich* (London: Penguin Classics, 2000)
—— *The Gulag Archipelago* (London: Harper Perennial, 2007)
Steinberg, Mark, *Petersburg Fin de Siècle* (New Haven, CT: Yale University Press, 2011)
Stites, R., *Revolutionary Dreams: Utopian Vision and Experimental Life in the Russian Revolution* (Oxford: Oxford University Press, 1989)
—— *The Women's Liberation Movement in Russia. Feminism, Nihilism and Bolsheviks, 1960–1930* (Princeton, NJ: Princeton University Press, 1991)
Sukhanov, N.N., *The Russian Revolution, 1917: A Personal Record* (Princeton, NJ: Princeton University Press, 1984)
Taubman, William, *Khrushchev: The Man and his Era* (New York: W.W. Norton, 2003)
Todes, Daniel, *Ivan Pavlov: A Russian Life in Science* (New York: Oxford University Press, 2014)
Tolz, Vera, *Russia: Inventing the Nation* (London: Bloomsbury, 2001)
—— *Russia's Own Orient: The Politics of Identity and Oriental Studies in the Late Imperial and Early Soviet Periods* (Oxford: Oxford University Press, 2011)
Tromly, Benjamin, *Making of the Soviet Intelligentsia: Universities and Intellectual Life under Stalin and Khrushchev* (Cambridge: Cambridge University Press, 2014)
Venturi, Franco, *Roots of Revolution: A History of Populist and Socialist Movements in Nineteenth Century Russia* (Chicago: University of Chicago Press, 1983)
Volkov, Solomon, *St. Petersburg: A Cultural History* (New York: Free Press, 1997)
Yurchak, Alexei, *Everything Was Forever, Until It Was No More: The Last Soviet Generation* (Princeton, NJ: Princeton University Press, 2006)
Zubkova, Elena, *Russia After the War: Hopes, Illusions, and Disappointments, 1945–1957* (London: Routledge, 1998)
Zubok, Vladislav, *A Failed Empire: The Soviet Union in the Cold War from Stalin to Gorbachev* (Chapel Hill, NC: The University of North Carolina Press, 2007)
—— *Zhivago's Children: The Last Russian Intelligentsia* (Cambridge, MA: Harvard University Press, 2009)

# INDEX

Abramov, Feodor, 120
Academy of Sciences, the, 7, 74, 144, 165
   and 'Academic Affair', 43–44
   destruction of its library, 141
   and Likhachev's elections, 111–112
   and the old Petersburg network, 75, 84–86
Adrianova-Peretz, Varvara, 51, 74
Akhmatova, Anna, 72, 91, 144, 179
Alexeyev (Askoldov), Sergei, 16, 23, 65, 69
Alexyi II (Ridiger), the patriarch, 49, 152–153, 173, 174, *see also* Orthodox Church, Russian
Andreyevsky, Ivan, 14–16, 23, 24, 29, 33, 65, 115
Anichkov, Igor, 15, 23, 24, 30, 91, 94, 107, 124
avant-garde, Russian, *see* Silver Age
Averintsev, Sergei, 128, 152, 179

Bakhtin, Mikhail, 15, 24, 111, 123, 125
Baltic republics, 150
   national movement and nationalism, 140–141
   and Russia diaspora, 166–167
   ties with Russian culture, 166–167
Barinov, Mark, 125–126
Barmansky, Mikhail, 52, 55
Belavin, Tikhon, the Patriarch, 21–22, 144, *see also* Orthodox Church, Russian
Benois, Aleksandr, 6, 127–128
Berlin, Isaiah, 72, 107, 179
Bibikhin, Vladimir, 152, 153

Billington, James, 94–95, 118, 141, 150–151, *see also* Library of Congress
Blok, Aleksandr, 1, 4, 12, 15, 51
Brodsky, Joseph, 88
Brotherhood of St Seraphim, 23, 28
Bulanin, Dmitry, 170
Bykov, Dmitry, 169–170

Charles, Prince of Wales, 170–171
Chernyaev, Anatoly, 125
Chukovsky, Dmitry, 122, 126
collaborationism, Russian 56, 65, *see also* Great Fatherland War
Congress of People's Deputies, the USSR, 138–139, 141–142
coup, August 1991, 154–155
Cultural Foundation (Soviet, SFC, then Russian, RCF), 129, 130–132
   financial problems of, 158–159, 161
   internal tensions, 131, 146
   and Likhachev's resignation, 161–162

*dachniki* (summer-folk), 6
Danzas, Yulia, 37–38, 40, 43
Declaration on the Defence of the Rights of Culture, The, 148, 174
Dmitriev, Lev, 123, 161
Dostoyevsky, Feodor, 3, 117–118, 194

emigration, from Russia, 20–21, 50, 63, 64, 116–117, 130, 155, 160
Eurasianism, 20–21, 50, 166, 179

Falts-Fein, Eduard, 160, 174
Fennell, John, 107
Feodorov, Lev, 45
Finland, 6–7, 53
Firsov, Boris, 98, 99
Florovsky, Georgy (George), 94, 95, 201
formalism, in linguistics
   campaign against, 81
   in St Petersburg, 15
former people (*byvshiie*), 9, 14, 24, 27, 28, 30, 35, 40, 45, 46, 48–49, 56, 63, 96
Freidenberg, Olga, 56, 57, 60, 65
Furman, Dmitry, 157

Georg, Leonid, 12
Ginzburg, Lidia, 18, 65, 80
Glinka, Mikhail, the Hermitage scholar, 60
Gorbachev, Mikhail, 121, 126–127, 132, 144, 148, 156
   and his election as President, 135–136
Gorbacheva, Raisa, 121, 129, 131–132, 135, 141, 145, 146, 151
   and her break with Likhachev, 157
Gorky, Maxim, 6, 38–39, 43, 45
Granin, Daniil, 55, 57, 97, 155, 175
Great Fatherland War, 6, 56, 64
Great Terror, 31, 45–47, 49, 50–51
Grekov, Boris, 74, 75, 85
Gubenko, Nikolai, 143, 149
Gukovsky, Grigory, 81, 83
Gumilev, Lev, 73, *see also* Eurasianism

Helfernak (*kruzhok*), 15
Holy Russia, a concept of, 3, 13, 64

Ilyin, Ivan, 162, 179
Institute of Russian Literature (IRLI/Pushkin House), 51, 61, 83–85, 91–92, 100, 170
intelligentsia, Russian and Soviet, 3, 115–116, 27, 127, 131, 134, 140, 146, 148, 158
Invasion of Afghanistan, 118–119
Invasion of Czechoslovakia, 110
Ionov, Ilya, 10, 16, 19
Ivanov, Vyacheslav (Koma), 98

Jews, in Russia and the Soviet Union
   and anti–Semitism, 11, 27, 28, 57, 80, 83–84, 125, 127, 139
   aversion to Russian patriotism of, 65, 87, 117
   contribution to Russian culture, 7, 116
   dissent and emigration of, 116–117
Josephites, Orthodox opposition in the 1920s, 23, 35, 40

Kalistov, Dmitry, 26, 27, 40–41, 44, 50, 67, 83, 86, 188
Karsavin, Lev, 20, 27, 144
Keenan, Edward, 104, 118
Khrapchenko, Mikhail, 112, 113–114
Khrushchev, Nikita, 93, 96
Kniazev, Georgy, 57, 63
Komarovich, Vassily, 15, 19, 51, 52, 58, 61
Konovalov, Sergei, 107
Konrad, Nikolai, 93, 95, 110–111, 201
Konyaeva, Aleksandra (Andrealetti), 12, 107–108
Konyaeva (Likhacheva), Vera (mother), 2, 39–40, 52, 67, 110
Korolenko, Vladimir, 36
*kruzhki*, of Russian intellectuals, 14, 16, 26, 43, 131,
Krylenko, Nikolai, 47, 48–49

Lapitsky, Igor, 84–86, 198
*Lay of Igor's Campaign, The*, 78, 122, 128
   and sceptics, 78–79, 100–104, 118
Lenin, Vladimir, 11, 14, 16
Lentovka (Lentovskaia School), 12–13, 17
Library of Congress, 141, 145, 150
   *see also* Billington, James
Ligachev, Yegor, 122, 130
Likhachev, Dmitryi Sergeievich (Mitya, Dima, Dmitry),
   ancestry of, 1–2
   and anti-Semitism, 28–29
   arrest and imprisonment of, 26–27, 28–30
   and Baltics, 140–141, 150, 166–167
   and Bulgaria, 122–123, 136
   and charity, 135, 159, 178
   and civil freedoms, 135, 176
   and Crimea, 5, 144
   and collapse of the USSR, 149–151, 156
   death and burial of, 178–179

and Department (Sektor) of Ancient
   Russian Literature at IRLI, 51, 84–85,
   91–92, 123, 170, 179
and dissent, 109, 115–116
and ecology, 120, 134–135
education of, 8, 12, 17–19, 30,
and ethnic minorities, 140, 148
and European culture, 153, 159
family life of, 3, 10–11, 41, 44, 49, 52,
   54–55, 67–68, 89–90, 124
and Gorbachev, Raisa and Mikhail,
   121–122, 126, 135–136, 138–139,
   151–152
and *kruzhki*, 14–16
and *Lay of Igor's Campaign, The,* 78,
   99–100, 102–104, 128
and *Literary Monuments,* 127, 139
and Moscow friends and connections,
   125–126,
and nationalism, 8–9, 63, 164, 119, 168
and Novgorod, 51–52, 70
and Old Belief, 2, 13, 145
and Old Russia's literature and art, 38,
   41–42, 136–137
at Oxford, 107
and 'patriotism of pity,' 8, 21, 58, 63,
   68–69, 83, 98, 180
and peasantry, 44, 128, 133, 171
political and parliamentary activities of,
   138–139, 141, 143–144, 154
publications and books of, 50, 53, 62,
   68, 101–102, 117–118, 123–124,
   124, 136, 146
and pre-Renaissance in Russian culture,
   95, 96
and preservation/promotion of culture,
   92–93, 97, 142, 144, 148, 150,
   163–164, 171–172
and *prorabotki*, 82–85
and reburial of the Romanovs, 173–175
religious beliefs of, 3, 17, 21, 30–31, 40,
   59, 126, 133, 135, 145–146, 177
and Russian Church (*see* Josephites)
on Russian national character, 19–20,
   117–118, 147, 174
on Russian national identity, 53, 140
and Russian Orthodox Church (after
   1943), 135, 136, 144, 148–149, 174
and St Petersburg (Petrograd, Leningrad),
   4–5, 9, 11, 18–19, 43, 45, 57, 97

sickness of, 43, 61–62, 84, 85, 89,
   99–100, 125
and Solovki, 33–40, 106–107, 108,
   *also see* Solovki
and Solzhenitsyn, Aleksandr, 108–109,
   111, 112–113, 147, 169, 176
and Soviet Cultural Foundation, 129, 130,
   146, 158–162
and Stalinist terror, 42, 43, 47–49
trips abroad, 94, 107–108
and Ukraine, 139
and Yeltsin *see* Yeltsin, Boris
Likhachev, Mikhail (brother), 2, 67,
   89, 133
Likhachev, Sergei (father), 1–2, 9–10, 17,
   39–40, 42, 52, 60
Likhachev, Yuri (Georgy, Yura), 2, 41, 89,
   60, 124, 179
Likhacheva, Liudmila (daughter), 90
Likhacheva, Vera (daughter), 90, 112
   and tragic death of, 124,
Lossky, Nikolai, 16, 119
Lotman, Yuri, 124, 127, 129, 164
Lurie, Yakov, 84, 125
   his criticism of Likhachev, 91, 123

Makarova, Zinaida (Zina, Likhachev's wife),
   47, 49, 51–52, 53, 90, 154
   death of, 179
   and her notes, 59
   during the Siege, 59–61, 195
Malevich, Kazimir, 18, 97, 160
Malyshev, Vladimir, 91–92, 100
Mankov, Arkady, 44–45, 53
Manuilov, Victor, 61, 69
Maxwell, Robert, 132, 151, 160
Mazon, André, 78–79, 82, 100, 103–104
Medvedeva (Tomashevskaia), Irina, 91, 103,
   111, 112
Meyendorff, Ioann, 150, 151
Meyer, Aleksandr, 36–37, 40, 43
Mikhalkov, Nikita, 161–162, 164
Milner-Gulland, Robin, 179
monarchism, Russian, 174
Myasnikov, Georg, 119, 130, 146, 159, 206
   *see also* Cultural Foundation

nationalism, Russian
   and Bolshevism, 11, 20–21
   after collapse of the USSR, 156, 162, 166

before the revolution, 7
during Great Fatherland War, 63–64
in late Soviet times, 119, 131, 139–140, 143
liberal, 3, 7, 11
in Likhachev's early works, 50, 53, 62, 80
*Novyi Mir*, literary journal, 133–134
Likhachev's essays in, 117–118, 136

Obolensky, Dmitri, 107, 203
Oksman, Yuli, 51
Oppenheimer, Harry and Nicky, 160
Orlov, Aleksandr 51, 74
Orthodox Church, Russian, 21–22, 136
Millennium of (1988), 135–136, 145
and restitution of property, 149
and the Romanovs' remains,
Osorgin, Georgy, 40, 107, 117

passportization, 47–49
*see also* Great Terror, secret police
Pasternak, Boris, 30, 60, 134
Pasternak, Evgeny, 134
Piskanovsky, Nikolai, 35, 42–43
Pokrovsky, Mikhail, historical school of, 19, 20
Prishvin, Mikhail, 27, 47–48, 76, 147
Prokhorov, Gelian, 123, 166
Pushkarev, Vasily, 161
Pushkin, Aleksandr, 51, 69, 78, 124, 136, 153
Putin, Vladimir, 179
protection of cultural legacy, 96, 98
*see also* Voronin, Nikolai

Rasputin, Valentin, 143, 145
Reagan, Nancy, 136
restitution of art, 163–164
Roginsky, Arseny, 125, 208
Romanov, Boris, 73–74, 82–83, 86
Romanovs, the royal family
controversy about their remains, 172–174
and pretenders, 174
and reburial, 175–176
Rozenberg, Eduard (Feodor), friend of Likhachev, 23, 24, 25, 35, 40, 41, 47, 91
Russophobia, in Western culture and politics, 180

Sakharov, Andrei, 113, 114, 129, 134, 142–143
funeral of, 144
secret police, Soviet (OGPU, NKVD, MGB, KGB), 16, 23, 34, 39, 40, 45–46, 112, 113, 125
and persecution of Likhachev, 26–28, 65–66, 67, 112, 114–115
Selivanov, Arkady (friend of Likhachev), 25, 62, 145–146, 161
Shakhmatov, Alexei, 25, 60, 68, 77–78, 122
Shklovsky, Victor, 15, 18
Shmeman, Aleksandr, 117
Shmidt, Sigurd, 126
Silver Age, concept of, 6–7, 128, 160, 170
Simmons, John, 107, 203
Sinyavsky–Daniel affair, 109
small homeland, concept of (*rodinovedenie*), 3, 13, 75
Sobchak, Anatoly, 138–139, 143, 154, 159, 167
Solovki (Solovetsky camp, SLON, STON),
cloister and monks in, 33
documentary film on, 43
and intellectuals, 35–38
Likhachev's reminiscences on, 108, 134
Likhachev's return to, 106–107
mass executions in, 39–40
nature of, 36
stratification of, 34–35
Solzhenitsyn, Aleksander, 109, 110, 147, 176
and the *Gulag Archipelago*, 108, 111, 112–113
his idea of Russia, 113, 116, 147
meetings with Likhachev, 108–109, 111, 113
return to Russia, 168–169, 176, 179
and Ukraine, 147, 168
Soros, George, 160
Space Academy (KAN), 24–26
St Petersburg (Petersburg, Petrograd, Leningrad),
and aristocracy
and August 1991 coup, 154–155
destruction and preservation of, 70, 97
in Great Terror, 43–44, 45–46
and imperial ballet, 4
and *kruzhki* of intellectuals, 14–15
and Likhachev's formation, 4

and Russian art
and Russian revolution, 9–11
the siege of, 57, 58–59, 60–61
topography of, 18, 155
in World War I, 7–11
Stalin, Joseph, 40, 42, 75,
and Cultural Revolution, 40–41, 44, 45, 49
death of, 85
denunciation of, 88, 92–93
and Likhachev's release from the gulag, 42
and Orthodox Church, 64–65
and *prorabotki*/anti–cosmopolitan campaign, 80–82,
and terror, 32
during World War II, 56, 64
Starovoitova, Galina, 144, 175
Steblin–Kamenski, Mikhail, 51, 118, 124
Stromin, Albert (aka Albrecht Heller), 26, 28, 29, 37, 44
*see also* secret police
Struve, Peter, 7, 21
Suleymenov, Oljas, 128

Tikhanova, Maria, 51, 62
Timashev, Nikolai (Nicholas Timasheff), 50, 63
Tolz, Vera *see* Zilitinkevich–Tolz, Vera
Tolz, Vladimir, 125
Tomashevsky, Boris, 83–84, 91
*tufta*, 35–36, 38, 45, 48, 56, 83, 133

Ukraine, 164
independence of, 155, 165, 168
nationalism in, 139, 164

Vakhtin, Boris, 98
Vaneieva, Elena, 93, 124

Vasilchikov, Georgy, 160
Vavilov, Sergei, 44, 75–77, 127
Veidle, Vladimir, 12
Veresh, Svetlana, 106, 107, 109, 110, 149
Vernadsky, Vladimir, 44, 50
and 'adviser to Genghis Khan', 93
Versano, Lidia, 160
Volkov, Oleg, 134
VOOPIK (All–Russian Society for the Protection of Monuments), 98
Voronel, Aleksandr, 116, 206
Voronin, Nikolai, 51, 70, 92–91, 110, 111

World of Art, 6
*also see* Benois, Aleksandr

Yakobson, Roman, 99, 100, 101, 113
Yeltsin, Boris, 144, 145, 152, 173, 156, 158, 163, 169
Likhachev's relations with, 157–158, 163, 165, 171–172, 175, 176
and Romanovs' reburial, 175
and Russian nationalists, 167
Yeltsina, Naina, 171, 175, 179
Yenisherlov, Vladimir, 125

Zabolotsky, Nikolai, 79
Zhdanov, Andrei, 55, 73
Zhirmunsky, Victor, 18, 19, 50, 53, 83, 90, 91, 110
Zhivkova, Liudmila, 123
Zilbershtein, Ilya, 130
Zilitinkevich, Sergei, 124
Zilitinkevich–Tolz, Vera, 25, 125, 129, 156
*see also* Tolz, Vera (Likhachev's granddaughter)
Zimin, Aleksandr, 91, 100, 101, 103
Zorza, Victor, 178